I0822219

Both Sides of the Bullpen

Both Sides of the Bullpen
Navajo Trade and Posts

Robert S. McPherson

University of Oklahoma Press : Norman

A version of part of chapter 11 was previously published in Robert S. McPherson, *Viewing the Ancestors: Perceptions of the Anaasází, Mokwič, and Hisatsinom* (Norman: University of Oklahoma Press, 2014).

Library of Congress Cataloging-in-Publication Data

Name: McPherson, Robert S., 1947– author.
Title: Both sides of the bullpen : Navajo trade and posts / Robert S. McPherson.
Other titles: Navajo trade and posts
Description: Norman, OK : University of Oklahoma Press, [2017] | Includes bibliographical references and index.
Identifiers: LCCN 2017001745 | ISBN 978-0-8061-5745-0 (hardcover : alk. paper)
Subjects: LCSH: Navajo Indians—Commerce. | Trading posts—Utah—History. | Trading posts—Colorado—History. | Indian traders—Utah—History. | Indian traders—Colorado—History. | Navajo Indians—Social life and customs. | Navajo Indians—Four Corners Region—History. | Trading posts—Four Corners Region—History. | Four Corners Region—Commerce. | Four Corners Region—History.
Classification: LCC E99.N3 M24 2017 | DDC 979.1004/9726—dc23
LC record available at https://lccn.loc.gov/2017001745

The paper in this book meets the guidelines for permanence and durability of the Committee on Production Guidelines for Book Longevity of the Council on Library Resources, Inc. ∞

1 2 3 4 5 6 7 8 9 10

Contents

Illustrations

Figures

Map

Acknowledgments

The cultural history found in this book depends heavily on the perspective of the people who lived it. Extensive use of oral histories lies at the heart of what is found here, the result of collecting materials for over three decades. Many of those interviewed are now gone, but their memories live on in what they have shared. Among those to whom I am most indebted are Stewart Hatch, Ray Hunt, Alan Whitmer, John Meadows, Lolla K. Noland, John Holiday, Marilyn Holiday, and Mary and Charlie Blueyes. Their insights into yesteryear were invaluable.

Institutions that provided photographs include the San Juan County Historical Commission, the Utah State Historical Society, the Cline Library of Northern Arizona University, and the J. Willard Marriott Library of the University of Utah. Appreciation is also extended to photographer Kay Shumway and artist Charles Yanito for their visual contributions, as well as to Clayton Long for his help with Navajo orthography. To all, and to many others listed in the endnotes and bibliography, I give thanks. In the same respect, any errors of fact or interpretation found within the pages of this book are mine, and I accept responsibility for them.

This has been an interesting and beneficial project, made possible in no small part by my wife, Betsy, and her continual support. She allowed not only me, but my research assistant, Buddy, to spend weekends and holidays working on the manuscript. I am indebted to both for their unwavering loyalty and assistance.

Introduction

Barter is as much a cultural expression as it is an economic necessity. Ever since the first two people walked on American soil, exchanging products and meeting needs have played an important part in that experience. Far-flung trade networks in Native America, the "discovery" of this continent by the Vikings and later Christopher Columbus, the colonial era, and every other aspect of American history has been deeply colored by economic development and exchange at some level. This book is about a very specific time, place, and people in that general process—the upper Four Corners area of the American Southwest between 1880 and 1940, as Navajos and Anglos traded goods in a system that employed cultural values significant to both groups.

Parts of this story have been told elsewhere. Traders have shared their life histories; Navajos are now world-famous for their creation of rugs and silverwork; old trading posts serve as prominent tourist sites; and books explore the development and dissolution of these stores as tied to specific personalities. Here, a different approach is taken. Ethnohistory, or the combining of history and culture to understand two different perspectives of the same cultural scene, allows for the creation of a rich tapestry concerning how and why this picturesque period of the trading post unfolded as it did. The "how," or the cultural side, investigates exactly what the Navajo customer expected as he or she faced the trader across the counter, and the "why" explores the reasons the trader organized the store's environment as it was. The trader, on the other hand, not only had to provide what the clientele wanted but had to meet the demands of the dominant society. Each participant had their own expectations, shaped not only by immediate needs, but by long-standing convention. Most important of all—beyond the wool and rugs, coffee and flour—was the establishment of cooperative relationships. Success or failure hinged upon this simple notion in all of its complexity.

The twelve chapters of this book represent a balanced exploration into two cultures. The first four establish a Navajo cultural perspective about trade, the next four are oriented toward the post and its products from both a Navajo and Anglo perspective, while the last four concentrate on the stores in the Upper Four Corners, as Anglo fortune and misfortune fomented their rise and fall. In every chapter, the participants share their experiences and thoughts in their own words. This heavy dependence on oral history provides a flavor that cannot be obtained otherwise. The result: an opportunity to go back in time and learn of a bygone era as it is examined under the microscope of ethnohistory through the words of those who lived it.

More specifically, what can the reader expect? The first chapter explores the realm of values. Traditional Navajo teachings tell of the nature of creation, its spiritual properties, and how everything in this world—both animate and inanimate (according to Anglo classification)—is based in a relationship. Whether weaving a rug, riding a horse, or trading at a post, there were songs and prayers that established a beneficial connection. Chapter 2 looks at Navajo trade practices with other Native American groups and how this barter depended heavily on relationships. Long before the first trading post became a reality, many of the customs that became standard practice in the store were already in play. While some readers may view events in a trading post as unique, much of what occurred derived from long-standing, expected behavior. In chapter 3, the reader is given the opportunity to consider both traditional Navajo and trading post architecture. These American Indians were acutely sensitive to their surroundings. Whether one looks at the four sacred mountains, local hallowed space, or the construction of, and teachings about, the hogan, there is no missing the fact that traditional Navajos were highly aware of their environment, which they imbued with significance. For these people, architecture was a man-made, but God-designed edifice filled with moral significance. Some of their values and teachings made their way into the posts—whether intentionally or unintentionally—creating a fairly standard and hospitable form of structure consistent throughout Navajo land. Chapter 4 discusses the conduct of business within the post from a Navajo perspective. This pattern was a highly defined and standard procedure.

The next four chapters begin the shift across the counter, from the bullpen where the customer stood to the elevated platform of the trader. Chapter 5 analyzes what it was like to be a trader in a post and what it took to meet both the trader's and the Navajo's expectations. What demands did the government place on traders, what was the rhythm of exchange in the post like, and how did owners become accepted members of the community? Learning to speak Navajo, the development of a specialized trade language, the bestowal of individual names, and the handling of disagreements were all important aspects faced by the men and women working in the posts. The next two chapters look at the heart of this economic system. But what the Navajo brought to sell and what the store owner sold were only part of the story. From a cultural perspective, traders had to meet the wishes of a variety of people. Besides the Navajo men and women who frequented the post, there were Anglo middlemen, other traders providing competition, and suppliers, all of whom vied for profit in a stingy land. Credit or pawn was the only way that customers and store owners could economically survive and mutually benefit each other. Was this barter system fair or unjust? What did the government do to ensure honesty, and what was the reality? Chapter 8 discusses humor, daily life, and conflict resolution as they seesawed back and forth over the counters of the stores. Women traders played a significant role in many of these businesses, healing the sick and supporting their husbands; Navajo diviners used supernatural power to locate stolen property; while cultural and physical isolation took its emotional toll on those unfamiliar with the land. These and other elements composed social life at the stores. Often, traders grew to enjoy the experience so that when they re-entered white society, there was a certain uneasiness and dissatisfaction that encouraged a return to the reservation and their former way of life. Here, the reader learns why this lifestyle became so appealing.

These first eight chapters draw from Navajo and trader experience lived in the general Four Corners region. They focus on cultural teachings and examples provided by trader and customer. The last four chapters look at the establishment, growth, and decline of posts in the upper

Four Corner states of southeastern Utah and southwestern Colorado. The reason for this selection is threefold. First, many of the books written about trading posts center on those that operated in Arizona and New Mexico. There were literally hundreds of them, as Frank McNitt's classic study, *The Indian Traders*, points out.[1] That seminal work covers some of the large trading organizations and major posts, so prominent in these states. The stores in Utah and Colorado, both on and off the Navajo Reservation, were usually smaller than, and in some cases more representative of, the general overall trading experience. Little has been written about the men and women who ran the posts in this geographic area. A second reason is that these stores had a steady flow of Ute customers, providing an interesting comparison with their Navajo clientele. The third reason is that the land and the white people who settled it represent a way of life that is more similar and interdependent when compared to the way of life found in New Mexico and Arizona. In other words, while everyone in all four states shared similarities in trading with the Navajos and often shipped goods out of the more-southern states, the history and the land of the upper Four Corners held more in common than with many of the posts in the other two states. Also, the more limited geographical area in the north allows for a more complete, unified picture of events, making the number of posts and telling of their history more manageable.

The rise and fall of many of these stores is often difficult to trace, given the unending change of owners and the posts' ephemeral existence. What follows is a chronology of their development as shared by knowledgeable traders, the only people who kept track of such things. Chapter 9 looks at the early businesses, where Mormons and non-Mormons settled along the San Juan River and began trading with the Navajos and Utes living there. In addition to comparing the differences in economic practices and cultural beliefs of the four groups of people, there is also a discussion of interpersonal conflict, weather and geographical issues, and economic trends that challenged stores and customers alike. The next chapter focuses on Ute trading as compared with that of the Navajos and looks at some of the prominent store owners—their successes and failures—as they exchanged goods with both groups. To ignore the presence of the Utes in the posts of this region would be unfair and inaccurate. While they did not have the same economic prominence because of lifestyle and values, the Utes played an important role in the history of the area and traded side-by-side with their Navajo neighbors. Chapter 11 examines the role of the trading post as a fundamental institution that served both Anglo and Navajo communities. These stores developed a variety of economic opportunities during the height of the trading post era. Sometimes perceived solely as an outlet for Native American goods, in reality many stores worked at the forefront in fostering prosperity, not only through economic development but in other facets of daily life. The role of the trader as a cultural and economic "booster" is examined. The final chapter glimpses a variety of events at some of the posts during the 1920s—a golden era of efflorescence—that began plummeting in the 1930s with livestock reduction during the Great Depression. While many stores remained operational in the 1940s and beyond, the nature of the trade, the growth of the wage system, the increasing dependence on the dominant society for off-reservation employment, the effects of World War II, the subsequent uranium industry, and changing technology had a mounting impact that either closed or modified the stores, moving them away from the traditional practices of the past. Many of the old traders noted these changes, seeing a clear differentiation between the cultural values of yesteryear and the new innovations being adopted. The era of older cultural practices, and the posts that relied on them, was coming to a close.

A brief discussion of sources, at this point, will be helpful. Each chapter is heavily documented to explain where the information comes from. Much of the material has been gathered over a long period of time and is not generally available. For instance, I have depended extensively on oral and family history, which is the primary means of getting into the nitty-gritty of daily store operation and life. A quick perusal of the bibliography shows that approximately half of the interviews—especially those with Navajo people—I collected in the upper Four Corners over the past thirty years. There were also some wonderfully detailed interviews with traders who shared their experiences, drew diagrams of a few of the posts, and provided the genealogy of some stores' ownership. Making this kind of information available is important, not only for its preservation, but also because it creates a personal reality of what life was like on both sides of the bullpen.

The trader, as a businessperson, has at times been unfairly maligned, being characterized as a sharp-eyed operator, just waiting to skin a customer. There is no doubt that there were those who fit this category, but as a whole, most of the men and women who approached their clientele this way were not in business for long, as the following pages attest. The Navajo people I have interviewed generally agree: few ever felt that they were abused or cheated, although there were those who complained of low return for their goods—particularly during the Great Depression.

What follows, then, is a look at a bygone era, when lambs, wool, and rugs supported a lifestyle based in Navajo traditional values. The people, for the most part, were not famous, wealthy, or dishonest. Traders and customers all worked hard to make a living that met their cultural, economic, and social needs. What one soon discovers is that the counters in a store served as a dividing line, but they were broad enough to accept fair exchanges for those dealing on both sides. The bullpen, or that place where the Navajo stood, had its own kind of power, as did the elevated floor on the far side for the store owner. For most who traded at a post, a mutual respect developed based on relationships of trust as well as the fulfillment of needs.

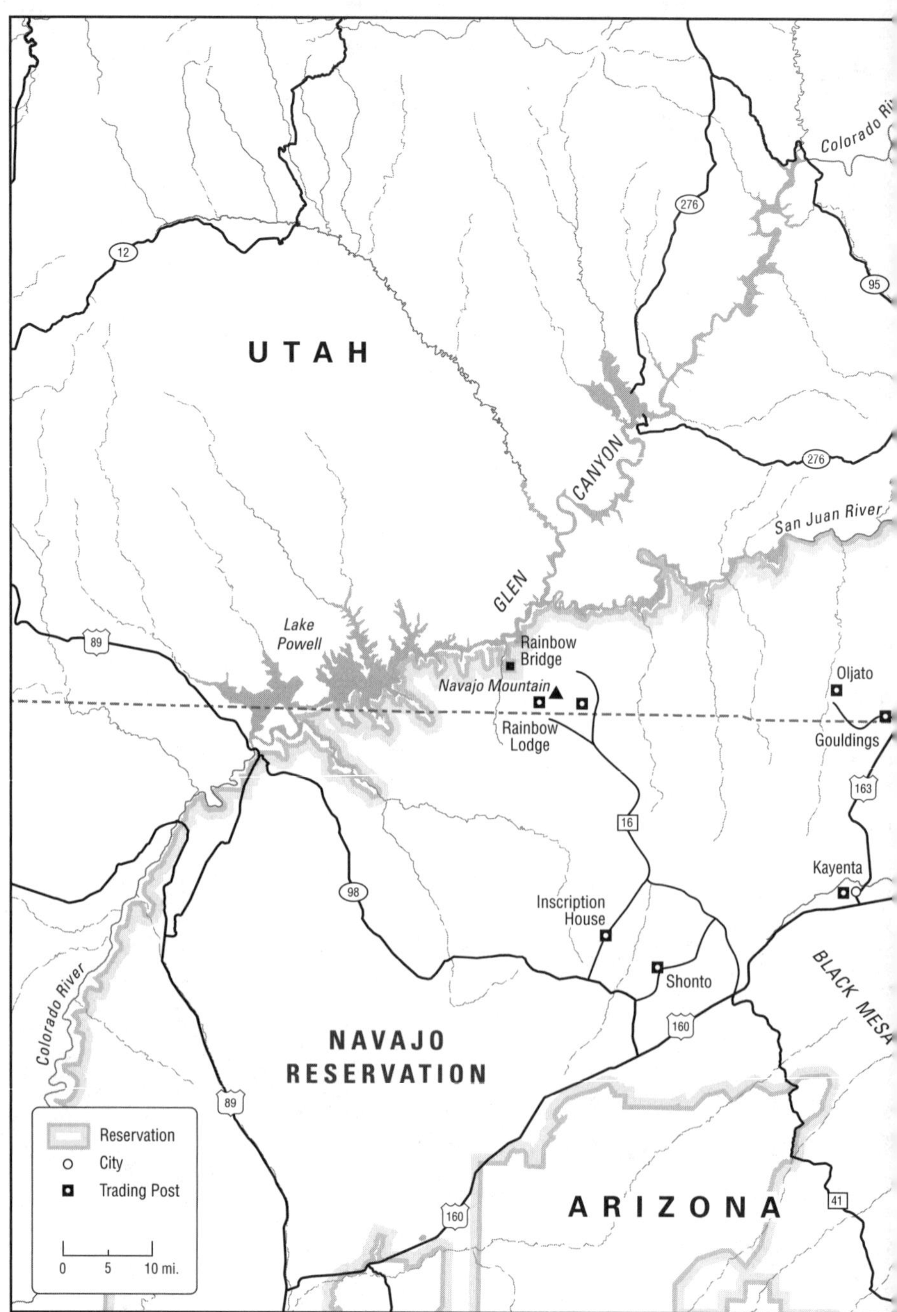

Trading posts of the upper Four Corners area. (Cartography by Erin Greb. Copyright © 2017, University of Oklahoma Press.)

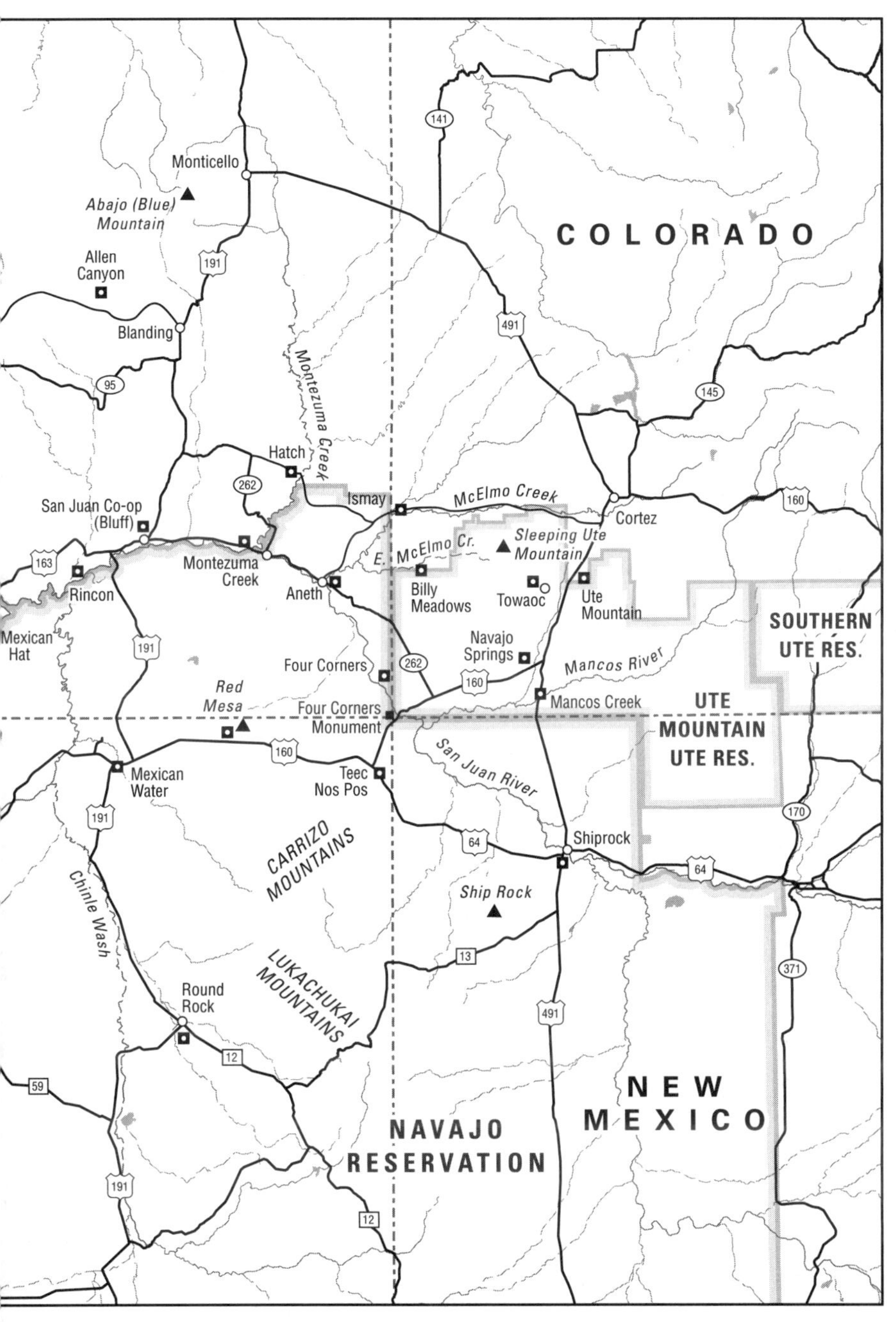
COLORADO
NEW MEXICO
NAVAJO RESERVATION
SOUTHERN UTE RES.
UTE MOUNTAIN UTE RES.
CARRIZO MOUNTAINS
LUKACHUKAI MOUNTAINS
Monticello
Abajo (Blue) Mountain
Allen Canyon
Blanding
Montezuma Creek
Hatch
San Juan Co-op (Bluff)
Ismay
McElmo Creek
E. McElmo Cr.
Sleeping Ute Mountain
Cortez
Montezuma Creek
Aneth
Rincon
Mexican Hat
Billy Meadows
Towaoc
Ute Mountain
Navajo Springs
Four Corners
Mancos River
Mancos Creek
Red Mesa
Four Corners Monument
Mexican Water
Teec Nos Pos
San Juan River
Shiprock
Ship Rock
Chinle Wash
Round Rock
141
191
491
95
145
262
160
163
170
64
13
371
12
59

Both Sides of the Bullpen

CHAPTER ONE

Of Songs, Prayers, and Spirit

Navajo Relationships and Property Concepts

Like fish in a pond, humans swim through culture on a daily basis. People are often unaware that they are participating in a select body of ideals, values, and beliefs that interpret experience and generate behavior peculiar to their society. Every culture in the world has its set of values that defines membership through a taught and practiced system of beliefs. For most people living outside of those limits but looking in, a culture may range from being mildly different and amusing to frightening and insane, depending upon compatibility with their own values. Those practicing within a specific culture experience expected behavior buttressed by ideals and teachings that circumscribe what is best. It is just normal and "makes sense," given their upbringing.

Take, for instance, shopping at a twenty-first-century American supermarket through the eyes of a fictitious character named John. He has been reading all week of the super sales now available for a limited time only. As he approaches the entrance of his spacious neighborhood market, he sees seasonal plants and bags of loam stacked on wooden pallets outside, as the doors open, automatically activated by an electric-eye beam. John picks out a large pushcart with a collapsible child's seat, rather than the plastic shopping cart built like a car with an inoperable steering wheel. In the background, he hears soothing nondescript tunes from Muzak piped in over an intercom as he selects produce stacked in a pyramid and advertised with florescent lettered signs hung from the ceiling. Oranges treated with chemicals that turn them a desired color, apples coated with wax to preserve freshness, and glistening fruits and vegetables sprayed with water are placed beside brightly colored packaging that screams "one-third off," or "fewer calories," or "organically grown, natural food." As John speeds through the express-lane checkout where his items are laser-scanned, he barely acknowledges the girl working behind the counter in front of the code-reader. Instead, he gathers up his purchases in plastic tote bags, glances at his watch, then sprints to his car, located near the handicap-parking stall. Weaving between other automobiles, he hits the main flow of traffic, never giving a second thought to the series of choices he has made, many of which were influenced as much by his environment and the store manager as by his own needs. John's value-laden decisions derived, whether consciously or subconsciously, from the culture in which he operated. Shoppers visiting a bazaar in Marrakesh, Morocco, at the same time, would find John's experience bizarre.

This book is also about a cultural experience—the one encountered in trading posts on or near the Navajo Reservation between 1880 and 1940. During this sixty-year period, while there were changes in products, transportation, and other circumstances introduced from Anglo-American culture, many of the traditional Navajo practices derived from their nineteenth-century agrarian-livestock economy were also present. Most of these values and customs had their origin in religious teachings and myths that framed Navajo culture. The term "myth," as used here, denotes stories that are sacred and true and that outline proper behavior and practices as given to the Navajo by the holy people. This point is central to understanding what follows. The first two chapters in this book revolve around some of those teachings as understood by both the Navajos and the traders who faced them across the counter. While there have been a number of excellent studies about trading posts as a frontier institution of commerce, as well as autobiographies and biographies of Anglo traders and their experiences, there has been very little done in analyzing the cultural scene from both sides of the "bullpen."[1] That is the task at hand.

Fundamental Navajo Thought

Since the Navajo perspective is unfamiliar to most readers, a brief description of relevant elements in Navajo thought will lay the foundation for what lies ahead. Navajo cosmology is complex, interconnected, and pervasive, explaining most aspects of life in this physical world. Through the stories, ceremonies, and songs, one encounters a deep philosophical framework of not just how to understand what has happened but also how to interact, influence, and direct both tangible and intangible elements. The world, and everything encountered in it, started at the beginning of creation with the holy people. This was a time when powerful spiritual beings established the physical world, its inhabitants, and all of the patterns and procedures necessary to make it a successful place to live. There had to be the opposites of good and evil, success and failure, right and wrong, but each side of these pairs complemented the other. One cannot know good without recognizing evil; one must know hunger in order to appreciate food, and poverty to value wealth. These qualities are viewed by the dominant American society as intangible properties that denote a state of being. In other words, they express how one feels.

Navajo culture looks at them differently in that although one cannot see hunger, just the results of it, the feeling is actually personified as a being that acts upon an individual. For example, in English, when one says, "I am hungry," what is really being communicated is that "I feel hungry," whereas in Navajo, the phrase is interpreted as "hunger is killing me." This can be understood as both metaphorical and literal—that an active force is working on an individual. The myth or story that explains why hunger exists comes from events during a period known as the "palm of time" as the holy beings prepared the world for habitation. Joe Manygoats from Navajo Mountain explained that during this time Monster Slayer and Born for Water, mythological warrior twins, traveled about, killing monsters that inhabited the earth.[2] Four of these monster groups were allowed to exist in order to foster appreciation for the things of life. The first ones, called the Hunger People, pleaded, "Let us live. Who can eat and live on one meal forever? Let us be the hunger that exists in humans so that one will crave the taste of all the different varieties of food. It is good for everyone's well-being." So they, as invisible beings, were allowed to continue to exist. Next, the Death People begged, saying, "Let us live. We will fill the void, the boring time, even if one is at home." They, too, were not killed. Next, the Poverty People pleaded to remain alive: "It is not good to wear one type of clothing forever. It is better to keep changing and renewing one's clothes because of the wear and tear. Besides, then one will have a choice." Finally, Old Age reminded Monster Slayer, "It is not good to be born, then remain as a newborn forever. Therefore, it is better to renew generation after generation through the aging and dying process." All of these beings are with us today, as each generation continues to ask why it faces these problems.

This type of story can be multiplied numerous times, as traditional teachings explain how and why things happen to the Earth Surface People, or the Five-fingered Beings known as humans. Continuing with this single concept of hunger, the holy people have provided a way to combat it. Women, whose domain is the home, have a number of tools (*habeedí*) that are essential for their role in this setting. Among these tools are the stone mano and metate, whose noise while grinding corn keeps sickness away. Stirring sticks used to mix ground cornmeal mush combine into another instrument that combats hunger. Made from seven peeled greasewood sticks two feet long and tied approximately six inches at one end, this utensil serves not only the practical side of moving thick cornmeal mush but also works as a "weapon to fight hunger," just as a bow and arrow serve a corresponding function for men. Nellie Grandson spoke of women praying for rain after mixing the mush and noted that, when the sticks were not washed, "it is said that there is hunger on them. The Hunger says, 'Eek' when she is washing her weapon. This is what was said."[3] The Navajo saying, "Healthy food makes me invulnerable," takes on a deeper meaning than just "eating right."

There are two additional points to be drawn before leaving this example. The first is that everything in the Navajo universe is either male or female. This includes what Anglos would consider both animate and inanimate objects, as well as dual parts of the same thing. For instance, it is male rain that comes in a downpour that scours the canyons and floods the land; female rain is a soft, nurturing, soaking shower that brings life to plants and animals. Everything from rivers and trees and clouds to homes and ceremonies and prayers is also classified in similar fashion, based upon their nature, shape, or origin as specified in the myths by the holy people. Even within an individual, regardless of sex, there is this male and female dichotomy. Returning to the example of the stirring sticks, women hold them in their right hand while stirring, but men grasp the bow, a corresponding weapon to fight hunger, in the left hand. In Navajo thought, the left side and those things associated with it are for males; those on the right, for females. Thus the left ear, eye, nostril, lung, leg, and arm are viewed as male; those on the right, female. In the hogan, the female's work area and place to sit is to the north, or on the right side as one enters, while the men move to the left or south side, a point that will be expanded elsewhere.

The male/female dichotomy extends into activities. Men are concerned with war, hunting, politics, and powerful ceremonies, while women are often herbalists, caretakers, weavers, and homemakers. Each has their realm of power and objects received from the holy people to perform their assigned roles. Both men and women can use some of the same objects, such as sheep shears and saddles, without a problem. On the other hand, there are other things that hold power and should not be used by the opposite sex. Women should not be involved with weapons like bows and arrows and other objects that may be associated with violent death, for their realm is one of birth, life, and nurturing. A knife used to kill a sheep for dinner presents no problem, since it is associated with food, so both sexes can use it. On the other hand, men are not free to use certain women's implements. Sam Black, a traditional Navajo from Monument Valley, noted that, after a woman has used the stirring sticks, she raises the implement to the east and prays for a "warm winter day so that her family will not be cold. After her prayer, she squeezes the cornmeal off of each stick and eats it with delight. If a man should use the cornmeal sticks, he will be afraid and shake all over. These sticks are not to be used by a man."[4] Thus, the universe is one of order and respect, with some tasks being shared while others are relegated to specific roles.

As the holy people made plans and established patterns, they created everything spiritually before it existed physically. The process started by thinking about what was needed and how it would help to make life on earth meaningful. Lengthy discussions followed, where abstract thought became concrete when expressed through words, which in turn became songs and prayers—the heart of existence. The world was literally first thought about, then sung into being with each object, place, or thing having its own songs and prayers that not only identify it spiritually, but also provide a means by which it can be approached and communicated with. Language holds a compelling power through which spiritual and physical things are controlled.[5] Frank Mitchell, Blessingway singer, explained that when the creative process ended, the holy people would no longer speak to the Earth Surface people but would be available to help. All one needed to do in the future was to go to a certain spot and leave an offering with prayers, and then these supernatural beings would provide assistance. He next said:

> You see, in the story [origin of the Blessingway ceremony] it says that whenever anything was established for the use of the Earth People, it required song and prayer. In that way they [the holy people] put it in motion; it became alive, just by the songs, the actions, and the prayers. Now with us, we cannot do that because we do not have the power to create anything. If we were singing and praying, it would not come to life at all. But we can keep the power alive today by using those songs that were used when the first Blessingway was created.[6]

At the center of everything in the physical universe—from rocks and trees to baskets and blankets—there lies an inner form (*bii'yistiin*), roughly glossed as "animate being that lies within." Humans also have an inner form known as "in-standing wind soul" (*nítch'í bii'siziinii*), which enters the body at birth, leaves at death, and during life controls a person's thoughts and actions, giving rise to individual personality traits. "The capacity to think 'far ahead' and speak a language is acquired from the wind soul dispatched at birth, and it is this capacity that distinguishes humans from other animals, who have only calls and cries."[7] Thus, while everything has a spirit or soul, there are gradations in ability as to what each spirit can accomplish. Navajo prayers and songs address both the outer and inner form of an object, or in other words, both its physical and spiritual essence.

A person's wealth and power can be measured by the number and type of songs that he or she knows. They open the gate of understanding and communicating with whatever the song addresses and calls upon for assistance. The entire world is energized and controlled through this power, which instructs the spiritual forces within. From birth to death and beyond, there are songs that influence and direct every occasion and every object. There are songs for traveling, from the time a person leaves home until their return; there are farming songs that cover each stage of the effort, from clearing the field to harvesting the crop; there are songs for war, hunting, gambling, bidding farewell, greeting the sun, and healing the sick; and there are "building songs, which celebrate every act in the structure of the hut [hogan], from 'thinking' about it to moving into it and lighting the first fire."[8]

Relationships (K'é) and Property

All of this leads to one of the most fundamental principles in understanding traditional Navajo life and values and one central to the trading experience—*k'é*. This simple word, translated as "relations, relationships," encompasses a wide variety of thought and action and identifies the ideal relationship that an individual should strive to achieve. Encompassed in this term is the meaning "compassion, cooperation, friendliness, unselfishness, peacefulness, and all those positive virtues which constitute intense, diffuse, and enduring solidarity."[9] Also inherent is the thought that all people are related, a feeling that is expressed through bonds of love and assistance. Navajos use kinship terms to describe this relationship, terms that show respect and commitment, so people do not address individuals by their "street names," as is done in Anglo society. Kinship, with its accompanying responsibilities, becomes the basis for all relationships.

The practice of *k'é* extends beyond the family to all other humans as they adopt this code of behavior. Social interaction of this nature produces harmony and brings people into a bonding relationship of peace, love, cooperation, and the ideal state of *hózhǫ*, a complex term that means far more than the gloss of "long life, happiness." Navajo people recognize that obtaining this point of perfection in this life, where there is a final state of spiritual harmony and equilibrium within oneself and with the outer world, is almost impossible. Rather, it is an ideal to strive for as one stays on a path of long life and correct behavior as outlined by the holy people.[10]

The concepts of *k'é* and *hózhǫ*, however, go far beyond human relations. Since everything in the Navajo world is animated with a spiritual essence, can communicate, assist, or deny, and enjoys certain ways of being addressed as established in the beginning, an individual needs to properly maintain those relationships. In a world filled with spiritual beings, ranging from the holy people to a tree to a human, it is imperative that proper respect be shown. Otherwise, the object and its

Jay Charles Holiday and family represent the fundamental importance of multigenerational relationships expressed in the term *k'é*. Longtime residents of the Monument Valley area, this family also illustrates the mixing of Navajo and Ute/Paiute ancestry so prominent in the region. *Left to right*: Jay Charles Holiday, Jenny Olds (Ute/Paiute from Navajo Mountain), Dee Ba (Frieda Cly) with child. (Used by permission, Utah State Historical Society.)

spirit can turn its power against the offending person. Thus, ceremonies establish a proper relationship with the holy people who can aid in healing an individual as long as care is taken to follow prescribed actions, the songs are sung properly, and participants provide offerings identified when the holy people performed the ceremony for the first time. The same is true when one crosses a river. Offerings and prayers for protection are said as one leaves the boundary of safety and moves into the water. The power of the being within the river can serve as a protective force as long as the person crossing shows proper respect and diligence in performing the prescribed ritual. This underlying concept of relationships is central to every aspect of traditional Navajo life, including the trading experience.

Words can attract both good and evil, can heal and sicken, can benefit and curse, depending on the ritual setting and how they are used. When acquiring property, which in Navajo thought can be either tangible or intangible, words play an extremely important role. Starting with physical objects, there are a number of ways of thinking about and using them. Since each object has an "animate being that lies within," it is capable of thought and action. Property can therefore make itself available or unavailable to an individual. Perhaps one of the best examples of Navajo thought about this subject is found in the two-volume autobiography about Left Handed, a Navajo man born in 1868 and interviewed in 1934. Walter Dyk, editor/author of *Son of Old Man Hat* and *Left Handed, A Navajo Autobiography*, has translated the thought and dialogue in these very personal accounts of an individual who would be classified as an "average" Navajo man of this time.[11] He was not a war leader, medicine man, or political pundit, and, aside from some of his youthful sexual escapades, he lived a typical existence of a Navajo from that era. While no two people's lives are alike, Left Handed did not seem to consider many of his experiences out of the ordinary.

One spring day after sheep shearing, Left Handed and his wife decided that they wanted to go to a trading post in Ganado to sell their wool. Before going, he wanted to go up on Black Mountain and retrieve a bundle of goods that he had placed in a tree for safekeeping and out of the hands of people who might want to steal it. Left Handed rode his horse up the steep slope as far as he could, dismounted, and walked to the spot where he had left the materials about six months prior. The tree was empty, although the cedar bark on which he had left the bundle resting was still there. Then ten yards away, he spotted his bundle, apparently undisturbed. There were no tracks around it, no tampering with the wrapping, and no sign as to how it had ended up where it was. After opening the large package, he found nothing disturbed and so repacked the contents and brought it home.

Left Handed talked to his mother, who believed that the bundle had just rolled out of the tree, but Slim Man, a clan relative, had a very different interpretation, saying that it was a serious thing, and that elders had taught him about this type of event. "They say all the properties are alive. Some of them are men and women so they are alive. You shouldn't leave your property all alone that long. They must have got tired lying in the bundle upon the tree where there wasn't anybody around, and maybe they couldn't stand it anymore. So they got down themselves. . . . Maybe you or maybe one of your relatives will die. That's the way I am thinking about it. When the property gets that way without anybody moving it, if it moves by itself even for just a little ways, that means something bad will come up."[12]

Left Handed never described what was in the bundle, other than it had three "robes" sewn around it and a buckskin tied around the contents. Most likely this was a medicine bundle (*jish*), an object that today is still viewed as alive. Anthropologist Charlotte Frisbie has written extensively about the care and use of Navajo medicine bundles and points out that keeping them in trees to safeguard against intruders tampering with the contents, that they should not be left alone for long periods of time, and that they should be "fed" with corn pollen and prayers were all part of customary care.[13] Inappropriate use of the medicine bundle leads to problems.

Another example of treating an object as one would a living person is seen with the Pectol shields reclaimed by the Navajos in 2003. Representatives of the Navajo Nation obtained these three objects after a long, contentious series of claims and counterclaims with other tribes. Medicine man John Holiday and Marklyn Chee from the Navajo Nation Historic Preservation Department drove the three shields to Window Rock as Holiday sang and prayed over them. "The songs were to revive them and tell them 'you're home.' . . . It felt like a good thing to bring them back."[14] Later, they were blessed with pollen, prayed over, and reintroduced to their role as protectors of the Navajo Nation.

There are three major types of property that an individual can possess: livestock, goods, and things intangible such as prayers, songs, and ceremonial knowledge. Stories from the Blessingway and other myths explain how many of these items originated, while also providing songs to obtain them. Two general categories—hard goods (*nitł'iz*) and soft goods (*yódí*)—are part of this thinking. Hard goods are composed of silver ornaments, precious stones, saddles, money, rifles, and other objects viewed as male and of value. Soft goods include blankets, cloth, rugs, baskets, clothing, and other objects crafted by or associated with women. This dual classification is used in ceremonial thought and prayers to obtain this type of wealth, which may pay for the ceremony.

Items obtained for daily use are not spoken of in this way; only those referring to ritual items that an individual can use in payment are classified accordingly.[15]

Livestock is the next category of property and one of great importance. Old Man Hat counselled his son, Left Handed, in the practical application of livestock care, but also the role of songs and prayers in obtaining and maintaining wealth on the hoof. The father instructed, "If you take care of them, you'll have sheep and cattle to live on and horses to travel around with. That whole thing will give you clothing of all kinds and all kinds of food. By taking care of all things, you'll soon be a man who has everything. . . . I'm telling you this, because I don't want you to be poor."[16]

To ensure his son's success, Old Man Hat taught him songs about different types of property. Realizing that he was old and not long for this world, he shared his songs about horses and sheep, jewelry and farms. "Even if you learn only one song of each of them you'll be fixed all right as long as you live. . . . If you don't know any songs, you'll soon lose all the stock."[17] He then began to teach a flurry of songs. The first six went easily, with Left Handed repeating them twice, then "counting" or recognizing an additional twenty-two that all had to do with livestock. After this, they were "put away" so that the pair could start on twelve new ones. These were "driving songs" used to move a herd to a new location. Songs and corn pollen are given to the animals to protect them and to help them be healthy. There were twenty-eight total, but Left Handed only learned four before morning dawned. The father ended with, "That's as far as I want you to learn from me. The rest of your fathers know all about these songs. . . . I know they will [teach you], when you ask them. A fellow shouldn't be stingy about the songs."[18] Left Handed practiced what he had learned as he herded the sheep that day and got the songs fixed in his mind.

He had been taught by a master who practiced what he shared. Previously, Left Handed had watched his father go outside in the middle of winter to his corral, walking around its perimeter and, amid the animals, singing the Owl Song to keep the sheep from being bothered by low temperatures. The song took its name from the owl because it can withstand the cold and appears impervious to discomfort. Old Man Hat sang away sickness; he sprinkled herbs combined in water over the sheep and around the corral so that the cold would leave them alone, so that they would grow fat and strong, and so that none of them would be lost. Left Handed noted that their herd increased quickly.[19]

Songs and prayers are part of the third category of wealth—intangible property—as are names. One individual may have three or four names that may be used for different occasions. For instance, the most frequently used names are kinship terms that denote relationships and affiliated responsibilities, a topic that will be discussed in another chapter. The same individual might have a name based upon a particular physical or temperamental characteristic, or an occupation, or where they live, or their clan, or a ceremony they perform. These names are used in everyday parlance, and although individuals are usually not addressed directly with these names, they are in general use and do not have any particular power.

The war, or holy name, on the other hand, is used on special occasions such as ceremonies, especially the Enemy Way ceremony. Both men and women have these titles and hold them sacred and primarily secret. They are bestowed on a boy by his father and on a girl by her maternal grandmother or maternal uncle (her mother's brother); it is the women in the family who have the responsibility to keep track of the names.[20] Examples of female names are War Bands Meet, Goes to War, She Arrived with War, while examples of male names are Warrior Catches Up, Warriors Came to Him, He is Bent on War. Enemies also have secret names, and by knowing them, these enemies can be defeated, just as the Twins during their mythological adventures used those names to bypass danger and defeat their adversaries.[21] Anthropologist Gladys Reichard suggests that the war name is used during times of extreme difficulty or danger, and in ceremonies, but to use the name often is to deplete the power it holds. Franciscan missionary Berard Haile, who studied Navajo ceremonial beliefs extensively, does not fully agree with Reichard's understanding of the power of the war names, but certainly agrees that they are important. At the same time, he recognizes that "injury by use of name formula is wishful of the killing of a victim," or in other words, there is more to a name and its use than just addressing a person.[22]

Most animals also have a sacred name that Navajos used in preparing ceremonial paraphernalia, during the ceremonies, and in special prayers and songs. All of these names originated from the myths and are used to show respect and to obtain power from specific creatures. The songs and prayers call upon that power in a very personal and sacred way. Thus, a bear, instead of being called by its common name *shash*, becomes Roaming in the Mountains or the Fine Young Chief; and a deer, instead of *bįįh*, becomes the Youth or Chief of the White Patch.[23] The knowledge of an animal's or an object's name provides a distinct advantage when trying to obtain it. That is why Reichard insists that "some very unusual individuals possess the 'sacred names' of property. There are sacred names for sheep, horses, and hard goods, the knowledge of which will cause the particular animal or commodity to increase for the owner of the name. These sacred names are not the same in different families."[24]

Left Handed helped teach this principle to a group of unruly Navajo friends who were giving him a hard time while he was on a trading trip. The young men started to examine the bow and arrows Left Handed was bringing to market, laughing about them, and passing them around in a joking manner. A man named Slow approached the group and chastised them, saying, "That's what you call a man's property. I know he's [Left Handed] a man. And that quiver has a name. It has got a name, and the arrows themselves have a name, and so has the bow. They all have names. Some of you don't know anything about it, so you mustn't laugh. A man who has things like that has all kinds of stuff. I know that fellow. He has got property. He has got stock. So you mustn't laugh at him, you evil spirits you, laughing about him."[25]

Other elements of intangible property include dances, medicine bundles, prayer sticks, the ability to use divination, and specific ceremonies. Berard Haile suggests that these incorporeal properties "found in the power of a name, in knowledge, ceremonial paraphernalia, witchcraft, divining and similar gifts, of which the individual or group may hold control, are perhaps valued more than tangible goods."[26] All of this understanding is owned by an individual and can be transferred to others, who apprentice to learn the information. The teacher is paid, although under no circumstances does he specify a price, but instead leaves that to the student.[27] There are two reasons for this. The first is that in Navajo culture, greed, stinginess, and wealth are often associated with people involved in witchcraft and other forms of antisocial behavior. A person with excessive livestock and with a lot of ceremonial knowledge, and who refuses to help and share, may have obtained what he had by using negative supernatural power.[28] Other people may be accused of not thinking of members of their group whom they should be helping. On a number of occasions, Left Handed's mother warned him about being selfish with his property: "When you have such a nice name, why do you want to be stingy? You mustn't be stingy. They will call you Stingy after a while, instead of calling you by my name. You will make yourself a name if you do not look out."[29] Thus, the instructor does not establish a price for his services, but the pupil should pay a substantial amount to show the value of what is learned.

A second reason for paying a good price is that the holy people are very much aware of this transfer of knowledge. The songs and prayers are living entities and understand their value, as do those who use them for the first time. A low price, or "bargain shopping," communicates low respect and little value for what is being shared, the exact opposite message needed for the songs and prayers to have efficacy. This will also make the learning of the material more difficult to attain and retain. As Left Handed prepared to learn more songs from a clan relative after his father had passed away, he realized that he had forgotten everything that he had learned. He reasoned, "I don't remember any of the songs. They are all gone away from me. I can't think of one. Perhaps the songs don't want me." He tried and had some success, but "I just couldn't get them straight." Eventually, he mastered a number of difficult songs. His teacher, Choclays Kinsman, comforted and encouraged his student through the process, saying, "You will get them straight sometime, and this isn't the only time to learn. . . . I want you to learn all the songs, because it's good to know. You can use them any time you want to, and everything is true about it."[30]

Left Handed gives another detailed account of learning the songs, only highlights of which can be shared here. This ongoing process and dialogue between him and Choclays Kinsman leaves no doubt as to the importance and the effort that each placed in this process. The two started out with some playful banter, underscoring the wisdom of medieval poet Geoffrey Chaucer's saying, "[M]any a truth is said in jest." After the student asked his teacher to instruct him, Choclays replied that Left Handed already knew enough songs, that he was not taking

Every aspect of this photo speaks of relationship: the sheep obtained through song and prayer; the care of their shepherdess (Lucy Benally); the nurturing of lambs; Ron Kennedy helping Lucy; and the guest accommodations in the background provided by Troy and Edith Kennedy, owners of the Red Rock trading post. (NAU.PH. 98.71.25, Northern Arizona University, Cline Library, Kennedy Collection.)

care of the livestock he owned, that he could not "handle what he had," and that the songs were just songs—that is all. The two continued until Left Handed's older sister stepped in, and Choclays agreed to stop the playful discussion and get serious. He started with the "lamb songs." "That's what you want to start on first. There is where it starts, because when the little lamb is born it will crawl around in the dirt. Soon he will get up and soon he will be running around and begin growing. Soon it will be a great big sheep and begin to grow lambs all the time . . . so there's where you start from, because you want to grow something, so we'll start from there."[31] There were multiple sets of four, each one to protect the sheep from accidents, sickness, and getting lost as well as to sustain individual growth and development of the herd. "All of a sudden it was morning."

The men slept for a short while, ate breakfast, then prepared the sweat lodge, where they spent the rest of the day, rehearsing the songs and sharing new ones. That evening, after dinner, they prepared the hogan for another night's practice. At one point, Choclays declared, "You called for the songs, which I didn't want to let anybody know, which I wanted to keep to myself. I didn't want anybody to learn my songs, but here you called for it, you begged for it, so you have to learn all of it, not just a piece of it." That night they reviewed what had been taught, with Left Handed repeating the songs until they were perfect; next they worked on pronunciation. Choclays insisted that certain words be said in a particular way so that they were correct and clear to understand. The teacher then sang them all again and then the pupil. Now it was time to move on. "Let's see you try the property songs, start on them. The properties have little ones, too. There is a baby in the property, and these little ones have songs, so start on that. Everything has got young ones. Everything has got a baby, sheep property, beads, horses, and all other things have young, and they have all got songs." The two continued, with the master wide awake and the pupil becoming increasingly drowsy, "almost dropping over." Left Handed, by this time, was experiencing real difficulty in retaining all the information. As the sun rose, they got some sleep, ate breakfast, and prepared the sweat lodge for another session that morning. By the end of this session, Left Handed was doing well enough for his teacher to say, "You will catch onto it yourself sometime. I guess we had better quit."[32]

John Holiday tells of how he worked, when a youth, as an apprentice for Metal Teeth, an accomplished medicine man. Holiday met this elder as he traveled with his helpers, herding his cattle, mules, horses, sheep, and goats with jewelry, rugs, silver belts, new cloth, and deerskins packed in bundles on the mules and horses. Holiday, dressed in rags, greeted his relative who invited him to accompany him on the "singing and ceremonial trail," performing rituals and healing the sick. The young man stayed with Metal Teeth through the winter and spring, learning the songs, prayers, lectures, rituals, and stories and how they came into being during the creation. By the time the entourage headed home, Holiday had reached the depths of poverty, or so it seemed. He described his condition: "My clothes were in shreds, my coat and pants patched, and my toes hung out of the front of my shoes. I was a sight to see. Hardly anybody took a bath, and our feet and hands and faces were sandpaper-rough because we never washed them. 'I'm ready to go home; I'm leaving,' I told my teacher, and he agreed."[33]

Before departing, Metal Teeth told Holiday that he had received a big present in payment for all of the tasks he had performed as an apprentice. The young man, standing in rags before his wealthy instructor, wondered exactly what he meant. Metal Teeth left no doubt:

> "There, I have given you everything, all the prayers, the life, the shield—the protector of life—the gift of a healthy life. I have given you everything. I have bracelets, money, livestock, and my medicine bag. But I will give you none of them. It's all out there beyond that hill. You have the songs, prayers, and all it takes to get these things. You can receive these valuables, but you have to get them for yourself. You will use what I've taught, and if you do it right, you'll have what you need. Someday you'll know what I'm talking about." I now understand what he meant by that. It is true.[34]

It actually did not take Holiday long to realize what the medicine man meant.

He left Metal Teeth in the Dennehotso area and traveled cross-country to the Mexican Water trading post run by a white trader named Red-Haired Man (*Hastiin Bitsii'łichí'í*). When John arrived, he saw a lot of horses tied outside the store, indicating there were many customers inside, and so he waited for them to depart. Holiday had no desire to have anyone see him in his present condition and so he remained at a distance, hidden in the sagebrush, peeking through its branches. Finally, the men came out, loaded their goods on the horses, and rode to a cluster of cottonwood trees at a distance. This was Holiday's chance, so he hurried over on his horse in time to catch Red Hair going to lunch. Known for his facility with the Navajo language and his ability to joke, the trader invited his customer to lunch and got started on him. "Where have you been, John? What happened to you? You look scary! Have you been dragged around in the rocks? . . . There are plenty of goods here in the trading post." The trader let him know that he had been to his family's camp and bought a lot of wool from them just the day before and that they had sheared John's sheep and he had thirty-three bags waiting for him that the trader was willing to buy.[35]

Holiday did not hesitate. He received pants, shirt, shoes, socks, a coat with a velveteen collar that "felt like bat hair," a new saddle, bridle, rope, silver concho belt, silver and turquoise bracelets, and a hat with a silver band. John knew that he had overdone it, but he felt, "I really look nice," and waited for the previous customers to return to see how he had transformed. He was proud of his appearance, but more importantly, he was aware of what Metal Teeth had meant about wealth being "just beyond that hill." He had found it, and it had found him.

Work and Property Values

Today's Navajo elders were raised at a time when traditional teachings implanted strong work and preparedness ethics. Their mothers and fathers awakened their children and had them roll in the snow, dressed only in a breechclout for boys or a skirt for the girls, after they had run long distances in the cold. They were cautioned that the holy people would not bring them blessings if they were found lying around in bed after the sun had risen. They apparently had all that was needed, so why should the gods assist any more? Left Handed remembered running at all times of the day, especially around noon, because that was when Sun Bearer (*Jóhonaa'éí*) was having lunch. "When he sees me running a race under him, he'll try to get me a horse. The sun that we see in the sky is our father, and I'm his son; that's why when I race under him, when he sees me running, he knows I am after something, he knows I am after a horse. And soon enough I'll get a horse from my father, the sun, and from there on I won't be on foot any more. It's as when you're working for something, trying your best to get it."[36]

Tall Woman remembered that as a young girl her mother taught her about always working hard—preparing meals, keeping the hogan clean, and becoming expert in weaving. "You will find you can support yourself with that. You can feed your children with it, even if there is no other way to acquire food."[37] Buck Navajo, a medicine man at Navajo Mountain, recalls the counsel he received:

> My father was very assertive. He would chase me out of the hogan even though there was snow outside and make me walk. He would say, "Let your eyes get cold. Let your body get cold. Let the cold freeze your total body. Your brother is not mercy. Your sister is not mercy. You are going among people who have no mercy. This world has no mercy and you are going into it. The Anglos are not merciful.

> Everywhere you go you will encounter people who have no mercy. It is all up to you to survive." This was how I was raised and what I was told.[38]

What has been presented in the preceding material provides a glimpse into the highly traditional Navajo beliefs surrounding how and why this world functions as it does. Relatively few of the people, even in the late-nineteenth and early-twentieth centuries, discussed the philosophical reasoning behind what occurred or knew the songs and prayers the way Left Handed learned them. Thus, for some, going to trade was an energized spiritual experience, especially when traveling out of familiar territory, coupled with the possibility of unanticipated events. For others, trading was a mundane necessity where one obtained useful goods, while the feelings of still others fell somewhere in between. What, then, were the concerns or teachings for those not as tutored in traditional thought? What values did they have to guide them in acceptable behavior?

Richard Hobson, in 1954, published an important study entitled, *Navaho Acquisitive Values* as part of a series of reports about Navajos living around Rimrock, New Mexico. Based on 335 statements made by 77 Navajos out of a local population of around 600, this study provides an informed view in the words of the contributors. Participants came from a broad socioeconomic background. "About 43 percent of these informants would be considered poor by Navaho standards, 12 percent rich, and 45 percent in the middle range. As to degree of acculturation, about 47 percent are conservative, wanting to 'go the Navaho way;' 15 percent are caught between two worlds, have conflicting values and indulge in delinquent behavior; 24 percent are fairly acculturated and accept one or both ways of life, and about 14 percent want to go the white way."[39] Consider that almost half of the participants followed traditional values, even though the dominant culture had made extensive inroads by 1954. In one generation, starting roughly about 1930, the Navajos experienced livestock reduction, the Civilian Conservation Corps, the World War II exodus from the reservation for wage work and military service, extensive boarding- and day-school recruitment, proselytization by various Christian denominations and the Native American Church, the effects of the Korean War, and general trends in

U.S. culture to include accessibility of radios, a proliferation of cars and trucks, and an increasing availability of electricity and phone services. Still, traditional values prevailed.

Since this study is the first quantitatively and qualitatively based report on how Navajos view wealth in a context that defines their own cultural ideas, it bears scrutiny. It is divided into two main sections—the first "Values Regarding Wealth Accumulation," and the second "Socio-economic Values." The dominant theme in "wealth accumulation" is to "make a good living." Hobson found that "poverty generates an uncommon degree of anxiety" and that "the desire to accumulate wealth is perhaps stronger among the Navahos than among most other similar groups."[40] At least for some, this worked into the older traditional values of wearing nice clothes, having a good horse and riding equipment, and accumulating sheep to live on—at a time when much of the practicality of the old values was waning. In order to obtain these things, a person had to first think about it, plan, then work hard. "Having lots of property," the next category, is obtained through songs and dreams as well as physical effort. Dreams may portend what a person is about to receive. While Hobson makes no mention of the influence of the holy people, the implication is that this kind of assistance comes from spiritual realms. He then quotes an individual who reflected John Holiday's sentiments at the trading post after receiving his new clothes: "I could go anywhere to a Sing without being ashamed. Without good clothes, you couldn't go anywhere there were lots of people. Might get ashamed where they had good times."[41]

Other categories concerning gaining and maintaining wealth teach that it is equally important, once things have been received, that they are taken care of. Failure to do so will bring sickness and death to livestock and loss of property through waste and gambling. "Navaho anxiety over losing things is closely related to their anxiety over poverty. Don't gamble because you would lose, one is advised, but the phrase 'you would go without and be poor' is usually tacked on." "Work hard and don't be lazy" are other key concepts, since a person who is a good worker is seen as a good person and, likewise, one who is lazy is most likely a witch. During the study, Bill Begay said, "It helps if you have a good mother and father who tell you lots of stories all the time. Then maybe you will know something by the time you are twenty." Hobson concluded this section by stating that the younger generation was moving more and more into formal education, speaking English, and learning mechanical skills—all of which was a shift of values in traditional culture into comparable categories in Anglo-American society.[42]

Hobson's second section on "Socio-economic Values" begins with a dichotomy—"Don't Be too Rich" and "Never Get Poor." Both are viewed as going against the norm of conforming and working together with other members in the society. Rich people are often feared and mistrusted, although their wealth is admired. Often, accusations of witchcraft as a means of obtaining the wealth circulate about the individual. The use of supernatural power to trick and steal, robbing graves of buried wealth, being stingy with relatives or the poor, having enough wealth to maintain more than one wife, and enjoying a relatively easy lifestyle all contribute to what may be viewed as antisocial behavior. Witchcraft and wealth are closely linked, with people suggesting that getting rich is one of the main reasons a person will turn to witchcraft. Poverty, as related earlier, is personified as one of the last remaining monsters left to plague the Navajos. Those cursed with it are rejected and ridiculed and may be accused of being apprenticed to the rich as accomplices in witchcraft. While there may be a tempering of negative attitudes toward the poor, their lot in life is accepted by both those who are poor and those who are not.

The next two values—"Look after Your Family" and "Help People Out"—are closely allied and do not require a lot of explanation. Family solidarity and economic cooperation come together, especially when people are preparing and participating in ceremonies, some of which can take no more than a night (or day) and some of which can last as long as nine nights (or days). Large amounts of food, ceremonial and nonceremonial materials, payment for the medicine man and other participants, and necessities for the occasion may be far beyond the means of the host family. Hobson estimated that 20 percent of the total family income of the Rimrock Navajos was tied up in paying for ceremonies. Cooperation was essential.

Anthropologist Gary Witherspoon provided some calculations, based on his views in 1975, of the expense of a single Enemy Way ceremony. He suggests that, for the ritual activities, more than thirty people are involved; on the logistical side, including construction of the cooking area, the hauling of firewood, and general camp and guest maintenance, another hundred people may be added; when guests and spectators join the list, more than five hundred people may be counted. Next, he calculated the time required:

> From initial planning to completion, the ritual requires around two weeks, with the last three days containing the major aspects of the ritual. By assuming that the ritual is performed an average of five times each summer in each community, and with approximately one hundred Navajo communities, it is likely that the ritual occurs five hundred times each summer. An average of two thousand dollars is spent or exchanged in the performance of each ritual, and so it is likely that a million dollars is spent yearly by Navajos in the performance of Enemy Way.[43]

Hobson concludes his 1954 study with a few final points. Navajos placed "a high valuation upon the possession of land, livestock, houses, clothes, and jewelry. . . . Moreover, *learning* [his italics] about livestock and property is a sure method of acquiring them. One is instructed to 'learn how old people found things out' and to learn prayers, songs, and stories."[44] This hearkens back to the experience of Left Handed, whom Hobson cites liberally, and others, confirming that even at this later time, traditional values and properties were still in vogue and sought after. Following a discussion about wealth and poverty, the author ends with a principle that was central to white traders and their experience on the reservation. He points out that Navajos placed a premium on assistance and cooperation as an expected means of maintaining *k'é* and other positive societal bonds. "This 'helping out' policy is extended [beyond the family] to include Navaho people who are friends, neighbors, travelers. One must help everyone and 'do whatever people ask'—feed them, give them goods, money, and horses; help with herding, shearing, farming, and especially assisting in curing ceremonies."[45] Traders became involved in each of these important cultural aspects.

A final example summarizes traditional Navajo views and practices concerning relationships and values. Anthropologist Edward T. Hall spent four years (1933–37) working with the Navajo and Hopi on their reservations. As a young man who had not yet had formal schooling in studying culture, he became instantly aware that he was now living in a very different environment. This experience eventually led him to a lifetime of studying peoples of the world as well as of writing about his life and observations among those with whom he had begun. Of the Navajos he said, "[They] struck me as a people with the capacity to consider with a high degree of objectivity the consequences of their acts without sinking into a moralistic and political morass. They had a vibrant sense of life, which we only occasionally attain."[46] Hall went on to share his experiences as a trader who worked with sheep and their byproducts of wool and rugs, but then admitted that he and his associates never knew sheep as sheep in the same way as did his Navajo customers.

Many times Hall would pass a young boy or girl tending a large herd of grazing animals. He wondered how the child could perform this responsibility but then answered his own question: "It was the Navajos' *relationship* [his italics] that enabled the six-year-old Navajo child to stand in the middle of the herd without scattering the sheep. I found this to be extraordinary. The sheep and the people reacted to each other as though they were the same species! . . . Having been around animals most of my life, I could see that the sheep not only were not afraid of their owners, but were actually comfortable with them, the way some people and horses are." Here Hall is describing the effects of *k'é*, in this case with animals but which can be extended to everything that has an "animate being that lies within." Since a successful relationship needs to go two ways, people must make an effort toward positive interaction. "Consider what it would be like to know all the sheep individually, with some your friends, as a person can be friends with a horse. Then you will begin to experience the way Navajos felt about their sheep." The anthropologist concludes by pointing out that Navajos love their sheep, just as Anglos love a pet dog or cat, and considers them members of the family. Even when an old ewe has lost her teeth, is no longer in her prime, and appears to have no value, she has a right to live "because she had produced so much." The concern was not to "improve the herd" and get rid of her but to take care of an old friend—a relationship that continued even when not "practical."[47]

Buck Austin, a Navajo elder from the Kaibeto-Navajo Mountain region, shared some of the old people's teachings he learned when he was growing up. These elders taught that a person should rise early and start the sheep and horses toward good grass and water. By doing so, the sheep supplied the necessities of life, while the horses provided transportation, the animals reciprocating because of their good care. "To be a part of his own livestock, a Navajo breathed his animal's breath and inhaled the odor of their dung. Through smell, a horse or sheep would recognize its owner anywhere and would not be afraid. They would accept him as one of themselves. During lamb marketing time, the sheep would not loathe the owner for selling the lambs; . . . The money a Navajo received for the sales would buy what he wanted. That was a payment or reward from one's livestock for being good to them."[48]

Navajos believe that this reciprocity continues until death; the animals eat to become fat in order to better serve their master when they are killed. Some Navajos even suggest that one of the sheep in the herd will separate itself from the other livestock, signifying it is ready to give its life for food for its owner. Before killing a sheep, some people take wool from the chest, flank, and rear as they pray to the victim, then place the fleece first in its mouth, then in another sheep's mouth, explaining that this is not the end and that the herd will continue to grow and prosper. The sheep or goat is killed by cutting its throat as the head faces north, the direction that departing spirits go after this life. The skull is not completely severed until the carcass is ready to be hung up and divided for cooking. All of this is done to show respect for the animal as part of this two-way relationship.[49]

Since *k'é* is one of the most fundamental concepts in understanding the Navajo universe, it is not surprising that it enters significantly into the realm of Navajo trade and trading posts. While each individual has his or her own personality, cultural traditions, and life-shaping events that compose their existence and attitudes, the modal personality of the traditional Navajo pays attention to the establishment of relationships in both the tangible and intangible world in which the individual exists. Failure to do so leads to problems and consequences that only the holy people can diminish.

CHAPTER TWO

Setting the Stage

Traditional Trading Practices

The Colorado Plateau is not an easy place to live. This high-desert environment, with its sand-covered landscapes, rocky canyons, piñon and juniper forests, laccolithic mountains, intermittent and perennial streams, and fluctuating temperatures, provides challenges to those who wish to wrest a livelihood from such surroundings. Adaptation to this environment requires flexibility, resourcefulness, and an understanding of what it takes to survive. The plants and animals of this region illustrate well the toughness and specialization necessary to find a niche in this often unforgiving land, where resources may be abundant one moment and nonexistent the next, where conflict over those resources may be deadly, and where extremes may be the norm. Mother Nature makes her demands on those who wish to live in this part of the American West.

Prehistoric Native American cultures, as they moved into this area, were ingenious in adapting to the rhythms of the land, whether as hunters and gatherers or later as horticulturalists. Still, there were items that could only be obtained from trade with peoples living in other areas and with different resources. The material record left by the Paleo-Indians (9500–6000 BC) is sketchy enough to raise the question as to whether there were active trade networks operating among the bands of hunters and gatherers stalking paleofauna throughout the region. While these people fashioned stone tools from rock quarries that were, in some cases, two hundred miles or more distant from where such quarries were recently discovered, they could have carried these implements from their source rather than trading for them. The same could be argued about the Archaic-Indians (6000–1000 BC) as the environment shifted to its present characteristics.[1] What was this limited trade like, what items did these people desire, and what was traded or carried in to the Four Corners region, where today's states of Colorado, New Mexico, Arizona, and Utah meet? As Archaic hunters and gatherers on a drying, warming landscape, what kind of trade took place within and outside of this region as new ways of working the land became necessary? There are limited answers for these and similar questions.[2]

Not until the Ancestral Puebloans, or Anasazi (1000 BC–1300 AD), developed a culture distinct from that of the Archaic peoples, does one find absolute proof of both extensive internal and external trade. While the relatively slow but extremely important introduction of corn, squash, and later beans may have been part of a gradual agricultural expansion of these people, there is no doubt that maize is a product originating in Mesoamerica. Whether initially introduced by or traded into this culture, these plants became staples of the Anasazis' livelihood. Other items are more easily traced, pointing to high-value, very desirable trade goods. In southeastern Utah, the material remains left by these Native Americans includes macaws, kilts made from their feathers, copper bells from western Mexico, chocolate from Mesoamerica, a type of domesticated turkey derived from Texas and points east, and turquoise from southwestern and Mexican sources.[3] At their height, from the late 1000s to early 1100s AD, Anasazi trade networks extended throughout the Southwest and into Mexico as part of what is known as the Chacoan Phenomenon. While archaeologists are still not in agreement as to who controlled this exchange system and how it worked, they concur that trade was a central component of this culture's economy. By 1300 AD, the Anasazis had left their homes in the Four Corners region, settling farther south along the Rio Grande and at Acoma, Zuni, and the Hopi mesas.

Navajos, Utes, and their cousins, the Paiutes, were the next to enter the scene. Again, there is controversy as to when these groups arrived in the Four Corners region. Initially, as hunters and gatherers, all three left few material remains until well into the historic period, but the general trend among archaeologists now is to attribute an early presence—some believing these groups to be contemporaneous with the last gasps of Anasazi culture before departing the San Juan Basin.[4] Regardless as to the exact time of arrival in the prehistoric period, during historic times, the Utes and Navajos established intense trade relations that threaded throughout the Southwest and Great Basin and onto the plains to the east, Mexico to the south, and California to the west. There can be little doubt that a wide-ranging trail network based upon previous groups trading in the area was handily adopted by these historic tribes. With the introduction of the horse, mobility increased, expanding commerce in both quality and quantity. Many early Euro-American exploring parties—Spanish, Mexican, and Anglo-American—who left a detailed written record, noted that during at least part of their journey, they were following heavily traveled Indian foot and horse trails. Ease of movement through a tortuous canyon country, the availability of water and grass for livestock, the location of game and friendly villages, as well as the exchange of different resources and manufactured products made travel possible and trade profitable.

In the Four Corners region, Navajos had a checkered relationship with the Utes and Paiutes living there. The Utes were often allied with the Spanish, and later the Mexicans, headquartered in Santa Fe, who viewed these Indians as allies who could assist against the Navajo raids into their territory. The Spanish, either intentionally or unintentionally, expanded the amount and type of warfare and trade by introducing the horse, as well as opening a market for slaves to increase production of goods and to work the land. The Utes were more than happy to serve as scouts and fighters for Spanish armies, who set out on punitive raids against their enemies. Navajos not only attacked Spanish settlements, but also those of the Pueblo Indians whom the Spanish had subjugated. Both the Navajos and Utes raided for slaves to be sold in Abiquiu, Taos, and Santa Fe. They often attacked and captured each other, but a primary source of slaves was the Paiutes to the west, who did not have horses, operated in an austere environment in small, defenseless groups, and had not obtained metal goods, including firearms, to the same extent as those living closer to Spanish settlements. During the two hundred years of Spanish domination in the Southwest, there were a few instances when the tables turned and the Utes fought the Spanish, and some Navajo groups assisted both the colonizers and the Utes. For the Paiutes, however, there was no end to their being captured and sold.[5]

Early Navajo Trade

Throughout the seventeenth, eighteenth, and first half of the nineteenth centuries, trade with various groups continued. The Navajos became particularly well known for their weaving of saddle blankets, serapes, woven sashes, and "chief blankets," as well as for providing buckskins and baskets. In exchange, they received from various groups buffalo robes, elk hides, bridles, beads, turquoise, white shells, foodstuffs—especially corn—horses, and raw materials such as ochre, mescal, and pitch. From the Spanish and Mexicans came horses, sheep, goats, cattle, brass, copper, silver, pack saddles, guns, and alcohol.[6] Products and rates of exchange varied from tribe to tribe. For instance, in barter with pueblo groups, the Navajos might trade a large blanket for a string of turquoise beads or a small blanket, and for a saddle blanket they might get a pair of turquoise earrings or strands of abalone and turquoise. A sheep might be exchanged for fifty to eighty pounds of unhusked corn, a sack of peaches, or a large plaque of wafer bread. A horse or calf might be swapped for a Zuni silver-coated horse bridle or some combination of silver bracelets and other forms of jewelry. The "chief blanket," manufactured primarily for trade by the Navajos, may bring five buckskins or a dressed buffalo robe or a horse.[7] At a later time, Mrs. Dan Tauchin recalls her people trading with the Utes after the Long Walk period (1860s). "The Navajos traded their old rugs and saddle blankets, and occasionally some knitted stockings—like leggings which covered the legs but not the feet—to the Utes for buckskins and buffalo robes and commercial blankets. When I was a girl I saw those Utes come in and they would have a powwow on the other [north] side of the San Juan River. Once in a while they crossed south of the river to trade. They didn't live in those areas and came in only on trading missions."[8]

Navajos also exchanged materials used for ceremonies or for healing. Anthropologist Clyde Kluckhohn noted that, in purchasing medicinal plants, "There is a tremendous range in the prices paid for [them], varying primarily with the rarity of the plant and with the distance which must be traversed to collect it. In the case of some plants, knowledge of the sacred name which must be used in addressing it, and of prayers and/or songs which must be employed in collecting it, is also a price factor. The highest price I have on record is that of a good horse. . . .

The medicine involved a number of plants and it must be noted that the price was not so much for the actual plant specimens as much as for *the knowledge* [Kluckhohn's italics]."[9]

In 1948, anthropologist W. (Willard) W. Hill published the only extensive study of the older form of Navajo trading practices with different tribes. His classic "Navajo Trading and Trading Ritual" is based on elders sharing their memories of how they performed this activity in the old days, before Anglo stores became established and intertribal trade decreased. Unless otherwise cited, the following information comes from this study.

Trading was not a casual, spur-of-the-moment affair. A number of aspects had to be taken into consideration, such as the preparation of what was to be exchanged. Blankets and other woven products had to be made, sometimes six to eight months in advance. Horses needed to be well fed and rested, while grass and water needed to be available while en route. The travelers had to ensure that the objects they wished to obtain would be available at the end of their journey and that there would be a large collection of people to barter with to increase competitive advantage. One way to capitalize on this possibility was to follow the trading group's ceremonial calendar, when tribal members gathered for a religious observance. Although some Navajo trading parties were small, with three or four people, larger expeditions composed of twenty-five to thirty men appeared to be normal. The important criterion was to have participants with the right personality: "When picking partners for a trading trip, you should pick a lively man; one who arises early and takes good care of his horse. He need not be a relative unless the relative fits the description."[10]

Prominent members in the party selected a leader who organized and approved of who was to go and when they would leave. Hill mentions that the group chose this man with the primary consideration of his having "knowledge of trading ritual, songs, prayers, and prescribed behavior . . . [who] commanded immense bodies of religious knowledge devoted to this activity."[11] From start to finish, two to three weeks were not uncommon for a trading expedition to be gone, and so preparation of food, clothing, animals, and weapons, as well as trade goods, had to be undertaken. Women, the makers of many of the objects traded, could accompany male family members, but usually did not, although they knew that when the men returned, they would receive some benefit from their labor. Part of the reason that women did not go on these trips was because of the danger of moving beyond Navajo territory and into the land of a potential enemy. Home and the country within the bounds of Navajo land was safe—physically and spiritually—whereas once a person left this refuge, the possibility of encountering dangerous situations increased.

Boundaries and Power

The importance of boundaries in traditional Navajo thought cannot be overemphasized. Their influence is found in many aspects of life—from the Four Sacred Mountains and the four rivers that encircle Navajo lands to the weaving of a rug, the performance of a ceremony, the offering of prayers, and the entering of a home. Underlying all of these examples are two primary concepts. The first is that there is usually a clear division between what is safe or holy and what is dangerous or mundane. The event that occurred in a particular place or the creation of a power that resides in a specific site or area is explained in songs, prayers, and myths. For instance, the Four Sacred Mountains, in Navajo thought, circumscribe Navajo lands. The holy people created each of these mountains, which hold different powers, are viewed as the home of specific deity, and are protective in nature while empowering the ceremonies performed within their bounds. To the east is Blanca Peak (male) near Alamosa, Colorado; to the south, Mount Taylor (female) near Acoma, New Mexico; to the west, San Francisco Peaks (female) near Flagstaff, Arizona; and to the north, Mount Hesperus (male) near Durango, Colorado. The East holds the power of positive thinking, planning, new beginnings, and life and is represented by white shell; the South is turquoise, health, learning, summer, and leadership; the West is adult life, power, strength, and autumn; the North is self-protection, guidance, old age, and winter. Blessings from these personified powers are bigger and stronger when living within the boundaries established by the mountains.

Navajo land is also bounded by four sacred rivers—starting from the east and moving clockwise: Rio Grande (female), Little Colorado (male), Colorado (female), and San Juan (male). As with the mountains, everything inside of these boundaries is safe, while across the river lies the land of the enemy and potentially dangerous conditions. This theoretical understanding is explained by Romanian philosopher Mircea Eliade in *The Sacred and the Profane.*[12] He postulates that religious man separates the mundane world of daily life from the sacred, spiritual, and religious aspects that potentially make it special. "Interrupted space" exists where the sacred is found. For the Navajo, this rests inside the boundaries, and by differentiating the sacred from the profane, the believer encompasses and identifies many values held dear. In other words, beliefs and religious practices are highlighted by the object, location, or action considered sacred, embodying the most important elements of the religious experience.

The second point gathered from this understanding of boundaries is that it directs behavior and allows a person to control the power associated with the object, place, or holy person. In the animated, personified Navajo universe, everything holds a power that can help or hinder, depending upon the relationship (*k'é*) created by an individual. Offerings and prayers create that positive relationship so that assistance is obtained. One type of offering called *nitł'iz* is composed of four finely ground materials—white shell, turquoise, abalone, and jet—associated with the four directions and their powers. This male offering, in addition to corn pollen, a female offering, when accompanied with prayers, establishes a positive relationship. Without going into detail, a person who uses nitł'iz combines the powers and elements of the four directions to provide assistance and establish a pattern of thinking and behavior. Take one aspect of this power, the North, for instance, as explained by traditional teacher Jim Dandy: "The black stone [jet] represents your weapons and arrowheads. Anything that is used in war or for protection in ceremonies and that a person 'sits behind' for safety is associated with the North. In an Enemy Way ceremony, the sacred stick that is carried to different camps always goes to the North because it represents a weapon like an arrow, against evil. Anything to do with protective black clubs fashioned from stone symbolizes the North."[13]

Another important aspect in establishing a correct relationship is to know the sacred name of the entity being addressed. The San Juan River—the river of the North—provides an example. Songs and prayers offered a number of different sacred names that unlocked its protective power. The San Juan River is known as Old Age River (*Są Bitooh*), Male Water (*Tooh Biką'ii*), Male with a Crooked Body (*Biką'ii Bits'íís Nanooltł'iizhii*), Decorated with Abalone Shells (*Bikáá' Hodiichíłí*), and One with a Long Body (*Bits'íís Nineezí*). It is a powerful river, described as an older man with hair of white foam, as a snake wriggling through the desert, as a flash of lightning, and as a black club of protection to keep invaders from Navajo lands.[14] To some, the sparkle on the surface represents the shine of lightning. Prayer and pollen invoke the spirit within, which may be connected to protection through "singing the ways of the snake."[15] Certainly its holiness is called upon to help the traveler obtain goods and enjoy safety. To Tallis Holiday, leaving an offering on the shore of the river helped him achieve his goals after he crossed: "When a person comes to the river, he offers his corn pollen for a good journey and prosperity. 'I will receive many things with this small amount of money or trading items.' The people pleaded with the river's holy being. A long time ago, the river was the boundary to keep the enemy out."[16]

Crossing to the north side of the San Juan River places the traveler in enemy territory. Before going to the far shore, a person offers a prayer asking that the spirit of the river wrap its protective shield about him before entering the land of the Utes and the white man. Florence Begay recalls how Navajos prayed against their enemy: "The prayers were a tool to defeat evil or to hide behind for a safe journey."[17] In addition to protection, rain, grass, and other good things come to the person who beseeches the river. According to Sally Manygoats, "Now that this practice of prayer for protection and assistance is no longer being performed, the land is dry, rain has decreased, accidents have increased, vegetation is short and withered, livestock is dwindling, drowning is prevalent, and harmony is scarce. When people paid respect to Navajo boundaries, life was safe and happy."[18]

Sacred names were also part of the preparation before trading with other people. The Navajos referred to the Utes, in songs and prayers, as Dwellers in the Cedar-bark, while puebloan peoples were Dwellers in the Earth. Navajos believed that, in terms of obtaining what they wanted, these names were "the most essential part" in ritually preparing for transactions before the physical exchange took place.[19] Indeed, once the trading party reached its boundaries and prepared to enter the land of the foreigner, the leader and other knowledgeable men led the group

Distant travel for the Navajos meant potential physical and spiritual harm if not properly prepared. A common motif in most of the traditional stories focuses on a person on a journey who encounters challenges that could only be overcome through prayer and song. (Used by permission, Utah State Historical Society.)

in songs and prayers that changed the entire demeanor of the group. The men put joking aside, became serious, speaking only of positive things and successful trading from the past, and ensured that the trip became a deeply religious undertaking. Songs and prayers built the relationships with traders and the goods to make the trip fruitful.

There was a variety of songs that came from the Blessingway ceremony to promote good bargaining, friendly relations, and safety. These included the Hogan Songs, Mountain Songs, Songs of Hard and Soft Goods, Talking God Songs, Corn Songs, and Journey Songs. All of them brought beneficial results, but, depending upon where the travelers were, different songs might be used to fit a particular occasion. For instance, when traveling over difficult terrain, Mountain Songs may be used, whereas if in a wide valley, songs about Changing Woman, a beneficent Navajo deity might be more appropriate. Another song tells of four horses—each made of one of the four sacred "stones"—white shell, turquoise, abalone, and jet—who will bring riches to the singer: "With its beautiful neigh it calls as it starts toward me; soft goods of all sorts are attached to it [white shell bead horse] as it starts toward me; hard goods of all sorts are attached to it as it starts toward me; it shall continue to increase without fail as it starts toward me."[20] Each of the four horses brings its hard and soft goods to the singer. A different song intones: "Of all the good things of the earth, let me have an abundance; of all the beads and jewels of the earth, let me have abundance; let my horses pasture in peace, let my sheep pasture in peace."[21] Prayers and short rituals followed a similar pattern, with offerings of nitł'iz and then prayers that ask that the horses will be fleet of foot, that all may return safely home, and that the "Dwellers in the Cedar-bark (Utes), or that Dwellers in the Earth (Pueblos), may I have success in dealing with them."[22]

Another class of songs that were not tied into specific ceremonial knowledge are those called *sin beena'iiniihí*, translated as "songs by means of which trade is carried on." These are owned by individuals and sung to acquire wealth.[23] Those learned by Left Handed, discussed in the preceding chapter, are of this type. The power of these songs cannot be missed. Left Handed, on one occasion, explained to G-string's Son, a clan relative, the necessity of knowing trade and property songs. "It is good to know them [songs]. If you don't know anything about the different things then you are not strong at all. If you know some songs about the stocks and properties or life then you will be strong. You will have power. You will not starve. You won't go ragged. So you had better learn some songs about these things, my nephew."[24] G-string's Son then compared the poverty of his father to the wealth of Left Handed, because the latter knew the holy songs. The young man resolved to learn them all to avoid the situation that his father had left him and his family in.

The sole act of traveling could be dangerous, requiring protection by the holy people. There was the possibility of physical harm, as encountered by Walking Man, who traveled north of the San Juan River to the vicinity of today's Cortez, Colorado, to trade with the Utes. There he exchanged blankets for buffalo robes, then started home. On the way, he stopped at a Paiute camp near present-day Bluff, Utah, to spend the night. Before morning, they had killed him.[25] There was also spiritual danger while traveling through strange territory. Navajo Oshley from Dennehotso encountered a frightening experience that illustrates why the Navajos insisted on obtaining supernatural aid. He left one day with some wool, a few sheepskins and goatskins, and a rug to be traded at the Chilchinbeto trading post. That evening he was in unfamiliar territory, the sun had set, and his horse became spooky. Soon Oshley heard singing close by, heard horses snorting, and saw a corral in the distance, but at this point his horse would not move forward. He gave up trying to join what he thought might be a friendly camp, so he backtracked on the trail in an effort to find the trading post. Eventually, he spotted it, stayed the night, made his exchanges, and headed out. Curious about what had happened the previous night, he retraced his steps, only to find that what he thought was a sheep corral was really part of a wash and there was no hogan where the singing had supposedly come from; his horse again became increasingly skittish. What he found, however, was that he had luckily avoided imminent danger the night before. On a piece of hard, flat ground, he discovered a small female footprint. As Oshley tells it,

> She had walked right onto the flat hard surface that had some leaves on it, but the tracks that left the hard surface were those of a coyote. The human footprints did not leave the hard surface, while the coyote tracks went toward the trading post. I believe it was a skin walker [*yeenaldlooshii*—a malevolent human who uses supernatural power to transform into an animal and practice witchcraft] that I had encountered the night before, and this was the spot where she put on her skin. Her singing was very soft; almost as if it was secret. I still did not want to believe this, so I rode around again to see if her footprints came out somewhere. I saw it with my very own eyes. The footprints showed that she was a very old woman. . . . I was a little bit scared after that experience.[26]

Charlie Blueyes summarized the reason for protective songs when he said, "It is so that everything will go your way and you will return home."[27]

Trade Procedures

Trading parties established camp before dark and often built a brush enclosure that followed prescribed ritual behavior. When the men unsaddled the horses, the animals had to initially face in the direction of their destination. The windbreak had its opening face east, the cut boughs of the wall had their tips going in a clockwise or sunwise direction, and movement within the shelter was similar to that in a hogan—also in a sunwise direction. The leader sat in the place of honor in the back on the west wall, and when it was time to sleep, the men lay with their heads toward home and their feet in the direction they were to travel, symbolizing that they wished to return without difficulties. Before retiring and after rising, the men sang more songs and recited prayers under the direction of their leader, with each person taking a turn.

W. W. Hill learned there were significant differences between trading with the Utes and the puebloan peoples. Although the Navajos had historically fought with both groups, there is no question that the most extensive conflict had been against the Utes, who tirelessly pursued the Navajos during the Fearing Time and Long Walk period (1857–68).[28] So it is surprising that there was a more relaxed atmosphere between them as opposed to the Navajos' relations with the pueblo people. An excerpt from a Navajo account of trading with the Northern Utes in 1870 is instructive. It begins with a trade party approaching the Ute camp. Three Utes accompanying this group left them about twenty miles away to announce the Navajos' intent and to let both groups prepare. In the afternoon, a band of mounted Ute warriors charged the Navajo encampment, firing their guns in the air to welcome. After dismounting, they greeted the traders and spent the night with them, exchanging stories and reassuring each other that the conflicts of the past were over. During this time, the Utes picked out different Navajo friends who became trade partners responsible for entertaining and caring for their new associate. Building friendly relations was at the heart of this interaction.

Once at the Ute village, there was a dance, after which the men stayed awake much of the night exchanging songs. The following day, the trading took place:

> The next morning, after the Navaho were fed, each was told to go to a Ute tipi and sing. Every time they sang they were given a present. . . . The Navaho did this until they were tired. Then they went to their camp. Then the chief of the Ute came to the camp of the Navaho and told them not to be afraid because these Ute had never seen Navahos before and were friendly to them. . . . Next he said that the Ute who had taken blankets from their Navaho friends the night before would have horses ready for them the next morning. The next morning, certain ones were notified to come to different tipis. I had three

> chief's blankets which were taken by three Utes. I got a mare apiece for two of the blankets and a big buckskin and an American blanket for the third. We stayed with the Ute for six days. Some of the Ute accompanied us as far as the Green River. The Ute asked us to come back again.[29]

It appears that this procedure was fairly standard among many of the Southwest tribes. Richard I. Ford has studied extensively exchange relations between different Indian groups and confirms these practices:

> The visitor placed himself into the custody of a stranger. This was done by making an initial gift. Since each gift was actually a request to trade, to accept the gift obligated the recipient to feed and protect his guest. The two might trade or the host might inform others about his guest's desires. Upon the visitor leaving, the host would give a present. If he wanted to obligate his visitor in the future, he might give something of greater value than the initial gift. Conversely, he could guarantee the termination of the association by giving something of lesser value. This type of visitation was common throughout the Southwest.[30]

Many of these partnerships lasted for years and passed on to future generations. Whether for a long or short duration, these ad hoc connections were based on one guiding principle from the Navajo perspective, and that is *k'é*. Just as much of the trading excursion followed prescribed behavior to keep the holy people working with the traders, so, too, did the Navajos' relationship with the Utes. Sexual relations with Ute women were forbidden, there was no sharp bargaining but rather an exchange of "gifts," and upon departure a farewell present of equal value to previous gifts confirmed the friendship. This "free gift," called in Navajo *t'áájíík'eh*, was a token of good will.

Trade relations with different puebloan groups had a different tenor. Between the Navajos and these people, trade was conducted on more of a commercial basis, where sharp trading and deal-making provided the tone, even though the use of "friends" was still employed. The Navajos did not find this atmosphere nearly as enjoyable, but felt it was necessary. "The Pueblos are greedy; they are not like the Ute. If you want turquoise beads or buckskin, you have to 'buy' it from the Pueblos."[31] Still, the rates of exchange followed a predictable pattern. While none

These two Southern Utes (Capote) from northern New Mexico present a graphic image of the importance of trade with the Navajos. The silver conchos, the blanket placed over the warrior's legs, and the buffalo hide at his feet were all desired elements of exchange. (Special Collections, J. Willard Marriott Library, University of Utah.)

of the values given here are absolute and were collected from Native Americans at different times, they give a sense of what was considered fair. Navajos would exchange with the Utes two large buckskins for a large blanket or a "chief's" blanket for a horse; from the pueblos a string of turquoise for a large blanket or a few strands of beads for a horse; the Yavapais gave a buckskin for a blanket and two buckskins for a large blanket; and the Havasupais, a large buckskin for a pony or one blanket for a poor horse.[32] Objects used for ceremonial paraphernalia, wood brought in by the Navajos to the pueblos, corn and other foods, medicinal plants, and many other items not necessarily abundant at the host's village were also exchanged.

The return home for the traders continued the ritual behavior, ensuring safety and that the goods obtained would remain with the new owners and not have a desire to return from whence they came. Prayers and songs were part of this procedure for safe arrival within the bounds of Navajo land. Horses obtained through trade were blessed with corn pollen so that they would have no wish to return to their previous owners. Once home, a Blessingway ceremony cleansed the participants, who might have been affected by non-Navajo influences. It also ensured future good luck, turned the products obtained into those of the owner, fixed the color and purity of any beads traded, and renewed spiritual strength. Turquoise beads, because they are used in ceremonies and are believed to hold particular power, were treated circumspectly. Once traded, they remained in a sealed pouch until they were cleansed at home through the Blessingway. "These beads are like tender squash. They are easily bruised until after the ceremony. . . . One of the first things you do when you get a good string of beads is to inhale its breath."[33] As mentioned previously, everything has an "inner being that stands within," and that, when treated in a respectful relationship, assists the owner.

Internal Navajo Exchange

Before leaving the subject of traditional trading practices, a few additional points should be made. The previous discussion focused on exchanges with people outside of Navajo culture. Within the culture, it was a more relaxed, less ceremonially prescribed system of barter. If an individual was unfamiliar with whom he or she was trading, the first step was to learn of their social identity—their clan and family relations. This is standard fare whenever people meet. Next the type and amount of goods to be exchanged was shared, followed by an inspection of the property. Left Handed followed this procedure when he met Mister Wounded Kneecap, a clan relative. After exchanging clan information, Left Handed determined, "Well then, I guess you are my younger brother, or older brother, or nephew or uncle," to which Kneecap replied, "then we are younger and older brothers to each other."[34] Once they had established their relationship, Kneecap laid out on a canvas some goods he had secured in a bundle. He displayed two nicely woven women's skirts and some blankets and robes with different designs. The skirts were each valued at twenty sheep, the blanket at ten. Left Handed next spent a lot of time visiting, which ended by his inviting Kneecap and some of his family members to spend a few days at his home, where he would sponsor them in trading with neighbors. The family agreed and made their way to his hogan. The next morning after breakfast, the trading began. Left Handed purchased a skirt and blanket for thirty sheep, his wife a red belt for two sheep, two boys each took a robe for three sheep each, and a girl purchased all the calico Kneecap had for two sheep. Before departing, Kneecap attempted to sell some other products, but by this time, Left Handed felt he had exhausted his saleable livestock.[35]

From this simple experience, one sees a diluted form of trading procedures practiced in intertribal exchange—the establishment of relationships; the friendly conduct of business; hosting the trader, even when not particularly well known; sponsoring an exchange with neighboring people; and paying what was considered a fair price without dickering. At one point, one of the women who was selling stated that the price being asked was totally in keeping with what was being offered elsewhere. On the other hand, there were no ceremonial restrictions or spiritual preparation for the undertaking. Generally, it was a nonthreatening, even friendly exchange held within Navajo territory. In future chapters, there is a discussion of interactions at white trading posts, where many of the qualities just mentioned were utilized by the traders.

A final point is that of the songs and singing. Many accounts from traders at various posts recollect customers traveling from afar, chanting right up to the door of the post. While traditional Navajo people love to sing, these songs could also be helpful in the upcoming exchange. A few examples of the dramatic nature of this singing helps one to visualize the nature of this cultural experience. Hilda Wetherill and her husband, Ben, ran the Covered Water trading post in Arizona during World War I. She tells of being in the post with some customers when a few faint notes from a song drifted across the desert and into the store. Those inside moved to the outside porch to listen in the still evening air, the "sweetest, smoothest notes . . . [that] seemed not so loud as they seemed powerful."[36] In the distance, an old man recognized by the customers as "The Singer" rode his pony through the piñons and toward the post. "Swinging his quirt, his head thrown back, he poured out the most beautiful, wild, paganish sounds. I can't begin to describe them. Straight toward us he galloped and, pulling his horse to a sliding stop directly in front of the platform, he sat swaying in his saddle until he finished his song. His audience never stirred. When the song ended, there was that second of silence that is more appreciative than any applause; and then the Indians seized upon and greeted their old friend." The Singer entered the post, received a can of tomatoes and some crackers, then explained that he had ridden a long distance, exulting in his recollection of the old days and the land he lived in. That was when "the old songs came back and I remembered that I was The Singer. Hear me now as I ride home. I'll sing you the song of the trails as I sang it thirty years ago. A-la-honi, my children, today I am young again."[37] With that he was gone, but Wetherill listened to the song, almost in tears, as he rode into the distance.

Trader Harry Goulding, whose post was in Monument Valley, shared similar feelings. He recalled how for years, men riding horses or in a wagon would approach, "training their voices." This was especially impressive early in the morning or in the still of the evening. "They had a special chant that they sang while they were riding. It's a beautiful chant, especially where you get it from an old Navajo. And then, boom, it echoes back in the rock, and there she is again, it's coming and going. That big old cliff in there carried the echo right back to us. It changes. It goes along, and then all at once a high, beautiful note, where most people can't go, chanting down low a little bit and then all at once away up she goes. And do it perfect."[38]

Traditional Navajo trading practices were a cultural manifestation of deeply rooted values. They stressed what was most important in the Navajo world—expressing relationships, recognizing spiritual aspects in life, maintaining harmony when interacting with others, and protecting oneself from harm or evil, while obtaining what was desired. Much of this was possible as Native Americans interacted among themselves. But what could be maintained and what lost when dealing with Anglo-Americans in a trading-post setting? The next chapter starts from the ground floor up, literally, to see what kinds of accommodations each group would make on both sides of the bullpen.

CHAPTER THREE

Thinking about Architecture
Navajo Values in the Home and at the Post

The Navajo trading post, as an institution, began in 1868 when the Diné returned from their exile at Fort Sumner (1864–68). With a rather slow start at the southern end of a continuously expanding reservation, the trading post had become an integral part of the Navajo experience by 1900, when it blossomed and then prospered into the 1930s, before it began its decline and transformation into what is today—for the most part, a convenience store. The social, cultural, and economic shifts that brought about this change will be discussed later, but here we want to look at an often-mentioned but seldom-examined aspect of this experience—the architecture and location of these posts. In spite of the plentiful studies concerning the trading experience, very little has been written about the post's architectural organization from a cultural perspective. Most stores followed a very distinct and widespread pattern, but few people have discussed it from the view of the Navajo customer. This chapter investigates Navajo architectural beliefs that reflect social and cultural values and how traders made practical application of those beliefs while accommodating their own needs.

Just as stores today are arranged and operated with the customer in mind, buildings then were designed and constructed for certain reasons. Architectural specialist V. B. Price reminds us that "the lesson that design has symbolic as well as utilitarian meaning is vital for the creation of a humane future. . . . Architecture can reinforce such values by representing them symbolically in the design of buildings . . . by creating structures that help to channel action in socially favorable ways."[1] How the space is divided, the play of light for visual purposes, the scale and dimensions of its features, the expression of relationships, and its purely practical function all add to the meaning derived from the structure. In 1896, when Louis Sullivan coined the phrase "form follows function," he was partially right, but he missed the more human aspect of cultural values that enter into construction and add a dimension that may have little to do with pure function.[2] Every structure presents its builder with a set of conditions—the materials that are available, the purpose of the building, and who will be using it—that is, its totality as embodied in the final product.

Like so many aspects of a society, there is a great deal of accepted and expected behavior and form that is determined by the values important to a people. The space in a fixed feature is organized according to the activities of the group designing its use. Anthropologist Edward T. Hall supports the architectural notion of V. B. Price when he writes, "[Architectural structure] includes material manifestations as well as the hidden, internalized designs that govern behavior as man moves about on this earth. . . . Architects traditionally are preoccupied with the visual patterns of structures—what one sees. They are almost totally unaware of the fact that people carry around with them internalizations of fixed-feature space learned early in life. . . . The important point about fixed feature space is that it is the mold into which a great deal of behavior is cast."[3] In other words, there is a uniform, predictable spatial plan that speaks to learned, but perhaps not verbalized, notions of proper behavior within a particular setting.

Architectural Considerations: The Hogan

There is no finer example of how a structure and the space within became imbued with value than that found in a Navajo hogan. The design itself came from the holy people. What follows is an illustration of the importance of architectural thought for the Navajos, according to how they define cultural and spatial patterns. These values were part of a standardized house form that, with small variations, has been repeated from the earliest structures identified as Navajo down to the present-day hogan. Later, while looking at trading posts, one will see that traders applied some of these same teachings and principles in order to appeal to their clientele. The result was a somewhat standardized architecture that blended Navajo beliefs with late-nineteenth and early-twentieth century Anglo mercantile practices.

Traditional Navajo culture demands orderliness. Before the holy people created this world, they carefully thought through what would take place in the human experience, defining rules of proper behavior: how to cure disease, handle conflict, find peace, and avoid chaos. The establishment of the hogan was part of this plan. There are a number of different stories that tell of its creation, but all of them concern the holy people during the formative time when they were deciding what would be best for the Diné. Thought, songs, and prayers were an integral part of its establishment in this, the Fifth World. In one version, First Man is credited with taking a Black Bow (symbol of the power to overthrow evil) and a Male and Female Reed (symbol of the male and female principles), then joined them in a structure, added more logs, and covered it with dirt. His wife, First Woman, provided white corn pollen and ground cornmeal that he used to sprinkle the new home from east to west, saying, "May my home be sacred and beautiful, and may the days be beautiful and plenty."[4] In another version, First Man built his home of rainbows and sunbeams, the former going from north to south, the latter from east to west.[5]

Franc Newcomb, trader and ethnologist, provided a lengthier treatment based on a different story. Briefly, after the First People emerged into the Fifth World, the holy people busied themselves in the creation of the mountains and other parts of the environment to give diversity to the land. The First People lived together, but eventually tired of the circumstances, so they went in search of dwellings more appropriate than the caves and alcoves they then inhabited. The population grew, so they divided into clan and family groups, making change even more necessary. First Woman led some of them in a search that took them first to the Bird People. Each of the birds was anxious to help and show how they built their homes. From the Eagle, they learned how it put sticks together to make the nest structurally sound; from the Oriole they learned how to weave material from milkweed pods and cliff rose to make baskets; from Woodpecker and his hollowing out of a tree came the knowledge of drumming; but none of these birds' houses would do for humans. First Woman moved on. From the Beaver, the People learned about domed roofs, but did not like having the entrance under the water; from the Caterpillar they learned about webs that protect the young, but they did not want to live under the bark of trees during the winter; from Spider Woman, the People learned how she had a spacious room beneath the earth that she divided into four areas with blankets that she had woven, and so from her they also learned weaving; and then there were the Ant People, who had a doorway in the roof, but another one that went out to the east. These ants covered their home with dirt so that the enemy could not easily find it. The People had seen enough. It was time to act on the teachings received. First Woman told them:

> Our houses will be round, as all the homes we have visited have been that shape. We will build the walls of logs and make them higher than our heads, as do the eagles and the beaver. We will have a dome-shaped roof with an opening to the sky, and we will have a doorway facing east so the sun can waken us in the morning. Our floors and walls will be plastered with adobe mud like the home of the swallows. Then when it is finished, we will cover the house with earth to resemble the land all about us, and we will hang a woven blanket over the doorway.[6]

This pattern is repeated with hogans built today. There are certain variations in building materials, numbers of sides, additions of modern conveniences, all of which are documented in Stephen C. Jett's comprehensive study, *Navajo Architecture, Forms, History, Distributions*, but the basic form of this structure remains.[7]

Home site selection for a hogan was important. Many Navajo families used both a summer and winter range for livestock that were far enough apart to require two different homes during an annual rotation to resources. Indeed, there were some Navajo flocks that were so large that there could be two or three family camps to disperse the herds, again requiring a number of homes. In the summer, family members moved their livestock to higher elevations in the mountains, where firewood, water, and rich pasturelands for sheep and goats could be used in order to give the winter ranges a rest. During the cold months, the family moved to its winter hogan. A sheltered valley, a nook in a mesa, the edge of a piñon grove, close proximity to a rock wall that radiated heat from the sun but was not so close as to be hit with rolling rocks, and sites with southern and eastern exposures were all considered in camp selection. Areas prone to strong winds, deep snow, frigid temperatures, and difficult access were usually avoided. Whether selecting a spot for a winter or summer camp, the general Navajo practice was not to build right next to its source of water, but rather to give some distance so that other people or animals could also use the spring or waterhole. Many families were careful not to disturb anthills, build on or near Anasazi ruins, upset patterns of animal traffic, or settle near recent burials.[8]

Once the family selected a site, construction began. There are two types of hogans that exist today, both of which are closely identified with the Navajo deity named Talking God. He is one of the most powerful of the holy people. He supplies answers and assistance to mortals, has compassion, and is the god who responds during the sanctifying of a hogan. He is also a prominent deity in the Blessingway ritual that is associated with the teachings of the hogan as well as other foundational Navajo thought. In a number of versions about the first home, Talking God, with the help of Calling God, created the mythic prototype of the male, or conical or forked-stick, hogan (*ałch'į'á deez'éí*) out of the four sacred "stones" of white shell, turquoise, abalone, and jet. He formed them in the shape of Gobernador Knob, New Mexico, ceremonially referred to as the "Heart of the Earth." Talking God also made the female, or round-top or cribbed-roof, hogan (*tsindahdiitł'in*), which he fashioned after Huerfano Mountain, also in New Mexico, and which is called "Lungs of the Earth."[9] Both of these structures are believed to be alive and so need to be cleansed through ceremony, fed through pollen and prayer, and treated with respect according to traditional procedures. The beginning of the Blessingway starts with the Hogan Songs referred to as "first" or "leading" songs that dedicate the structure for ritual purposes. There are two sets of Hogan Songs, the first being called the Chief or Hogan Songs of Planning and the second, the Hogan Songs of Talking God.[10] "The songs remind the occupants that orderliness should not cease with the close of a ceremony and that man's appreciation for orderliness, beauty, and regularity should not be confined to the immediate surroundings of his home. They extend this appreciation to earth and sky, to cardinal points and their phenomena, to all things in the universe."[11]

The construction of a hogan is well documented and so will not be repeated here, other than for those elements that had an impact on trading-post architecture and thought.[12] The four main posts (the doorposts on the east are considered as one) each have a deity, are connected in power to one of the four sacred mountains, and represent (going from east to north in a sunwise direction) thinking, planning, life, and the future. The doorpost slabs are referred to as door guards (*chéʼ étiin siláí*), with the one on the left (south) side representing soft goods of various types (*yódí ał taasʼéí*) as well as First Man, while the one on the right (north) represents hard goods or the four types of sacred stones (*nitłʻiz*) and First Woman. Together, they portray man and woman living and working together.[13] A bow and arrow to keep evil at bay is hung above this east-facing door. Covering the doorway hangs a woven blanket, which notifies the holy people that this is a Navajo home and that they are welcomed. Thus, the doorposts facing east not only have the power to summon property when blessed, but also function as guards for protection and provide the portal for the sun to enter and awaken people in the morning. They face the direction from which the holy people travel to visit a home, where blessings and teachings come from, and the direction in which all creation began.

Of Property and Etiquette

Wealth and property are also part of the material that fills in between the main structural posts. Father Berard Haile, who spoke the Navajo language fluently and understood ceremonial perception of the intangible, used the word "shelves" in describing how the holy people built the first hogan. "The legends let the spaces between the poles be filled with shelves of white bead east to south, with shelves of turquoise south to west, with shelves of abalone west to north, with shelves of jet north to east." The four poles are prayed to as living female beings who can bring blessings from their respective mountain into the home and to the family. Haile continues: "The poles move to this mountain at the bidding of the builders who lean them in position as living symbols of vegetation, soft goods or apparel, jewels or ornaments, as symbols of the source of rain, water and pollen, in fact symbolic of all that carries long life and happiness with it."[14]

The interior space within a hogan is divided according to both daily functions and ritual activity. Just as the main poles are emplaced starting in the east and ending in the north in a sunwise direction, it is proper etiquette for those entering a hogan, especially during a ceremony, to also move in that same clockwise manner. The cardinal direction used in building the structure continues inside with space allocation. The south side is generally viewed as the males' area, where they sleep and store much of their property. The west is the place of honor, where respected elders (male or female), medicine men, and influential leaders sit, while the north is the women's work area, where much of their household equipment and cooking utensils are stored. That is why Left Handed commented, "My place was always on the south side, my mother's place was always on the north, and my father's on the west."[15]

During ceremonies, occupants removed much of the daily household equipment to maximize floor space for ritual procedures, but even then the seating was sexually segregated. Traffic flow under these conditions would always follow a sunwise, or clockwise, movement, but during non-ceremonial times, with daily activities and objects limiting space, a person could enter and go either to the north or south without summoning the evil that would otherwise be attracted by going counterclockwise.[16]

The point to consider here is that there are definite cultural patterns that became ingrained as second nature and as the correct way to do things. Just as in American society today, driving on the right, walking down a crowded hallway on the right, yielding the right-of-way at an intersection, and allowing women to pass through a doorway before men are all culturally derived and approved patterns to diminish chaos, avoid accidents, and show politeness, so too did Navajo culture form its own expected behavior. Anthropologist Gladys Reichard put into perspective a Navajo view of when one approaches a hogan for a ceremony. The ritualistic points start before even reaching the structure:

> If we consider the home from the viewpoint of one approaching and entering, we may find some such sequence as the following: "to the place where the trails converge," "to the trail that leads up to the home," "through the door," "around the house in a sunwise circuit," "to the foundation of the house," "to the four sides of the house," to the center of the house," to the place for the one-sung-over at the west behind the fire." These are points to which a god returns with me after accompanying me on a dangerous journey. . . .
>
> I consider my door from two viewpoints, one the trail leading out of it; the other the trail leading in, both being mentioned in prayer. As

> I step out I pray for "safety one step before me," then "safety the step beyond that one." These two phrases mean "may my road be safe step by step as I move along it," or they may be explained as a request for safety this moment and in the future.[17]

This movement represents the person traveling through time and space during a sacred ceremony that has both physical and spiritual outcomes. Comparable ceremonies that ritually institutionalize religious patterns of movement are found in the fourteen Stations of the Cross as practiced in the Roman Catholic faith and the Condolence and Installation of Chiefs ritual of the Iroquois.[18] In all three, core religious beliefs are expressed through the approach, entrance, participation, and exit of the structure in compliance with teachings and shared experience with supernatural powers. Sacred space in architecture teaches values as humans participate with the holy people.

Inside the hogan are symbols of healing and comfort that also express spiritual relationships. The fire (*kǫ'*) built in the middle floor space represents the center of the universe, the floor being the land and the walls the sky, while the opening at the top is where the holy people look in to see what is happening. The fire is also the heart of this living structure, giving warmth and light, cooking food to sustain life, and creating a desirable place where *k'é* (relationships) are maintained. Jim Dandy, a traditional Navajo educator, told of the teachings he received from his parents and grandparents concerning the home fire: "Fire, like a grandparent, is a provider and must be respected. Every time my great-grandmother cooked, she would stir the coals with her fire poker, pray, then place on the coals any food that was left over so that the fire, too, could eat. She thanked it for being a holy person, a great-great-great grandfather who provides. When my grandparents prayed it was always addressed as a male in the prayer, thanking it for its help. Another way we showed respect was not to play with fire."[19]

The fire poker (*honeeshgish*) is another symbol that has both spiritual and practical application in the home. There are two types—one used for daily stoking and banking of the fire and is associated with the female principle, while the other used in ceremonies is considered male. In both cases, they serve as protection against evil and as an object that holds power through prayers. Jenny Francis, a traditional grandmother from Monument Valley, counselled, "You pray and pray with the fire

The interior of this hogan—with its peeled juniper logs that cast a warm glow, its cribbed roof and symmetrical visual balance, and its multitude of metaphorical images, ranging from a representation of a womb or bird's nest to the world and sky—gives proof of First Woman's wish: "May my home be sacred and beautiful and may the days be beautiful and plenty." (Used by permission, photo by Kay Shumway.)

poker. Everything goes according to the way you pray. If you pray in the good way, without harsh words, it is good for your children. You pray for them from the bottom of their feet to the top of their head."[20] Even when a parent must leave for a short time, a fire poker can be used to watch over the home and a sleeping child. It is placed next to an infant to protect it through the love and prayers left behind. In the old days, when a hogan was abandoned for a season, the occupants placed a poker in a crevice between the logs to protect the structure until they returned, addressing it saying, "Grandfather or grandmother, protect our home while we are away."[21]

Another basic element that is part of traditional Navajo homes and thinking is water, a substance that is a source of life-giving power. As with the other things already mentioned, there are extensive teachings and a number of dos and don'ts associated with it. Water, whether it falls from the sky or rests on the land, is vital to life and is to be treated with respect, just as grandparents should be. The reason water is referred to as a grandparent or parent is because it provides for the Navajos. Rain and snow add to other sources of water on the earth, and together they care for it and work together to sustain life. Both earth and water are grandparents and are addressed that way when Navajos pray. Water is considered female in the prayers, and so is treated as a living grandmother who holds lots of power.[22]

Navajo thinking about architecture and related elements is embedded with intense symbolism, much of which is contained in the songs and prayers of the Blessingway. These ritual teachings are fundamental to traditional thought and are well known to knowledgeable Navajo people. Even in a nonceremonial environment, correct behavior and established patterns were taught and practiced by many. In summarizing the discussion above, there are numerous points to consider. The first is that patterns and expected behavior limit confusion and offense. Navajo culture has a very strong set of beliefs that describe how to do things correctly, as prescribed by the holy people. Site selection of a home is not just one of convenience but also one that expresses relationships with the gods as well as with creatures in the natural world. For example, homes were not built right next to a spring, but at a distance in order to allow others to make use of it. The importance of an east-facing door (true for every hogan), a large, open space inside the hogan for ceremonial and social gatherings, the sunwise movement within the structure, the doorposts associated with hard and soft goods, as well as the "shelves" along the wall mentioned in the songs, the four divisions of space, the fire, fire poker, and water as part of the protective and social imagery taught by these objects were all part of the values found in Navajo architectural thought. How much of this transferred to the trading post?

The Trading Post: Location

What follows is proof that many of the early traders understood enough about Navajo culture to create an environment that was familiar and friendly to their customers. When one considers that there were hundreds of Navajo trading posts over a span of the roughly seventy years under consideration here, that these were built by white men who may or may not have understood Navajo culture, who came from a very different background and had different priorities, and whose resources were often strained, then one can marvel at the consistency that many of these posts shared in their architectural form.[23] There were, of course, differences in placement, materials, and structures, but even a quick perusal of posts still standing shows a very close conformity to a particular pattern conducive to Navajo trade and values.

The process started with proper site selection. Elizabeth Hegemann, a trader at Shonto during the late 1920s and early 1930s, made it sound quite easy when she wrote that "In those primitive days, there were two essentials for existence on the reservation—water and Navvy trade."[24] While these were crucial, there was more to it than that. The Navajo Reservation covers a vast expanse of land that requires skill to navigate. Since the Anasazis in prehistoric times, there has been a network of trails that crisscrossed this high-desert environment. Canyons, ground conditions, traffic-ability, snow depth, prevailing westerly winds, river crossings, grazing areas, springs and waterholes, and interconnecting trail and road systems all had to be considered. Looking at Hegemann's Shonto as an example, she is quick to point out that the post did a steady but not spectacular business. Because it sits in a sea of piñon and juniper trees, piñon nuts became one of its main items of export. The topography was rough, making it suitable for goats, and so the traders sold many goatskins and much less wool when compared with posts located in prime sheep country. Navajo customers in the Shonto–Navajo Mountain–Inscription House region frequented the post, maintaining a steady, local business, while the store provided a service to people who would have otherwise had to travel a very long distance on a regular basis. The big drawback to its location was getting in and out of the canyon. Thus, road construction and maintenance were ongoing tasks necessary for the post to get its supplies in and purchases out.[25] Other stores, such as the Wetherill post in Kayenta, were in a position to catch the natural flow of a number of intersecting trails that brought a large clientele with their substantial flocks of sheep and bags of wool to sell.

Father Leopold Ostermann of the Franciscans shared why the Catholic Church established a mission at Chinle, mentioning many of the same reasons used by traders. That is why, in 1916, there were four active posts within a very short distance of this Catholic station. Ostermann explains why. Chinle was near the center of the Navajo Reservation and enjoyed excellent accessibility. Chinle Wash had been famous for its planted fields of corn and other vegetables since the mid-1870s, and with Canyon de Chelly providing access from the east, the Hopi mesas to the west, and Chinle Wash offering a north-south route with a predictable fording location across the San Juan River to the north, it was a natural location for trade. Peach harvests in Canyon de Chelly served as another magnet to draw people from all over the reservation along this network of roads and trails and into Chinle.[26] Add to this, a growing number of tourists at the turn of the century interested in exploring Canyon de Chelly, the introduction of the automobile, and a growing fascination with Native American culture, especially in the Southwest, and one can understand how this location supported that number of posts. While it violated the generally accepted dictum among traders that there should be roughly twenty-five miles between each post, since that was considered a day's travel by horse and wagon for a Navajo family, the resources and situation allowed multiple stores to exist.

The second of Hegemann's necessities—water—was absolutely crucial. Traders established posts because there was a large enough population to sustain the business. Water was a major reason why people stayed in an area, and so it would often take an agreement with the local population to allow a store owner to enter the community and have access to a site with water. Many traders tell of how they established their post at a distance from a spring or waterhole, in keeping with traditional Navajo values of having the precious liquid available for others. Mildred Heflin remembers carrying water about a quarter of a mile to her home and trading post at Navajo Mountain; in another instance, she hauled water in barrels seven miles to the post at Star Lake, while at Shonto, Elizabeth Hegemann noted that the earliest source of water at this post required the individual to carry it a couple hundred feet up a sandy slope.[27] Some posts were located on a river or lake, where availability of water was no problem, but the majority of stores operated near a well dug in the desert soil.

The experience of John Hunt, a trader in northeastern Arizona, gives a good example of how some posts had to obtain water. He bought the Mexican Water trading post around 1913, after an earlier trader had built the store next to a wash on a slick-rock hill. The well on the south side of this wash provided water for the animals in a nearby corral, but it was unpalatable for humans. The rock potholes around the store held rainwater for a short time, which the Hunt family used for drinking, but a half mile from the store, there was also a rock formation with a cistern twelve feet deep and eight feet wide where water collected. This "Jacob's Well" also provided drinking water from snow and rain runoff that family members carried back in pails. When this, too, dried up, the Hunts sent their bucket brigade to another wash at some distance and secured water from a good spring. The trail to this source changed every time it rained, while its steepness added to the difficulty of carrying heavy buckets out of the wash.[28]

Other times there was too much water at Mexican Water. Summer storms brought intense flash flooding that scoured away the bank of the wash. John built a dam to slow the rampaging torrents until one storm poured five feet over the top of it and carried the remains down the wash, making a twenty- to thirty-foot-deep chasm fifteen feet away from the store. There was no choice; the family had to move. Hunt and his partner, John Walker, went to the local Navajos and asked them where they would like a new store to be located. The Indians selected a spot three miles to the south of the previous site, the traders received approval from the agent in Shiprock, and built a new structure with the materials from the old one. Twenty yards to the north of the store, the men dug a well, struck water, and retrieved the precious liquid from the open hole with a bucket until it was eventually covered with a wooden top and fitted with a hand pump.[29]

A final example of posts and water comes from Hilda Faunce Wetherill, who, with her husband, Ben, moved into an already established store. One day, a Navajo woman approached them with a demand that they start paying for the water from the spring in the wash below the store. Her family had dug it, and the previous trader had paid an annual fee of one hundred dollars in merchandise, and so she argued, the Wetherills should do the same. Ben calmed the situation by giving the woman some food and told her he would talk to her another time, but he knew that without access to water, the store and all of its trade would dry up and blow away. Eventually, Ben found a likely spot that he, with some Navajo help, could explore for water. After digging down ten feet, they struck water, went deeper and increased the flow, built a wooden top to place over the hole, then celebrated their success. Not only did he get out of the fix he had been in with the Navajo woman, but his store received a name. Ben announced that, in the best tradition of Navajo practices, "anyone who came would be welcome to fill a keg or a canteen or to water a thirsty horse, for this water was the old, old spring that belonged to Hosteen Blue Goat [a deceased but highly respected neighbor] and that we should all know this and call it Covered Water."[30]

Another concern in site selection for some traders was the post's proximity to Anasazi ruins. Traditional Navajo people practiced a general avoidance of the dead.[31] Bill and Sally Lippincott encountered this at their post at Wide Ruin when they were excavating for a pipeline. Navajo workers soon discovered that there were Anasazi artifacts beneath the soil. All work stopped, the men refused to touch the objects that had belonged to the "Pueblo Old Ones," and business at the store dropped off. Bill had to entirely reroute his pipeline to avoid any further disturbance that might anger the prehistoric Anasazi spirits. A visit from a medicine man helped allay local fears. Unfortunately, a little later some insecticide with nitroglycerine exploded inside the store, badly damaging it. The Lippincotts decided to renovate what was left, increase their stock of goods, and add electricity to power refrigerators, an innovation. Still, the customers did not frequent the store. The owners learned that many of the local Navajos believed that it was the Anasazis who had caused the explosion, and it was not until the Lippincotts employed a medicine man to ceremonially cleanse the area by putting the spirits to rest that business returned to normal.[32]

The Trading Post: Spatial Organization

Not until the future operator of a post and the local Navajo community had agreed on a site and the Bureau of Indian Affairs had approved it, did construction begin. Many posts followed a general pattern of the trader living in the area first in a tent from which he sold goods. This tested the viability of customer traffic and trade without having to make a large investment. Assuming all went well, the next step was to make a more permanent structure out of local materials such as cottonwood logs, rocks, and dirt—or, in later years, slab lumber brought in by wagon. One popular form of structure that was relatively easy to build and inexpensive was called a stockade-type. Builders trimmed cedar (juniper) posts, inserted them three feet into the ground, chinked the spaces with mud and bark, and put on a flat roof made of boards covered with six inches of soil. Windows could be added to provide sunshine, while as in the interior of a hogan, the blond color of the peeled logs reflected light and gave a warm glow to the room. Theft was always a concern, and so as soon as practical, finely carved rock or adobe walls, laid by Navajo labor, provided the thickness necessary to prevent break-ins. Small windows placed eight to ten feet high and fitted with iron bars prevented people from crawling inside, while some posts had a small skylight on the roof to give added light.

While no two posts were exactly the same, there were many similarities shared by all. Stokes Carson, a trader who operated a number of stores in the Four Corners region, gives a particularly good description of a "typical" store and how it evolved. His biographer, Willow Roberts, summarizes his experience at one site in New Mexico:

> On the Gallegos, the Carsons put up two tents, one for the operation of business and one to live in while they completed the trading post. Stokes built two rooms, one for living quarters and the other for the store, into a shelf of sandstone that formed the base and part of the back wall. Later a small storeroom was added to the other side of the store, also dug into the sandstone, its floor a foot lower so that stepping into it was like going into a cool, dark cave. In front of the trading post, the sandstone sloped unevenly down a few yards to more level and sandy ground above the wash, a bumpy approach for wagons. The building was long, low, and sturdy; its rough-hewn stone block walls, eighteen inches thick, were carefully squared on the outside corners and rounded with adobe plaster on the inside edges of windows and doors. The plaster was whitewashed. The living quarters adjoining the store, partitioned out of an area thirty-six feet square, consisted of two little bedrooms, a kitchen, and a room for eating and sitting in. The ceilings were low, and though it might have been small for a family of four, it was larger than a hogan.
>
> A door led into the slightly smaller shelf-lined store. Goods hung from the ceilings: coils of rope, lanterns, tin coffee pots and buckets, bits, and pieces of harnesses. High counters were built on three sides around the front door so that they enclosed a space for people

Inside the H. K. Warren trading post, Kayenta, Arizona, one finds the elements common to most stores of the early twentieth century—the bullpen with its well-worn counters, a stove to warm visitors, scales to weigh goods, stocked shelves beyond the reach of customers, merchandise suspended from the ceiling, and the room bathed in natural light. (NAU.PH. 412.5.86, Northern Arizona University, Cline Library, Warren Collection.)

to gather in, buy, sit, and smoke; this was referred to in all trading posts as the bull pen. The floor behind these counters was raised a few inches above ground level, a psychological vantage point because it made the trader taller than his customers. A wood stove stood in the center of the bull pen, its tin smoke pipe running up through the ceiling and several feet above the flat wooden roof.

The windows set into the thick walls in both house and store were not large. They let in only enough of the brilliant dry sunlight to see by without also letting in too much heat in the summer and cold in winter. In the back wall of the store a window peered like an eye over the sandstone shelf, almost at ground level. In the opposite wall was the front door, and another lower window facing south across the wash. The wash in those days was narrower than it is today, and water, which appeared in it more frequently, was drawn up into a well. The water was even drinkable, though it tasted a little sulfurous.[33]

A study published in 1936 examined sixty-four posts in operation at that time and found that thirty-five were built with rock, sixteen of adobe, five of logs, and eight were frame buildings. Based on information provided by forty-nine traders at the time, two of these posts were established between 1870 and 1879, two between 1880 and 1889, seven between 1890 and 1899, fourteen between 1900 and 1909, fifteen between 1910 and 1919, and nine between 1920 and 1929, with another thirty posts not visited or accounted for. All but three of these stores were licensed, the unlicensed ones being on deeded land on the reservation. But there were also a lot of posts that were not on the reservation, many of them in border towns.[34]

The Bureau of Indian Affairs approved the licensed traders and gave instructions for a post at a specific location. In 1943, there were ninety-five such traders.[35] The store and inventory may have belonged to the trader, but the land surrounding it was the tribe's, and the license was the government's.[36] Anyone caught trading on the reservation without a license forfeited all merchandise and paid a fine of up to five hundred dollars. How much money was actually lost in such an incident varied from post to post, but one trader estimated that his store cost him five thousand dollars, with two thousand down and a 6 percent mortgage, along with an inventory of fifteen hundred dollars. On the other hand, a person with a license was never guaranteed that it would be renewed at the end of the tenure, which could last from one to five years.[37]

The store was the central pivot from which many activities radiated. Most posts had their main trade room, the warerooms where pawn and other exchanged items were kept, and the living quarters of the trader and his family. The 1936 study related that, of fifty posts examined, thirty-seven had living quarters incorporated as part of the store area under one roof, with only thirteen traders living in separate houses.[38] This provided security for the goods and convenience for the trader, since customers appeared at many different hours, making eating and sleeping sometimes irregular events. Franc Newcomb described her impression as a newlywed bride as she entered her trading-post home: "My first view of the interior was something of a shock as I had never seen anything just like it before. The original two rooms were of logs papered with blue calico held in place with slats taken from 'Four-XXXX' coffee boxes, with no attempt to conceal the lettering. The floors were of wide, badly-worn planks covered with beautiful red-grey-and-black Navaho rugs. Planks were also used to make the door, which swung on iron hinges and fastened with a heavy iron bolt. There was a small square window in each room with half inch iron bars outside."[39]

Once the trader completed the main building, there were other facilities necessary to support the business. A long shed or barn housed large sacks of wool purchased from the Navajos, as well as the bales of hay and bags of grain that had to be kept out of the weather and secured. Corrals used for livestock, for sheep shearing, and for impromptu rodeos became centers of seasonal activity. Some posts might have a sheep-dipping vat nearby, and most had a tall pole frame to hold sacks used to support the bags while stuffing them with wool. The indispensable outhouse was another featured edifice, until indoor plumbing with sufficient water arrived. The "two-seater" at Shonto provided amusement for the white occupants and their guests. When the wind blew just right, there was enough open space behind the structure that the updraft "would have launched a glider, and the lee side of any sagebrush would have been preferable. . . . One joked about putting a piece of the paper down behind and then seeing it float overhead; even the heavier sheets from the mail order catalogues fared no better."[40]

One structure that really struck home with the Navajo clientele was the guest hogan. People wishing to trade at a post may have had two or three days' travel before arriving at their destination, followed by a day of trading. To not only assist but to encourage people to stay, many traders had Navajo workers construct a hogan in near proximity to the post as a sort of free motel room for weary travelers. Built according to Navajo specifications—an east-facing door, peeled cedar logs, small metal stove or fireplace, and some basic cooking utensils—this shelter helped the guests feel cared for and fostered a desire to return. Add to this, wood hauled in for cooking and water made available for drinking, and the Navajo customers literally had all of the comforts of home. The structure, with its amenities, was similar to what Gladwell Richardson called a "travelers" hogan, often found at trail junctions in isolated areas, where Navajos would stop and rest. This building did not necessarily belong to anyone but was available for free use. "According to custom, a baking powder tin, containing coffee and a small amount of salt, should be buried to the right of the door. This was for emergency use—afterward to be replaced for the next hungry person. A can for boiling coffee stood against the log wall over the cache."[41] A sleeping blanket might also be there for added comfort. The guest hogan, like many other practices, showed that the traders were aware of the values and beliefs of their customers.

At Home in a Post

How much of what traders did was a result of studied practice and observation, how much was based on following what other traders did, and how much was just good luck will never be entirely known. But common sense suggests that many traders understood important Navajo values and applied them to their business practices. Since relationships are central to Navajo thought, the architecture and the experience at the post for the Navajo customer helped to foster a sense of acceptance and well-being. Unlike the round hogan described in the myths and used for ceremonial purposes, most Navajo trading posts were either square or rectangular, a type of structure called *kin*, and were not considered sacred. Still, in Navajo thought it was a home—"a home for merchandise" (*naalyéhé bá hooghan*)—just as a bank was "a home for money" (*béeso bá hooghan*), a drugstore "a home for medicine (*azee' bá hooghan*), and a church "a home of prayer" (*sodizin bá hooghan*).[42] Navajo etiquette and procedure was not dropped at the door, but continued from start to finish.

The orientation of the trading post is another good indicator of sensitivity to tradition. Underscoring, again, that Anglo owners brought their own cultural values and economic desires to the business—which included the building of the store—it might be surprising that over 55 percent of the doors used by customers faced east.[43] Given all of the possible considerations when building a post—access roads, rock formations, prevailing winds, space for loading and unloading merchandise, area needed for turning wagons, exposure to heat and cold, layout of supporting structures, and other concerns—this percentage seems to indicate more than just chance. The second-most-popular direction for the door to face was south at 27 percent, while those facing west and those facing north were tied at 9 percent. There are certainly physical considerations as to why the east was favored—morning sunlight coming in to illuminate the store, more exposure to the sun of the south-facing wall in the winter, and away from the prevailing winds that generally come from the west—but there is no missing the cultural teachings of good coming from the east, the direction associated with the holy people.

The first area encountered, once inside the post, was the bullpen. Just the name connotes a certain set of Anglo cultural values—the control of cattle or a temporary place to hold prisoners. While this gives a feeling of animosity linked with power that was not intended by most traders—indeed, many held just the opposite sentiments—the name remained standard throughout the posts of Navajo land. To the *Diné*, this open space mimicked, in a sense, the same arrangement found in a hogan, a large open area where social interaction took place. The bullpen's size varied according to that of the structure, some being twenty-five by fifteen feet, others twelve feet square, others longer and narrower, but a central feature to most was an iron stove that radiated heat in the winter just as a fire or stove did in the center of a hogan. The importance of the fire with its accompanying imagery, along with that of the fire poker used to stoke it, were transferred in Navajo thought to these features in the store. Many posts in the early days also made a bucket of water with a common dipper or cup available for customers, another symbol of home and traditional values. To Elizabeth Hegemann, "This was sloppy business at best and an extra chore for the trader," but a necessity until water became more available or other types of drink could be sold.[44] A few benches might line a wall of the bullpen, but many traders talk of their customers sitting on the floor in small clusters around its perimeter, just as in a hogan.

Some Anglo people going into a post for the first time might be confused as to how to approach this open space. Teresa Wilkins mentioned that when she entered the Hubbell store for the first time she felt "dwarfed" by what she saw and observed that "the few hasty visitors who rush headlong through the entry, stop short in the center of the bullpen and stand looking confused. When I did this myself, I wondered, 'What do I do? Where do I go? What is this place? What do I do now that I am here?'"[45] On the other hand, Edward T. Hall, who spent a number of years as a young man as a trader on the reservation and who has studied the use of spatial arrangements in cultures, had a different view:

> After your eyes adjusted, you found a visual feast. All manner of tack and other goods hung from the vigas (logs used as roof beams), and what light there was came from a couple of small barred windows

> about ten feet above the ground, high enough to discourage break-ins. The only other space that left me with a similar visual feeling was years later when I visited the Le Corbusier's magnificent chapel at Ronchamp. Naturally, the early trading post was diminutive in scale and lacked Corbusier's touch, but the effect was still evocative (there is no term in the English language to express that amalgam of visual and emotional responses elicited by certain architectural spaces).[46]

Traders often describe the activities in the bullpen almost as if it were a stage. When people entered, they would usually find a seat against a wall after shaking hands all around with whoever was present. There did not seem to be a standard traffic flow in a sunwise direction, but in keeping with traditional Navajo patterns, the men congregated in one part of the space and the women in another. Talk was generally soft-spoken and unpretentious as people discussed the latest price of sheep and wool, what trader gave the best prices, where the next ceremony would be held, or any other news—personal or community. There were also opportunities to make new acquaintances. "Here in this bullpen, many a young Navajo couple had met and sedately talked over marriage while seated on the floor with a bottle of pop between them. It would have been considered immoral and scandalous to have been seen together outside the trading post. Afterwards their parents would get together and arrange the wedding ceremony."[47]

Surrounding the bullpen, usually on three sides, were counters approximately three feet wide and four feet tall. Small posts might just have one counter that went the length or width of the room. In either instance, access to space behind the counter was controlled by a hinged countertop that lifted upward, so that this motion was highly visible. Counters worn smooth by the sliding of rugs, small sacks of wool, jewelry, and other items made by the Navajos, as well as the trader's wares, were the focal point of business. The width of the wooden counters was important. First they had to handle bulky, heavy items passing to and from both sides of the bullpen. Second, they served as a barrier between customer and owner so that only those things handed by the trader to the Navajo were in reach.[48] Third, counters kept the bullpen free from clutter so that, as in a hogan with its seating arrangements around the periphery, the trader could deal with one person at a time.

Counters serving as a defensive barrier between trader and customer occasionally proved necessary. In 1902–3, Arthur L. Chaffin operated a small post forty-five miles below Hite on the Colorado River. Above his counter was an eighteen-inch open space through which objects of trade were passed. Above this opening was a wire screen stretched across the length of the counter, then up to the ceiling. Its purpose was to protect the trader from a customer throwing a noose around his neck and strangling him with the ten-foot rawhide lariat that many Indians carried to lead their horses. According to Chaffin, this occurred a number of times on the eastern part of the reservation. How quickly a dicey situation could arise became apparent to this trader when, one day, he conducted business with a group of Navajos. One of them spied a bottle that he thought was alcohol in a trunk, and although the trader tried to convince him that it was not, the man did not accept the explanation. Some of the customers asked to go across the river to their temporary camp, and so Chaffin had his assistant, Mike, take them in the post ferry, a small rowboat. When one of the Navajos came back, he slipped on the landing, thereby revealing a rawhide lariat wrapped around his waist.

Chaffin became uneasy as a large group of men entered the store. Mike pretended to clean his rifle, while Chaffin, wearing a six-shooter and keeping a shotgun within easy reach behind the counter, continued to serve his clients. Soon the truth came out—the Navajos wanted the whiskey and they wanted it now. Chaffin unlocked the trunk and handed them the bottle, protesting all the while that they really did not want to drink its contents. A few quick gulps by the first imbiber convinced them that the trader was right—the vinegar in the bottle just was not what they expected. The counter, with its protective wire, had helped maintain sufficient space for the incident to play out peacefully.[49]

In a store with an entrance in the east, the counters would be on the south, west, and north walls, patterning the social division of space found in a hogan. On the west, the place of honor, stood the trader, waiting to greet his customers; to his sides and behind him were shelves of goods. These were placed high enough so that the customer could have an unhindered view of what the store had to offer and point to the item without having to know its specific name. One distinct disadvantage to the trader was that the counters blocked most of the heat radiating from the stove during the winter. While the Navajo customers sitting on the floor were comfortable, the man or woman behind the counters was cold from the waist down.[50]

The floor behind the counter was raised approximately six inches above that of the floor of the bullpen, giving the trader a visual and psychological advantage. Hall explains: "Counters were chest-high on a small man and undercut so that it was possible to rest your folded arms horizontally on the counter as though it were a wide mantelpiece. The effect, although comfortable, was to reduce your psychological height to that of a child. The trader, meanwhile, stood on a raised platform behind the counter like a parent or a king surveying his subjects below. When he put his hands on the counter, he had to lean over and look down at you from twenty inches above."[51] Much of this was done for self-protection as well as to monitor the flow of traffic and activities in the bullpen.

Hall divides spatial relationships into four categories—intimate, personal, social, and public—all of which apply in the interaction that occurs in a post. Intimate space in the bullpen is very much in keeping with the type of relationships found in a hogan. This is characterized by being in close enough proximity to feel body warmth, experience personal smells, sitting or standing side-by-side, and being within easy touch. The next phase of personal distance (two-and-a-half feet to four feet) characterizes the space between the trader and a single customer over the counter. Hall explains: "Keeping someone at 'arm's length' is one way of expressing the far phase of personal distance. It extends from a point that is just outside of easy touching distance by one person to a point where two people can touch fingers if they extend both arms. This is the limit of physical domination in the very real sense. Beyond it, a person cannot easily 'get his hands on' someone else."[52] This is an important point for the trader when conflict arose. The counter provided the necessary safe distance between trader and customer, allowing time to react if necessary.

Close social distance (four to seven feet) was where impersonal business dealings occurred in which the trader talked to customers in the bullpen as at a casual social gathering, whereas the far phase of social distance (seven to twelve feet) gave a "more formal character" to business conducted at this range. The voice was raised, people at this distance could hear clearly what was being said, and eye contact was a means of judging if the listeners were involved in the discussion. The distance could also "insulate or screen people from each other. This distance [made] it possible for them to continue to work in the presence of another person without appearing to be rude."[53] In a trading post, this allowed the trader to maintain his position and work behind the counter without having to insert himself into the interaction in the bullpen unless invited or until a customer approached to do business. Finally, close public distance (twelve to twenty-five feet) provided time for a person to take evasive or defensive action if threatened.

In summarizing Navajo and Anglo values embedded in the architecture of the trading post, it is safe to say that it was a joint amalgam in which both cultures found expression. The Navajos, with their deep philosophical and physical understanding of the origin and organization of traditional structures, paid a great deal of attention to everything—from site selection and spatial orientation, to powerful symbols of protection for that space, to communication of important values in a fixed structure. The traders paid attention to these beliefs, while implementing their own values of functional utility, security, customer satisfaction, and profit. These values were literally expressed on both sides of the bullpen, one side of the counter having a Navajo orientation, the other Anglo-American mercantile concepts and products. Here they joined together for mutual benefit.

CHAPTER FOUR

Building Bonds, Trading Goods

The Navajo Post Experience

This chapter and the next look at the trading experience from two different perspectives—that of the Navajo customer and that of the Anglo trader—on each of their sides of the bullpen. It is immediately apparent that, for the Navajo, relationships of many different types guided the process, even though there might be some sharp-eyed trade accompanying the banter and goods pushed across the counter. Previous chapters have noted the concept of spiritual property and the preparations made to ensure harmony in trade and success in obtaining desired materials. Much of this occurred in a Native-to-Native setting and was based in traditional procedures of exchange. There were, of course, other times that required none of the complexity and preparation, but just a simple swap. Shifting to the trading-post scene, one finds many accounts that indicate traditional values frequently came into play, determining what Navajo customers did. What also becomes apparent is that they were equals in bartering with the Anglo traders who had their own concerns and cultural ways of dealing with the exchange.

The introduction of the trading post on the reservation brought white neighbors into an otherwise totally Navajo environment. Previous experience with the dominant society had primarily been warfare, which etched deep scars into the memory of who these white people were. The "Fearing Time" (roughly 1857–64) and the incarceration at Fort Sumner (1864–68) of over eight thousand Navajos placed perhaps half of the tribe in exile from their homelands, forcing them to live in very difficult circumstances.[1] Those who did not go to Fort Sumner in east-central New Mexico lived in different, but equally challenging, conditions on the periphery of Navajo lands. Once these scattered and chastened groups reunited, thoughts from these now-past events remained embedded for decades.

Initial Impressions

There is little wonder that, when trading posts began to appear on the reservation, there was at least some hesitation by those who had shared these earlier experiences as well as by those who had only heard about them. In March 1906, when John Wetherill approached the Navajo people living in the Oljato area about his establishing a post, he met with initial resistance. At first, a group of men who had fled to Navajo Mountain and returned after the signing of the peace treaty told him to load his wagon and go back to where he had come from. John remained calm, sponsored a rabbit hunt-then-feast, providing coffee and bread for the occasion, and listened to the old men speak. He pointed out the long distances people had to travel to trade, while some argued that this was their land, they had done well without white men present, and they did not need them now. Then an old man spoke:

> There were hard days long ago, days when the People gathered piñon nuts and built platforms of sticks in trees to protect themselves from the wolves; days when they dug roots for food and made clothes of cedar bark; days when the rains did not come and the grass failed and we had no food. . . . The white men brought us sheep, and we had meat and wool for our clothing. It is not hard now as it once was. . . . It will be better still if this white man comes among us. Then we will not have to go so far to sell our skins and our wool, our blankets, and our cattle. We can get food when we need it. It is good to have the white man here.[2]

Not only did John Wetherill receive permission to build the post in Oljato, but a few years later, he built another one in Kayenta, as he and his wife, Louisa, became fast friends with the Navajos living in the area. Together, they did much to preserve the culture. Certainly, the Navajo reasoning for letting him stay—more plentiful food, easier trading circumstances, less travel, access to more and better goods—resonated not only with this group, but others across tribal lands.

Still there was a sense of fear that accompanied the white presence. Left Handed, son of Old Man Hat, arrived for his first time at one of the very early posts at Fort Defiance to sell some wool. Although he was very impressed with all of the merchandise—"What wonderful things they are"—the trader scared him: "I was afraid of the white people."[3] The first time Tall Woman and her sisters, who were living in the Chinle Valley, saw Anglos, she noted, "We didn't know what they were doing. They were just full of hair, and their beards were big. That scared us and we told our parents about it when we brought the sheep in. . . . Some of the People said those white people were spies or something like that."[4] Initial mistrust of traders continued for some time. Samuel Holiday in Monument Valley remembers his mother saying that, although they were friendly, she did not trust them because they very well could be spies for the white government, which was looking for children to put in school. Samuel's first trip to a trading post in Oljato gave him his initial introduction to Anglos. "The first day I went to that post with my mother, I was shy and frightened. I stood by the store door and saw a white man laughing and talking to Navajos inside. Afraid to enter, I watched and studied this man known to the Navajos as *Bilagáana Tso* (Big Whiteman) or in English Reuben Heflin. . . . I must have been about eleven or twelve years old before I stopped being afraid of white men."[5]

While there might always be an opportunity for mistrust, for the most part, the Navajos welcomed traders into their communities because they were viewed as a positive addition. Harry Goulding knew that the Monument Valley community had accepted him when he and his wife, Mike, had to leave their trade stock for a number of days. He tied the flaps of his tent that held all of his goods, told a Navajo neighbor to watch his property, and departed. When he returned, he found everything in order. Goulding knew "that by that time, I guess they thought we were alright."[6] From a practical standpoint, life just became a whole lot easier. The closer the post, the less travel and the more convenience in obtaining what was needed for daily existence. As one Navajo noted: "The necessities of life, it seems like, is always there: shovels and tools and hoes, something that made your job a lot easier. . . . And that's what the trading post was to us, is a convenience for us. Everything that we need, it seems like it's there. It's always something you look forward to. And, of course, as little children, we'd cry because the wagon was leaving and we wanted to go."[7] Fred Yazzie from Monument Valley agreed. He was happy that traders had moved in: "When the supplies were coming, people would tell each other that they were coming. I liked it when the money was still coin, because of its jingle. It made me sound like a rich man."[8]

Finally, Navajo people appreciated the post as an agent of change—not that they were consciously trying to leave the old ways behind, but they accepted innovation and readily adapted. Navajos recognized the material benefit that came with that change during the first half of the twentieth century. When, in the last quarter of the nineteenth century, Left Handed's mother gave him a pouch with fifteen matches, she explained, "Those matches are from the white people. That's what they use to make fire with. . . . A white man who came and is living [in Keams Canyon] said he was going to put up a store. He has all kinds of things, different kinds of grub, flour, coffee, sugar, all different kinds of calico and colored blankets and dishes, and these matches. He has a great many matches. He wants to buy wool, skins, and blankets from us. . . . So now we can buy anything that we want."[9]

Greetings with Amenities

The trading experience of a family or individual began long before they arrived at the post. Spiritual preparations through prayers and songs for safe travel and profitable exchanges as well as gathering and packing the items for trade were part of the process. Many traders noted that as travelers approached the store, they lifted their voices in song characterized as a "falsetto . . . together with rapid, pulsing, bounding movement, and restless, beautiful melodies."[10] Hilda Faunce Wetherill's experience with The Singer at the Covered Water Trading Post and that of Harry Goulding in Monument Valley, both previously cited, provide good examples of how important song and prayer were to the business of trading.

Once a customer reached the post, and if activities in the store allowed, the trader might come out to welcome the new arrival. Navajo greetings with strangers were restrained and dignified when compared with the loud voice, tight grip, and shoulder slapping commonly found with enthusiastic Anglo greetings. A slight touch of hands and a short verbal exchange were often enough. Wearing Spectacles (John L. Hubbell) at the Ganado post walked a fine line one day in terms of enthusiasm, but there was no missing his happiness when he greeted Left Handed and his companions. He emerged from the store, ran among the visitors shaking hands, addressing them using kinship terms, and thanking them for coming. Then, in keeping with the best of Navajo traditions, he told them to unload the horses and turn them loose, remarking that there was abundant feed and water nearby. He then offered, "There's wood behind the building, plenty of it, so get some wood and build yourselves a fire anywhere around here where you can find some shade, and I'll go in and get you something to eat. Come over to the store, and I'll let you have some buckets and you can get some water." In addition to the pails, Hubbell gave them a large Dutch oven and a big pan of flour with salt and baking powder added to make bread. Following a hefty lunch, he had them stay in the shade where it was cool and later invited them to come into the store when they were ready to trade, all of the time laughing and joking and promising to give them a good price for their wool. Hubbell wanted his customers to know he understood that "you've come from a long way. After you're through trading you can stay here tonight. You can spend a day or two or three or even four, because I like to have company all the time." The men finished their trading that day and planned on leaving the next since they had lots of things to do at home and did not want to loaf around the post eating the trader's food for days, because, "then you wouldn't have any more store." The trader replied, "Well, I don't care about feeding you. I only care for friends, that's all. Even though I run out of grub I can get more, because it's not far from here to where I get it. But it's up to you. If you hurry home it's all right. I know you have many things to do." Before they left the next day, the trader gave them additional food for their journey.[11]

More common and in keeping with Navajo tradition is the entry into a store as described by Edward Hall. In this case the customer would ease into the store in a subtle way, harmonious with what was taking place inside. Direct, prolonged eye contact by the individual entering was avoided:

> As two men approach each other, eye contact is broken—at about the point where it is possible to begin to pick up details of facial expression. Once this boundary is crossed, they look past each other, holding the approaching figure in their peripheral field of vision. To look

> directly at the other is tantamount to swearing at them (to a child, a sharp look takes the place of a hard slap). The handshake is gentle and held for quite a while—held but not squeezed—as each soaks up the emotional tone of the other. When each has both sent and received the warmth and pleasure of meeting as well as a sampling of each other's underlying mood, then they have in a subtle way also communicated mutual respect.[12]

These small scenes of greeting encapsulate many traditional values important in Navajo relationships. Anthropologist Louise Lamphere named her study of ritual and economic cooperation in a Navajo community *To Run after Them*, "[alluding] to the Navajo concept of cooperation, which is expressed in phrases like 'I'll help him' or 'I'll run after him' (*bíká 'adeeshgwoł*) and 'After me they are running along' or 'They are helping me' (*shíká 'anájah*)."[13] Foundational to what has been described here are fundamental Navajo beliefs of how people should be treated. In addition to her own research, Lamphere cites a study of core values conducted in the 1950s by John Ladd, who identified seven values central to Navajo behavior. They are:

1. Take care of your possessions.
2. Take good care of your children.
3. Children should take care of their parents.
4. People ought to help the aged.
5. One ought to help a person who is in dire need.
6. Help one's wife's family.
7. In general, help anybody who needs or requests it.[14]

At least four of these seven concepts are found in the previous account of Hubbell's greeting and dealing with Left Handed. The initial greeting began by using kinship terms, a topic to be discussed in more detail shortly. At this point, it is enough to indicate that, by doing so, both the customer and the trader place responsibilities and obligations to act in certain ways as if those involved were actual relatives. Providing firewood, offering food, ensuring comfort, using joking relations, and lending equipment are all part of assistance expected of relatives. Making food and water available for the animals is a matter of caring for one's possessions. All of this falls into the general category of helping people in need. The trader did not want them to miss these points and so assured them that the barter and cost of feeding them was not what he cared about, but only watching after his friends. Another way of looking at this relationship is to view the opposite, or negative, side, which expresses uncooperativeness. Lamphere, in her study, determined that a Navajo person should not be "stingy," "mean," "mad," "jealous," or "lazy"—none of which fits the description of Hubbell.[15] Edward Hall's experience in trading posts and working with Navajo people in a variety of circumstances confirmed his belief that "when a Navajo doesn't know you, he has no particular reason to pay attention to you. It is as though you don't exist. . . . When Navajos act pleased to be with you, you can believe them. They must know you first in order for you to become a friend."[16]

When a customer arrived at a post, he or she might take a little time outside before entering. This is a Navajo courtesy, still practiced today, that discourages hurrying to the door and pushing one's way in, only to find that something is going on that is personal in nature. A newcomer may not know what is happening inside and so a leisurely approach gives people a chance to collect themselves and prepare. Once within, low-spoken greetings and handshakes with people in the bullpen established a welcome with those sharing the space. Some might take seats around the periphery, others might circulate to a group of their own sex. Elizabeth Hegemann paints a colorful picture in her description of the atmosphere in the Shonto post before actual trading begins:

> The quiet self-effacement of the younger women was noticeable; any other behavior after they had passed the giggling little girl stage would have been considered bold and far from decorous. When they entered, they walked around to the right [or north] side of the bullpen, because the right side of the hogan is the woman's side. They kept their Pendleton blankets pulled over their heads, not for warmth, but to protect them from any unseemly stares from young bucks in the store. A few old matriarchs, however, were a law unto themselves. They would sweep into the store, their wide hips and skirts filling the doorway, and go straight to the counter with their rug or sack of wool. Then after glancing around at all the men as if they did not exist and emitting a loud "Yah-de-luum" [equivalent to English "Oh, well"], they went right to trading. After all, most of the men other than blood relatives in the store had been their husbands or brothers-in-law or fathers-in-law. It took more than these to faze such a Navaho dowager.

> The customers watched each other and their possessions like hawks because stealing was not looked upon as a sin, and we watched all of them for the same reason.[17]

Most of the Navajo clients were not quite as brash as an occasional older woman could be because of her prominent standing in a matrilineal community. There was no hurry in getting down to business, since people came as much to socialize and learn about events in the area as they did to obtain goods. Fred Yazzie recalls, "You didn't run in there and then out. You would ask what an individual was doing and in turn he would like to know what you were doing—are there any social events like sings and Enemy Way ceremonies. That's how Navajos had their togetherness. You would see if your neighbors were well and good. Navajos depended on each other in health and sickness."[18]

Gifting Relationships

From a white man's perspective, the trader was on Navajo time. Tom Kirk, in discussing his family's experience as traders, believed that exchanges with the Navajos in a post were different from anything else in the United States. He felt one had to "think like a Navaho," disregard most Anglo business procedures, and accept that they felt like they had "all the time in the world." He continued, "Getting the best price for their merchandise was not the most important thing, after they got to know and trust you, but you had to prove yourself first. They would wait for hours for you, and only you, to take care of them. Each has his or her own personality and, like anyone else, had to be dealt with as an individual."[19]

Once a customer approached the counter, known as "on top you buy or sell" (*bikáá nida'iiniihígíí*), a new set of dynamics came into play, but central to all was still relationship. Navajo culture emphasizes specific ways of acting based upon kinship. Anthropologists have spent a great deal of time in analyzing proper behavior between husband-wife, mother-child, father-child, in-laws, grandparents, and many other kinship combinations. For purposes here, suffice it to say that by using kinship terms—whether mother-daughter, grandmother or grandfather and child, or son- in-law—there were expected behaviors and obligations that accompanied these titles. For example, the responsibility of a

Ray Hunt, speaking here to a crowd of customers visiting his Chilchinbeto trading post, was well known for his fluent Navajo. Having been raised on the reservation, he was very aware of the social amenities expected in Navajo culture that encouraged return visits. (Courtesy San Juan County Historical Commission.)

mother to provide for and nurture a child is a strong bond in traditional culture that is reinforced by the example of Changing Woman in Navajo mythology. Respect, love, caring, and service are the expected bonds that hold son and daughter to mother through childhood and adult life. Fathers are also affectionate, teach their children, joke with them on certain topics, and train them in hard work and responsibility. A father's bond is often not nearly as close, however, as that of mother with child. Grandparents are kind, caring, wise, and sought after during times of trouble. They receive a great deal of respect and share traditional knowledge that is important in maintaining Navajo values.[20] Thus, a customer using these terms of relationship expected the recipient to respond in a culturally acceptable way, according to how they were addressed. Deescheeny Nez Tracy, an elder raised in Ganado, explained, "When I speak to people at meetings or talk to students, I traditionally greet my audience with 'My friends,' 'My grandchildren,' 'My children' or whatever relates to brotherhood. Being friendly and respectful to everyone can prolong a person's life while jealousy and hate are evil and lead only to loneliness, ill health, and tragedy."[21]

Hilda Wetherill at Covered Water re-created a classic dialogue of what transpired at the counter. Although she tired of "listening any day and many times a day to monologues" (like the one that follows), she also allowed the customer to establish the atmosphere and relationship that was conducive to his or her need. Here, Hilda becomes "Grandmother."

> "My dear Grandmother, come into this corner with me. We will speak slowly and not get mad. The children at my house who call you mother are hungry. They cry and call for candy and bread. One has a stomach. He said his mother would send medicine and apples and candy to him by me. Your children need shoes. In six months I shall sell my wool. Allow me, my mother, my sister, my pretty younger sister, to owe you twenty dollars until I shear my sheep. This will make all your children who live at my house warm.
>
> "Other Navajos may lie to you and never pay their bills, but I am not like those crows and coyotes and gamblers. I never lie; I do not know anything about cards; I never go where cards are.
>
> "See. My coat is worn out and no good. Let me have a new coat. Let me owe you four dollars for a new coat. Is this four dollars? It is very thin and ugly for four dollars. But I am poor so I will take it. I tell all Navajos how nice you are, how you feed anyone who asks it, and give apples and candy to all children who come to your store. The Indians all say you are good. Put some sweets in a bag and I will take it to your children and tell them their mother sent it.
>
> "Is this good flour? It looks black; it may be wormy. Give me a knife and I will cut open the sack and look at it.
>
> "How much do I owe you now? Twenty dollars plus four dollars plus three dollars and a half? Twenty-seven and a half? I will trade two dollars and a half more and then I will remember thirty dollars. I could never remember twenty-seven dollars and a half.
>
> "Have you a sack? What shall I carry all this stuff home in? Give me a sack, mother; a poor ugly gunnysack will do. None? Then I must use my robe, and I shall be cold riding.
>
> "Give me some strong twine to tie this robe so I won't lose my sack of flour. More than that; make it strong enough for a hair string. See,

> my hair string is dirty. I need a new one. Now I am ready to go. No, wait. I forgot tobacco. Mother mine, give me tobacco.
>
> "It's a long way to my house and my horse is tired. While he rests I have time to eat. Give me a can of pears and a box of crackers, because I live a long way off and come all this distance in the cold to trade with you because I know you are good and we are friends. That's right, that's good. This is for friendship. My mother doesn't want money for this, because she feeds her friend. Have you any coffee made? No? Then bring me a cup of water and pass me a spoon and a can opener. May I have the spoon? Your little boy that lives at our house lost the best spoon we had. I'll take this one. Thanks, my mother—good, good. Now I go."[22]

There is much to be learned from this monologue, in addition to the expression of relationships through kinship responsibility. Another prominent part of this conversation is the series of requests and how they are made. Hilda Wetherill, obviously harried by this approach, categorized it as "the wily savage way of wheedling us out of everything movable on the place." She failed to mention that the way these questions were phrased was very much in keeping with the Navajo way of avoiding conflict and embarrassment. Louise Lamphere suggests that "An obligation to cooperate is binding on all adult Navajos, regardless of kinship status or situation. Not only is there an expectation that an individual request will be performed with good will and generosity, but there is little or no effort to calculate the 'debits' and 'credits' resulting from the sum of exchanges between two individuals."[23] Wetherill, like most Anglo people, was no doubt keeping score as she assisted her customer.

What she may not have recognized is the suggestive manner in which the requests were made. The individual asking does so in a way that the need is made known without directly confronting the person. The one who is to fulfill the request is not forced but can choose as part of his or her free agency. Ambiguity arises. Both parties now have an interest—the one who has asked, the other who feels an obligation—with the chance that if the need is not met, participants may feel discredited. The more ambiguous the situation is, the less chance of offense. Wetherill's customer made her aware of the situation at home with the children, something that any "mother" would want to correct.[24] How the trader handled that information was left to her.

Another factor that worked on behalf of the customer was public opinion. This was particularly important to traders, whose reputation and the number of visitors at the post depended upon how they were portrayed in the community. There was a direct correlation between how people felt the trader was as a friend who provided assistance and how much the trader was just out for gain. A bad reputation hurt and became part of the news spread about. One trader noted, "In spite of the fact that there were no telephones, communication on the reservation was amazing. News was spread by word-of-mouth and spread rapidly. It was nothing for a Navajo to walk twenty or thirty miles just to visit another trading post to learn what was going on. Each trading post was a social center, a gathering place where news was relayed back and forth from all parts of the reservation."[25] That is why Hilda Wetherill, in a continuation of her account of trading-post dialogue, stressed that she felt a strong obligation to be reasonable in meeting customer needs. She explained that, "in a conversation I have about twenty times a day," the customer had spent all of his money. Yet, he or she continued to ask for items off the store shelf, hoping they'll just be thrown in as a bargain or that the trader has miscounted. Frustrated and yet concerned, the trader grants more leniency. According to Wetherill, "The women are the worst, and how they do rant and rave if they think they can make me believe they are short a half dollar. They'll argue for hours and it's often cheaper to give them the money outright than to have them go home angry and tell everyone they have been robbed."[26] Social and economic pressures existed on both sides of the bullpen.

To offset any ill will and to establish a positive reputation, traders provided free food or items to show their friendship and generosity. Many posts had a tin fastened through the counter with the nails protruding up through the can, where tobacco was available for the taking, along with free cigarette papers for rolling a smoke. The nails prevented too much tobacco from being taken all at once. In later years, when soda pop, known to the Navajos as "sweet water," was available, the trader might offer some, with customers requesting "red" (strawberry), "black" (coke), or "orange." The trader might also open a can of tomatoes and add some sugar or a can of fruit, or perhaps give some small items for the children and something for the adult members of the family. Some posts kept tight control on a few spoons and cups that customers could use for eating right there, as they sat in a circle on the floor and consumed the gift.[27] Even those not present might have something sent home to them, hence Wetherill's previous mention of the "apples and candy for all of the children who come to your store," a point made a number of times. Word spread about that kind of generosity. At the conclusion of a trading session, another gift might be given. This harkens back to the traditional practice discussed in chapter 2, where two trade partners each gave a present before separating to confirm their friendship. This "free gift," called in Navajo *t'ááji̧íik'eh*, was a token of good will. Franc Newcomb explained this in her dealings with *Asdzáán Nez*: "When the full price of the blanket had been paid in yard goods, groceries, and shoes for her two small girls, she [Nez] requested that something be given her '*tseegisigie*'—free—as a token of good will. How this custom started, I do not know, but when a Navaho woman sold a blanket, she always expected a gift. I added a box of frosted cookies to her pile of purchases and she nodded happily as she spread her Pendleton shawl on the floor."[28] Trader Billy Meadows did likewise. Two young boys, ten and fourteen, after traveling a long distance, appeared at his post one day with a quarter to invest in candy. With an additional fifty cents obtained from selling a bow and three arrows, they purchased food. Meadows insisted on helping them more by giving them a good meal and adding a couple of cans of tomatoes and some baked crackers akin to hardtack, for their long return journey.[29] Generosity and friendship gifts were common fare at the posts.

Hilda Wetherill, however, was not enamored with this traditional practice and felt that the spirit of developing a lasting spontaneous friendship based on goodwill had degenerated into "wheedling" again. She tells of when Mrs. Little Crank came to the store to trade. No initial offer for a blanket was ever accepted, but rather there would be a series of offers and counteroffers that eventually led to an acceptable price for both. Mrs. Crank assumed there was a strong friendship between her and Hilda so that she was comfortable in asking for an additional half-dollar for a seventy-five-cent goat hide. It is not surprising that she used gifting in the same way. This practice, called *shik'isígíí* (literally, "the one that is my friend" or friendship), is a gifting that represents and strengthens the bond of friendship, although Hilda looked at it as more of an obligation bordering on nuisance. She explains:

> Another good bit of business on her part was to give me a quarter for *sekissigie [shik'isígíí]. Sekiss* [shik'is] means my friend, and anything given for *sekissigie* or friendship is given as a flattering tribute. Mrs. Little Crank liked to have others see that we exchanged *sekissigie.* She came up to me, just as she did immediately after the boy's death, grasped my hand, leaned her head on my shoulder and after a long moment put the twenty-five-cent piece in my hand. "For *sekissigie,*" she whispered. "Not to buy anything. I give to my mother, to my kind older sister. Oh, no, it is not to buy anything but because my sister, my older sister, is good and kind."
>
> After that she stood around and waited for what I should give her. I tried her out on various things and she insisted on a full twenty-five cents' worth, or a little more. If I gave her a can of peaches worth twenty cents, she said, as she accepted it, "And some candy, five cents worth of candy in a paper bag, and an orange, two oranges for the children." If I gave her a nickel's worth of stick candy, she said, "It is very little. There are not enough sticks in the bag."
>
> Then she stood around another hour or two and whispered, "For *old, old* friendship, give me two cans of peaches." Ken [Hilda's husband] said we were not to allow ourselves to be wheedled out of too much, so I had to play I didn't hear her. After the *sekissigie* exchange, Mrs. Little Crank did her buying; then she shook hands and promised to come again.[30]

Smoking was a common practice among both men and women and an important part of the post's social scene. People sitting in the bullpen would talk and listen to each other while rolling, then smoking their cigarettes (*nát'oh bił da'asdisígíí*—wrapped tobacco) or perhaps puffing on a cigar (*nát'oh daniłchonígíí*—ill-smelling tobacco). Bull Durham mixture was the brand of choice, which the Navajos called "bull" or "cow" tobacco because of the seal on the package. After adeptly creasing the cigarette paper, pouring some tobacco in, then sealing with a rolling motion of thumb and two fingers of the left hand and a lick, the smoker would light the cigarette in the fire or on the stove, if matches were unavailable, and sit back to relax.[31] Most posts purchased the tobacco in long slabs that were then cut into five-, ten-, or twenty-five-cent slices. Free papers and tobacco were kept on the counters, a gift that never seemed to be abused.

Transacting Business

Two final examples of the trading-post experience from the Navajo perspective illustrate the give-and-take of the exchange, as both parties came to a final agreement. In this first instance, note the efforts of the trader to meet the needs of the customer and the honesty of both partners during the exchange. A Navajo, Old Mexican, had been traveling for some time in winter weather before he arrived at the post in Crystal, New Mexico, where he wanted to trade three buckskins. He asked the trader what they were worth, and learned that they were a scarce commodity in that area. After the store owner examined the hides a few times, he offered thirty dollars for two, more than twice what his customer would have received elsewhere. Old Mexican responded, "'All right.' At home I sold them for seven dollars apiece. Then I took over the other one. He said, 'I'll give you three strings of white beads with many turquoise among them.' I told him, 'These beads aren't enough. There are some black turquoise among them. They aren't worth much. If you give me some cash to boot I'll take it.' He was awfully anxious to get the buckskins. He put them behind the counter, got five dollars from the cash drawer and put it beside the beads, and a pound of coffee, a loaf of bread, two cans of fruit and a box of crackers. 'Is that all right?' he asked me. I said 'Yes.' He said, 'The reason I have done this for you, is because you have come a long way. I could tell by your ears. Your ears have turned black from frost.'"[32]

There are three points to be gained from this episode. The first is the honesty with which the transaction took place. The trader did not mask his desire to obtain the hides, Old Mexican told the store owner that he had sold skins for a lot less money than was being offered, and both worked toward an equitable price. Second, when the trader understood what his customer thought was a fair price, he went far beyond the mere cash requested. The amount of money approached what a whole hide would bring "back home," but then he added a lot of foodstuffs that ensured the price was more than acceptable. Third, both men "read" each other. The trader knew that he was dealing with someone who had come from far away with the type of goods that he wanted, and so did what he could to ensure this customer returned. Old Mexican, on the other hand, wanted to sell his skins and understood how to approach the trader when the initial offer was not enough. Once he got what he considered fair, the transaction closed.

A second example offers additional insight into establishing and maintaining relationships. Left Handed traveled a fairly long distance to trade with Old Mexican (a second name for John Lorenzo Hubbell) at Ganado. When he arrived, the trader came out to greet him, saying, "I am very anxious to see you and glad that you came. You used to be my father or son-in-law by a woman that we used to call Little Lamb No Mother, Doggie Lamb had Bow Legs."[33] By greeting him in this fashion, Hubbell opens up a joking relationship. In Navajo culture, a son-in-law is often viewed as an outsider to the family, a person who is expected to do all of the menial work around camp, and an individual who has to earn the family's admiration. There are many in-law jokes that speak to the issue of being in a subservient position. Add to this, the funny name of his fictional "mother" and one understands why Hubbell laughed, then continued to pour on the humor by suggesting that Left Handed had been "running around with this woman all the time," another tabooed behavior in Navajo culture. The greeting was a way of putting one at ease by joking about the unseemly.

Left Handed escaped the humor by saying that he had traveled two days to get to the post and that he was very hungry. The trader told those in the party to unsaddle their horses and spend the day resting, that he would get food for them and that the next day or two they could spend trading, all the time referring to Left Handed as "my partner, my friend." A leisurely approach kept the customers at the store, buying some things and receiving other items for free. After eating, the visitors went to the store with their wool tied in blankets. Hubbell began asking questions about his other customers—those not present—what they were doing, were they planning on bringing their wool to him, and how much longer they would be shearing sheep? Then he got Left Handed to do some advertising: "Will you tell all of these friends of mine to bring all of their wool to me and tell them I will give them a good price for their wool and I will give them so much for their trip too, so will you tell them this

Left Handed, although neither rich nor powerful nor a medicine man, provided an extremely important view of daily life and practices in his two-volume autobiographical account edited by Walter Dyk. His experiences at trading posts in the nineteenth and twentieth century are foundational in understanding Navajo thought. (Photo courtesy University of Nebraska Press.)

for me?" The customer agreed to help. A word-of-mouth endorsement from a friend could pay significant dividends.

Hubbell next weighed the wool on scales outside. As for the Navajos, "nobody knew what he was doing, only himself. None of us knew anything about the weight." Once this was accomplished, he had everyone come into the store, where he gave a large stack of silver dollars, half-dollars, and quarters, a rare act since most posts did not have access to sufficient cash for this kind of transaction. Left Handed gave some money to his wife, his wife's brother ("He was awful thankful for it"), and kept some for himself, even though he did not know exactly what it all totaled collectively. Left Handed purchased things first, followed by his wife. The trader encouraged him to buy a saddle for fifteen dollars, which he eventually did. Hubbell gave the money to a Navajo who had made the saddle and was there in the store at the time. This man began spending his money as soon as it was his turn at the counter. The trading took all day and so the party stayed that night in a guest hogan.[34]

Three additional points come from this part of the story. First, although Left Handed knew the general outline of what was taking place, the world of weights and measures and money was foreign. This raises the question of the honesty of traders, a topic to be discussed in the next chapter. Hubbell, like other traders, knew that the customer had to be satisfied with what came from the barter. Whether in money or goods, customer satisfaction led to return visits, and while the Navajos may not have been totally aware of trader costs and market prices, they did know what other posts were offering and what, at that time, would be considered a fair deal. Second, when someone had money or buying power at the store, it was good not to be stingy. Each person received something from the transaction and was free to spend it as they saw fit. Still, there was a cultural pressure to make sure everyone got something. Third, Hubbell, by helping another customer to sell his wares—in this case, a saddle—could almost guarantee that that person's money would circulate back into the store while strengthening the friendship of the man he assisted. Good business meant good business for all.

Naming by Knowing

Part of any relationship was knowing how to address an individual. Navajos had a keen ear for determining exactly how they were going to refer to a person, and traders were no exception. Within Navajo culture, one might have three or four names, each used in a different way in a different setting. The sacred/secret name has already been discussed, as have kinship terms that serve as the day-to-day titles used among family members and friends. For public use, a person might receive a name such as Son of So-and-So, or be addressed by a clan designation or by more general terms of endearment such as "Friend" or "Younger Brother/Sister," or have an adopted white man's name—all of which were used in a friendly, accepting manner without causing offense to the individual. In the past, people within the same family did not necessarily have a name that showed connection. Father Emanuel Trockur tells of a soldier, Pvt. Allen Necly, who died during World War II in North Africa. Following his death, the government needed to pay his insurance claim, but faced a difficult situation. "Surviving him are four brothers, Jim Hale, Hashke Yichihaya, Ernie Nestachie, Hashke Yidoya; and three sisters, Yilhanaba, Carrie N. Taliman, and Hazba. His father and mother were Tabaha and Asdza Yazhe, respectively. Thus in this family there are not two names that suggest relationship."[35]

Many people also had a Navajo name that they received from the observations of others. The person may have a physical deformity, exhibit a certain personality quality, been involved in a specific incident, wear an item of clothing, and so forth, that gives them a distinctive identity. Some of these names are complimentary; more often they may not be, and supposedly, the individual to whom it belonged did not know it or at least was very hesitant to tell a person inquiring. The same individual may have two or three such names by which he is known on the reservation. Berard Haile recognized that these titles may be offensive, were imposed by others, and were forced upon an individual. If a man was approached and asked by an Anglo what his name was, and there were others around, the man being questioned might respond, "'They know, why ask me, they did it, let them tell you.' Hence, it is customary to ask a man's companion for the name, not the bearer himself, or get the information in the bearer's absence. It doesn't seem polite to ask a man's name from himself, nor to expect him to speak his own name either privately or in the presence of others, especially strangers. It is done, to be sure, if they are pressed, but not without reluctance."[36] Many either tried to avoid receiving such a title or did all they could to shake it once they had it. The Navajos were just as quick to give white men and women the same kind of names, in all their variety, with traders receiving their fair share. The store owners reciprocated, creating their own names for their customers, as they stood on their side of the bullpen, a topic discussed in the next chapter.

Navajo trader names are both amusing and instructive—in the sense that they not only point out individual qualities and characteristics, but may also speak to relationships. Some of these names are easy to understand. Curly Head (Will Evans in Shiprock), Big White Man (Arthur Spencer in Mexican Hat), Old John (John Wetherill in Kayenta), Slim Woman (Louisa Wetherill, John's wife), Red Woman (Hilda Faunce Wetherill in Covered Water) and a host of others—Red Beard, Little White Man, Strong White Man, Hairy, Long Beard, Worn Out Hat—are just a few of many. Other names are less clear, until one meets the individual. For instance, Ray Hunt, who owned a post in Mexican Hat, was called Swinging Arm, or simply Arm, because when he was three years old, he had suffered from a bout with polio that withered his left arm, making it less useful than his strong, right arm.[37] The mother of Whip Wheeler, a trader in Montezuma Creek, had a round face, pointed ears, and short whiskers protruding from her nostrils that reminded people of a cat, and so Whip received the name of the Cat's Little One, and the store took on the name of *Mósí*, or Cat. Bill Young, another Montezuma Creek trader, also passed his name along to the post he worked in, which was called Black Hat. Bruce Bernard in Shiprock had the name of Wind because he had a tilt in his neck that caused him to hold his head to one side, as if the wind were blowing strongly.[38] John Hunt received the epithet of Little Mexican because, even though he did not have an ancestral link to those people, his facial features, dark hair, and swarthy skin, coupled with his roving about, fit how the Navajos viewed Mexican men.[39] Mister Yeast (Con Shillinburg) could be proud of his name, since he was a baker who took pride in his work.[40]

Perhaps most intriguing are the names derived from events or personality traits. In Monument Valley, Clyde Colville, a trading partner with the Wetherills, was known as Hurry Up, since he tried to move the Navajos along in the purchasing process; his second name, The Man Who Drives Around, he earned because the store was constantly running out of supplies and so he traveled long distances to purchase replacements. The Navajos called O. J. (Orange Jay) "Stokes" Carson, who also traded in the area, The Poor One because when he was approached to extend credit, he "made a poor mouth," saying that he could not lend any money.[41] Harry Goulding, whose Navajo name was The Hungry One, had an ingenious trait. If he had a lot of customers in his store, but not a lot of trading going on, his wife, who was in their home above the store, banged on the floor, calling to him that dinner was ready. That cued him to tell everyone that he was hungry and they had to leave the store so that he could close and eat.[42]

Elijah Blair tells the story of when he first arrived at the Mexican Water post as a new trader, and was still trying to learn the Navajo language. When he drew up in front of the store that he was going to take over, an old man approached him, pointed at the store's wagon, and let it be known that he wanted to take it. Blair told him he would have to pay for it; otherwise, the wagon didn't move. The man went off but returned shortly with the same demand. This went on for three days, the Navajo staying in the guest hogan while making continuous requests, but receiving the same answer. Finally, one night Elijah's brother and his wife, who had more experience with the language, came to Mexican Water and talked to the elated Navajo, who was so happy they were there. He told them that he had already paid the previous store owner for the wagon and all he wanted to do was have permission to drive it off. Elijah ended his tale by saying, "You know, a Navajo is the most tolerant person in the world, the most accepting person in the world, and [the Indian] finally said, 'Your ears are just round and nothing goes in!' And that's when they first started calling me 'Ear.'"[43] Fred Scribner, who worked for Stokes Carson, received a similar name, Ears as Hard as Crystal, because he had trouble differentiating Navajo sounds in the language as he tried to learn it.[44]

Divining the Truth

Another place where culture from the Navajo side crossed the counter was in divination. This process is difficult to explain to people unused to experiencing the supernatural, but many traders speak very openly about the power and what they witnessed. There are three major types of divination—listening *(íístsʼąąʼ)*; star (*sǫʻnílʼį*), with its subsidiaries of sun and moon gazing, and their affiliate, crystal gazing (déstʼįįʼ), literally, to see, understand; and hand trembling, or motion-in-the-hand (*ndishįįh*)—all of which are related in that they are spiritually based and serve a similar function. Performance of this ritual allows the diagnostician to explore the unknown, to find lost people or objects, to identify a thief or witch, to locate water or other desirable resources, to prevent danger or evil, and—most important—to determine the cause of an illness so that the patient can be cured.[45] Each one of the forms of divination is performed differently, but all are accompanied by songs and prayers, with special abilities given to those who have been empowered and understand how to use them.

Many of the old-time traders have encountered, and even sought after, Navajos who use this power, usually in association with lost or stolen articles. One of the most complete accounts is provided by Franc Newcomb, trader-turned-ethnologist, who devoted an entire chapter in her book, *Navaho Neighbors*, to this phenomenon. Hosteen Beaal, a local medicine man and friend of the family, one day used divination to locate three missing horses belonging to the Newcombs. Both Franc and her husband, Arthur, were skeptics at the time. Still, the couple approached Beaal to find an answer. He agreed to help, and had clean sand brought to where he performed the rite. Squatting in the midst of the sand, he blessed it and himself with corn pollen. As he began to chant, his body shook, until, suddenly, the trembling ceased and his hand drew lines and trails in the sand. He then told in detail who had taken the horses, where they had gone, and what was happening to them at that time. Once Arthur heard the explanation, he felt it was just a simple deduction—that two boys he knew were then racing the horses at a ceremony and would return them when the ceremony was over. As far as the trader was concerned, he "should have guessed where they were myself! There was no magic in finding them, just a matter of good common sense."[46] His wife was not convinced that it was that simple.

Two months later, someone stole a valuable saddle and three Pendelton shawls from the Newcombs. Once again, they summoned Beaal, who again was not really interested in payment, just in helping. Arthur admitted that, this time, he could never have guessed what had happened in an event that occurred so far away from the post. The medicine man performed his hand trembling and gave a minute-by-minute description of how the thief committed the crime, including the movement of the individual, the pawning of the materials, and where the thief went afterward. An actual movie could not have been more explicit. Arthur traveled to the Coyote Canyon trading post, where he had been told his property would be; paid Mr. Grey, the trader, for the pawned items; and returned home a far stronger believer. As for Franc, she believed it was ESP, or Extraordinary Spiritual Power, that allowed the old man to know these types of things. She asked a Navajo friend how it was done and learned, "Everything that happens leaves its picture in the air. So he goes to sleep and sends his spirit out of his body to find that picture. When it returns, he knows all about what has happened."[47]

News of Beaal's involvement spread throughout the community. When someone stole an object, the mere mention of this medicine man's name was enough to have the item suddenly reappear. Beaal also used his powers to find missing people; to solve crimes such as the clubbing of a trader's wife and the burning of an unoccupied trading post; and to determine if an individual would live or die after sustaining injuries. He answered all of these questions in detailed accuracy, the result being the capture of the culprits and the confirmation of what he had said. Beaal went on to assist in the capture of a man who had murdered a trader selling bootleg whiskey and the capture of others who had committed multiple thefts. He solved many problems in the community—all for usually little reimbursement. He eventually became tired and worn from the use of this spiritual power. He was blind and incapacitated by the time he died at the age of 104. But to the end, he was highly respected by both Anglos and Navajos.

Hosteen Beaal was an exceptional individual whose life, fortunately, was recorded by a trader whose experience went from doubt to conviction. The same is true of traders like Richard and Marietta Wetherill, Con Schillinburg, Hilda Wetherill, Vernon Jack, the Lippincotts, and a host of others who could testify of the truthfulness of the powers these diviners held. Their testimonies track closely to what the Newcombs described. As part of the trading-post experience from the Navajo side of the counter, these people brought a power and strength that was foreign and unexplainable to the Anglo side, but one that was very useful in discovering, explaining, and deterring crime. The traders caught a glimpse of that intangible part of another culture that seemed so foreign, and yet it "worked." So, too, did their way of viewing the world from the Anglo side of the counter, but in a different way, as will be shown in the next chapter.

CHAPTER FIVE

Standing behind the Counter

The Qualifications and Qualities of a Trader

Anglo traders arriving on the Navajo Reservation for the first time transported their own cultural assumptions and practices with them. Their ability to understand, adapt, and adopt to what they encountered foretold of their success or failure in dealing with a way of life foreign to the dominant culture. The Navajos proved to be patient and willing teachers, who were themselves learning about the world beyond the reservation and what it had to offer. Together, these worlds joined hands over a three-foot-wide counter that allowed both sides to interact while adjusting to the other's expectations. There was little coercion, little interference to force one side to accept another; more often it was give-and-take, accept-or-leave what was proffered. In this atmosphere, a general sense of trust arose, with traders depending on the Navajos for their livelihood and the Navajos selecting what they wanted or going elsewhere. This chapter examines the traders' world on their side of the counter, a world based on government regulations as well as their own personal standards and their customers' expectations.

Indian Traders and the Government

During the early years of establishing posts on the reservation, the men and women who ran the stores were known as Indian traders. They came from all walks of life with different reasons for wanting to work in this capacity, but for the most part, they did it because they enjoyed the lifestyle and were good enough to make a living at it. The Indian trader lived in tenuous circumstances. In order to operate a post on the reservation, they had to apply for a license from the U.S. Indian Commissioner and follow all regulations outlined by the government. These regulations could be onerous at times. For instance, in 1876, traders received directives that they had to supply the Indian Bureau with price lists of the principal articles they sold in their stores and that they could not sell alcohol. They also had to submit testimonials with their application that they were of "'unexceptionable' character and fitness to be in Indian country." They had to serve a year's probation before receiving a five-year license, which could be revoked any time before its expiration; they provided a bond of ten thousand dollars (the fee varied over time) and had to maintain responsibility for the actions of anyone in their employ. They had to notify the Indian agent of any new goods they were stocking, and they owned only the merchandise on the shelves, not the buildings or land.[1]

How detailed these instructions could become are illustrated in a circular of 1905. After counselling the traders that many of their stores were "dirty even to filthiness," C. F. Larrabee, acting commissioner, gave orders as to the storing and handling of food, the necessity of insuring weighing scales for accuracy, and proper account keeping. He concluded by discussing the sale of medicine with alcoholic content—especially one called Peruna—that became "absolutely prohibited." Other items on the same list included "Jamaica ginger and flavoring extracts of vanilla, lemon, and so forth [which] should be kept in only small quantities and in small bottles and should not be sold to Indians, or at least only sparingly to those who it is known will use them only for legitimate purposes."[2] Posts on the reservations had to be closed on Sundays, although a number of traders indicated that when customers had traveled long distances in difficult circumstances, the post doors were sometimes opened as an exception.[3] No doubt this specificity arose from real problems, but it is interesting to see how the long arm of Washington, D.C., extended all the way to some lonely post in the middle of the Arizona or Utah desert.

On the other hand, a full-blood Navajo wanting to open his own post did not require a license or a bond, just enough capital to line the shelves of his store with merchandise.[4] How many Navajo traders existed during the time period of roughly 1880 to 1940 is unclear. Klara Kelly and Harris Francis have collected extensive data on this topic, and in their listing of traders who were Navajo and who fall into this era, they have identified around forty-five.[5] These traders faced a different set of problems in operating their own posts, problems rising from family expectations, Navajo cultural expectations, the extension and collection of credit, and other issues. This is a topic ripe for investigation, but it moves beyond the subjects covered here.

Part of the government's attempts at control rose from Washington's bureaucratic view of traders across the United States at this time. According to this view, "The licensed trader is a survival from the old days of the wild frontier, like the rickety stagecoach and the wolf's-scalp currency, and among more modern conditions seems almost as much of an anomaly."[6] The primary reason for maintaining this antiquated form of barter was to have a place that the government controlled to ensure that American Indians received fair treatment, sheltered from the evil influences waiting to prey upon them beyond the bounds of the reservation. Recognizing that traders often had a generally bad reputation with the public, men in the Indian Office countered that most were no more and no less trustworthy than store owners who operated in the broader society. At the same time, traders took care of their charges, extended credit in such a way that it did not harm the Indian, and slowly introduced elements of white society along the road to acculturation.

While the growth of posts on the reservation can be fairly well documented, that of posts surrounding the reservation on public or private land is close to impossible, given their fluid condition. Often the traders provided the best record of the opening and closing of different stores, since many of them were linked in one way or another. The best study of the development of posts on the Navajo Reservation is by Frank McNitt in his *The Indian Traders*.[7] Trader involvement in a particular post varied widely. Many of these men exchanged stores often, taking their stock and moving to a new location to see if business was better there. Others remained in the same location for years, sometimes their whole lifetime. Demographically, of forty-three traders interviewed in 1934–35, six had been involved in trading from one to five years; seven from six to ten years; eight from eleven to fifteen years; nine from sixteen to twenty years; six from twenty-one to twenty-five years; five from twenty-six to thirty years; and two between thirty-one and thirty-five years. As for the ages of forty-five men responding, nine were from twenty-six to thirty-five; fourteen from thirty-six to forty-five; twelve from forty-six to fifty-five; and ten from fifty-six to sixty-five years old.[8] What these two sets of figures provide is a snapshot, when trading posts were at their height, of a mature group of men who remained in the business for a lengthy period of time. Managers (not owners) of these stores received a salary ranging from a low of forty dollars to a high of two hundred dollars a month, with room and board and fuel a part of their wage.[9] The average salary of these managers was $120 per month, and this during the depth of the Great Depression. There are no general statistics on what each post owner earned, and given the multiple variables for each store, it is difficult to determine that amount. A handful of posts, like that of J. L. Hubbell, who was involved in a network of stores, who tapped into the tourist industry through partnerships, and who drew large Navajo populations from a wide area, would have a greater income that buffered them from fluctuations in different markets. Diversity provided more protection.

In the northwestern part of the reservation, the three big trading families were John and Louisa Wetherill in Oljato, then Kayenta; the Richardson family, whose operations centered in Flagstaff, Arizona, with posts in Cameron, Kaibito, The Gap, Inscription House, Rainbow Lodge, and Shonto; and the Babbitt Brothers Trading Company out of Flagstaff. The Wetherills will be discussed later, but while their trading post did a good business, it was Louisa's astute running of that post, the family's political connections, and John's packhorse trips for tourists to Anasazi ruins and Rainbow Bridge that allowed the Wetherills to prosper. Gladwell Richardson refers to his father, brothers, uncles, and in-laws as a "dynasty of traders"—an appropriate phrase that describes the multifaceted connections this family established throughout much of the reservation.[10] The Babbitts began their business in the livestock industry, expanded into purchasing wool, and eventually became involved in operating trading posts in Tuba City, Cedar Ridge, Red Lake, Cow Springs, Kayenta, Piñon, Jeddito, and Indian Wells. Their expansion, coupled with diversity, helped them to prosper.[11] While these larger groups were economically more significant than the smaller, individual posts, it is those littler, less-well-known stores of southeastern Utah and southwestern Colorado where the majority of this study will focus, since they are more representative of the general trading-post experience encountered in hundreds of stores serving the Navajos.

Every post was different, with varying clientele and resources to draw upon. Vernon Jack provides a good example of what one trader went through to finance his store, an experience that is probably illustrative of what most individual traders went through. Jack, already a seasoned trader, joined in partnership in the mid-1930s with Carl Ashcroft, another veteran trader, to buy the Round Rock trading post. This type of risk-share of expense between traders was common, since many were aware of how each store owner functioned, who could be trusted , and what their personality was like. Jack writes,

> We gave six thousand dollars for the entire post, including the building, merchandise, and fixtures. However, everything was pretty well run down. We did not have any money of our own, so we borrowed the entire amount from Carl's [Ashcroft] Greasewood [Trading Post] partner, Burt Dustin. That was when I actually went to work for myself. Carl sold me a third interest in the store. I signed a note that I would pay two thousand dollars that being one third of six thousand, plus six percent interest until the note was paid. Immediately we had to go into debt again to buy merchandise to put into the post, so we borrowed another six thousand dollars. It was on an open note or account. We would buy and sell rugs, sheep, wool and what have you. Anything that the Indians had to sell, we would buy and anything they needed to buy, we would sell. So we traded with them, but very little money exchanged since most of our trading was in Navajo blankets, wool, hides, sheep, and cattle.
>
> We were there for nine years until we sold out. We paid off our first third in four and a half years. Then we paid off all our bills. Carl Ashcroft sold me the other 17 percent which, added to my third, gave me a half interest in the post. I paid something like nine thousand dollars then for that 17 percent of the business. So we had to work for a little over four years to pay off the indebtedness.[12]

Trader Qualities

From the trader's perspective, what were the qualities of an ideal store owner? There are a number of prominent characteristics, among the first being willingness to help. Mildred Heflin recalled how the trading post was the center of a community, and how the Navajos depended upon the trader not just to have the supplies they needed, but also the advice necessary to deal with the government and other outside influences. This advice also extended to family problems, issues in the neighborhood, and general counsel on monetary and social matters.[13] But advice often turned to action. Ray Hunt remembers driving Navajo patients to distant hospitals over dirt roads, all hours of the day and night, to save their lives without receiving any form of reimbursement.[14] Many traders purchased a little girl's first rug, no matter how rough it might be, to encourage her to continue to learn to weave. Paul Begay recollects entering the local post as a child with a cohort of friends and the trader taking a couple of fistfuls of pennies and throwing them to the children. "Now we had money to spend. And he did that to us every time we went over there. That won our hearts, and we wanted to go see this man again."[15] Begay summarized his feelings about traders by saying that if they understood, respected, and appreciated the cultural teachings, then "he's truly a Navajo trader . . . he understands the Navajo in this way." From an Anglo perspective, Shiprock trader Will Evans explained how he saw his role. "A trader and his post are the center and heart of the Navajo community. He is their creditor, advisor, and at times their midwife and undertaker. He supplies them with flour and coffee, sugar and salt; he measures out their cloth, fits their feet with shoes and stockings, clothes them with shirts and trousers, shades them with hats and umbrellas, protects them with coats and shawls, dispenses their medicine and soft drinks, satisfies their sweet tooth, weighs their nails and bolts, and supplies their tools."[16] While neither Begay's nor Evan's views are mutually exclusive, they do illustrate the difference between the two—one is fundamentally built upon relationships, the other economics.

J. L. Hubbell felt that the Navajo viewed Anglos as a race of people who were "workers of miracles, to whom nothing is impossible." For example, handling the dead, an action dangerous to perform in Navajo culture, had no impact on the white trader asked to bury a corpse. The powers of witchcraft had no effect. And when one considered the new inventions made out of strange materials that might arrive at a trading post to surprise its customers, one can see why this attitude developed. Hubbell, a veteran trader of fifty years at this point in his career, who had witnessed great changes himself, put it this way: "The Indians many years ago ceased to marvel at the accomplishments of the white man. They have philosophically accepted the fact that the white man can do anything under the sun, and are surprised at nothing. Their reasoning along such lines is simply: If you can build a wagon that runs better without a horse; why bother with the horse? If you can talk without wires; why go to all of the trouble of stringing them? If you can fly through the air like a bird; why travel any other way? So quite logically, the Indian has come to regard the white man as a worker of miracles, to whom nothing is impossible."[17]

Certainly these and the examples from the previous chapter provide the positive side of interactions between the traders and their customers. There was another side to consider. Some Navajos felt the white men were intruders and even unfair. "They knew that many Navajos do not understand the value of money or what they want to buy; they often have been cheated by the traders who gave the Navajos only half the value of a rug or a piece of jewelry and then sold them for much more; that way the traders made more of a profit, especially when they made Navajos take payment in food and merchandise which is priced very high."[18] The topic of fairness, prices, and customer service is discussed in a future chapter, but the subject is raised here to show that there were contrasting views that were not always friendly.

William Y. Adams, trader-turned-anthropologist, acknowledges that the Indian trader was often either romanticized or vilified, but believes the truth lies somewhere between. Above all, the men—and it was by far predominantly a man's trade, with wife serving as an assistant—were small business owners or managers. The Navajo title for a trader—Sits or Stands in Place for Merchandise (*naalyééhé básidáhí*)—describes very accurately how his customers viewed him. To white visitors at the post, many traders seemed taciturn and uncommunicative, speaking only when spoken to. Adams points out, however, that "As we all know, Navajos are not given to effusive greeting or to making chitchat with strangers; they like serious conversation with known friends and kinsmen. Traders simply fell into the same mode of discourse, for day in and day out most of their interaction was with Navajos. The trading post often hummed with activity, but it did not hum with conversation."[19]

The trader had to have the ability to say "no." Adams correctly identifies that in the early days, when Left Handed and others were trading with posts using a strictly barter system, the competition between traders

This old photo, taken between 1893 and 1896, shows the interior of the Aneth trading post with (*left to right*) Gussie Honaker, Anna Ames (wife of part-owner Arthur J. Ames) and Jesse West (also part-owner). This spur-of-the-moment picture taken by local photographer Charles Goodman captures the reality of a trader's environment—bolts of cloth, picture-labeled cans, a sign promoting the sale of coffee accompanied by a variety of gift dolls, and rifles in the corner, all lit by sunshine from a distinctive skylight above. (San Juan County Historical Commission.)

could be fierce because it was a direct exchange transaction as opposed to a later time, when credit on a six-month rotating basis was the expected. In this latter period, it is conceivable that a trader could extend so much credit that the customer could not work his or her way out of debt. It was up to the trader to monitor accounts and be able say "no" when necessary. Many store owners assumed this paternalistic role of watching out for the welfare of the customers, developing a "father-knows-best" attitude that today would never be tolerated, but at the time was acceptable because both sides of the counter had a stake in ensuring that a good relationship continued. In Adams's view, "The trader exploited his status advantage in all commercial dealings by maintaining an attitude of detachment and indifference which forced the customer to take the initiative and come to him. It was always up to the customer to open negotiations; traders almost never spoke to Navajos until they have been addressed."[20]

Friction was always a possibility, and so one of the necessary qualities of a trader was to be fearless. In a number of different interviews, J. L. Hubbell drove home this point. He felt that if a store owner showed the slightest bit of fear, he was on the defensive, no matter how many or how few antagonists there might be. The Indians would have him "on the run" as soon as it happened. To illustrate his belief, Hubbell told of when a large Indian "buck" came into the store and demanded a sack of flour, even though he had nothing to trade. When the man seized a sack and walked out, Hubbell knew that he had to act quickly, realizing that if this man got away with it, a precedent would be set. There were seventy-five other men outside waiting to "back up" the culprit. The unarmed Hubbell bounded over the counter, chased the man and seized him by his hair, forcing him to the ground. He twisted his ear and marched him back into the store with the sack, where he had him deposit it on the pile from which it had come. Another man stepped forward to challenge the trader and received the same treatment. Hubbell knew it was a big bluff, but said in Navajo, "Come on any of you who think you can steal from me. I'll twist the ears of any Indian who wants to try it—and, I'll twist all your ears at once if you want them twisted." The crowd dispersed.[21]

One also cannot ignore the competitive nature that existed between traders. Gladwell Richardson provides a couple of examples of this internecine conflict. All traders tried to maintain their local client base, while bringing in new customers to expand business. Navajos, being a highly mobile group of people, were not averse to traveling a longer distance for a better deal, but if they did, it meant that their normal trade relationship with the local trader was harmed. That is why, when Luke Smith, who was managing the Shonto store, hit upon selling Arbuckle Brothers' coffee at a greatly reduced price—three one-pound packages for a dollar, when the coffee usually retailed at sixty cents for a single package—Navajos began to flock to his store. Smith reasoned that he would make up the monetary difference on other goods he would sell and on the sheer volume of new customers attracted to his store. All of the other traders in the region suffered. Determined to teach Smith a lesson, they maintained their agreed-upon price, but every few days sent a different Navajo armed with a few blankets to Smith's store to stock up on the inexpensive coffee. After two months of this, with Smith none the wiser, the traders had their warehouses filled with his coffee, which they could now sell for a reduced price to their customers. Eventually, Smith learned of the trick and went back to selling his wares at the standard prices charged by the other traders.[22]

Just how tit-for-tat this rivalry could become and how the traders used Navajo beliefs to further the rivalry is seen in a second example. A trader at Red Lake, Arizona, viewed Gladwell Richardson as a competitor worth troubling. Richardson, at Shonto, obtained some army-surplus World War I–vintage wool pants that he sold to Navajo customers. The trader at Red Lake sent a Navajo to Shonto, who waited for a good crowd of customers to be in the store before exclaiming that these pants had been taken off dead Germans. Playing on the extreme fear that Navajos have of the dead and items associated with the deceased, the opponent had put Richardson on the defensive. His customers stopped purchasing the pants and began trading elsewhere. Richardson soon retaliated with his own show of force. He produced a paper that no Navajo could read, but which Richardson said testified that these pants were new (it actually said "reconditioned"—but obviously had nothing to do with the dead), and then told them a story about how the other trader ate a lot of fish because he had served in the navy, which they knew. For many traditional Navajos, eating fish was taboo because of teachings in mythology where Navajo people and other Indian groups had been eaten by them. The Red Lake customers began bringing their business back to Shonto or Tuba City, and the wool-pants business boomed again.

Sometime later, Richardson was traveling in the Red Lake area when his wagon became stuck and he needed a rope. He went to the post, where his rival blandly smiled that he did not have a rope, but there was a lariat he could purchase for full price—an affront, since traders usually exchanged for wholesale. The seventy-five-cent lariat cost Richardson a dollar and a half, ensuring the next round of revenge. Time passed and Richardson was about to give up on getting even when a Red Lake Navajo customer appeared in Shonto, wanting to pawn a valuable string of shells and turquoise. The trader had his chance. Recoiling in horror, he demanded, "Take them out of here! You bought those beads at Red Lake!" He let the customer know that they had come from the grave of a wealthy Navajo, buried the previous year. He swore they were just like the beads that this man had pawned earlier at Shonto. The word quickly got out; no one would buy jewelry from the Red Lake store.

Eventually, Tuba City Indian police investigated and determined that there had not been any grave robbery, but the ruse had its effect, the damage done. "Never again, however, did that trader pull any tricks on me [Richardson]."[23]

Post owners also had to keep an eye on where their customers were shopping. Jot Stiles went to public gatherings to see his customers' clothing and other possessions. This allowed him to determine if they were trading with his competitors. A new shirt or hat indicated that the person was borrowing from another post without settling his debt. If they owed Stiles a lot on their pawn or money, he talked to them, encouraging them to straighten their accounts and adjust their dealings until the money they owed was paid. He also kept a sharp eye on the animals he purchased, unlike one of the traders at the Cow Springs post, who purchased the same cow three separate times from different Navajo sellers, who stole the animal back at night, then waited a while before making the re-sale. Word of the incident was too good to hold back; the perpetrators let the joke out on the "sagebrush telegraph," and the practice halted, but not before the Navajos had a good laugh.[24]

Trader Navajo

One important quality necessary for any trader was the ability to communicate with customers. This took a variety of forms. Trader Elijah Blair believed that to really learn to interact with Navajo customers, "You learned to speak body language and that's the first thing you learned. You learned by watching them, what the feel was, and then you learned to speak orally. And after you learned to be able to communicate in that way, then you had to learn what I refer to as 'speaking [understanding] the culture' . . . after that you can speak the language."[25] Harry Goulding experienced firsthand the power of Navajo kinesics. During the early stages of his establishment in Monument Valley, a group of Navajos visited him, asking about his presence there and exactly how long he intended to remain. It was not an overly friendly discussion, but was ambiguous enough to avoid direct conflict. Goulding noted, "A Navajo can put out an atmosphere—oh, it's like a breeze if it's nice, or it's like a terrible whirlwind when they want it to be. They have the ability whenever they want to use it. . . . They left it so that the atmosphere would tell you, if you're going to leave pretty soon, well it's all right, but don't hang around too long." Goulding did not budge and so the group showed up again, this time expecting him to fold his tent and depart. Asked when he was going, Goulding, who spoke poor Navajo at the time, gestured to his white tent and let it be known that when his hair was the same color, that would be when he would leave. The group broke into laughter, shook hands all around, and dropped the demand.[26]

Edward T. Hall identified what the first stage of reading body language meant in his experience. It included everything from avoiding eye contact when in close quarters, to "synchronizing body movements with the Navajo rhythm and tempo," entering and exiting groups politely, and following other patterns of social interaction. He further illustrated how he put this into practice. "I soon acquired the habit of opening the door quietly in the Navajo way, squeezing in sideways so as not to let in too much light or disturb the air, and waiting for the proper amount of time for people to get used to my presence. I let the trader—when he was ready—ask me where I had come from. It was in this context, whenever I was working with another culture, that I first acquired the habit of letting others set the tempo, as well as the order of events." By doing so it promoted a spirit of friendship and respect for the culture.[27]

The next stage in communication—oral language—provided a greater challenge, which some people barely, or never, attained, depending on their circumstances. Those who learned the language best were immersed in it outside of the store experience. Ray Hunt, a trader highly fluent in the language, never had to "learn" the language, since he was raised in a trading family. "I just more or less kind of grew up with them [Navajos]. My brothers being much younger than I was, I played quite a bit with the Indian kids. I just picked it up. I didn't try to learn it; it just came automatically."[28] Compare that with the experiences of his wife, Grace, who learned only the names of most of the items that were frequently purchased and a few phrases, one of the most important ones being, "He'll be back soon."[29] When Ray and Grace had to leave their store in Mexican Hat, he would ask relatives to cover for him. One in-law, Freda Hunt, used the point-and-grab technique, where the customer read no English, she spoke no Navajo, and so he would point and she would grab what he wanted, one item at a time. Later, she learned how to count out change so that both parties could keep track of where they were in the transaction.[30] Colors and pictures on labels played an important part for the Navajo; that is why Borden's canned milk, with a cow on the label, sold better than Carnation canned milk, with just writing.

Like Grace, who used "He'll be back soon" as a fallback position, some traders capitalized on their "inability" to their benefit. John Kirk at Chinle claimed he knew only four phrases: "Hello," "No," and "I don't know." The fourth one was his favorite—"I don't understand." He learned this phrase quickly after watching his brother, Michael, listen to all the woes of his customers and then have to provide some type of assistance. John deduced, "If the Indians thought you didn't understand, they didn't bother to tell you their troubles, thus saving you money."[31] But ignorance was not always bliss. Mary Stiles Bailey spoke little Navajo when she was left to mind the counter in the Tuba City trading post. A Navajo entered seeking *tó azis*. "Now *tó* means 'water.' *Azis* is a sack. So it was over an hour that we went through everything in that trading post. . . . Anyway, what he finally wanted—he found a potato, I took him to the back of the counter, and he found a potato, and there was an empty pop bottle, and he put 'em together and then I knew he needed kerosene in a bottle with a potato stopper. Now how you could get from *tó azis* to that, without knowing the kerosene part, was a real battle."[32]

Mary was not alone. Gladys Jack, in learning the names of some of the store's merchandise, had problems in distinguishing different words. One man approached her asking for bacon, and she thought he wanted mutton. Even the picture he drew of a pig looked like a sheep until he drew on body parts under the stomach that helped Gladys to know what was wanted. The intonation of a word and some slight variations could also be confusing. Gladys found that the Navajo words for hay, string, sardines, and prairie dogs were almost impossible to differentiate, but the man finally got his bale of hay. Her husband, Vernon, a more accomplished speaker, struggled to learn the word for dye, with its variations in color. Counting change had its own procedure and vocabulary. A nickel was called "yellow" and a dime was "blue" because of the color of the paper script introduced by the army at Fort Sumner. A quarter was two bits, a half dollar was four bits, but a dollar was never eight bits. The word *neyáál* was often used for a dollar and a quarter.[33] These were all part of a specialized vocabulary and a way of viewing the trading scene.

There was, however, help for some of the confusion. Arthur Newcomb had a strong friend in Hastiin Klah, who arrived in the afternoon to visit the new trader and to assist with the language. Klah would stay into the evening after supper, teaching Newcomb, who made lists of words and phrases to carry around in his pocket during the day. Harry Goulding appreciated his two Navajo workers—Little Boy and Big Boy—who had an interest in learning English and so helped Harry and his wife, Mike, to learn Navajo. "We'd sit by the campfire at night and make lists of words and whenever they quit laughing at us we figured we had said it pretty good."[34] After the trading post was built, Harry continued his education with any Navajo who took the time to teach him, but it really ended up being only three who visited the store regularly and who already spoke a little English. "They had long hair, and they wouldn't talk English if another Navajo was around. The Navajos gave an ultimatum: you're either a white man or you're an Indian, we don't like anybody with two tongues. So those were the ones who would teach me Navajo when I could get them alone."[35] In Shonto, Donald Tsayutcissi entered the store for the first time to trade with Harry Rorick. The customer priced a lot of the merchandise in Navajo and approached the task leisurely, taking a full two hours to complete the deal. As he left the store, he looked back and asked in plain English, "'Wha' time is it?' And Harry answered with a broad grin, 'Why, god-damn-you! It's four o'clock.'"[36] The two men later became fast friends.

Thus, there was a large variation in the ability of traders to speak the language; where some were extremely fluent, others barely got by, while most were somewhere in between. William Adams provides the most informed analysis of what is known as "Trader Navajo." He refers to it as a specialized form of speech used in the posts between trader and customer that both had to learn. While Navajo was the only language usually spoken throughout the day, this pidgin, or marginal, language was a specialized form of communication. Its lexicon was pure Navajo, "nouns and verbs occur only in a single form, and the syntax is generally reminiscent of English."[37] Sometimes referred to as "Navajo baby talk," this language could be learned in three or four months and was essential to post transactions. Adams estimated that at Shonto during the early 1950s, only half of the Navajos spoke the simplest English during a trade, while in earlier years, Ray Hunt had placed the figure at ten out of a thousand. Hence the necessity for "Trader Navajo."[38] For traders who spoke only this language, they could converse very little beyond the counter. Vernon Jack explained: "The conversation that goes on in a store and that goes on outside is so different that while I could catch words of an outside conversation and catch the thread of the conversation, I couldn't interpret it for you. But as far as the words for the things that were in the store, I could interpret those."[39] That is why Navajo matriarch Gladys Yellowman, when asked if Navajos understood what the white trader was saying, replied, "The white men talked poor Navajo. Where they learned it, I do not know."[40]

Using Trader Navajo sometimes led to interesting circumstances. Adams noted that 90 percent of all the communication in the post was Navajo, but that when a Navajo customer who spoke English preferred to use that language, traders would at times insist on using Trader Navajo. Since many store owners were not able to understand a lot of what was being said in their post, they might depend on someone to interpret for them. Unless a Navajo customer specifically addressed him in Trader Navajo, there was a good chance he might be oblivious as to what was transpiring in the bullpen.[41]

Names and Relations

Just as the Navajo customers gave names to traders, so too, did the store owners have names for the customers. And they were not alone. Government officials, school superintendents, missionaries, and many other Anglos serving in official capacities were given to simplifying Navajo names that could be either spelled or replaced with something familiar in English. The Navajos themselves might latch on to a name that they liked. Here, only a cursory look is taken at the naming process. Traders often shortened names or translated them into English, giving rise to names such as Shorty, Little, Red Woman, and Salt. Like his Navajo neighbors, the trader might give a customer a name based on a quality, a physical ability, or an occupation—Slim, Shorty, Weaver, Singer, Blue Eyes, Many Goats, . . . Others were given names of people the traders respected, such as Woodrow Wilson, Lew Wallace, Mark Twain, and Jack Johnson.[42]

Trader John Kirk provided his own name to a worker who admired him. He was trading in Gallup at the time when a Navajo employee, who had no English name, asked if he could use his—John Kirk. Kirk agreed, and years later, when his son accidently met John Kirk the Navajo, there was also a John Kirk Jr.[43] Carl Hines reports having three Indians at his post named John Joe. But there was only one Mrs. Beaver, whom the traders named for her broad tail.[44] Other Navajos earned their name, like Charlie Tso. He was a peaceful individual who befriended a trader, Frank Noel, and advocated for the store. One day, Tso entered the post to find his friend beset by a group of Navajos, who first intimidated the trader, then ran about the store, "upsetting things and knocking them into splinters and smithereens." Tso sized up the situation, grabbed an ax handle, and went to work, clearing the crowd and saving his friend. Noel dubbed him Charlie Mitchell, a famous English prizefighter at the time, and the name stuck.[45] Mister Bent Knee, on the other hand, was appropriately named but the name caused his wife some problems when she went to the hospital in Ganado, where they thought her name was an ailment as opposed to a title. A call by the trader straightened out the confusion.[46]

Before leaving the business of naming by traders, there is another facet to look at—that of the "stealing wife" (*ach'ooní yineezįį'*). This is the translation of the Navajo name for a woman who was not married but had a child by a trader. The fact that this happened cannot be disputed, but the extent and frequency are open to further research. With men in lonely posts, women selling and trading products, and differing codes of ethics in terms of sexuality, illegitimate children resulted. On the Anglo side, there is little mention of it, with the name of the father rarely transferring, but Navajo families kept close track of parentage through their oral tradition. Author Martha Blue, who studied J. L. Hubbell, gives a glimpse into what she discovered. There are a number of stories about how he fathered many children, ogled young women, and chased a few of them around the store. The Franciscans at Saint Michael's Mission recorded six offspring by him on their books, but there may have been more.[47] Hubbell was not the only one to take advantage of the situation.

The previous chapter has already discussed much of the trading scene from the Navajo perspective. Here, a few additional insights are gained from that of the traders. A visitor watched Joe Hatch conduct business in one of Billy Meadows's posts. He noted that the tobacco bill for that year must have been tremendous, since both trader and customer started, ended, and conducted the entire lengthy trading process in a cloud of smoke. "This method of trade, the customer paying for each article as he received it and smoking a cigarette after each purchase, was carried on until he bought more canned goods, and some sugar, tobacco, and candy for his wife and children."[48] J. L. Hubble's greeting to visitors was a can of tomatoes with a scoop of sugar or some bread or canned meat, as well as candy for the children and a plug or twist of tobacco for the men. At the same time, he introduced new products that might be of interest and supplies that the family might need for children going to school or some other activity.[49]

The accepted practice as customer and trader started to deal for a blanket or some other item across the counter was that the trader started low, the customer started high. Then, during the discussion, both would reach a price they were comfortable with. Everyone knew what a product was bringing at other posts and what constituted a fair ballpark figure. It was also given that the trader had to make some profit in order to exist. On the other hand, there had been a lot of time and effort that went into the item the Navajo was selling. The customer could trade wherever he or she desired, and traveling another day was not a terrible inconvenience. So there was room for choice and negotiation. If the trader appeared too anxious to sell his goods, the Navajo might become suspicious and wonder why there was such a good deal—there must be a trick. The Lippincotts at Wide Ruin put it this way: "The trading business might lack the strain of Big Business, but nonetheless even its smallest transaction had all the elements of a major fray in collective bargaining. All of the canniness on both sides was called into play."[50]

The previous chapter discussed a number of extended dialogues that focused on the typically Navajo side of a transaction. Will Evans provides a similar dialogue from the trader's perspective. Here, a fictitious Navajo woman has brought a rug for sale, wrapped it in a flour sack, and concealed it under her Pendleton shawl as she enters the post. When ready, she sidles over to the counter and shakes hands with Evans, who initiates the discussion.

> "Hello my cousin."
> "Yes, my friend."
> "Where did you come from?"
> "Beyond Shiprock."
> "Unh" [meaning, "I see"].

"On what day did you come?"

"Yesterday, by horse; I came alone."

The trader unties the flour sack, weighs the rug, and spreads it on the floor.

"How much do you want for it?"

"That is for you to say; you are buying it."

"It is not straight; that end is wider than this one. Nine pesos and four bits [$9.50], I think."

"Nine and four bits. I thought it was worth at least eleven."

"No, it is narrow at one end and there is a mistake in the border in the corner."

"I will take the blanket. Perhaps the white man at the Hogback [post] will pay more. I will leave it for ten, my friend. Ten is good. I have come from far away and weaving is hard work."

"All right, ten."

All right, my friend."

The trader pulls out a small pad of paper making note of the purchase, continues a light conversation that is leisurely in pace, and waits for the woman to start purchasing.

"How much is the flour?"

"For money, one beso (dollar) and nine blues."

"The little sack is how much?"

"One beso."

"Bring me a big one and some baking powder for one blue."

While the trader has been recording the deal with the woman buying each item one at a time, her fingers have been moving deftly counting, lips moving silently. Under her breath she whispers to herself the results of her subtraction from the blanket's price. She asks the trader for verification as to how much she has left. The process continues until all of the money earned by her sale is spent.[51]

In addition to sales across the counter, there were also acts of friendship that brought customer and buyer together. Some of John Hunt's family members collected ration stamps for coffee during World War II. Since a number of them were Mormons (The Church of Jesus Christ of Latter-day Saints) and did not drink coffee, they funneled the tickets to the posts and their Navajo clientele.[52] Letter writing for families with

Navajo customers as well as traders understood clearly the value of the products they brought to a store. During a sale, while each side bartered back and forth, they knew what was fair and acceptable. Failure to reach an agreement on either side of the counter could affect future relationships and loss of business. (Painting by Charles Yanito.)

children in school became another responsibility for the trader and his wife. Mothers and fathers would miss their child and want to know what was going on, or a child might request some item from the post that would be added to the family's ticket until they could sell their wool. The trader provided the correspondence in both directions.[53]

As the 1936 *Survey of Conditions on the Navajo Reservation* by the federal government pointed out, many traders served as counselors, whether they wanted to or not, with the potential of becoming embroiled in marital difficulties, illness, death, and inheritance issues. Apparently, the government approved of this, recognizing that "The Indians insist upon the counsel and advice of the trader or of an employee of the Indian Service."[54]

For many traders, the responsibility of being a judge was a difficult task. In each case, there was the very real possibility of making an enemy of one customer, while satisfying another. The interconnectedness of large, extended families could drag in other groups not directly involved in the issue and commit them to taking sides. Loss of business was a real concern. Also, the trader who understood Navajo culture might arrive at a solution unlike the determination that might have been found in an Anglo court. S. I. Richardson, who detested being a judge as a trader, provides two examples. One time at Rainbow Lodge, near the base of Navajo Mountain, Slim Fingers approached S. I. about a man who had stolen his wife. He wanted revenge but not necessarily the woman. Following some deliberation, S. I. suggested that he go to the offending man's hogan at night, stealthily unscrew all of the taps from the four wheels, and leave the place. Slim Fingers returned to the store the next day with a bag full of wagon-wheel taps, feeling at peace with the outcome. In a second instance, a man with two wives offered a visiting friend an opportunity to sleep with the host's older wife, whom he did not care much about. Instead, the visitor slept with the younger one. When the host found this out in the morning, he brought the friend and wife to the post, asking S. I. to determine fair damages. The trader, who knew the economic situation of both parties, suggested that the angry husband receive a burro from his friend. All agreed that this was fair, and the culprit made the payment. Later, the trader learned that the man who had offended no longer had his large herd of burros—his friend, the husband, had them all—but both parties were satisfied.[55]

Traders also subsidized part of ceremonial gatherings that could last from one to nine nights, depending on the ritual being performed. They donated flour and other foodstuffs, attended when invited, and welcomed the sale of all materials—from cloth to baskets to hardware—needed for the large gathering. The Enemy Way (*Anaa'jí Ndáá'*), a three night–four day ceremony, lent itself particularly well to trading activities, since the participants moved to three different Navajo camps over a wide territory. Thus, two posts might benefit, depending on their location, and at least one post received significant business in the sale of goods.

The posts also became a place of learning and an introduction to the world beyond the reservation. New tools and equipment made labor easier and better. For instance, Old Mexican in Aneth dug an irrigation ditch for a garden. He obtained a level and a board from the trader who showed him how to use them to determine a good grade for water flow. He also worked for a plow, wagon, shovels, and axes that made his life easier. He paid for all these new tools in freighting and road repair.[56]

Hilda Wetherill, on the other hand, provided newspapers telling of current happenings to make residents aware of national and international events. During World War I, she laid newspapers on the counter with pictures of marching soldiers, crowds of people in Paris amid tall buildings, and flying airplanes. She marveled at the Navajos' "real intelligence," as her customers studied the paper and tried to figure out how many people were in a picture or how tall a building was. To determine the number of people, a soda-pop bottle and a pencil circumscribed a part of the picture so that the Navajos could count the heads inside. Then they drew another circle, counted the heads, and added the two totals until all the people in the picture were included. They next counted the stories in a building by the windows defining a floor, and then related it to a rock formation nearby, which seemed comparable in height. They finally determined that "the stars were the only thing more numerous, or maybe the grass," when it came to the white population. As for the airplanes flying in a military formation, "The Indians asked if they [planes] would come down at the waterholes. They couldn't get away from the idea that things that flew had bird habits even if men did ride in them."[57] It did not take long, however, before the Navajos encountered the car and airplane in their own life and realized just how this technology worked.[58]

Respect in the posts went in both directions. Gladys Jack had trouble nursing her babies. Canned milk with a touch of Karo syrup and a banana seemed to be the only things that her infant son, Rayburn, could keep down. Shortly after his arrival, an Indian mother gave birth to a young daughter whom she could not feed. Knowing that Gladys struggled with the same issue, the Navajo mother brought her baby to Gladys and asked that she care for her until she could handle a regular diet. Gladys agreed, returning the baby when she had grown sufficiently. Years later, the mother presented a rug to Gladys with the Jacks' names on it in gratitude for saving the infant's life. She also told her daughter, "It doesn't make any difference what Mrs. Jack asks you to do; if she ever asks you to give her anything or to do anything, you just do it. You owe all your life, everything that you have and everything that you will be to her, because if it hadn't been for her, you wouldn't be here. You just would have died."[59]

There were always special events in the community, with children going off to school, ceremonial celebrations and gatherings, sheep shearing and lambing time, and Anglo holidays like "Little Christmas" (Thanksgiving). One of the most prominent holidays, mentioned by many traders, however, was Christmas, what Franc Newcomb called, "one of the great events of the year." A few days before December 25, Navajo workers would dig a deep pit in the ground, slaughter and barbecue a beef provided by the post, and keep the fire burning at an even heat. Once the meat was ready, the store provided bakery bread, a couple of galvanized tubs of cooked beans with chilies, a washer boiler of coffee that had to be refilled two or three times, and frosted cookies for dessert. Each individual received a sack filled with an orange, apple, a handful of peanuts, a package of gum, and some mixed candy. When the festivities ended, many families moved on to the next post for a similar celebration.[60]

Hilda Wetherill provides a vivid image of one Christmas at the Covered Water Trading Post in 1928. Although sometimes not as sympathetic to her neighbors as other traders, she leaves a memorable picture:

> There were wagonloads of women and children and scores of men and young folks on ponies. Everybody was dressed in his best: beads, bracelets, and silver belts glistened against bright-colored velvet shirts and glossy sateen skirts with miles and miles of flounces. . . . By dark

> there were some two hundred Indians here. . . . The adults came and took what they needed for their families for supper and Christmas morning breakfast. What they did not eat at once they were afraid to put down because someone would steal it, so all the evening they strolled around with great red raw beefsteaks in their hands. . . . Big fires were made on the level space where the dancing was to be, and the fires and the full moon made the night so light we could see the whole landscape round. . . . The music was made by a clay water jar with water in it and rawhide stretched over the top . . . rattles [were] made of paper bags with beans in them. [Christmas morning the men raced horses and the women cooked.] When dinner was ready, [the men] charged in, the ponies running pell-mell between the campfires and jumping over the clutter of camp stuff, the Indians yelling like pirates and quirting on both sides.

Following the meal, the traders handed out the obligatory bags of candy that ended the day's celebration.[61]

Other traders took a modified approach to the Christmas season, seeing it as an opportunity to teach giving and not just receiving. Gladys and Vernon Jack was such a couple. That is not to say that they did not feed the five hundred to six hundred people that arrived at their post for the celebration. They kept track of the number of attendees by the bags of treats put together and handed out by a committee. Each man, woman, and child got one and only one—the committee members ensured that. But by the second and third Christmases, the traders noticed that Navajo families were exchanging small gifts among themselves. Even the traders received gifts from Navajo friends, like small rugs and pieces of jewelry, which "meant an awful lot to us." One year Gladys ordered and sold forty turkeys, but did not save one for herself. A Navajo woman came in to purchase one and heard that they were all gone—not even one for Gladys. Thinking that the trader was in a difficult position, she went home, killed the family's tame rabbit, and presented it to her so that she would have something better than mutton for Christmas dinner. To Gladys, "That was one of the things that lasted me a lifetime and I never will forget that."[62]

The experience and attitudes of the traders were as varied as the posts they worked in and the people they served. Underlying all of the variety, however, were fundamental views and actions that allowed the Anglo trader to be successful. Among these was the acceptance of Navajo culture and its emphasis on relationships, while the customer had to realize that the traders were running stores for their livelihood. Both sides of the bullpen needed to obtain what it wanted but still be fair to the other side. Whether following government directives, driving an individual to a hospital, serving as a judge, learning Trader Navajo, donating for a ceremony, bargaining across a counter, or preparing for Christmas, traders and their families were a central part of Navajo communities. They were either successful or failed, respected or rejected, prosperous or impoverished, depending on their ability to accept the needs and understand the cultural expectations of the people among whom they lived.

CHAPTER SIX

Exchanging Wealth

Stock and Livestock

The operation of trading posts and the preparation of Navajo products to sell were multifaceted undertakings. What might seem like a simple store in a picturesque—or not so picturesque—setting actually required a large amount of knowledge and effort to be successful. The same was true for the Navajos who had to use their understanding of the land and livestock as well as their own innate ability in weaving and craft production. This and the next chapter delve into what was required on both sides of the counter to be successful. Chapter 6 looks at Navajo livestock practices and their cultural implications, the processing of wool for sale, and other items brought to the trader for exchange. For the store owners, their merchandise did not miraculously appear on the shelf. What did it take for that can of tomatoes sitting behind the counter or a washtub hanging from the ceiling to get to their respective places? What were traders stocking, why, and at what price? This cultural scene required far more than just freighting to achieve an equitable return. The next chapter discusses the sale of rugs, blankets, and baskets, the role of the trader in encouraging their manufacture, how pawn met the needs of both parties involved, and what each considered a fair expectation in the other. Together, these two chapters bring to life the financial operation of the trading posts up to the beginning of livestock reduction in the 1930s.

"Sheep Are Life"

Following the Fort Sumner era, Navajo traditional values greatly intensified in emphasis on sheep, as the culture moved from a hunting, gathering, and raiding lifestyle to an increasing reliance on domestic livestock and agriculture. Both of these elements had been present prior to this time, but with the establishment of reservation boundaries and a sedentary way of life, stock raising and agriculture increased in importance. As a girl, Navajo matriarch Ella Sakizzie remembers her mother saying, "I will not live for you forever. Therefore, learn to take care of the sheep, for it will be your mother and father and support you. Its meat you will use as food; its wool you will use in many different ways. If you are willing to learn how to card, spin, and weave with your hands, you will have all that you need and want. If you are careless, you will be begging for handouts from other people. . . . Your wealth will not diminish and die, for this is the 'life of life' and 'strength of life.' It is the 'life of life' because these animals are alive."[1] Her teachings cannot be overemphasized—livestock was central to Navajo existence. Paul Begay tied this way of life to the trading post when he referred to sheep as dollar signs or a ticket. "If we had about fifty head of sheep, we were secure; we knew we could make things work. . . . Yeah, sheep were very important to us; they were our ticket to the store."[2]

But sheep were not just a ticket. They permeated every aspect of Navajo life, either directly or indirectly. The importance of sheep in a pastoral lifestyle, regardless of how much capital was derived from this source, was seen in the emphasis an owner placed upon his herd. Total family involvement was required during certain times of the year (shearing, dipping, and herding) and, although ownership was maintained on an individual basis, personal acquisition was a source of group responsibility and family pride. Thus, livestock operations were the "most important cooperative enterprise of the 'outfit' [defined as one or more extended families that worked together]; the animals were normally herded together, though owned individually, and children were started in the whole process at about the age of five."[3]

Navajos obtained social prominence from the ownership of sheep, so a person with a large herd was often respected as wise in management and supernaturally blessed. Also, since the Navajos lived in a matrilineal society, wives often owned more livestock than husbands, while members of the extended kin group, or even unrelated groups, combined efforts in maintaining their animals with those of their relatives or associates. By 1915, goats, cattle, horses, and mules served as another basis for wealth. Although herds of these animals were numerous, sheep continued to be the pillar of the economy. Perhaps the most complete study of Navajo attitudes toward wealth is found in *Navajo Acquisitive Values* by Richard Hobson, who argues that the Navajo possess a strong desire to accumulate wealth and to "make a good living." This motivation is interpreted by some Navajos, Hobson notes, to mean "The Navajo way is just to want enough to have enough to eat for your family and nice things to wear sometimes."[4] On the other hand, those who acquired excessive wealth and broke the injunction against being "too rich" were the first to be accused of antisocial behavior.[5] Thus, Hobson sees wealth accumulation as a primary preoccupation controlled through social means: "A high valuation is placed upon the possession of land, livestock, houses, clothes, and jewelry. . . . Sheer accumulation of wealth is of less importance than its display or its generous distribution."[6]

When the Navajos returned to their homelands after the Fort Sumner experience, they received 30,000 sheep and 4,000 goats from which their herds expanded. By 1915, Agent Peter Paquette conducted an extensive census in four districts (Window Rock Agency, Chinle, Saint Michaels, and Ganado) that composed the heart of the Navajo Reservation population. This study listed 382,044 sheep and 119, 228 goats, as well as other livestock, including horses, cattle, mules, and burros. In the monetary terms of those days (a sheep cost $3.25 and a goat $.75), the value of these two types of animals was $1,331,064, while the value of the remaining categories of horses, cattle, mules, and burros amounted to $1,101,487.[7] When the livestock owners in these districts are divided into ten equal increments and placed in ascending order on the basis of wealth, a high concentration—54 percent (averaged over the four districts)—is found in the wealthiest decile concerning sheep; a similar pattern is found for goats. These wealthy livestock owners or "ricos" often hired poorer Navajos ("pobres") to herd their livestock on either their own lands or, when available, on public domain.

In 1928, District Superintendent Chester E. Faris spoke about this distribution of wealth, noting that some families had from three thousand to five thousand sheep and goats. "These men are leaders in thought, application, and influence. . . . Such leaders are found among every people. There are industrial chiefs among white people—the Fords, the Morgans, the Rothchilds. These men have much and they give much."[8]

So, while Hobson and others have emphasized cultural leveling mechanisms that encouraged sharing and wealth distribution leading to equality, the reality was that there was a concentration of wealth among a few powerful men, while many others had to depend on more meagre means.[9] Those with large herds had to constantly monitor range conditions, dividing the herds into a number of different camps or bases of operation so that grazing conditions would not be ruined. Charlie Blueyes understood the importance of the range when he said, "From the sheep and cattle, life renews itself. You get many lambs and calves from the plants around here. On the tip of these plants are horses, cattle, and sheep. They are made of plants."[10]

Marketing Influences

The federal government constantly monitored the Navajo livestock industry and how their advisors, the traders, were conducting business. A cursory look at ten years (1919–29) of correspondence from the Western Agency to the Office of Indian Affairs indicates the volume of letters and the tenor of how the government viewed this economic activity as well as the types of problems Navajo shepherds faced. The government tried to advise both the Navajos and the traders as to how to conduct their business. In 1919, Superintendent Walter Runke of the Western Agency estimated that there were 200,000 sheep and 40,000 goats on his part of the reservation after a 15 percent loss from that winter's severe weather.[11] He felt that the sheep on the Western Navajo Agency were inferior to those that Anglo ranchers had, and so over the previous five years he had introduced seventy-five Lincoln rams, which he sold to the Navajos to upgrade their herd. Trader Stewart Hatch in southeast Utah agreed with Runke's observation. Hatch mentioned how traders drew a marked distinction between what they called "American" and Navajo sheep. The former were larger, grain-fed animals that yielded ten to twelve pounds of wool at a shearing, while the latter foraged for their food, became very thin over the winter until spring brought increasing access to grass. These animals yielded from four to six pounds of wool.[12]

By 1923, on the Western Navajo, there was no appreciable difference in the sheep's quality or the amount of wool from the experimental breeding practices, while the traders across the reservation were paying a standard price, as established by Babbitt Brothers in Flagstaff. The owners of chain trading posts often established the price, with the independent traders agreeing to go along with what was decided. The produce from southeastern Utah, southwestern Colorado, and northwestern New Mexico would, in turn, go to the Colorado-New Mexico Wool Marketing Association, which sold to the National Wool Marketing Association in Boston. All of these connections influenced the price and acceptance of the Navajos' product.[13] Trader Tom Kirk told of the dealers' surprise when they came to his post from the East. They saw copies of *Kiplinger's Letter*, the *Congressional Record*, and *Boston Wool Market Report* in the store. As to why he had them, Kirk's answer was simple: "They didn't realize that we had to know what was going on in the sheep market in Denver and Kansas City, what the wool market was in Boston, and what the silver market was in Los Angeles and New York. We had to know these things in order to base our prices in buying and trading."[14]

The uphill struggle to improve the quality of wool continued. The government introduced good breeding stock with the idea that Indian livestock owners would be reimbursed for the expense, but this proved difficult to enforce and caused bad feelings between agent and owner. Stewart Hatch recalled this program and felt that the "Navajos kind of resented it."[15] From problems in the corral to fluctuations in market prices, selling wool could be a tenuous livelihood. Traders reduced payment by two or three cents per pound of wool in order to clean and ship the wool to market, where they still received lower prices than Anglo breeders using superior stock. The agents encouraged Navajos to change their normal livestock patterns by using new corrals not infected with lice, vermin, and diseases that lingered and tormented the animals.

Scabies was a particularly troubling disease. These microscopic arthropods feed on the blood and skin of sheep and are highly contagious, causing intense itching, patches of fur to fall out, and subsequent sores and crusted scabs. An application of lime sulfur and nicotine sulfate kills the mites, but it may take years to remove the last vestiges. In 1905, agents in the Southern and Northern Navajo Districts reported the disease's presence.[16] The government launched a reservation-wide program that called for dipping vats and a trough approximately forty-eight inches deep and thirty feet long filled with a nicotine-and-chemical medicine. Navajo herders forced the sheep to swim through the bath, with the solution covering every inch of the animal, including its head, which was pushed down with a forked stick. Harry Goulding in Monument Valley, like other traders, was highly supportive of this program to improve livestock; he spent a month and a half constructing the necessary facilities. He recalled, "I don't think the Navajos had ever seen sheep-dipping before, but they were willing to do it because it [scabies] was just murder on the sheep. If you leave it on there too long, it'll kill a sheep."[17] Although dipping throughout the reservation was mandatory, some Navajos initially resisted.[18] For approximately fifteen days after the treatment, the meat from the animal tasted like the dip as the solution dried, then killed the mites. After that, the meat tasted normal, but it still went against the grain for some of the more traditional families.

Some elements of the livestock-improvement program were successful, others less so; regardless, Navajo herds grew. Scabies eventually became a concern of the past; the quality of mutton meat and wool slowly improved; and Navajo weaving became increasingly popular. However, this success led to other problems. By 1929, as large herds of sheep, goats, feral horses, and other animals expanded over the range and the boundaries of the reservation became solidified, with white settlements established on surrounding lands, resources shrank to the point that livestock reduction appeared to be the only solution. That gray day in Navajo history will be discussed in a later chapter.

Wool at this time (mid- to late-1920s) sold for between thirty-two and forty-five cents a pound in Boston or Philadelphia markets, depending upon its quality, but the best price in Boston for Navajo wool was between twenty-five and thirty cents, while in Philadelphia, the highest quotes were from thirty to forty cents. There were a number of reasons for the lower prices. Navajo wool was coarse in quality, light in quantity, and showed no preparation for market. Agents hoped that, by breeding superior stock, the first two problems could be solved, estimating that the yield might increase three- or fourfold. The third problem fell squarely on the shoulders of Navajo stockmen.[19]

Navajo Livestock Practices

Herding customs met the needs of certain cultural beliefs but also had their drawbacks. In traditional society, a person avoided staying out at night and traveling during darkness because of potentially evil influences. This necessitated having animals back in the corral before the sun went down, limiting the range that the flock could travel to find food. Whether in a summer camp, located at higher altitudes, or at a winter camp, where it was either flat or in lower elevations in canyon country, the general radius of travel from a base would be no longer than five miles if the animals were to be returned to the corral in the middle of the day or ten miles if they were to remain on the range for the entire day.[20] Within that radius, the herder would use a cloverleaf-loop approach known as the Savory method, where alternate routes were taken each day in order to give the range a rest, at least in theory.[21] The location of a water source as well as the corral and different terrain limitations could alter the pattern. Some herders did not follow this practice at all, but took their herds wherever they could find grass while moving and sleeping on the range with their flocks. Navajos referring to the rangelands for their herds would say, "*shikéyah kodóó*," meaning "This is where I put my foot down," establishing a certain location as their range.[22] In the old days, there was a sense of cooperation free from disputes over the land and its use, but as the range became increasingly restricted, conflict between neighbors proved to be more prevalent.

Many traders accumulated large herds of sheep, either from sales at their posts or as part of a separate business venture. They often hired Navajo herders, who had a reputation for knowing their business and caring for the flocks. Navajo Oshley was such a man, and so trader Ray Hunt hired him. When Oshley began herding, he found that the trader had different expectations from what he, Oshley, was used to. Hunt's sheep were accustomed to just wandering about; he did not specify where the animals should be taken; they were not used to being returned to the corral before sunset; and Oshley feared coyotes would get into the herd. But the trader did not share those concerns. Oshley's upbringing did not fit with the ways of the owner. "Then Hunt came to me and said that they just let the sheep out and let them roam around by themselves, and that all I had to do was keep an eye on them. I said that I was afraid of what might happen to them, but he said that he didn't think there was anything to worry about."[23] Oshley enjoyed a long relationship of mutual respect with Hunt, who depended on the Navajo's knowledge of the terrain and the animals to safeguard his herd.

Livestock was so central to traditional Navajo life that it has now become one of the most popular images portraying the people's ties to the land. Herding animals in Monument Valley, Utah, with Totem Pole Rock in the background, this couple provides one of many iconic scenes that dramatize Navajo dependence on sheep and goats. (Used by permission, Utah State Historical Society.)

On an individual level, what did the livestock industry look like for the Navajo stockmen and traders who went about their seasonal business? Most ewes gave birth between February and April, while the shearing of winter coats occurred between mid-April and mid-May, in a process that took about a half hour for each animal. Anthropologist Louise Lamphere noted that Navajo shepherds using hand clippers could shear 200 to 250 sheep in two days, with six to nine people working together to accomplish the task.[24] In the early years, sharpened knives or even a tin-can lid did the job, but when single-piece shears became available in posts during the late nineteenth century, traders began to stock this popular item. Each sheep, once secured, came under the control of the shearer, who "with bent knees, or in the case of a woman, with a leg folded under them hidden in their full skirt [the polite way for Navajo women to sit as first demonstrated by Changing Woman], clipped with one hand while the other pushed back the fleece and held down the sheep. . . . Each fleece was tied separately with hard twine that was glazed to prevent its fibers from getting mixed into the wool."[25] Workers then stuffed the product in a six-by-three-foot-long sack suspended on a frame, which held the sack open and allowed a person to jump on the wool packed inside. When filled, the sack weighed around two hundred pounds. Traders differentiated between types of wool.

> Black and brown fleeces, bought from the Navajos, would be put in separate sacks. Dark wool could not be dyed and the mills paid less for it. They also paid less for bags that on inspection proved to contain mixed dark and white wool. Stokes's [Carson] sheep were white, but the Navajos used the dark wools for weaving, and their flocks of sheep and goats contained many with rich brown or black fleeces. Traders kept back a little wool, often the dark wools to sell to weavers who ran short over the summer. The filled sacks would be sewn up and rolled aside into a great pyramid of bulging burlap. Wool will keep, though not indefinitely. In the damp it molds and grubs and moths will discover it eventually. However, with the dry air of this country, it was safe for months.[26]

In the spring, Navajo shepherds drove their sheep to the most convenient place for the shearing and selling of wool. It was hot, dirty work in which the owner tied the animal to prevent movement, clipped the wool, then tossed it on the ground until it was bagged. During the process, sand, manure, twigs, and other debris either already in the wool or picked up off the ground in the corral mixed into the fiber. Some traders gave the shearers extra money to remove what they called "tags," where "on the rear end of the sheep there are a lot of little tags falling, maybe you got a sheep turd to it or something."[27] The trader paid a small amount for a bag of tags, so wool sacks were marked separately, showing that their contents had been cleaned. The stockmen shoved the wool into a six-, seven-, or nine-foot bag, the latter when filled weighing 300 to 325 pounds, and brought it to the trader, who weighed it and purchased the contents with a three-to-six-cent margin per pound to cover shipping costs and profit. Many Navajos brought small amounts (up to forty pounds) of wool wrapped in a Pendleton blanket stitched shut with yucca fiber, a tough material that, once dried, was impossible to untie, so had to be cut.[28]

There are plenty of stories about how sand or a rock or a hide might be added to give additional weight for a higher price. Ruth Claw remembers a man called "Very Tall One," who was shearing sheep. As the wool went into the sack, he tossed in two shovelfuls of dirt, declaring, "The white man isn't the only one that can cheat."[29] Another time, J. L. Hubbell paid for a sack that had a large rock placed in the midst of the wool. He instructed a clerk to put the same rock in a sack of flour and sell it back to that customer. He did, and the man never complained.[30] Many traders had a bag's contents dumped and examined, but generally, most post operators felt their Navajo customers were honest. Bags that had substantial foreign matter added would bend in the middle, indicating uneven weight. To counter part of the problem—whether intentional or unintentional presence of debris—the traders might deduct some pounds from the total to compensate.[31]

Once the buying house purchased the wool, it was cleaned and graded, and a final price paid for the wool. The estimated loss in weight could be as much as 50 percent by the time the buyers had removed all foreign matter and the wool readied for sale to a manufacturer. Special Advisor F. E. Brandon tells of other problems encountered in the process of selling Navajo wool: "As an example of the reported losses sustained by the traders from time to time, one firm, Richardson and Lowery, purchased their share of the 1920 and 1921 clip from the Indians, paying 35 to 40 cents per pound. On account of the drop in prices they held the wool in storage one-and-a-half years, paid one-and-a-half cents per pound for freight to market and other expenses as storage, insurance, commission, etc., and sold the same wool for 9 cents a pound. Mr. Lowery told me their losses were $38,000 and that they were forced to close one of their stores on account of it."[32]

By March 1, 1923, Agent Byron A. Sharp reported sales by the Navajos under his charge, giving a sense of the volume of production and monetary gain in the Western District. He obtained these figures from the traders in his jurisdiction: Sheep—2,240 ($8,850); sheep and goat pelts—24,568 pounds ($5,007); wool—178,488 pounds ($21,824); and Navajo rugs—23,080 pounds ($41,038).[33] This was a low year for the Western Agency.[34] There were other times when fluctuations in the market pushed prices so low that many Navajos became angered at being "cheated," since they were not aware of the world conditions that caused the drop in sales. Even when prices were at their very height, such as during World War I with its seemingly insatiable demand for wool and meat, there could be problems. Some traders worked tirelessly to ensure that their customers did not sell too much, crippling their ability to have a successful crop the following year. They would go to market with the livestock owners, marking animals that could be sold while still maintaining a healthy breeding stock.[35]

There were some bright spots in the livestock industry. Selling young lambs was often more profitable than selling wool, choice lambs bringing a price of $12.25 each in 1922, but more often around five dollars for a forty-pound animal. Moving them to market required herding on foot and horseback to the nearest railhead—Thompson, Utah, and Durango or Farmington, Colorado, in the upper Four Corners area, where the animals then shipped to Kansas City. Between August and the first part of October, this process reached its height.[36] Stewart Hatch recalled, "Maybe a family would bring a hundred lambs to pay off their bill. I think some of them traders, they'd get maybe two or three thousand head of lambs in the fall. We always contracted for 1200 head because I knew we would get that many. Then we had to drive them to Farmington."[37] Stewart's brother, Joe, hired three Navajo helpers, brought along a chuck wagon, and received permission to bring the herd across Ute Reservation lands to the market. Vernon Jack recalled herding sheep one fall following a heavy rainstorm. After waiting a day, he moved his wagon into the swollen Lukachukai Wash, where the horses balked as items floated downstream out of the wagonbed. He recouped everything but a bale of hay, eventually caught up with his herders, who had not eaten for a day and a half, and continued his journey.[38]

Goats—A Mainstay

Before leaving the corral, brief mention should be made of goats. Sheep dominated the Navajo livestock scene because of the size of the herds, the amount of wool processed, and their connection to weaving. There is also ceremonial knowledge surrounding the care and use of sheep. Goats do not carry that background, and yet this animal was an important part of the poor Navajos' diet. Goats were able foragers, ideally suited to eking out their subsistence from a stingy desert environment.

They provided meat and milk, and cost a third of what a sheep might cost. A report written at the end of livestock reduction underscored the importance of goats and their loss during this time. Following Navajo testimony about the harm done in killing so many goats, the report summarized the issues:

> The goat, traditionally, is the property of the poor shepherd and roams the poorest range, surviving where no other animal can survive. It was the proverbial food supply: not only does natural economy prevent the Navajo from killing his sheep, but he prefers kid meat to all other food. The goat is highly productive, bearing two and sometimes three kids a year. Goat milk was widely used both by adults and children, and as a means of feeding orphan lambs. There are evidences that a crude kind of cheese was made. The loss of this native milk supply has resulted in increased purchases of canned milk from the trader.[39]

Harry Goulding agreed, saying that goat meat was "choice meat," superior to mutton.[40] They were choosey eaters, great browsers, cleaner animals, and were "top meat," and that is why he always kept them around his home as "camp food." Like sheepskins, goatskins served as currency at posts. The owner of a freshly slaughtered goat staked the hide into the ground until it dried, rolled it up with other hides, and brought them to the trading post as "pocket change" to buy incidentals not part of the larger transactions of wool, lambs, and other products. Left Handed tells of shearing a large herd of sheep with some helpers near a post. "When they started in they killed a billy goat and sold the skin at the store. They got a dollar for it and bought some grub. Skins were worth a whole lot, and after they'd sheared all the sheep, they killed ten billy goats, all at once, and the fellows who helped us got a skin apiece. We kept five and the wool. We sold the wool and hides and bought more stuff, flour, baking powder, coffee, sugar, and other food, and a lot of dry goods, calico and things like that, and different kinds of dishes."[41]

Piñon Nuts

Beginning in the early 1900s, another source of income for the Navajos was the sale of piñon (*Pinus edulis*) nut crops available in certain areas of the reservation during different years. Trader Elizabeth Hegemann, who worked in Shonto, a heavily productive area for this crop, suggests that these trees were on a seven-year cycle, with two bumper crop years, two fair years, and three without any nuts. Others insist that the size of the crop depended on the amount of moisture received through the winter and in early spring rains.[42] The nuts were ready to either be picked off the tree, or as in the old days, just picked up off the ground, after a hard frost broke open the cone, usually in October. All nuts had to be picked before the first snow, since wet nuts quickly became moldy.

"Camping parties" composed of a number of families with members of all ages received word as to where the crop was located for that year, then remained at the groves for as long as a week for daylong picking sessions. Some traders sponsored families, providing them with food and supplies, with the understanding that they would return with their harvest to that store. Navajos did not throw sticks to knock down the nuts because the tree may be hurt or offended by the treatment, and they did not shake the branches to drop their nuts because that is how bears acted.[43] Each person would have a small sack that held ten to fifteen pounds of nuts, which would then be dumped into a larger burlap sack that held about eighty pounds of nuts. Once the harvester removed the sticky outer cone, workers parched the nuts by a fire and placed them in a bag for sale at the post. Navajo pickers welcomed the additional income, spending it quickly and freely. While wool and lambs and rugs were staples of their economy, piñon nuts provided an opportunity to go beyond the necessities of life and try some new products.[44]

When the trader purchased an eighty-pound bag, he quickly consolidated his load, readying it for shipment to an outlet such as Santa Fe, Albuquerque, Flagstaff, Gallup, or other railhead cities. Buyers purchased the nuts according to their weight, so the sooner they were sold, the more money a trader received, since the nuts started to dry and lose up to 10 percent of their weight in a month's time. They could be stored for a year, and even though their flavor became stronger during that time, the nuts were still sold. After two years, they became rancid and oily and were no longer marketable.[45]

New York City was a particularly well-known destination for shipments because of its Armenian and Syrian populations, who had similar nuts and recipes in their own countries. Trader Tom Kirk regularly shipped back East sixteen railroad cars, each with at least forty thousand pounds of nuts. Elizabeth Hegemann, in her small post, purchased seventy thousand pounds of nuts each year during the 1930s, paying between twelve and thirty-five cents per pound, depending on the market. Gladwell Richardson remembers one year he sold almost all of his merchandise off the shelves to Navajo customers bringing in their harvest. He had to contact a fellow trader to obtain additional supplies and a whole lot more eighty-pound burlap sacks to hold the nuts. His friend came to the rescue, took a truckload of nuts with him after delivering the supplies, and brought them back to the warehouse. By the end of that season, Richardson had shipped eight hundred sacks to the main store.[46]

Supplying the Posts

To this point, the discussion has been primarily about what the Navajos did to bring unprocessed materials—wool, lambs, hides, and piñon nuts to the store. On the other side of the counter stood the trader and his wife, stocking the shelves, extending credit, bartering with customers, and eying regional and national markets. What did it take for these traders to stay afloat? They, first and foremost, had to meet the many different needs of their customers. That meant they had to know what, how much, and when certain supplies were required. A wide variety of goods provided the customer a practical source of products as well as a visual display of what the store had to offer. While there are many descriptions of posts' inventories, one of the best is provided by Sandford L. Hassell, who describes an unnamed store in New Mexico run by "Tooth Gone, a white man, one of the 175 licensed traders on the Navajo Reservation." Hassell starts:

> The trading post was well-stocked. From nails driven into the logs that supported the ceiling hung saddles, bridles, lariat ropes, harnesses, buckets, tubs, cooking pots, and other articles. Tooth Gone smiled when his eyes rested on half-a-dozen dust-covered brown crock chamber-pots suspended by strings. Years ago these had been good sellers. The Navajos had used them as mixing bowls when making bread, until somebody mentioned what the white people did with them; then they immediately went out of style.
>
> The shelves behind the counters were divided into departments: groceries—including canned goods, consisting mostly of tomatoes

> and fruit—hardware, and dry goods. (Flour, sugar, coffee, and lard were kept underneath the counter.) The dry goods section was largest. Shelf after shelf stacked with piece goods, and there were shelves for shirts, trousers, and shoes. Shoes were not much of a problem, for the trader carried only a couple of styles, and the foot sizes for both men and women were so uniform that he rarely had any trouble with the fit. A five or five-and-one-half would fit most of the women and a six-and-one half or a seven most of the men. If the children didn't get a good fit, it didn't make much difference. Often a mother would come to the store and with nothing to guide her but her eyes pick out a pair of shoes for the little boy or little girl who was left at home herding sheep. Rarely did she select a pair of shoes that did not fit.
>
> Tooth Gone usually kept a large stock of robes for men and shawls for the women. The only difference between the robes and shawls is that the shawls have fringe and robes do not. He also had robes and shawls for children. The dress of Navajo children is the same as that of their elders.
>
> On each end of the counter in front to the dry goods were two old-fashioned, round-topped glass show cases. These were packed with notions, novelties, and Indian jewelry. A little box in one corner of the showcase contained sleigh bells. In years past, unmarried Indian girls often wore these tied to the fringes of their belts. . . .
>
> In the trading post, both men and women used the "complimentary makings" freely. Tobacco, cigarette papers, and matches were kept in a one pound coffee can nailed to the counter. Seldom did an Indian come into the trading post and go directly to the tobacco can. This would have shown an unbecoming lack of restraint. Usually he would wait fifteen minutes or longer before taking a smoke. After the first smoke he felt free to visit the tobacco can as often as he liked.[47]

The purchasing of goods was not only conducted in a culturally defined manner, as discussed previously, but Navajo society also determined what was desired and the form it came in. Charlie Blueyes, when asked to name the first things he looked for upon entering a post, responded flour, sugar, and baking powder, three staples of the trade.[48] Add to that Arbuckles' Coffee, canned tomatoes, salt, and hard candy, and one has the mainstay of the diet—other than what the Navajos raised for themselves. Flour came in twenty-five-, fifty-, or one-hundred-pound sacks, from which it could be scooped; sugar, called "sweet salt" (*áshįįh łikan*), also came in various size sacks and was often dipped out of a large bag, weighed, and placed on the counter, where it was scraped into a buckskin container, a seamless twenty-five-pound flour sack, or a heavy canvas sack. Sometimes customers combined the sugar and flour. Vernon Jack remembers,

> The Indians would buy a twenty-five pound bag of flour, a ten cent can of baking powder, which was usually an eight to twelve ounce can of KC Baking Powder. . . . They also added a ten cent or two pound bag of salt. They mixed all these together, but they would not put all of the salt in, only part of the salt. They would mix it together by turning the sack up and down and turning it around. Then when they got ready to make their bread, they would just pour so much water on top of it and mix the dough and everything right in the top of the bag. They would put the dough either in hot grease and make fry bread, or if they did not have a frying pan, they would roast it over the coals.[49]

While trading posts sold lard, often there was enough fat already available from the roasting of mutton that many Navajos just used what they had. Some women used ground corn to extend the store-bought flour and to increase the flavor of their tortillas.[50]

Arbuckles' Coffee, a cheap grade shipped from Brazil, was a standard commodity. Still in the whole-bean state (called *níyizígíí*—the round one), the beans had to be ground with either a mano and metate or a store-bought grinder. To John Holiday of Monument Valley, coffee beans looked like the piñon nuts that his family roasted in a pan until they split open and were ready to be ground. Just as popular as the coffee were the wooden crates it came in. The wood from them served as cupboards, shelving, dressing tables, cradleboards, furniture, fences, chicken coops, and every other imaginable purpose in both the posts and Navajo homes.[51] Since almost every store sold the Arbuckles' brand of coffee, it was used as a comparative indicator of the pricing at a particular post. Vernon Jack gives a good sense of what this product cost the Navajo and the trader in the 1930s. "We would get the coffee in hundred pound wooden boxes. It would cost us about twelve-and-a-half to fourteen cents a pound; we also had to pay the freight charges. We paid about twenty-five cents freight on a hundred pounds, so it was not all profit. . . . On coffee, freight would only add about two cents a pound, so if we paid twelve cents a pound, coffee that we sold for twenty-five cents would actually cost us in the neighborhood of fifteen or sixteen cents a pound."[52]

Other items that sold well were potatoes, onions, and canned tomatoes and peaches. Grace Hunt never could figure out the fascination for canned tomatoes, but they sold quickly. Before the introduction of soda pop, they were the entry-level food when a person arrived at a post. "They'd come, and there was a can opener we kept on the counter. They'd get a can of tomatoes and open it. The trader kept sugar. They would put several spoons of sugar in the tomatoes. We sort of had a community spoon. . . . They'd go sit in the corner of the store and have their tomatoes."[53] Hard candy also came in bulk, and the harder the better. Traders distributed it as a sort of bonus to literally "sweeten" a deal and to win the children over as customers. In general, store owners stocked the brand of goods that the Navajos knew and trusted, no matter what the item. A familiar picture on the label was literally worth a thousand sales.

Before leaving the food section behind the counter, one has to recognize that there were also problems as new items entered the diet. A few stories can illustrate this. Left Handed remembers when his mother first learned about coffee. The trader provided instructions and she did the best she could, but she burned the beans before grinding and boiling them, then tried to cover the taste with far too much sugar. She made bread only from flour and water, with no salt or baking powder. The family and guests sat down to eat, but the bitter coffee had "everybody making faces and spitting it out; you couldn't swallow it." Even with added sugar, the drink did not improve. Next came the tortillas, but they were thin, as hard as a rock, and had no taste. "It was so hard you couldn't chew it, and it didn't taste good. So we couldn't use that, we had to let that go too, and just eat our own food, meat and cornbread and other food we always had."[54]

Joe Lee at Red Lake remembers when one of the men working for him tried to persuade Hastiin Nibbyjhay (*Nibijéí*—His Heart Said), that the newfangled jelly that he wanted to try for the first time came in a different tin than the one he was pointing at. The Indian thought the trader was tricking him, so demanded that he get the can he wanted, along with a box of soda crackers. He then seated himself on the bullpen floor and ate it all. "Smacking his lips, he said, 'It isn't sweet like candy as I was told. I don't think I am going to like this white man's jelly.'"[55] But why the axle grease did not taste good with soda crackers, no longer had to be explained. Hastiin Nibbyjhay was probably no worse off than a Navajo at the Shonto trading post who stole a small box with the picture of a kitchen on it, thinking he was getting cake flour. His wives attempted to make fry bread from it, but the product was as hard as a rock. They could not break it apart with their hands, much less eat it. The cake flour was actually kalsomine, a calcium carbonate (chalk) substance that was mixed with glue and used to whitewash interior plaster walls.[56]

Moving farther down the counter of the post, one finds the dry goods section, with the cloth and clothes preferred by Navajo customers. Popular store-bought fabric included calico, sateen, and velvet, which were at times sold by the bolt. If the customer only wanted to make a dress of velvet, for instance, the material could be cut from bolts forty yards in length, twenty-seven inches wide, and dyed in dark red, scarlet, purple, or midnight blue, because these colors did not show the dirt as readily. If making a skirt, women required eight to ten yards of cloth because of the pleats they sewed in, while it took two-and-a-half yards of velvet for a blouse. Some wholesale houses provided this material already cut. Unbleached muslin came in two grades, with men's pants fashioned from the heavier one, while women's dresses came from the lighter fabric. Muslin was inexpensive, could be dyed, and was easy to sew. Eventually, calico replaced muslin as a cheaper material. Print cloth was not popular with the Navajos, but it was with the Utes; sometimes local traders exchanged dry goods with each other to satisfy their customer base.[57]

Navajo women preferred to make their own clothing, tailoring it to their needs, while men were more accepting of store-bought clothes, like Levis and cowboy shirts. In the early days, and when a family lacked the means to purchase clothing or material from the trader, women made do with the fabric at hand—flour sacks. Tom Ration, when growing up, did not have the luxury of manufactured apparel. "Our clothes were not very fancy. My mother saved all the empty flour sacks and made crude-looking shirts and pants from them. No one could afford luxuries. . . . Our wardrobes consisted of flour-sack trousers and blouses. Each had huge printed flowers, or a bird or a bunch of wheat as a design, and we were proud of those clothes. Probably there would turn out to be a bird on the side or seat of the trousers, or a flower or a sheaf of wheat on the back of a shirt. All these were hand-sewn, of course."[58] Max Hanley remembered wearing similar clothing, with a "crisscross design of wheat on the back." He liked the looks, but in the winter, there were no coats to cover the torso, so his family used blankets. "Lambskins or sheepskins were sewed together, just the right size for me, and I wore the garment under the blanket, which was really warm."[59] Increased inventory at the trading post eventually changed much of this.

Both men and women appreciated new clothing. When a woman made a new dress or a man purchased a pair of pants, they would quickly slip the new garment on over the old, and go on their way. For men working outside, this provided more warmth, and for women, their skirts could serve as everything from a hot pad to remove a pan from a fire to a symbol of wealth. The value of cloth was emphasized again when a medicine man received the fabric used in a ceremony. Paul Begay tells of how "towards the end of a ceremony on the last night, they would fold these blankets, fabrics, within about one yard square, and the patient will sit on top of that, and the singing and the prayers go on all night. At the conclusion of the ceremony in the morning, the patient gets up and the medicine man rolls this fabric and blankets together and he puts it on his horse, ties it on the back of his saddle, and rides off. It's used as part of the payment for the job or service rendered."[60] Much of the cloth, food, and other necessities for a gathering or ceremonial activities came from a trading post.

Shoes replaced moccasins as traders began to supply their customers. Women wore "squaw shoes," brown, high-top leather shoes that laced all the way to the top. The soles also had to be leather, since rubber ones were uncomfortably hot in the summer. Navajos did not like to wear black shoes, because the Utes preferred that color; they had no desire to be mistaken for their traditional competitor. In 1936, traders introduced a low-cut shoe for women. Those who stayed around camp and did not have to herd the sheep began to buy this type, but those who had to move through the brush and over rocks, chasing animals, preferred the old high-top. Men, on the other hand, bought a high-grade of boot, such as those made by Ryder, because they wore well and could be resoled.[61] A high-crowned felt hat—either black or brown—with a wide brim was very popular, and when a band of silver went about the base of the hat above the brim, a man considered his attire complete. These hats, now referred to as "*cheii* (grandfather) hats" have become a symbol of the old traditional dress of a Navajo man.

Freighting

A major concern for many posts was the issue of freighting—getting the supplies to the desired destination. Reservation roads were notorious in the early years for being rough, having steep sections, requiring constant maintenance, being vulnerable to the elements—blowing snow, shifting sand, mud—and extending far into the hinterlands. Traders and Navajos alike ended up not only creating but also maintaining the roads, and helping the agent keep his network of travel options open. In the early days, before wagons, horses and mules served the Navajos well. After making their purchases at the store, customers would fill a seamless bag three-fourths full, so that the load was evenly distributed on both sides of their horse or burro.[62] But once wagons became available, the owner exchanged more mobility for volume of goods and transportation of the family. A round-trip might take two or three days or two weeks, depending on the distance traveled, weather and road conditions, strength of the animals, and amount of goods transported. Traders faced many of the same limitations in getting their merchandise to the store.

An example from Ray Hunt during the horse-and-wagon era illustrates what many other traders went through in traveling on the reservation. Ray often freighted for his father, driving a wagon pulled by a horse and mule. To go from Aneth, Utah, to Fruitland, New Mexico, for resupplies required three days' travel, then a day of loading, and another three days to return—if everything went well. The road wound around various terrain features to avoid cliffs and canyons or to reach waterholes. In attempting to follow this road, Hunt sometimes had to go a mile-and-a-half out of his way to bypass an obstacle. Often the creeks ran high in the spring and summer, so travelers had to wait for the water to subside. One time, Mancos Creek was on the rampage, and so Ray and his companion, Clarence, waited for the water to go down. For a day and a half, the men bided their time, waiting for the water to recede, but it remained high. Hunt decided he would try to make it across, but

Clarence warned that he would fail. According to Ray, "He took a shovel and started across. The current was so swift it almost washed him downstream. After he reached the far shore, he shoveled the edge off, because the water had washed the road out and left about a two foot bank. Back on the other side again, Ray got the horses ready and said to Clarence, 'Get a good holt, we're goin' across.' He popped the horses with the whip and away they went. They barely edged out on the other side." It was a good thing—the waters were rising again.[63]

There were certain tricks to the trade when freighting with wagons. For instance, Navajo Tom Ration often helped his father with long drives during the winter. To stay warm, they walked beside the wagon. Hilda Wetherill remembers hiring Navajo men to bale and tie stacks of sheep, goat, cattle, and horse hides. These she had placed on the outer part of the load, while the Navajo blankets were baled in burlap, the sack sewn shut and placed in the middle of the hides, then covered so that they were rain-proofed and there was nothing to attract the eye of a thief. Another important point was for the trader to have an equally good return load. A well-prepared shopping list and prior arrangements made the return trip just as profitable.[64]

Once the era of trucks arrived, things became somewhat easier, but still there were challenges. In the early days of automotive shipping on the reservation, there were many instances where a team of horses or mules had to come to the rescue to pull a car or truck out of the sand or through the snow. John Hunt, on the way to Flagstaff, had two 250-pound sacks of wool slide off the back of his truck. Too much for him to lift, he waited for help. "There was not much traffic in those days and many times when we were stuck in the sand or mud, we would just have to sit and wait it out. Navajos would come along usually in wagons and were always good to help." This time it was a car traveling from a movie location in Monument Valley. Five men—three of them big—emerged from their vehicle and hefted the heavy sacks into the truck and fastened the load. Hunt remembered that movie stars Lee Marvin and Ward Bond joked a lot as they helped the trader get on his way.[65] Arthur Newcomb was not so fortunate. On his way to Gallup with a double-decker load of sheep, his truck hit soft sand, laying it over on its side, then its top, then its other side, and finally rolling into a gulch, killing a lot of the cargo. Newcomb sent helpers to surrounding hogans, recruited thirty Navajos

Whether by wagon or, later, by truck, traders faced serious challenges in moving freight across hundreds of miles of dirt and sand roads in all types of weather. This truck, loaded here with sacks of wool, would return a few days later with just as much weight in store-bought goods to line the shelves of the post. (NAU.PH. 98.71.3, Northern Arizona University, Cline Library, Kennedy Collection.)

to extricate the animals, then kill those that were badly injured, and sent for a truck in Gallup to ship and deliver the uninjured sheep. The workers kept the meat, while Arthur got the pelts.[66]

There were also problems with mechanical breakdowns that only ingenuity could fix. Once, Joe Hunt left the Greasewood trading post headed for Mexican Hat. Well into the journey, he and his companions blew a hole in the truck's radiator; nursing the truck along to a trading post, they purchased two bags of Bull Durham. The trader there advised putting one of the bags into the radiator to help seal the hole. But the travelers figured that, if one was good, certainly two were better.

Resuming their journey, they realized that the truck could not go far before overheating. After it cooled, it started again and was driven until it overheated and had to stop to cool. This went on for some time. As night approached, the group halted to build a fire, but there was only one match, which they thought they should save for a greater emergency. By accident, pliers in the trader's pants pocket struck the match, burning Joe's leg and doing no good. He pulled some of the wires under the hood and got a fire started. But everyone still had a cold night—except for the one who was charged to keep moving the truck until it overheated. Eventually, the vehicle made it to another trading post, where the owner gave them a wonderful breakfast and blew out the clogged radiator with exhaust from one of his engines. The travelers were again on their way and eventually reached Mexican Hat.[67]

Vernon and Gladys Jack felt safe driving on the reservation, secure in the knowledge that Navajo passersby would always stop to help. This was not as true with white motorists. One time, Vernon's truck bogged down in sand, and so he walked to a friend's home to spend the night. When he returned the next morning, he saw that the tarp covering his heavy load of supplies had been removed, the flour reloaded, and his truck driven out of the mud. Suspecting the worst, he guessed that half his freight would be missing. Instead, it turned out that somebody had unloaded part of the flour, shoveled out the truck, jacked it up, put rocks under the tires in order to move the vehicle clear of the sand, then reloaded the flour, and left the canvas unfastened so that the owner would know that the cargo had been shifted. The only clue that Vernon had as to the culprit were the tracks of an Indian wagon. The trader continued down the road, and when he emptied the freight at Round Rock, there was not a thing missing from the load. It took him ten years to find out who the Navajo was that performed this kind deed.[68]

Gladys Jack had similar experiences. Once, when she was driving alone from Gallup with a heavy load, a young man, Victor Begay, who lived near her post, pulled up beside the truck and was about to pass, but, instead, fell in behind. He followed her vehicle with its ponderous burden until about twenty miles from the post, when it had a blowout. Victor got out of his car, told Gladys he had decided to follow her in case she had a problem, and fixed the tire, then trailed her all the way home. Another time on a snowy, blustery winter day, she was driving a heavy load that caused a blowout one hundred miles from home. Navajo friends spotted Gladys in trouble, changed her tire, and followed her to her post. This was one more reason she testified, "I was never worried about traveling and going places alone because I knew that they [Navajos] would help me and they did. . . . I was never afraid of them; I was never afraid to stay alone. I felt like they were my friends."[69]

Keeping trading posts in operation was a full-time job that required savvy, determination, and communication skills. As Navajos and Anglos met on their respective sides of the counter, a mutual trust and respect often grew through long-term relationships of exchange. The raw products of Navajo industry—wool, lambs, hides, and piñon nuts—wore the counters smooth, added grease that polished the wood, and allowed the manufactured goods from industrial America to slide more easily into the hands and culture of the Navajo customer. Both sides benefitted, each meeting their respective needs in a physical and relational sense. When each understood the expectations of the other, both could exult at the end of the transaction, "*Tł'ę́į nizhónígo i'iilyaa*"—"In a good way we did it!"

CHAPTER SEVEN

Weaving a Lifestyle

Rugs and Pawn

To the general public, the word "Navajo" conjures images of a Navajo rug or a blanket that showcases the acquired skills of the weavers within the culture. At the same time, when the term "traders" is introduced, what comes to mind is the issue of fairness in a system where credit was extended for months or years at a time to a Native people unaccustomed to financial dealings with the dominant society. When the two images are put together—that of a woman engaged in back-breaking labor and that of the shopkeeper holding a certain advantage—the outcome of dealings in the post can become suspect. This chapter embraces these two large topics. It will not examine in detail the evolution of the weaving industry with its different styles and materials nor will it focus solely on the issue of fairness, since there is already an extensive literature on both.[1] Rather, the emphasis here is on a more cultural approach to Navajo weaving that considers what weaving meant to the Indian, and how traders actually encouraged innovation in weaving. Navajo jewelry and basketry is also briefly discussed. The second part of the chapter looks at the system of pawn from both sides of the counter, examining the ebb and flow of materials and what that did for both customer and trader. The chapter concludes with a summary of relations between the two sides.

Weaving

Since the introduction of sheep in the Southwest during the second half of the sixteenth century, Native Americans have availed themselves of this animal for its meat and wool. No group caught on more quickly to the potential that particular livestock offered than the Navajo. Their mobile lifestyle, small-group orientation, strong family values, and innovative adaptability, allowed them to become the most successful weavers and livestock owners in the Southwest, capitalizing on expanding herds and reservation lands, starting in 1868 and continuing to the present. While many other American Indian groups practiced weaving, none did it on the scale and intensity, and with as much variety, as did these people. That is why Martha Nez, a woman born at the beginning of the twentieth century, who never went to school, but made her living from livestock said, "The only things in my life that really count are the sheep and weaving rugs. The sheep and weaving rugs are related to the story of Spider Woman. It is from the Navajo rug that trading started. . . . This was what was told to a woman and that is a form of wealth [work] that women hold on to. If a woman does not weave, she will be poor as I am now."[2]

The origin of weaving from the Navajo perspective began when the mythological being, Spider Man, drew cotton from his side, then framed a loom whose upper cross-pole was fashioned from the sky, the lower cross-pole from the earth, and the warp sticks from the sun's rays, with other elements, including two types of lightning, rock crystals, and rain, supplying additional parts. All of the elements of this first loom, including the batten stick, comb, spindle, warp and weft materials, came from sacred elements that were living, sentient, and powerful. Spider Woman then taught the first Navajos how to weave and incorporate elements from the earth into a living product.[3] Indeed, the loom has "all the requisite elements of life," including moisture, heat, and physical substance. As Maureen Trudelle Schwarz pointed out, "The loom is animated when it acquires air and vibration from its maker in the process of construction. The maker sings a song and says a prayer as he constructs the loom, thereby imbuing the loom with a breath of life." Citing medicine man Wilson Aronilth, Schwarz continues, "A loom can 'see, feel, move, and grow just like all creation. So it is considered holy.'"[4]

The product of the loom, for many weavers, is also alive and holds power. The term "*naaskaa' bik'inidzisgai*" (literally, "they are there in *ntł'iz*") is the name of the group of chants associated with rug weaving while *dah yistł'ǫ biyiin* ("the rug loom's songs") are established songs sung at the beginning and the finishing of a product. These bless the weaver and her ability as well as the object she is creating and giving life to, just as everything that the holy people created started out in this same fashion. Women are also encouraged to create new songs as they work on the loom.[5] This aspect of weaving is not taken lightly. Improper use of, or a mistake in, the songs can offend the holy beings and, instead of helping the weaver, can cause harm or spoil the product. When asked if she used songs when weaving, one woman replied that it was too dangerous and that, though her weaving would probably be much improved, she preferred not to get involved but just to take her chances in the market. Another suggested that she never let children touch any of her blankets before trading because they would handle them playfully and so the trader might not want them. She then associated playing with poverty.[6]

In the past, Navajo women followed weaving practices to avoid problems. Certain symbols could be woven into a textile without angering the holy people. Rainbows, sheet lightning, the four sacred mountains, squares, crosses, diamonds, serrated lines, and many other designs gave the weaver a wide variety of geometric figures to choose from in her creative application. On the other hand, zigzag lightning, harmful creatures from mythology, animals that may be offended, and creatures with strong powers were avoided.[7] The disastrous results of copying and profaning sacred symbols and offending the deity is seen in what the Navajos teach about the Anasazi Indians, who were destroyed for treating cavalierly the sacred symbols given them by the holy people and by abusing their power.[8] Teresa Wilkins summarized nicely through the thoughts of Navajo women, the relationship between the loom, the rug, and the weaver, when she wrote:

> In the same way that First Man originally created possessions, livestock, ways of making a living, ideas, and plans through the action of his thinking, Navajo weavers bring life to their products. This is why Navajo designs are usually left open in some way. "Your design is your thinking so you don't border that up. It's your home and all that you have. And so if you close that up you close everything up, even your thinking and your work. . . ."
>
> Many weavers articulate this sense of life when discussing their work. The loom, tools, and materials are powerful persons who, along

> with weavers' prayers, songs, and actions—their thinking—produce other persons in the form of rugs. Some weavers speak of weaving as a process of communication with the loom. Juanita Paul told me, "I can't force it. The loom has to communicate to me what it wants to do." Collaborating with their loom persons, weavers instill in their rugs an inner being that is part of themselves and of their looms. As long as the rugs remain within the Navajo sacred geography, they embody this relationship to their producer. . . . Some weavers can "feel" their rugs in the trading post. Upon entering the trading post, these individuals often feel the locations of their rugs among the many there for sale.[9]

Compare this perspective to that of Anglo author George James who, in the early part of the twentieth century, studied Navajo rugs and blankets. Speaking of the songs for weaving, he commented, "It does not lessen the value of a good blanket in my estimation to know that it is probable that songs of blessing and benediction and prayers of helpfulness have been sung and said over it. I like to think that the Navaho woman thought of the beautiful poetic symbols of the first blanket when she made my blanket and that before she began work on it she prayed that only beautiful things should come in touch with it."[10] Thus, even in James's economic arena, the blanket, with an added dash of romanticism, was appreciated for its spiritual essence.

The designs of a Navajo blanket come from the mind of the weaver—there is no illustration or pattern to follow. Exactly when a new color or another geometric element is introduced in the pattern comes from the creator's intuition. She uses only her fingers and hand to measure. An irregularity might be woven in to avoid perfection, which would offend the holy people; a spirit line may be put into the design to prevent entrapment of the blanket's spirit, and no exact duplicate of another blanket is made.[11] These and a host of other taboos can be generally summarized as showing respect for the product being created, for the holy people, and as positive thinking about the trade and the skills required to successfully weave.

Weaving varied from region to region, from family to family, and from person to person, some individuals commanding better prices at the post than others. Blankets called "quickies" or "bread and coffee rugs" were loosely woven, poorly designed, and bought according to weight, varying from fifty cents to a dollar a pound. A well-woven rug, carefully designed and skillfully woven, brought a significantly higher price.[12] Tall Woman (1874–1977) spent much of her life weaving and tells of its impact on her and her family in her autobiography. She stresses that her mother and older sisters were in constant production—"that was about all they did." They were excellent weavers, knew how to prepare the wool, would each have two looms to work on, and wove nonstop, finishing a blanket and immediately going on to the next, while others worked nearby, carding, spinning, and dying the wool. At times, two of her sisters wove on a large rug together. The piles of completed rugs, saddle blankets, and other textiles grew to the point that the women knew it was time to take them to J. L. Hubbell in Ganado. They intentionally waited to amass a large number so that they could get a lot of money and trade goods all at once. The women felt it was not just a matter of volume, but that the trader would give better prices to his valued customers. Tall Woman was right. In those days her family did not have a wagon, only horses and donkeys. She describes these animals returning home. "When the horses or donkeys came back, you couldn't even tell it was those animals. All over, in every little place available, things were tied on to them. All you saw in the distance was these big things all covered with bundles. You could not even tell where the horse or donkey was."[13]

Training for this kind of productivity was progressive and rewarding. Tall Woman taught her daughters just as she had learned, by starting with observation, then receiving a small loom to practice the basics, then moving to bigger looms, obtaining individual recognition and financial rewards for her labor, and improving her product with assistance from the trader and his wife. Sometimes Tall Woman and her mother wove at the same time, with Tall Woman's daughters watching and learning. She recalled, "When Ruth sat next to my mother, she'd often tell her to sit on the other side of the loom. Every now and then she'd stop and tell Ruth to take over and do it from the other side, to bring it up from that side." Tall Woman's father was also in the mix, building progressively bigger looms for the girls and keeping their work separate. When he finally determined that their weaving was good enough to bring to the trader, he went to the post, then brought back their reward in the form of food and merchandise. Eventually, he took them with him so that they could learn "how to trade, count money, and other things. My oldest girl, especially, really started working on her weaving because of those things. My father and mother really encouraged her in that; they said even in her crippled condition, if she became good at weaving, she could support herself and any children she might have later in life by means of her rugs."[14]

Evaluating, Purchasing, and Coding a Textile

While Navajo weavers had their concerns, so, too, did the traders. But theirs were, in a number of instances, markedly different. When a Navajo customer approached the counter with her blanket or rug wrapped in a flour sack, the trader followed a protocol expected by both. With the unveiling of the rug, the trader laid it on the counter, flattened it out as he inspected it, weighed the product (even though that was more for the customer's benefit), and offered a price. All of this was done slowly and earnestly. Things to consider were its size, tightness of weave, fine or coarse texture, wool (preferred) or cotton warp, straight edges, and flaws. The tightness of spun wool made a big difference in the tightness of the blanket. "A good weaver always notices a good spin."[15] A light, well-woven, and visually appealing blanket brought a high price, while a coarse, heavy one brought lower. To Frank Noel, "Your success as a trader depended on your ability to classify that blanket. After you decided what the blanket was worth, you put the number of dollars you were willing to pay on the counter beside the blanket; and then the trader kept his eye on the deal. If the Indian took the money, the trader rolled up the blanket and put it under the counter. If the Indian took down the blanket, the trader put the money back into the drawer. Sometimes not a word was spoken by either party."[16] On the other hand, when a young girl with her first rug approached the counter, the trader, even though realizing that it would have little resale value, paid several times its worth, just to encourage her to continue weaving.[17]

Once the trader purchased a blanket, he entered a code signifying what he had paid for it. This code was based on a phrase that had ten different letters, each of which represented a number from nine to zero. For instance, if the word were "Black Horse," then B would equal one, L was two, A was three, C was four, K was five and so forth, with E being zero. Using just these numbers for an item that cost five dollars, the coded price would be KEE. Trader Will Evans used the cost-mark phrase of "hope and try," while another trader used the phrase "bad whiskey," and another "trade quick."[18] This system came in handy when remembering what had been paid and in determining markup and sale price.

The trader had other considerations when purchasing a woven product. Some wholesale houses became overstocked and would take no blankets. This was hard on Navajos, whose money came in twice a year—the wool season and lamb season. Weavers sold blankets any time of year, giving them needed supplies and the stores a chance to make money in between the two big credit-paying times. Traders understood that if they wanted to keep valued customers coming to their store, bringing their wool and lambs, a generous payment for woven products had to be considered. If the Navajo was well known and respected in the community, that was another important factor that boosted the status of the post. Poor Indians often followed the rich in their trading patterns, shopping where the well-to-do went.[19]

Some Navajo weavers saved wool for future use after their spring wool harvest was completed. If not, a good trader maintained two or three seven-foot-long sacks of the best weaving wool for the customers who came to the post for supplies. The most preferred was either white or black long staple wool because it was easy to hand-spin into yarn. A special dye, called Diamond Wool Dye, with a mordant sold for ten cents and made five gallons of a particular color. The individual doing the dying immersed the wool in a boiling tub of solution until she achieved the desired shade. In the 1920s and 1930s, traders purchased poor rugs by the pound, regardless of the color, so some weavers added white clay to make the wool heavier and brighter.[20]

In 1922, Special Government Supervisor F. E. Brandon conducted a survey covering wool and weaving production in the Western Navajo Agency. He noted that "The Indian is a shrewd trader" who availed himself of going to different posts to find the prices that he liked. In the same breath, Brandon said that he found no evidence of traders involved in price-fixing. Instead, he learned that two entities regulated the market: the first was the curio collectors who, because of sentimental value, "pay most any price to secure one [rug]." The second was "those people who

Navajo women, skilled in the art of weaving, were highly valued. This photo illustrates a number of steps taken to produce a rug. After obtaining the wool, the women dyed, carded, then spun it (pictured here) to form a tight yarn before weaving it on the loom (in background). The sheepskin seen behind the child was another product sold at trading posts. (NAU.PH. 412.5.52, Northern Arizona University, Cline Library, Warren Collection.)

regard the rugs from a standpoint of the service they render combined with the quality, design, and workmanship that goes into them. . . . The traders treat the Indians well in buying the blankets. The fabulous prices are tacked on after they have passed out of the traders' hands and reach the curio dealers." The best blankets at that time were the light, tightly woven, and uniformly colored articles, selling for five dollars a pound, while at the other end of the spectrum, the loosely woven, heavy blankets brought in as little as fifty cents a pound.[21]

Elizabeth Hegemann remembered when a three-by-five-foot rug sold for six dollars, and a good nine-by-twelve for not over twenty. "Our big problem at Shonto, as at other isolated posts, was to dispose of these thousand pounds of rugs which we had to buy even though we had no retail outlet." Part of the solution lay in human nature. She or her husband selected "an ugly rug, perhaps badly woven but with a good pattern" and hung it high over their counter in a difficult-to-access spot, and waited for an Anglo customer to come into the store. Once he or she spotted the textile, "No other rug in the piles on the floor would do. After Harry had gone through the gymnastics of getting it down and the satisfied customer had departed, another hard-to-sell-rug would be selected from the pile on the floor and laboriously hung in the same spot. It always worked."[22]

Stewart Hatch, a trader who bought and sold in posts all of his life, even into his nineties, told of purchasing rugs for thirty dollars and selling them for the same amount, with the hopes that the weaver was happy, the word would spread, and other blankets or rugs would show up on his counter that were even better. He estimated that, on average, he bought four to ten rugs a day and that in a normal year he purchased around fifteen hundred, with a monthly average of 160 rugs. With each one, he noted the month and year of purchase, what he paid, and the weaver's name. The best months to obtain good rugs were in the winter because people stayed home to work on weaving instead of traveling, and so their products piled up, ready for spring, when buyers from all over the West and California appeared at his door, anxious to stock up for the tourist season. Now his annual average of rugs is three hundred per year, with most of them inferior compared to what the old weavers used to sell.[23]

Marketing Value

As they did with the quality of livestock and wool, traders worked tirelessly to improve woven products and sales, thus benefiting both the store and its customers. The dependence of the weavers and their families continued to increase, no matter the fluctuations in the national economy. Gladwell Richardson estimated that 60 percent of the Navajos' income came from weaving, but all the trader could pay was what the market would bear. That is why traders were constantly in search of new ways to sell Navajo blankets. According to Richardson, "We did it all the time, even advertising in magazines and newspapers. When blankets failed to move and hit rock bottom prices, weavers' families were often hungry and traders could go flat broke."[24] Just how popular Navajo blankets had become on a national level is illustrated in the 1942 Spring/Summer Sears and Roebuck catalog that advertised them in different varieties with patterns that could be ordered.[25] The government kept tabs on these activities and helped promote the industry. For instance, in 1914 Navajos collectively earned about $700,000 a year from blankets; to prove to the buying public the authenticity of these wares, the government agent ensured that a linen tag and lead seal were attached to each rug that left the reservation.[26]

Agents encouraged other efforts to increase sales. Over the years, synthetic aniline dyes and commercially dyed wool appeared in Navajo weaving. The colors were brighter than those obtained with natural dyes and did not have variations from different dying sessions. However, around the first decade of the twentieth century, some agents began encouraging weavers to return to more traditional practices. They had received word that businessmen in California could obtain much higher prices for rugs and blankets whose wool had been colored with vegetal dyes. Softer in tone, these naturally dyed materials were more "authentic."[27] Another marketing boost came when William T. Shelton at the Shiprock Agency sponsored a regional fair. Trading posts from different areas had booths that competed in all types of industries. Shelton's reputation for carrying out the ethnocentric process of "civilizing" the Navajos became abundantly clear in some of the categories of exhibits. In addition to prizes for the best general display of Indian products and vegetables and the best team of workhorses and mules, there were also entries such as the "prettiest Navajo baby" and "cleanest Navajo baby." He awarded a cookstove as first prize for the best wool blanket, a washtub for the best Germantown blanket, and a handsaw for the best wool. The fair drew Navajo contestants from over a hundred miles away and was so successful that it became an annual event. Traders and their clients took the cue, starting preparations months in advance. Specialty rugs declaring the name of the post and products from that area fostered regional pride and competition. Shelton invited tourists to attend, encouraged the Navajos to sell traditional artifacts such as bows and arrows and silver work, and allowed some Indian dances, even though he tried to stamp out many other traditional practices. By 1914, seven hundred blankets graced the traders' booths, five of which were purchased and sent to the Panama-Pacific Exposition.[28]

Changes in design brought both action and reaction. Gladwell Richardson encouraged the weaving of "fuzzies," blankets with central and corner designs and a different type of weave. He had a half-dozen women create these blankets as examples for other weavers to follow, paid extra for those woven in this style, and started a new line of textiles that was not only unique but sold well, lifting his blanket trade out of the doldrums. Bill and Sally Lippincott at Wide Ruin also became tired of the diminished quality of the weaving in their part of the reservation. They began insisting on going back to an old style of simple striped patterns, rugs without borders, and using vegetal dyes. Elizabeth Hegemann began having weavers create matching pairs of rugs, going against the usual practice of no-two-rugs-alike. Those weaving these pairs, who considered "twins" unlucky, inserted enough difference to satisfy the holy people. Hastiin Klah, a powerful medicine man who knew how to deal with negative supernatural repercussions, dared to reproduce an old material fragment woven by the Anasazi and found in Chaco Canyon. A large rug reproduced this design, a highly dangerous act of both copying and utilizing something that came from the dead. An equally dangerous undertaking was his weaving of two *Ye'ii bicheii* dancing figures into a rug. To capture the image of holy beings on a textile was absolutely taboo, and yet traders, especially in the Shiprock area, encouraged other weavers to follow suit. The initial uproar over Klah's weaving did not subside until the trader told Navajo customers that the rug was sent off the reservation to Washington, thus removing from their presence an item offensive to the holy people.[29]

Entire sand-painting designs with built-in modifications to appease the deity became increasingly acceptable over time. Some Navajo weavers were anxious to fill a niche in the waiting markets of the commercial world. Stewart Hatch one time bought a rug depicting part of a sand painting. "There were certain things that a medicine man put in there that they'd leave out when they wove that particular design. I bought a rug one time, and it was a kind of ceremonial rug, and they wove something in it, then they took it out, and then they rewove it in there. It left a mark where it had been removed—just where they took those stitches out and left a mark."[30] For better or for worse, traditional Navajo practices were getting swept into the dominant society. Success in weaving brought change that would have been unthinkable in previous eras.

Navajo Basketry

While rugs and blankets were an important part of the economy, there were some items that traders carried more for the use of local Navajos than for sale in the dominant society, a prime example being baskets. As with the evolution of weaving, the history of the Navajo wedding, or ceremonial, basket, as well as the introduction of different features, such as animal figures and various geometric designs has been dealt with elsewhere.[31] Historically, basket making (technically, *not* basket weaving) was centered on the northern part of the Navajo Reservation and its perimeter, because of the nearby Ute and Paiute populations who made many of them. There were some Navajo women who were also accomplished in the task, but baskets remained a more important trade item with the Utes and Paiutes, since there was a time when there were so many taboos that Navajos needed to follow in creating a basket that the art was left to their northern neighbors.[32] Baskets also became increasingly less practical in day-to-day life for the Navajos, except on ceremonial occasions. Even today, there are few extended rituals that do not use these containers for holding religious paraphernalia, for mixing water and herbs for drinking, for washing with yucca soap, and, in the case of weddings, for holding ground cornmeal mush.

A Navajo medicine or wedding basket has extensive symbolism, with many interpretations. Its origin was with White Shell Woman. Talking God gave her sumac and instructions on how to fashion the material to make something useful. After debarking the three-to four-foot-long straight branches and splitting them into thirds, she began wrapping the pieces around a thin rod core that represented the earth. Next, she looked about and saw black storm clouds, which she inserted in the design. As the basket maker fashioned the container, there were songs and prayers infused amid the split sumac. Next, White Shell Woman placed a red rainbow into the pattern, followed by more storm clouds, and then white, the symbol of dawn. Through the entire design, she placed a trail or "road" (*atiin*) so the basket's spirit would not be trapped. She ended her creation by using the image of the leaves from the juniper or cedar tree she sat beneath to finish the rim. All of this was done in a clockwise fashion, the same direction that the sun follows, with the butt ends of the inner-rod framework going in the same direction, just as the plant grows. The basket, with its twelve- to fourteen-inch diameter and three-inch height is viewed as alive with a spirit, which holds the songs, prayers, and thoughts of its creator. That spirit is free to depart through the basket's pathway.[33]

Traders realized that baskets played an important role in the Navajo ceremonial world, and so they stocked them whenever possible. At the end of most rituals, other than a wedding ceremony, where the container remained with the family, the medicine man kept the basket as part of his pay and could later sell it. Dorothy Hubbell remembered, "We used to have a stack [three feet high] of wedding baskets. They just kept going back and forth as they were used. We sold a few to tourists, but mainly to the Navajos. We bought them from Ute country—from traders up there."[34] John Hunt sold both new and used baskets made by Navajos and Utes from the Tuba City, Navajo Mountain, and Blanding regions, while Elizabeth Hegemann, from Shonto, specified that Paiutes from that area made most of her baskets. She sold them for from two to five dollars, depending on the tightness of the weave and the basket's size; if it had been used in a ceremony, she charged a dollar less. She recalled, "Another custom of the traders was to insist that the baskets be washed clean of the cornmeal sticking in the cracks, as they did not want ants or bugs attracted by this on their shelves."[35] Carl Hines spoke of the popularity of the baskets: "Soon after the 'sing,' the medicine man's wife would sell the basket. During the summer months when there was less sickness among the Navajos, we would accumulate possibly twenty medicine baskets. This was hardly enough for the winter season even though we would buy and resell the same baskets many times. Most of the medicine baskets were made by the Ute Indians."[36]

During a ceremony, a basket is oriented to the east. This means that the pathway points in that direction, as does the ending place of the weave, which is a protruding bump that aligns with the "road." By starting at this end and retracing the concentric circles through the basket to the center, one follows a clockwise or sunwise direction. Some baskets are made just the opposite—in a counterclockwise direction. Often in Navajo culture, when something moves in this manner, it is considered dangerous or evil, going contrary to the correct sunwise pattern. Baskets created in this opposite fashion are used in a special ceremony called *Wooltáád* (unraveling, or coming undone), a part of the Evil Way group of ceremonies. Jim Dandy described it as "like wringing a deer hide tight, then letting it unravel"—in other words, a loosening or reversing of tension to get away from the thing that created a problem in a person's life.[37] The pain and evil causing the sickness is transferred to the herbs in the water that is drunk from a basket. This removes what is wrong and restores the patient to health, just as it was done in the beginning, or the first time that the holy people performed the ceremony. By following a "backwards" path, or counterclockwise movement as woven into the basket, the sick individual is healed by going back to the time when all was well.

Traditionalist Don Mose tells of an instance when his father was apprenticing to learn part of the Enemy Way ceremony. As he tied beads onto the rattle stick, he accidentally dropped one and soon became dizzy and weak. His wife scolded him for doing things he had not really been trained to do; they knew now that he needed a ceremony. The couple traveled to Low Mountain, where a person performed the unraveling rite. Part of this entailed drinking a cleansing agent of spruce medicine mixed in water from a counterclockwise-woven basket. Songs and prayers returned the patient to a time when things had been normal, and soon he was healed.[38]

Trader Stewart Hatch remembered that, in the posts where he worked, he carried a number of different types of baskets, which he kept separate. All of them had to be tightly woven and have good colors. The Utes used brown instead of red for part of the design, while the Navajos preferred red, but both used black—all of which came from packets of dye purchased for a dime. At the very center of the basket, where the weave started, there was a pinhole that the medicine man filled with a little piece of cloth to make the container leakproof. The color difference between red and brown was not an issue, but the store separated the baskets according to new or used—determined by cornmeal, pollen, or other material stuck in the cracks of a used basket—and by the clockwise or counterclockwise weave. Hatch commented, "Every time we bought one that was made in reverse, we kept it separate from the other baskets, and they'd come in and tell us they'd want one that was woven in reverse. Then we'd usually have a little stack of them, and they could pick out the one they wanted. We'd never get too many of them."[39] The price for a basket ranged from one to four dollars; there was very little profit in carrying them, but there was great customer satisfaction in obtaining one when needed.

Silverwork

Another item that came across trading-post counters was silverwork. Navajo metalcraft grew in importance for both the trader and the customer over the years. Not until after 1868 did Navajo silversmiths really get started in silverwork, and not until sometime in the mid- to late-1880s did they start to stamp their work with designs. This newly discovered craft began to blossom during the early years of the twentieth century, as new material and techniques, coupled with tourism and an increasing dependence on the Anglo economy, gave it added importance.[40] The general trend over the years was for Navajo silverwork to move from heavy to lighter pieces that were more skillfully decorated, going from plain to stamped and etched, to turquoise and coral embedded with more intricate designs. Silversmith Tom Ration did not feel like Navajo artists were necessarily benefiting from the increasing sophistication of the product. An old man himself, he remembered his elders telling him, "'Learn how to be a silversmith so we can have concho buttons on our bridles.' Many Navajos have become silversmiths. And all Indian stores carry a lot of Indian-made jewelry. But, instead of the Indians making good profits, they help to make the white traders rich. This has happened because we have forgotten the songs of the soft goods and of the sacred stones. We are deprived of the riches by our own carelessness."[41]

The art of silversmithing fits nicely into Navajo lifestyle. First, it required very little equipment, and that which was necessary was light and highly transportable. A small forge, bellows, anvil, crucibles, molds, stamps, and a blowpipe were all it took. Smiths carved molds from sandstone, stamps could be fashioned from any harder metal, the silver came from either American or Mexican dollars, and later, turquoise and coral, as trade items, found their way into the designs. Second, both Navajo and Anglo culture readily embraced the finished products. For the former, beautiful pieces of artwork held high value and made a statement about an individual's status and economic well-being. Dressing well was an important trait in Navajo society. Jewelry for both men and women provided a visual representation of beauty and wealth. For the latter, silver translated very nicely into the Anglo economy, with its monetary status based in gold and silver specie. A third point is that silver was a malleable art form, which allowed the same type of Navajo creativity that was found in weaving and the same skilled, detailed "art" work that appeared in sand paintings. In metal, these "hard goods" provided a more permanent form of artistic expression. Silver bracelets, necklaces, brooches, bow guards, bridles, concho belts, hatbands, buckles—the list goes on—moved from being not only functional but a statement of beauty.

Even the simplest form of silver found utility while beautifying, but in at least one setting, it put the trader in an awkward position. The Navajos loved silver coins, which they used as buttons and decorations on clothing. The federal criminal code clearly stated that anyone who "fraudulently defaced, mutilated . . . or lightened" U.S. currency could be fined two thousand dollars and imprisoned for up to five years. Agents contacted traders, requesting that they discourage the Navajos from drilling holes in coins and putting loops of copper through them to fasten to cloth. The traders did not like the practice any more than the government did, since banks would not accept mutilated currency because of decreased value and because the product did not stack well. Yet the traders had little choice but to accept it when Navajos in need cut dimes, quarters, half dollars, and dollars off their clothing. The only solution was to circulate this money among their clients, since few people accepted it off the reservation. Some posts even created their own money, stamped with a unique design, and used these tokens in place of regular U.S. currency, another practice frowned upon by the government.[42]

Apparently Mrs. Manygoats, and many Navajo women like her, was not overly impressed by the government's attempt to control its currency. "Her necklaces of shell beads were spaced with the finest grade of turquoise. The ten buttons on the front of Mrs. Many Goats' [*sic*] silk plush blouse were half dollars with a small copper loop brazed on the back of each. On the cuffs of her blouse were rows of five dimes. Each of her three skirts contained sixteen full yards of the best quality of brown sateen, and each was trimmed with yards and yards of rick-rack."[43] Some Navajo women might have as many as two hundred "buttons" on their

The simple, portable tools of this silversmith plying his trade near Bluff City, Utah, at the turn of the twentieth century does not hint of the beautiful ornaments turned out with such basic equipment. A small bellows, a log for a table, a small metal pounding surface, a hammer, stamps, and pliers were all it took to open shop. (Courtesy San Juan County Historical Commission.)

blouse. At the same time and in the same post, Tooth Gone followed his own interests when he "hefted a bridle and guessed that at least thirty-five American silver dollars had gone into the making of it. He was sure it was made from American money, for it had a brighter sheen than jewelry made from Mexican pesos."[44] While silver coinage was an important source of the precious metal, some traders, rather than depending on a good Navajo silversmith to find his own, advanced a bar of silver with the understanding that the artist would return to the post with his wares in a finished form for sale.[45]

Pawn and Tokens

The heart of most economic transactions at the store lay in the system of pawn that allowed Navajo customers and traders to work together the entire year, not just when wool and lambs and cattle were sold.[46] In terms of how it functioned, the system was simple and flexible enough to meet needs on both sides of the counter, but underlying it all was the customer-trader relationship that made it work. To Harry Goulding, Navajos were skilled traders: "They're shrewd, shrewd traders. You don't take an Indian too much. If what he brought in was enough to take his pawn out, or if he wanted to pay a little on his pawn, he'd do that first. He'd always ask how much his pawn was in for."[47] Hilda Wetherill struggled with the concept of customers who sold a bag of wool for forty dollars, paid the forty-dollar pawn ticket to get a bridle back, then pushed it across the counter, putting the bridle back in pawn for forty dollars. This customer now was free to spend his money in the store, while having renewed his pawn ticket. She pointed out that "the trader does not want a silver bridle. It is no good to anyone but the Indian" and that this customer would need it only once a year for a particular occasion.[48]

Edward T. Hall, who spent a number of years participating in and observing trade interaction at the posts, goes to the heart of the Navajo-trader relationship: "It seemed to me that the traders eventually became programmed by the people they were trading with, and whether they were aware of it or not, they adopted the moral codes of their customers. . . . On the reservation, in the words of those times, a man's word was still his bond. People trusted each other and depended on each other not to take unfair advantage. The traders were living fossils existing in a backwater." He goes on to point out that there were members from the dominant society who criticized the traders as men anxious to squeeze every cent from their customers and who were often dishonest, because that was the normal business ethic in mainstream America. Hall refutes these attacks, a topic that will be discussed momentarily.[49]

When Navajo customers could not pay directly for the goods they needed, there were choices. One possibility was to borrow money from a relative or neighbor, putting up some type of collateral that would be given back once he paid the loan. While there was liberal sharing among Navajos, especially among family members, as a business proposition, there were problems with the internal pawning of an item. Father Berard Haile felt this was rarely done, simply because "tribesmen will pocket the security as sure as the sun goes down," whereas the traders were more flexible and open to argument in their attempt to keep customers.[50] If an individual did not redeem his or her pawn when the period of grace was over, the object became "dead pawn" and technically could be sold. However, for a number of reasons, most traders carried dead pawn for years after, depending on the object.

One of the most important reasons was the idea of relationship. There were many different types of items that customers pawned; indeed, anything that a trader could sell on an open market might be accepted. Objects like silver jewelry, rugs, and other crafts were more likely to be sold to tourists or curio shop owners than things like a medicine bundle or something else that had intense cultural value but little extrinsic worth. Ideally, the trader had to ensure the debt would be paid and the object redeemed, or otherwise, he would be stuck with an item that held little sale value for outsiders. Many objects used as security were heirlooms important to a family who had every intention of eventually repossessing them—and the trader knew it. To sell an item as soon as it came due was legal and agreed upon by both parties at the time that it became pawn, but to do so was unethical from the trader's standpoint because of his relationship with the individual. Indeed, some people turned over prize possessions to a store owner just for safekeeping. They knew that if the trader lost it through theft, fire, or accident, the owner received full value without having to worry about its security.

Along those same lines, when a person pawned an object but then needed it temporarily, some traders loaned it for the occasion and then took it back. For instance, if there was an important social event to which a woman wanted to wear her jewelry, she could approach the owner and ask if she could borrow it until the event was over. Often, the trader would oblige. The same was true for a medicine man who needed his medicine bundle or a certain object for a ceremony, or for a man who wanted his rifle back for deer hunting. Other traders used the same situations to turn up the heat on their customers to pay off their tickets and remove the items from pawn. Trust and relationship were important principles; if a person betrayed that trust, future dealings were jeopardized. Ray Hunt put it this way: "The Navajo as a whole are honest people and it's only the ones that you let in too deep that don't pay. They can't pay out and so they run away from you; they don't want to pay. Several years ago I probably had two or three hundred Indians on my open account, and I explained it to them this way. 'I don't ever cut you off, you cut yourself off. Whenever you fail to pay within a reasonable length of time, or don't ever pay me, then you don't ever get any more credit until that is paid.'"[51]

Many posts had a pawn room, a secure area where the trader tagged items and hung them in such a way that they were easily accessed and visible for the Navajo owner who wanted to go into the room with the trader and check on its status. A visitor to a post could quickly determine how the economy of the Navajos in that area was doing by the amount of pawn—the more there was, the harder the times. Some items might be worth more than the credit extended on them, creating a temptation, if there was a default, to immediately sell it for a higher value. Most traders avoided doing this in order to maintain good customer relations. Six months (later changed to a year), by law, was the soonest that an item could be sold, but given the two-season economic pattern of the Navajo economy, this time period came around very quickly. Thus, "How [the trader] administered his pawn was as close as one could get to a bottom-line appraisal of whether the trader had the welfare of his Indian customers at heart or not."[52]

What if customer or trader chose to take advantage of the other? On the Navajo side, he or she accepted the loan on good faith and was expected to pay down the debt—either gradually or all at once—whichever was most practical, given their financial situation. Sometimes, when an Indian sold large amounts of wool, lambs, and cattle, the entire pawn ticket—often a tag written on each item as well as in a notebook or on a customer's tally on a paper bag—was redeemed. More often, the Navajo paid a little at a time on a number of pawned objects. The customer was also free to shop at any other store, but there was an expectation that if there were objects at a place that needed to be reclaimed, the owner should be working toward redeeming them. Just as Navajos knew what the prices were at various posts and what goods were available, traders understood where their customers were shopping and what they were buying. Store owners could do little about any breach of faith against them. If a Navajo failed to redeem the pawned object, the trader could sell it, hoping to get at least equal value for the goods initially given, or could refuse future credit and deny assistance, but in a monetary sense he was hamstrung. Father Berard Haile pointed out that even the government stacked its chips against the trader. "There are laws protecting the Indian but which apparently consider the trader a natural shark bent on exploitation of the government wards. Thus the government insists that it will not collect in court the Indian's debts, that they cannot be forced to pay them, which leaves the expressed alternative of having the trader see as best he can how debts may be collected. The trader is thus at the mercy of the Indian."[53]

Some posts introduced tokens or tin money that had its own unique design and value assigned—often in denominations of one dollar, a half dollar, quarter, dime, or nickel—redeemable at that store. This *seco* (dry money), or *béésh t'ą'í* (thin metal), as the Navajos referred to it, was meant to be used at a specific place, but many traders accepted it from Navajo customers who had traded elsewhere, with the understanding that the trader could go to its point of origin and be reimbursed in money or material. The idea behind this form of scrip was to have the customer trade at the same business. The federal government first discouraged its use then banned it, but in a cash-poor economy, tokens filled a void and fit in the setting because many Navajo people were raised on hard currency instead of paper money, which they did not trust. Tin money also made sense, because it looked like the currency they were accustomed to. Wool, sheep, lambs, skins, and piñon nuts were usually cash sales while rugs, jewelry and other slower-moving merchandise were tokens. Trader Tom Kirk noted, "A popular method of buying a rug or bracelet was to offer three different choices: one, an all cash offer; two, a half cash, half trade deal; or three, an all trade price. The Indian would choose the method he desired or declined the entire offer. If he owed the trader a bill, he naturally took the all trade deal. If, however, he had a payment due [elsewhere], he would take the cash offer. Rugs were always wholesaled at the purchase price. The trader used his trade margin for his profit."[54]

Store owners had to be careful as to how much credit they extended. They watched the prosperity and spending habits of their customers, gauging how much each could really afford, given their specific amount of income. The trader had to ensure that he did not lend out more than he could collect; if it was worth it to the customer to not pay off his bill, then he would stop coming.[55] At his post, Vernon Jack assisted families that struggled financially but were a good financial risk. After some pawn went dead and there was no attempt to redeem it, he selected a certain individual who was a good stockman, hard worker, and understood business, and let him take the dead pawn on credit. Many posts had thousands of dollars of unredeemed pawn that sat in the "vault" and did nothing for the trader, who had to watch his own credit rating. Jack let the Navajo man take it and trade for livestock in other parts of the reservation, build his herd, and repay the debt for the jewelry at the time of sale. "It did two things for us: we sold the pawn that we would have held anyway, and we built the herds of certain individuals. . . . We never misjudged anyone . . . they all came through and paid us."[56]

While each post was different, a few statistics give a strong impression of volume of sales and credit. Trader Mildred Heflin visited with twenty-six traders in the Farmington, New Mexico, area and found that "traders carry all the way from $5,000 to $12,000 or $15,000 in accounts during the period from wool season to lamb season and the period from lamb season to wool season."[57] The average trader bought 30,000 pounds of wool, with a total accumulation from all twenty-six traders of 780,000 pounds; the average trader also bought 1,000 lambs and $3,000 worth of rugs. A survey of fifty traders conducted in 1934 estimated that a post served between 120 and 135 families, although these figures were questionably high because the same family might frequent a number of posts and be counted by two or more different traders.[58] A government survey conducted at this same time reported the percentage of products being taken in at two average posts. The figures for one post included wool (35 percent), lambs (35 percent), hides (10 percent), piñons (10 percent), rugs (7.5 percent), and silver (2.5 percent). For the second post, the figures were wool (50 percent), lambs (25 percent), hides (12.5 percent), and rugs and silver (12.5 percent).[59]

Stewart Hatch, when asked about his experience with pawn and the volume of trade, described it as "kind of sacred between you and the customer. Ninety percent of the time you won't lose, he'll pay you." As for the amount of trade: "I'd say that livestock was our big part and the next thing for this particular place was Navajo rugs. We bought thousands of Navajo rugs from all over the reservation."[60] Anthropologist and trader William Adams, speaking of his own experience, tells of a "universal understanding among traders that particular families 'belonged' to one store and one store only, and could get nowhere else except by pawning. Popular literature may suggest that Navajo credit accounts were regularly secured by pawn, but this was very far from the case: at Shonto only about 10 percent of our accounts receivable were covered by pawn."[61] The variety of responses to the questions of volume, of products, and of families frequenting posts underscores the diversity of experience as well as the period under discussion.

Trader Character

This chapter opened with the question of the honesty of the traders as a collective group. Certainly, some people believe that these men and their families were intent on taking everything from the Navajo that they could. All was pure business, and "let the buyer beware." By now it should be obvious that, although there is no doubt that there were people like that—just as there were Navajos who were dishonest in some of their dealings—a trader with those qualities would not last long. The government, on a number of occasions, sent inspectors to the reservation to obtain an accurate picture, expecting to find that a populace that was unfamiliar with reading, writing, and economic practices was being taken advantage of, but that was not what was found.. For instance, in 1939, Horace Boardman, trading supervisor for the Navajo Service, reported that there were 150 Indian traders, 85 of whom were living on the reservation and held a license from the government. One of Boardman's responsibilities was to check the accuracy of the weighing scales in the posts. He reported finding a few irregularities, but 90 percent of the scales that were inaccurate weighed in favor of the Navajo—in other words, lighter—and that only two seemed skewed for the benefit of the trader.[62]

Boardman continued to paint a picture of the volume of pawn that the traders were carrying, reminding people that this was money from their "pockets" on loan to Navajo customers. "Based on one hundred twenty-five traders, and realizing that 78.4 percent are actual figures reported by the traders themselves, we show that the Navajos at the close of 1938 owed these traders almost $350,000 dollars on unsecured accounts; pawns almost $196,000, making a total indebtedness to the traders alone of $546,000. . . . The outstanding unsecured accounts and the pawn on traders' books show a direct ratio of 86.35 percent to the total value of merchandise inventories of these one hundred twenty-five traders." When asked if he had found any traders who showed a profit at the end of the year for rug sales, he replied he had not. Indeed, a number of them took a $900 to $1000 loss. Still, to one of the traders present during the discussion, "The Navajo is a friend and neighbor of the trader. We need them and they need us."[63]

Another report, given by a neutral government observer five years earlier, pointed out that "as a percentage either of costs or sales, the gross profits of the trading posts were not materially different from those realized by similar lines of business in towns and cities."[64] There were, of course, differences. Post owners had higher wholesale prices, charged higher markup and retail prices, and had different freighting responsibilities. They did not, however, have to pay rent on the buildings, pay wages for help, since family members assisted, and they had lower taxes. Edward Hall addresses part of this issue: "Possibly because their prices were double or more than those for similar goods in town, Indian traders had a reputation among whites for skinning the Indians. Ten-cent sardine cans were twenty cents. A nickel box of soda crackers was ten cents. A fifteen-cent can of tomatoes was thirty cents. Gasoline was even worse: standard gas selling for twenty-five to thirty cents a gallon on the railroad was eighty cents to a dollar on the reservation."[65] So, after all was said and done, what was in it for the trader? In 1933, the annual net profit for a trading-post owner was $4,587.38.[66]

Paul Begay adds a Navajo perspective. He raised the issue of the weaver, who spent a lot of time making a rug, sold it at the post for a hundred dollars, purchased some goods, and felt satisfied—until she came back a few months later and saw her handiwork being sold for twice as much as she had received. Not understanding that the trader also needed to make a profit, she concluded that she had gotten a bad deal. Begay posits, "I think that the Navajo people think they were being ripped off in many ways by the trader. But then again, they also understand that they can't do without the trader, because then it seems like they're not advancing with the changing times. . . . There was always a little animosity, there's always a little anger set towards the trader. But then it's also understood we cannot live without the trader."[67]

The final word comes from Edward T. Hall, whose experience as a trader in the 1930s gives his observations credibility. He assured his reader that the image of a trader cheating his customers will remain, although undeserved. He attributed much of it to white tourists, often from the East, who wanted to superimpose what they encountered in the dominant culture to what they expected to find on the reservation. "It is difficult to disabuse ignorant or misinformed travelers or romantic intellectuals of their misconceptions." After going through a number of reasons as to how difficult it would be to fool a Navajo customer—everyone knew the current prices, the approximate weight of things, government inspectors' and agents' sympathies—he concluded that it was almost impossible to cheat someone on a significant scale. He recognized that there were some itinerant traders who might venture onto the reservation for a quick, high-pressure bargain, and that, just like in the Navajo society, one could always find a crook. "But," he concluded, "like most businesspeople, who have a close relationship with their customers, in my experience the traders were honest."[68]

During the 1970s, when trading posts operating on pawn and extended credit finally came to an end, circumstances changed dramatically. Not that the traders were any less honest, but they demanded more security if they were to make loans. Indeed, the entire reservation economy had shifted, as had the way of life for the Navajo. The old-style trading days had ended thirty-plus years earlier.

CHAPTER EIGHT

Social Life at the Posts

Ladies, Law, and Laughter

Beyond the business of barter and sales lies the very human side of the life of those who ran the trading posts. Each life was as unique as the individual who lived it, yet there were some common themes and experiences threaded through what the men and women serving customers in the bullpen encountered. Their "trader stories" about living at an isolated post and, for the novice, trading with a different, even strange, culture speaks of the social gap that both groups experienced. This chapter provides a view of some aspects of this life—women, work, medicine, humor, and conflict—but what can be said conclusively is that much of what happened was unique to Navajo circumstances and had a strong impact on the white traders and their families. Rather than viewing traders solely as agents of change, introducing aspects of the dominant culture in an attempt to bring their customers into Anglo society, one should also recognize the strength in the Navajos' way of life and the impact it had on those white men and women living on the reservation.

Women of the Posts

Most traders who lived and work among these people had their wives by their side. Since Navajo culture is matrilineal, with some of its most powerful personal relationships emanating from female kinship and social bonds, having a woman in the post and acting as trader was a positive aspect.[1] Even so, there are few recorded instances where a lone woman entered a Navajo community by herself, without having the ability to call upon the assistance of a man. Even Louisa Wetherill, the quintessence of a woman trader, who will be discussed later, always had her husband, John, or his partner, Clyde Colville, readily available for help if needed. Potential conflict was never far away, and so, although women held their own in the trading arena, the necessity of being able to summon a man for protection was a fact of life.

Isolation is often discussed by women who worked the posts. Unless there was sufficient trade to support more than one store, a trading post had to be isolated in order to avoid attracting another post's customers. Traders mention a twenty-five-mile separation as the ideal, but not as a hard-and-fast rule. What this meant in terms of female companionship was that for the white trader's wife, her peers were Navajo women—often her customers. These American Indian women were highly independent, had their own accounts at the store, "were far tougher traders, drove harder bargains and raised more hell when they thought things were not right . . . [yet] were by no means unfeminine, but they were strong and tough, often a match for a man in a fight."[2] One gets the impression that, although there were friendships that arose between traders' wives and Navajo women from the community, for the most part, the latter had their own concerns and lifestyle that did not closely intertwine with those of their white counterparts.

Attitudes about being a trader's wife and living at a post ran the full gamut—from feeling totally isolated to fondly embracing the situation. Listen to Hilda Faunce Wetherill's impressions when she first arrived at Covered Water Trading Post, Arizona: "Black Mountain on the horizon seemed threatening. I tried to trace the road, forty miles of it to [Hubbell's trading post] and another sixty-five to Gallup and the railroad, but I could only see a yard or two of it on top of the humpy little hills or in the breaks in the scrubby piñons. It was a big country and getting bigger every minute. There was not a moving thing in sight. . . . I turned back to the desert. It was bigger than ever and lonesome. . . . I was feeling sure there was not another human being in the world."[3]

However, even in this isolation, she never gave up her feminine pride. On another occasion, after the post had become second nature to her, Hilda had put in a full day and then some. She and her husband had bid the last customers farewell at 9:30 at night and were getting settled for bed when a group of Navajo freighters arrived. They had supplies that needed to be unloaded, so as Ken got dressed, Hilda stopped her cold-cream application in order to find a string to hold up her stockings, then donned a kimono and headed for the store to help tally the incoming goods. She describes the scene, then asks, "Can you see the picture? Almost midnight, coal-oil lamps, piles of freight, savages, and the one woman present in a kimono and a pigtail." She tried to understand what the Navajo men were saying about her appearance, but fortunately, she could not glean much.[4]

Compare that with Gladys Jack's experience. Gladys recalled, "I thought it was wonderful; I loved it right from the very first. It never bothered me to be out and to be away from the family." And when asked about her life after she and her family went to Farmington, New Mexico, she spoke of the change: "It was a big difference and I never got over wanting to go back to the reservation. . . . I wasn't afraid to stay on the reservation alone; but in town . . . it worried me, and there was a lot of adjustment to make, but we lived through it."[5] Mildred Heflin, on the other hand, adapted in a different way to the isolation. When asked what it was like for her to spend her childhood years on the reservation, she responded, "I think I grew up with a terrible fear of people. I didn't like people and it has taken me years to overcome it. . . . I didn't know how to associate with other youngsters, really. I had to watch and see how people got along with one another and see how I could conduct myself in order to make friends. . . . I only had my sisters to play with, and occasionally a Navajo or two."[6]

Mike (Leone) Goulding, Hilda Wetherill, and others kept a sewing machine in their posts to teach Navajo women to sew and to foster goodwill. Navajo Ted Cly, speaking of Mike said, "She go to town, bring us some boots to wear in the snow, heavy clothes, and tee shirts, socks, gloves. Oh, they used to take good care of us. We all coming and going together, all feeding each other, help each other."[7] Julia Holiday shared similar feelings: "[Harry Goulding's wife, Mike] made dresses for me; I would tell her how to make it and she would do it on the sewing machine."[8] Hilda Wetherill won a large following with her sewing skills. One cold winter day a father and son came to the post in search of a warm jacket for the boy. The owners only had men's sizes which were impossibly large for the small lad—when he tried one on that caught his fancy, it hung all the way to the floor. Still, the boy would not be dissuaded. Hilda offered to shorten the sleeves, shorten the body, and lap over the front until the vestment fit, but she knew it was not going to look good. The father encouraged her to make the alterations, she sat at the machine until they were completed, then put the coat on the boy. Hilda knew enough Navajo to get the gist of what they were saying: "She is a friend to the Navajos." "She likes small boys." "She is grandmother to your small son, my friend." . . . "A-la-honi [ahéláani'(?)], our grandmother has made good work on the big coat." The father happily paid the five dollars for the garment, the boy was proud of his new possession, and Hilda was glad that only her Navajo customers would see the job she had done, commenting, "It was terrible, but they liked it and they loved me for doing it. I wanted nothing else."[9]

Women also had concerns about safety in a number of forms. For instance, Grace Hunt had a woman working for her whose husband had tuberculosis. Grace became a "nervous wreck," fearing that the disease would transmit to her family. "I was always trying to figure out ways to scrub and keep things so that my children would not come in contact with it."[10] Old Lady Nez liked to argue in the store about prices; she also sold sheep that she would take back at night for resale on another occasion. One time, she took Gladys Jack's family dog home, where it remained until Vernon Jack retrieved it. She also had a penchant for stealing chickens and eggs out of the trader's coop. Not until Gladys's son put on a bearskin and waited by the roost for the Navajo woman's return, was that problem solved.[11]

For most women, however, a typical fear was for personal safety. Franc Newcomb attests to that. She tells of being alone at her post, when a non-Navajo Indian, smelling of bootleg alcohol, came into the store to get gas for his car. The pump was dry, she offered food, which he took and demanded to stay inside instead of eating in his car. Franc became increasingly on edge. Luckily, her friend and protector, Hastiin Klah, learned of the situation and came to the store to make sure everything went well. She carefully armed him with a knife, fed the two men, and let them sleep in the living room until Franc's husband returned late at night. She resolved at that time to never be left alone at the post again.[12]

Living conditions at some stores were primitive. There were, however, ways to solve problems and achieve comfortable circumstances. Before refrigeration, a wire box covered with burlap sacks received slow drips of water from a pan that had small holes in it. Placed in the shade where a breeze blew over the container, the evaporating water kept the "refrigerator" cool. A can of milk poured into a fifty-gallon water barrel, when stirred in, caused suspended sand and dirt particles to drop to the bottom, making the water clear and potable. Small empty cans with kerosene in the bottom placed under the four legs of a bed prevented bugs from crawling onto the mattress.[13]

Washing clothes was often a day-long chore. Even when Ray Hunt bought his wife, Grace, a washing machine from a Montgomery Ward catalog, it only simplified part of the task. Their initial post in Mexican Hat was a couple of tents beneath a bridge spanning the San Juan River. The shade from the bridge and close proximity to the water made life more comfortable, but the water still needed to be hauled to a fire. "Grace heated the water outside in a boiler (a two foot deep, oblong, galvanized, sort of tub) over an open fire. She put lye in the water which formed a scum on top. We'd skim that off and it left nice soft water. She boiled the diapers, dish towels, and dish rags. It was very hard to start the washer, about like a lawnmower. We had to step on a pedal about twenty times. (We used a scrubbing board before we got our washing machine.) The machine had a long tube like a hose on a gas pump to let out the fumes. We had to stick this out the door. I don't know how we ever fit the washer in the small kitchen tent, but that is where it was."[14] While this young couple struggled with the process, there were many posts that had limited water that had to be hauled. Parents employed their children in doing chores like hauling water just to keep them out of the store. Marilene Blair remembers that, as a young girl, she gathered eggs, milked cows, brought the milk to their springhouse, weeded the garden, chopped wood, and raised an abundance of rabbits.[15] Everyone had a part in making life comfortable and in obtaining a livelihood.

Many women were prime movers in the social life of the posts. Gladys Jack shared how she and her husband rented movies, charged a dime for admittance to pay for the cost, and sold candy, popcorn, and soda to the crowds that flocked to the show. "We always tried to get a cowboy picture or something they could understand, and they would laugh and enjoy that. They'd all sit down in the bullpen and we would put the screen up on the counter where they could all see it. . . . That was really one of the highlights at that time. They would plan for weeks to come in and see that." Gladys also decorated the Christmas tree with candles, helped with the presents put in a two-yard-long seamless sack carried by Santa, and prepared the large community dinner. On other occasions, she had the unpleasant task of sending her children to school far from home. One daughter felt alienated from her Navajo friends while getting her education in town, so her parents relented the next year, letting her stay on the reservation.[16]

Louisa Wetherill—Protector and Judge

There were many unsung heroines who manned the counters of isolated posts, remaining at a husband's side from dawn to dusk. But there is no female trader better known than Louisa Wetherill, who operated stores in Oljato, Utah, and Kayenta, Arizona. Her fame was well earned; she wrote a book about her experience, was featured in numerous articles and stories, and received national recognition for her efforts in preserving elements of Navajo culture. Her work, and that of her husband, John, was extensive. They toured Anasazi sites and the natural wonders of the Four Corners region and were able to attract archaeologists, famous writers and artists, even the president of the United States, to their home in Kayenta. Louisa's life can be viewed as that of a female trader who won the greatest respect from the Navajos she dealt with. Indeed, her multifaceted accomplishments were exceptional, illustrating the power women could achieve when working in the matrilineal society of these people.[17]

Louisa (1877–1945) and John Wetherill (1866–1944) moved to Oljato in 1906. In August 1908, Lt. Col. George Hunter arrived at their trading post as one of his stopping points on his Black Mountain expedition. The purpose of this show-of-force was to ensure the tranquility of the Navajos, following an earlier disturbance at Black Mountain. A number of powerful local leaders, such as *Hashké neiniihí* (Giving Out Anger) and his son, *Hashké neiniihí Biye'*, had lived through the tumultuous years of the Long Walk, when they fled to Navajo Mountain (*Naatsis'áán*—Head of Earth Woman) to avoid conflict with the U.S. military and the Utes assisting them. Forty years later, the Indians still feared a recurrence of hostilities. One Navajo man had earlier been detained, then released, by cavalry moving through the area. To the Navajos, "Nat-sees-an (Navajo Mountain) had influenced his release from the soldiers. [Navajo Mountain] and Asthon Sosi (*Asdzáán Ts'ósí*—Slim Woman—Louisa Wetherill) have power. . . . We want to get behind you. We want the soldiers to find you first."[18] What the Navajos under *Hashké neiniihí* were suggesting goes back to the time of the myths, where traditional teachings tell of how the holy people placed Navajo Mountain in its isolated position to serve as a shield of protection against those fighting the Navajos. Many groups of refugees fled there during the Long Walk period and avoided detection from their enemies.[19] Both the mountain and Louisa were credited with providing protection against the approaching soldiers. After repeated urging by Louisa, *Hashké neiniihí* agreed to deliver a letter she wrote and meet with Lieutenant Colonel Hunter. Floodwaters in Laguna Creek prevented him from actually delivering it, but after the deluge subsided, Hunter came to Oljato and delivered his message of peace and cooperation to Louisa and her Navajo neighbors. She translated and gave a promise on their behalf: "I have said that you are not warlike, that you are not renegades, that you are not troublemakers. You must never make me a liar."[20] There is no missing the respect, power, and position this woman held when she was compared with that of a mountain and a person that a band of warriors wished to have represent them.

The Navajos came to her for advice and judgment. They felt comfortable doing this, not just because she spoke their language fluently—far beyond "Trader Navajo"—but because she learned to think like a Navajo, using her understanding of the culture as her basis. Her friends said, "Asthon Sosi is like a Navajo herself. Even when she speaks English, she speaks with the tone of the Navajo. She nurses them. She helps them. She sometimes scolds them. She never patronizes them. Two of them she has adopted into her own family. Hundreds of them she has taken periodically, into her own home."[21] Until her dying day, Louisa embodied both the nurturing assistance, as personified in Changing Woman of the myths and in the ideals of Navajo motherhood, and the sharp-edged wisdom expected of the tribe's elders.

A few more examples illustrate this cultural understanding and wisdom. When Tall Singer died at the end of a Night Way chant he was performing, people understood a special ceremony had to be held to remove the spiritual issues this created. One of the requirements was to use seawater, and so Louisa wrote to friends in California, who mailed some to

Louisa Wetherill in her prime while living in Kayenta, 1912. As a trader and student of Navajo culture, she was influential in helping these Indians during difficult times, while also preserving elements of their culture. She may have dined with Teddy Roosevelt and dignitaries from many walks of life, but her heart was with the Navajos. (NAU.PH. 643.4.14, Northern Arizona University, Cline Library, Stuart Young Collection.)

her, solving the problem. Another time, a group of Navajos brought a Paiute man to the store, accusing him of killing a cow and eating part of it. The Paiute, on the other hand, claimed the cow was sick, even dying, and was not worth the horse the Navajo owner claimed he should be paid. After hearing both sides, Louisa told the parties to each send a representative to retrieve the bones of the animal, with this instruction: "If the bones are yellow, the cow was fat, and the Paiute will give the Navajo a horse. If the bones are white, nothing more need be said about it." The Paiute went no further and paid with the horse he owed.[22]

A final example: A Navajo man with three wives was constantly embroiled in marital strife. The two younger women were nieces to the older one, their ages ranging from thirty-five to nineteen to thirteen. The "judge" after a long session of hearing everyone's complaint, decided that the man had shown that he could not handle three wives and so should only have one. He wanted the youngest, prettiest one, but Louisa said that she was too young and would later be able to get a husband of a comparable age. Instead, he needed to take the one in the middle, because she would make a good wife and was not as edgy as the oldest one, but she also would be able to handle her husband and not be overwhelmed by his personality and demands. Everyone agreed this was fair, with all four of the disputants accepting the decision.[23] Louisa Wetherill, at a time when, in the dominant society, women took a backseat to men in legal, social, and economic situations, found wide acceptance and heightened respect among the Navajos.

Assisting the Sick

Both cultures shared concerns about sickness, the trading post becoming a place for a different kind of exchange. Most of these stores were far from doctors, hospitals, or any type of medical help, and so traders were often on their own in assisting their neighbors. Many of them commented on their involvement in burying the dead, in their support of ceremonies, and in their respect for Navajo medicine men, but Gladys Jack provided an interesting evaluation of the shared benefit she witnessed from both sides. "We learned of things to do for illness. The Indians had lots of things that helped, too. You'd be surprised at how many medicines and how many things they have. We helped them and they helped us."[24]

Most posts carried "over-the-counter" medicines, such as Vicks VapoRub, Vaseline, Mentholatum, Ben-Gay, and Sloan's Liniment. Each had an advantage and disadvantage. For instance, Sloan's was very strong and, according to one trader, could "cook your skin." An old woman came into the Round Rock post one day, made her purchases, and then left. Not too far from the store, her horse bucked her onto the ground, breaking two or three of her ribs. The trader brought her back to the post, where he applied his best first-aid knowledge, which meant putting some Sloan's Liniment on the painfully bruised area and then wrapping it with adhesive tape. He helped her on her horse and sent her on her way. Three weeks later, she was back as angry as a bear. The liniment had proved uncomfortably hot, so she removed the tape, her skin peeling off with it. When she lifted her blouse, the mistake was evident—the location of every piece of tape was painfully apparent.[25]

Difficult living conditions on the reservation caused traders to stock medicines and teach practices to relieve the suffering. Head lice were a real nuisance, and so posts carried two types of remedies—one for the "blue lice" and one for the "white lice." Nits crawled around in the hairline of some customers and then dropped on the counter, to be passed on to others if they were not careful. Cough syrup, especially if it was sweetened and had a tinge of alcohol, sold readily in the winter, as did castor oil. Zinc oxide helped combat impetigo after the scabs had been removed, the area washed, and ointment applied. One day a man came into Ray Hunt's store, requesting the "medicine that boils." The befuddled trader finally realized that what his customer wanted was Alka-Seltzer. He obtained some but could not keep enough of it on the shelves, until he eventually ordered eight cases at a time. Joe Lee tells a similar story having to do with Hostetter's Bitters, a patent medicine that did not sell until Mister Blackgoats came to the store sick and ready to try something new. He bought a bottle, returned cured the next day, and purchased six more bottles. Others caught on, and a brisk sale over the counter kept the store ordering cases of the medicine until Lee learned it was actually colored alcohol with bitters added for taste.[26] No post, by law, could sell alcohol.

Some field doctors traveling out of specific agencies left basic medicines and supplies at posts so that the traders could act as first responders. That is what Harry Rorick at Shonto used when a young Navajo man appeared at the store with a flap of skin hanging over an eye, cut loose from the kick of a horse. The trader bathed the wound, cleaning out the fresh manure stuck in it, and cut strips of adhesive tape, which he applied lightly so that air circulated around the injury. He commented that his patient must have fallen just right in order to have so much horse manure spread throughout the wound. That was when he learned that the opening had been intentionally packed with horse droppings because of their medicinal properties. The next day, when the field doctor inspected Rorick's work, he complimented the trader on doing a good job; the wound eventually healed without a scar.[27]

While Harry Goulding obtained a self-help book for diagnosing and curing illnesses, no such volume prepared Hilda Wetherill for what she encountered at Covered Water. In March 1928, a smallpox epidemic engulfed the Navajo community. In a letter she explained that she had obtained vaccines and waited for the people to come to the post. The smallpox "has come upon us suddenly," she wrote, "and almost immediately, dozens have died. The Indians come to the store with their bodies covered; they lie down on the floor beside the stove sick as can be, and we have such a time getting them to go home. It's raw and cold and wet outside, and our stove is red-hot inside. May you never know the odor of drying clothes, none-too-clean bodies, and disease." The Navajos readily accepted the vaccinations as well as any solace the trader's wife could give. With soap and water, she washed an area on the arm and then scraped a small spot where she rubbed in a little vaccine. For others, all they wanted to do was hold her hand and receive comfort for lost family members. Even though she understood the contagious nature of the disease, she grasped their hands for several minutes before letting go. "What could I do but console them in their way? I'm covered with smallpox germs. One woman, who was covered with sores, laid her head on my shoulder and leaned against me. Her husband died last night. What use precautions?"[28]

Traders, in many instances, were just as susceptible to diseases as the Navajos and so trachoma, tuberculosis, and dysentery—as well as epidemics of measles, whooping cough, diphtheria, meningitis, smallpox, influenza, and typhoid—were a concern as they played across the reservation. That is why Frank Noel would leave his store on Sunday and ride thirty miles to Shiprock to have a doctor use a blue vitriol pencil to combat his case of trachoma. "Then I would have to sit all day with my eyes covered with a wet cloth, and when the sun went down, I would ride back to the store, making sixty miles in one day, as I had to be ready to run the store Monday morning."[29] Vernon Jack's wife had an infectious sore that refused to heal. A Navajo gave her some red mold that grew on old oak trees, and the sore cleared up right away. Navajos often used this same medicine for gonorrhea; it was nothing more than a form of raw penicillin.[30]

The men and women staffing the posts were also involved—some directly, others indirectly—with the medical practices of the Navajo people. There were two types of treatment for sickness—those derived from the use of plants and physical objects and those that required ceremonies, although the treatments were not mutually exclusive. No doubt, the traders understood best the things of a physical nature being done, since that was more in keeping, in general, with their worldview. If a bone was fractured, it needed to be splinted; a particular herb reduced inflammation or lowered a temperature; certain foods or drinks restored health. Stewart Hatch remembers a young man suffering from gonorrhea to the point that he remained prostrate and could not move. A medicine man from Arizona visited him at the confluence of Montezuma Creek with the San Juan River, boiled herbs in a Navajo pot, encouraged his patient to drink a large quantity of the liquid, then left. Three days later the sick man was back to normal and riding a horse. Another time a child burned his knee on hot coals. A medicine man scorched the hair of a rabbit skin, placing the powdered residue on the wound, which healed the burn. At other times, Navajos used plants to cure toothaches. Hatch explained that he did not understand how any of this worked, but he and his father and brothers—all of whom were in the trading business—held medicine men in great respect.[31]

Cecil Richardson at Inscription House also felt admiration and gratitude for them. His wife was flush with fever, weak, and barely responsive when he learned of a Navajo woman having trouble in childbirth. Family members requested he come and help, since he had successfully assisted before with births, but he was reticent to leave his ailing spouse.

Hosteen LeChee (*Hastiin Łichíí'*), a medicine man, encouraged Cecil to go and do what he could, while he cared for the trader's wife:

> "I promise you she will not die, if you will but go," he said, and his aged face became stern and grim and purposeful. "I will stay here, for I too, am a medicine man, and of this kind of sickness I know much. Your wife—your store—leave them to me. I promise—on my life!" The trader left, worked with other medicine men, and helped the mother deliver a healthy child. Upon returning, he found LeChee waiting for him with his wife remarkably improved and resting comfortably. When asked what the medicine man had done, she answered, "I wish I had saved some of that awful stuff he brewed on the stove and made me drink, but gosh I went right to sleep soon after, and well—I'm a lot better."[32]

The intangible, ceremonial side, for some Anglos, was difficult to grasp. As with most aspects of the posts, there were some traders who understood accurately what ceremonies did, how they worked, and what was required to support such activities. Others did not have a clear picture of these procedures and did not put much faith in their power to heal. Most carried supplies they had access to for the rites and willingly donated food for those attending, while others even participated when invited. For the traders, this could also pressure them to extend credit to a family holding a ceremony. Families and friends were expected to participate as part of the healing process, which meant feeding a large group as well as buying cloth, baskets, and other items. In some cases, if there were a lot of "sings" or ceremonies taking place for a family, credit might be denied, rather than allow the family to go into unbearable debt.[33]

Still, many traders felt like Jack Manning, whose father told of a little boy horribly sick with running sores from impetigo. "The little kid was pitiful to see." After a three-day ceremony, the trader saw the boy and found him with perfectly clear skin. From then on, "anytime anyone came in and said, 'We need money for a sing,' if at all possible, we made sure they had it."[34] Hilda Wetherill had her faith stretched when she witnessed a miraculous healing, but was hard-pressed to explain it. A fifteen-year-old boy was putting a dozen mules in the corral at the post when one of the animals kicked him in the shoulder and the back of his head, almost killing him. His father and grandfather left the youth there, called everyone into the store, and forbid anyone to look or go outside. Unfazed by the instructions, Hilda watched from her bedroom window as a medicine man entered the corral in a zigzag manner, sprinkled the prostrate figure with powder from his medicine bundle, then made "motions in the air as if he were driving something away. I think it was about ten minutes before he stooped down and helped the boy to his feet. The lad walked slowly and painfully about. The doctor followed him, making signs and pushing away something imaginary. . . . The next morning he was sore and aching, so the father got an Indian to drive his team and took the boy home. During the treatment, neither boy nor doctor made a sound, and there was no emotion on the part of anyone except myself."[35]

Navajos, Traders, and Death

Navajos feared death and tried to avoid having anything to do with it. There are numerous accounts of Indians asking traders to bury the deceased so that they would have no contact with the body or anything associated with it. Father Berard Haile, in his study *Soul Concepts of the Navaho,* provides an excellent discussion of beliefs concerning the spirit of the dead, the afterlife, and the actions that the living must take to prevent problems.[36] Briefly, when an individual died, there was a spiritual essence of evil that remained with the body and affected anyone who came in contact with it. Property that belonged to the deceased, the place where the person died—especially if it was their home—and even improper mention of their name, could attract this malevolent spirit that haunted the wrongdoers. In Navajo thought, Anglo people were not susceptible to this influence the way they were, and so as long as the white man buried the body according to traditional teachings and the Indians avoided the grave site, then spent the expected four days in mourning, they could resume a normal life.

Traders, if they were not already aware, soon became intimately associated with these beliefs, especially since they could affect their livelihood. For instance, one trader received very hostile treatment from his customers when he made the mistake of burying an important medicine man's body oriented in the wrong direction, instead of having the head to the north, the direction that the deceased's spirit traveled upon death.[37] Jot Styles, in his Tuba City post, watched a Navajo man have an epileptic seizure in the bullpen. "Jot was behind the counter at the time and as he watched the rest of the Navvies almost tear the front door apart in their scramble to get out, he vaulted the counter, grabbed the fellow's legs, and pulled him outside."[38] Associating this event with death, the Navajos would not have returned to the building had the man died inside until the trader held an expensive purification ceremony and the store's contents replaced, since they would now be *ch'į́įdii*, or haunted by the disembodied spirit and no longer usable. Will Evans applied this knowledge when he faced dire circumstances during the establishment of the post at Sanostee. Alone, inexperienced, snowbound, and besieged with hungry Navajos, whom he dubbed the "handout gang" because of their constant visits to the store for free food, Evans did the unthinkable. Short on firewood, he traipsed through the snow to a nearby hogan that the owners had abandoned because of a death. He carried a log that was now *ch'į́įdii* from the structure and used it in his stove to cook food. His neighbors found out what he had done, so no longer bothered him for meals.[39] When trader Joseph Heffernan died at his post in Oljato, Harry Goulding drove from his store in Kayenta with a box to put the body in so that none of the Navajo customers would learn of the man's death. Goulding drove the remains to Cortez, where he obtained a real coffin. A similar incident occurred during the1918 influenza epidemic, when Tom Turpin died in Kaibito. His wife closed the post, notified relatives, who were also traders, and kept it all a secret until the men removed the body at three o'clock in the morning in a touring car, so that no one would suspect what had happened in the store.[40]

Traders did what they could to assist bereaved families. An Arbuckles' Coffee crate served as a good coffin for a child, while two, each with an end removed and joined together, worked well for an adult.[41] If a person died in a hogan, the traders, according to custom, broke a hole in the north wall to carry the corpse through and then went to the burial place. There, the men lowered the body into the grave, along with valuable jewelry, clothing, blankets, a saddle, or other items important for the deceased's journey to the North. His favorite horse then might be shot over the grave. The site was not visited after interment, and the hogan where the death occurred was burned. Anyone who later went to the burial site might be accused of grave robbing, witchcraft, and other antisocial behavior, a dangerous situation in the Navajo community. At Covered Water, a family found tracks going directly toward a grave and asked the trader to investigate, concerned that the remains had been disturbed. After a thorough search, the trader assured them that nothing was amiss. At that point, a Navajo in the bullpen spoke up, saying that a man from a distant community had been in the area when his burro had wandered off. He had gone in search of the animal, unaware that he was trespassing on a burial site. With that, the concerned family relaxed.[42]

Humor—A Two-Way Bond

Life was not always serious at the posts. Indeed one of the most effective tools that the trader had in fostering positive relationships with his customers was joking. Navajo people love to laugh, and although humor takes on a particular form or twist in every culture, when common ground is reached between two different worlds, it builds a bond of friendship and opportunity to share a happy situation. Trader William Y. Adams observed that there were certain acceptable as well as unacceptable things that could be spoken of on the respective sides of the counter. For instance, the trader might joke with his male customers about liaisons with prostitutes or tell some in-law jokes, while the men on the other side might kid him about why his wife stayed so long in Flagstaff when she went there on business—an even exchange. Navajos might joke about physical things, such as a trader's looks, but they could not make light of his honesty, industriousness, and wealth, and they could not play practical jokes or touch him in a jesting fashion. The trader, on the other hand, had freer rein to joke with his customers—except about topics concerning religious beliefs. He could tease them about their run-ins with the law, about problems in the community, and mistakes made, all in the hopes of being perceived as "one of the gang" and solidifying his status as an important figure in the area.[43] Along with this, he liberally praised and rewarded individuals for positive behavior, saving humor to defuse hostility and suspicion.

From the Navajo perspective, teasing was an important part of life and was in keeping with traditional kinship-based values that defined who could be teased and what form of teasing was appropriate. Paul Begay remembered Elijah Blair teasing the people in his store, that Blair and the Indians would playfully grab at each other's clothes, and that the Indians came as much to visit as they did to trade. The men respected Blair, as did the women who joked,

> "Ah! Forget about that white man! He's no good; he doesn't know nothing about the Navajo," to which the men retorted, "I will go over there and talk with him, *shaadaaní*, my in-law," they call him. This is a way of when you say "in-law," you're basically saying, "Oh, he's good enough, so I wish he could be my in-law." . . . Maybe he's grabbing this Navajo's clothing because he owns a lot of jewelry and has got a big concha belt. Huge! Looks like a wealthy Navajo. "I want him as my in-law." And so this is the way to build good rapport, a good relationship between the trader and the Navajos, to win their hearts.[44]

A few examples from both sides of the counter make it apparent that rough play and slapstick, bawdy, and witty humor were all accepted. One also has to understand that, especially with verbal jokes, what is funny in one culture goes flat in another. There may be little transferred humor. For the Navajo, mother-in-law jokes were one of the most common. A Navajo husband, according to tradition, should never see his mother-in-law, and so a person leaving a post might approach another man and tell him that she was inside. The son-in-law would hide in a place where he would not be seen, but after a while might approach another individual to see if she had left, not realizing that she had never been in there in the first place. The trickster might return after a while, saying he did not know because he never knew all the wives of the son-in-law.[45] Or it could be played just the opposite. A mother-in-law would be in the store, the son-in-law was told that she was not, and then the two met. "She turned around and there he was. She grabbed one of about nine skirts she was wearing, and over her head it went. She screamed. He turned around and screamed and ran out."[46]

One popular story, heavily circulated on the reservation, gave birth to three different endings. It seems there was a father who had been able to marry off all of his daughters except the last one. She was most undesirable, being extremely heavy, having few teeth, little hair, and with "a face that would scare a varmint." The father located a man who lived

Navajo people love humor, and there was a lot of it in the bullpen. Here, Shine Smith, who came to the reservation in 1917 as a Presbyterian minister and eventually adopted many Navajo customs, entertains a crowd. His happy demeanor earned him the epithet of "Sunshine" from his Indian friends. (NAU.PH. 85.3.366.32, Northern Arizona University, Cline Library, Fronske Collection.)

far away, and he carried on at length about his daughter's beauty. The potential victim had heard of her, which now leads to three different endings: (1) "You go back home and tomorrow you bring me her hair and teeth and I will give you the best horse in my corral. You can keep the rest of her." (2) "My friend, you are such a wonderful man, I know you would not lie about your daughter. But I have one piece of advice. Don't let me take her from you because I am moving today over in Dead Goat Canyon where the buzzards are so bad they will carry off anything but a human being." (3) "I have nothing to give you for your wonderful daughter. All I have left is a flea-bitten yellow dog and a goat. When you arrived the goat ran away, and that was my dog that just backed up to your horse and let him kick him over the horizon."[47]

Other Navajo humor took the form of fooling a trader by selling mule or horse meat to him, while claiming it was beef, teasing the trader's wife about how she needed to groom slovenly customers, and making a task difficult by speaking Navajo when they knew English very well.[48] Walter Scribner gave a classic example of this. When Reuben Heflin was putting a new roof on his post at Oljato, there was a lengthy discussion in Navajo about how it should be done. A shaggy old man in the background, who appeared to be the least likely candidate to speak English, participated in the discussion. At the end of the dialogue, he surprised everyone when he chimed in in perfect English, "You failed to take into consideration the difference in climate and soil." The trader was amazed.[49] Another time, Louisa Wetherill was amused, as were her guests, when a Navajo woman walked around her home, which was decked out for Christmas, and carefully examined the silver, the dishes, and the food as she imitated how a Hopi, an Anglo, and a Ute would do it. Slapstick gave an intercultural flavor to humor.[50]

Traders had their own brand of jokes. Along the same lines as slapstick, Maurice Knee enjoyed physical pranks. He drilled a hole in the counter at Goulding's trading post and fastened through the hole a quarter that had been made into a button, attaching it to a magneto grounded to a piece of steel, with water on the floor as a conductor. Knee waited for a man to come in to sell a blanket, but also ensured that there were sufficient witnesses in the bullpen to suppress any anger that might rise in the victim of the joke. Invariably, the man would spot the quarter, lay the blanket he was selling on the counter, and during the transaction, slip his hand under the covering and try to grab the money. Knee would quickly tap on the magneto, and three shocks went through the quarter to the man's hand, while everyone there enjoyed the scene. On another occasion, Knee took a piece of straw and "pecked" *Hashké neiniihí*'s neck; the old man thought lice had bitten him. After three "bites," he declared, "Ah, that's a smart louse," then removed his shirt and "just shook the hell out of it." The trader did not have the heart to do it a fourth time.[51]

A Navajo customer brought in a small sack of wool and plopped it on the counter. The trader knew that the contents had been watered to give it extra weight, but said nothing, went to the back room, emptied the wool into a pile, returned to the bullpen, and put eight cents on the counter. The man was irate, telling the trader he was cheating him, that the wool was really worth a dollar and a quarter, and that he wanted higher pay. The white man responded, "The wool in that sack came from the backs of two sheep, but the water in the wool came from my spring. I saw you dipping it out a little while ago. Now, if you had brought your own water I might have paid you ten or twenty cents more, but do you think I am foolish enough to pay for water that already belongs to me?" Everyone in the store appreciated the wit except for the seller, but he too, eventually, joined in with the laughter.[52]

There were also stories the traders passed around among themselves. One features a German trader named Fritz, who sent a note to his partner in Flagstaff that read, "Dear Fred, Sand the wool, sand the blankets, sand the hides, and sand the money," knowing that more weight meant a higher price. The return message said, "Fritz, like you said, I sanded the wool, I sanded the blankets, and I sanded the hides, but doggone it, Fritz, you never showed me how to sand the money."[53] A trader posted a sign that read, "Mike Kirk—Product of 49 Tribes," without recognizing that he had forgotten to put an "s" on the word "product." When Will Rogers read it, he quipped, "He must be quite a guy."[54] Another trader yarn tells of when a Navajo man went to heaven and met St. Peter, who asked what he wanted as a reward for being faithful. The reply: "A million dollars," which he received. Shortly after, a trader appeared at the pearly gates, which was a first-time occurrence. After checking credentials and seeing all was in order, St. Peter asked what the trader wanted as his reward, and received word that "Unusual as it may seem, I don't want any money, just please show me which way the Navajo went with the million bucks you just gave him."[55]

Crime and Punishment

There was also a grim side to life in the posts, where conflict, fights, and even murder were potentially around the corner. In subsequent chapters concerning specific stores, it will become apparent that, while relations in general were pacific, isolation, limited personnel, community dynamics, and individual temperament were all factors in how incidents played out. Historian Frank McNitt, when analyzing the killing of traders, believed that, prior to 1900, few were murdered, but following that date and with the increased availability of alcohol, there was a steady increase. Between 1901 and 1934, Navajos killed over twenty traders.[56] In most instances, the circumstances were the same—the murderer was drunk and wanted to rob the store; the victim was alone; the guilty party stole all of the pawn; the deed took place after sunset; and the culprit burned the trading post with the body in it to hide the evidence. These facts led to two cardinal rules followed by most traders—close the post at dark and never open the warehouse at night.

Father Berard Haile studied Navajo ethics extensively. He found that the moral system at work in the culture valued certain qualities differently than did Anglos, and there was not a particularly strong feeling of censure for crimes like lying and theft. "Small thefts should not be customary in families of good parentage and standing. . . . By similar standard, the ethics of adultery, slander, rape, murder, assault, cheating, and the like, are gaged. These are crimes and evils because they are resented by others." The Navajo vocabulary, rich in descriptive words that emphasize many aspects of life important in the culture, has very few terms that have an ethical bearing. "The language has no word for law, order, justice, penalty, for right and wrong, for just and unjust or associated ideas like conscience, conscientious, conscious, guilty, and a host of others. The wrong and injustices done are felt by the perpetrator, but not as a conscious guilt. . . . The idea is to get away with anything, if you can, and have the laugh on yourself if you can't get there first."[57]

While Haile makes these general, somewhat critical, statements, one should also recognize that there were many Navajos who were honest and faithful, in the best sense of the Anglo code of ethics. Vernon Jack tells of the time he and his family were sitting at the breakfast table when an old Indian man from the community knocked on the door. He inquired if the trader was going to go back into the store, since he had been in there for a half hour and no one was there to trade. Jack suddenly realized that the door had been unlocked all night, and the man who stood before him was trying to help.[58] When discussing Navajo values, one should also consider that religious practices and things of a spiritual nature were of far more concern to them than to Anglos. Navajos have a rich vocabulary that describes intangible powers and events, as well as many of the "dos and don'ts" of life.

Conflict took many different forms. It might start with a cranky customer who wanted more money for a sale or when an important figure like Black Horse entered Will Evans's store, demanding that he be allowed to sleep inside while his four companions stayed in the guest hogan. (That night he slept outside.) It may take the form of a young boy who stole some beads, buried them in the bank of a wash, then went to church, where he sat for three hours waiting for the coast to clear. The police soon caught him, he confessed, and the trader repossessed his property. It might be a teenager who broke into a post and took three concha belts and some bracelets, then fled directly home, where he was apprehended the next day. A stiff penalty of a year in reform school changed his demeanor dramatically. Or it may be as blatant as when Taddytin (*Tádidíín*—Pollen) became angry with what he considered an unfair price for a blanket, leaped over the counter and took the money he thought covered its worth, then traded it out for supplies. The next time he tried that trick, trader Joe Lee hit him with a pickaxe handle filled with lead, then dragged him to a shady spot outside of his store to recuperate, ending any future incidents.[59]

Most of the problems, however, were over petty theft and were handled with diplomacy. Philip Johnston stood at the counter when two Navajo women came in with some very clean wool, which he weighed and paid for. The women wanted to look at some rings, a dozen to be exact, so the trader laid them on the counter. When he put them away, there were only eleven, but he said nothing. The ladies sat down in the corner of the bullpen, conversed with each other, then came back to the counter and paid four dollars for two sacks of flour. Johnston brought out one and let them know they were now even. The women were irate, demanding their second sack of flour, but the trader made it clear that they had gotten what they paid for, pointing out that the ring also cost two dollars. "Well, I never saw such indignation in my life. They berated me, told me what an evil person I was, and that they would not think of stealing a ring, and that they had never stolen anything in their lives." The trader held firm, the ring reappeared, and the ladies obtained their second sack of flour. Peace prevailed at the post.[60]

There were also full-blown confrontations, such as the time Will Evans and two other men started to build the Sanostee trading post. A powerful medicine man and community leader named *Bizhóshí*, with a group of men, demanded that they stop construction and leave. One of the white men sat on a nearby fence with a rifle across his knee, while the other two men proceeded with the construction. The Navajos wheeled their horses, shouted threats, and made intimidating gestures, while *Bizhóshí* rode close to the workers. Evans recalled, "I can still visualize that fierce old fellow's bristling gray mustache and his out-thrust jagged teeth as he grated out his words with all the venom he could muster: 'If you don't stop this work, I will slit your throat like I would a sheep!' He emphasized his threat by jerking the edge of his hand across his throat. To say that I was scared is putting it mildly." The men continued to build, the threats of the hecklers ceased, and soon they were welcomed into the community.[61]

A third cardinal rule for traders was to never let a Navajo know you are scared. Another time, two of *Bizhóshí*'s sons decided that they wanted to give Evans a hard time, and so they waited until the end of the day, when everyone was filing out of the bullpen. Evans walked toward the door to shut it, joking with the two men, when they suddenly grappled and threw him on the floor. They were large in stature and had the element of surprise, but Evans grabbed one by the throat, while kicking the other in the stomach, which momentarily took him out of the fight. Concentrating on squeezing the neck of the one on top, he rolled him off, got to his feet, vaulted the counter, and reached for his loaded rifle. When he rose up ready, the bullpen was empty, and his assailants were mounting their horses. No further repercussions occurred.[62]

Alcohol often was a factor in problems at the posts. Tom Ration, an elder, told a traditional story of when Coyote the Trickster first introduced alcohol and hallucinogenic plants to the Navajos. Before relating this story, Ration stated that "drinking among our people is one of the biggest problems they face" and that in the past, getting drunk was called "spitting the medicine into the mouth of another." He then listed a number of poisonous plants that the people used to "go crazy," like jimsonweed and sow thistle. He next told how Coyote had the Navajos meet on Mancos Creek, boil the juice from these plants, and put the contents in a container. The Trickster arrived and was the first to partake. Coyote, in his usual impulsive way, "gulped it all down too fast. Some dripped from his mouth. Not long afterward his eyes crossed, he began to stagger, and his mouth foamed. . . . He was drunk." Ever since then, alcoholism and drugs have been a problem. Ration concluded: "Now we have the sickness called alcoholism which has spread widely among Indians, both young and old. The horrible habit can destroy a person's physical being and dignity and make him unwanted and a dangerous person."[63]

Grace Hunt agreed. She remembers that, at Chilchinbeto, fermented raisins initially provided the brew, but later, with the introduction of cars into the area, border towns and bootlegging became primary sources. The traders tried to keep those drinking away from the store, but it was difficult when a group had imbibed and wanted to socialize. Grace recalled how scary it was when a gang of drinkers came to the store to have her husband referee an argument. Ray wanted nothing to do with it, locked the post, packed his family into the car, and drove to Kayenta to spend the night. Two days later, the Navajo police arrived, but everything about the incident by that time was history.[64] Elizabeth Hegemann had her own experience with a man who came to the Shonto post for his Christmas gift. High on jimsonweed, he aggressively demanded a second gift, lunged at her, swung at Harry, her husband, and did not stop until Harry's fist sprawled him on the floor. He soon rose and departed.[65]

A final point to be made is that when a theft did occur, often Navajos helped regain the lost items. In a previous chapter, divination was discussed as both a means to capture a culprit and a way of preventing theft. Although difficult for Anglos to believe, many traders testify to the power. Mary Bailey remembers when two men broke into her father's store during a windstorm that destroyed all traces of their travel and prevented the dogs from hearing them enter. Her father discovered the break-in and told his family, "You know, all my life I've heard of these crones among the Navajos who can tell exactly what happened. I'm going to find out if it is true." In a little over an hour, he was back with a woman who sat in his living room with an example of each of the missing items and performed hand trembling. She told of the direction they had come, how they broke into the store, what they had taken, and even gave the trader their names. He went to their home, confronted them, and received all of the missing goods back.[66]

Ray Hunt had a similar experience. When someone stole an expensive collection of pawned beads from his store, the trader had a relative of the owner search in a one-hundred-mile radius of the store to see if the beads had been hocked, but without success. He then called in a hand trembler who performed the rite, told Hunt exactly where the stolen objects were located, and received fifty dollars for his service—the beads at that time being worth ten times that amount. The trader sent a trusted worker to the Black Mountain trading post. Soon the items were back where they belonged. To Hunt, "How on earth the wizard [hand trembler] ever knew the beads were up there, I will never know."[67]

A little less mysterious, but equally effective, was the assistance rendered by Navajo trackers. Edward T. Hall shared an event that happened on March 21, 1919, as told to him by Lorenzo Hubbell. Lorenzo's Uncle Charley ran a post at Cedar Springs, southeast of the Hopi mesas. One night, two Navajos entered the store, killed the trader, stole pawn and goods, and burned the building with the body inside. A day-and-a-half later, Lorenzo arrived at the scene, where "lots of people—large crowds of whites and Navajos—wagons, buckboards, and tethered horses" had been milling around. He had everyone leave except for two men—*Bohokishi Biyé* and *Quinani*—who examined the site, where "for almost two days, a hundred or more persons added millions of footprints in an area of roughly two acres." From this tangled mess, the two trackers determined that a couple of men had committed the deed and identified the direction they had gone. *Bohokishi Biyé* and *Quinani* followed the trail for eighty miles, arrived at a hogan that had three of the stolen horses in the corral, "slowly dismounted, and tied their mounts in the shade of a large piñon, singing a little song so that the occupants of the hogan would know visitors were approaching." Inside, the two trackers found the thieves who admitted to the deed and willingly returned to Hubbell's post, where they were handed over to the law. Adams concludes the account by saying, "White men could never have sorted out the original tangled mass of footprints in the first place, nor could the white sheriffs and their deputies have been able to track their quarry over a distance of almost eighty miles. They [the thieves/murderers] had not counted on Lorenzo, who thought like a Navajo." Hall, as a well-respected academic, offers no doubt as to the truthfulness of these events.[68]

Life at a trading post during the first part of the twentieth century was filled with challenges—perhaps more so for the women than the men. Yet in spite of isolation, disease, physical danger, differing cultural values, environmental hardships, and economic pressures, the Indian trader and his wife weathered the storms and, for the most part, enjoyed this very different way of living. Because of these challenges, a couple had to depend on each other, strengthening their marital bonds. No doubt there were some couples who shattered. The same was true of customer relations, where those traders who remained on the reservation to work grew in admiration for, and friendship with, the Navajo people, forming close-knit relationships. There are relatively few traders who did not conclude their accounts—even though there were difficulties—with a positive attitude toward both the lifestyle and the people with whom they shared it.

CHAPTER NINE

Beginning Relationships

Early Posts along the San Juan, 1878–1900

As the San Juan River winds its way from the mountains of Colorado through the high desert of New Mexico, its course approaches the Four Corners Monument, where Colorado, New Mexico, Utah, and Arizona meet. The next stretch of river, known generally as the Lower San Juan, passes through gray, tan, and white sandstone formations, rolling hills, and wide floodplains before it drops through the dramatic red cliffs of the Mexican Hat and Goosenecks area on its way to the Colorado River, now contained by Lake Powell. Attached to this perennial water system is a network of large canyons with intermittent flows, dependent on spring runoff from melting snows in the mountains and summer and fall rainstorms. Equally important is the ability of these canyons to make travel possible through an otherwise impossible jumble of mesas, plateaus, rock barriers, and deep incisions in the land. At the mouth of each of these canyons, where they dump streambed materials, there is usually a gravelly bottom that serves as a fording site across an otherwise silty mire. Thus, water and access have made feasible human use of this land.

The story of human life in this region goes back through all of the various prehistoric stages of Paleolithic (until 8000 BC), Archaic (until 2000 BC), and Anasazi (1000 BC to AD 1300), as well as the prehistoric and historic periods of the Paiutes, Utes, and Navajos. By the time the Spanish entered the Southwest in serious enough numbers to start colonization (1600s), the Utes, Navajos, and Paiutes were well entrenched in this region, utilizing its resources as hunters and gatherers. The Spanish brought with them horses, sheep, goats, and cattle, as well as metal tools and different forms of technology that began to change the life and values of American Indians as they encountered new possibilities.[1] The Spanish period, ending in 1821, and the Mexican period, ending in 1848, were tumultuous, riven by intercultural warfare among the tribes as much as against Euro-American forces. By the time Anglo-Americans assumed responsibility for settling the Southwest, many of the Indian peoples were well practiced in resisting any type of external control.[2] This led to further warfare, and, for many of the Navajos, incarceration at Fort Sumner (1864–68), with their subsequent release. Bands of Southern Utes, Paiutes, and groups of Navajos now populated the Four Corners region, in general, and the areas of southwestern Colorado and southeastern Utah, specifically. This high-desert country, which had been hitherto considered wasteland and undesirable for Anglos, became increasingly noticed by those interested in mining, cattle ranching, and limited agriculture. Along with them came their brand of civilization and an insatiable desire to make money.

The territory on the northern part of the Navajo Reservation proved to be particularly challenging because of its distance from the agency at Fort Defiance, Arizona; the rugged canyon country that divided the land; and the lack of geographical knowledge surrounding it. Army doctor Bernard J. Byrne, stationed at Fort Lewis, Colorado, during the 1880s, said it well when he wrote that local folks called this region the "Dark Corner" because "a man makes his own laws there. There ain't no pertection 'cept what a man makes himself. . . . Down in the Dark Corner, if a man kills another man he just steps over to Utah. If he steals a horse in Arizona he slides across to New Mexico."[3] During the same time, Agent Dennis M. Riordan, sitting at the Navajo Agency in Fort Defiance, commented about the problems created by this type of isolation. Referring to the territory beyond reservation boundaries that encompassed primarily northern Arizona and southern Utah, he wrote in his1882 annual report about "a lawless remnant of the Pah Ute Indians and the Navajos affiliating with them." Given the lawlessness of the area, all he could do was "hope that murders of prospectors and others in that heretofore land of death will be less frequent."[4]

A Rough Start: Henry L. Mitchell

During this unsettled era and into this unsettled area came the first trading posts. As the wild side of the Wild West breathed its last gasps, there were those who entered the upper Four Corners region in search of land and opportunity. Settlers—Mormon and non-Mormon (gentile)—found both, but each also paid a price. The earliest posts were simple ad hoc businesses that had potential for raising money in a primary economy based on growing food, raising livestock, and exploiting niches, such as mining or ranching, that could leverage cash from the outside. Navajo industry, with its wool production, blanket weaving, and animal husbandry, fit one of those niches, providing an opportunity for white businesses to capitalize upon the Indians' desire to obtain manufactured products and various foodstuffs.

Central to this nascent experience was the formation of relationships, as new Anglo players entered an arena that had previously been hostile. As these newcomers shined light into the "Dark Corner," the type of experience they often encountered revolved around their ability to understand and adapt to the Navajos, Utes, and Paiutes living there. At a time when disagreements were often discussed over the barrel of a rifle, both sides worked for an advantage. Some people were able to resolve differences peacefully, while others prospered from turmoil. The posts, as a frontier institution, played a significant role where different cultures met and formed friendships or broke into hostility influenced by attitudes emanating from the bullpen. This time of turbulence, colorful and volatile, provided the basis for trading posts whose grassroots expansion developed over the next sixty years.

Peter Shirts, the first recorded settler on the Lower San Juan, was unfazed by potential Indian hostility. In 1877, he built a log cabin at the river's confluence with Montezuma Creek, lived off fish caught in his front yard, and enjoyed the isolation. Earlier, he had been active in the settling of Paiute County and in claiming land in Dolores, Colorado, where he met Henry L. Mitchell, living in Montezuma Valley.[5] In less than a year, Mitchell, who already owned property at the northeastern end of McElmo Canyon, joined Shirts upstream, at the confluence of the San Juan River and McElmo Creek. Mitchell, a cantankerous settler from Missouri, named his settlement Riverview (today's Aneth) and made trade an important part of his livelihood, although he seemed to fail in every aspect of diplomacy. For six years, he created, embellished, and fueled more incidents concerning Indian issues in this area than any other individual.[6] His importance lies in his correspondence and as an individual who serves in direct contrast to other traders living in the area at the same time. Mitchell wrote letter after letter to Indian agents, military commanders, and political personalities, relating—and often exaggerating—conflicts between white settlers and their Indian neighbors. By doing so, he provided a well-documented source of events that explained how he was either directly or indirectly involved with almost every incident with Navajos in this area until his departure in 1884.

Mitchell served in the Civil War, was wounded, and dishonorably discharged, which may explain his penchant for aggression. As early as 1879, he wrote to Utah governor Arthur Thomas, requesting that the territory supply fifty rifles and two hundred rounds of ammunition for each weapon for protection against hostile Utes, Paiutes, and Navajos. The purported reason was to assist the eighteen families living along the river in resisting Navajo demands that the whites leave. The Navajos responded by aggressively herding twenty thousand sheep around the Mitchell household, an act that "cleared away all grass several miles back from the river."[7] Each year saw other claims by Mitchell against the Indians, with a hope that he would receive some type of remuneration from the government.

One of Mitchell's sons, Hernon C. Mitchell, usually referred to as Ernest, appears to have been of a nature similar to his father's, but more interested in prospecting than in farming or operating a trading post. On December 29, 1879, Ernest and his partner, James Merrick, met an advance party of Mormons heading to Montezuma Creek, intent on settling there the next year. The two men invited one of the Mormons, George Hobbs, to join them in a search for silver mines in the Monument Valley area, but he declined.[8] The prospectors moved on to meet their fate. Two months passed and Henry had not heard from his son or Merrick. Mitchell wrote to Navajo agent Galen Eastman, saying that both the Utes and Navajos were acting "sassy" and that if fighting occurred, most of the settlers would be in trouble because the men were out looking for Merrick and Mitchell. However, if nothing happened in the next couple of weeks, there would be two hundred men present to hold out against Indian attacks until soldiers arrived.[9] As February drew to a close, Mitchell's fiery rhetoric grew more urgent. The search party found the two men dead in Monument Valley, adding to the anger and frustration. Following the burial, Henry Mitchell launched into another tirade, claiming that five other men had been killed (although no bodies were found), that the Utes were in league with the Navajos, and that both were equally bad. Eastman sent out representatives to investigate the murders. They returned with word that the guilty party was composed of renegades who were not attached to any agency. A second inquiry by a Navajo and a Mexican named Jesus Alviso confirmed that three or four Indians of Ute-Paiute ancestry, living north of the San Juan, had killed the two miners.[10]

The activities in the spring, summer, and fall of 1881 were not an anomaly. The next year, military forces of various sizes spent time at Riverview, stationing "a detachment of infantry of not less than 25 men to the Lower San Juan River to remain for a month to six weeks to give temporary protection and endeavor to restore confidence to the settlers. An equally important reason was to send an intelligent officer to investigate the trouble arising in that locality and report same to the District Commander."[11] Given Mitchell's penchant for requesting assistance, fostering controversy, and sniffing out an opportunity to sell goods from his trading post shelves to troops stationed nearby, it is not surprising that he had the military at his settlement for five years in a row, until he finally departed.

On April 15, 1884, shots rang out at Mitchell's store. Some transient white men visiting the post killed a Navajo and wounded two others over a misunderstanding. *Ba'álílee*, a local medicine man whose home was approximately four miles east of the post, had gone to the store to trade, accompanied by three other men and two women. One of the Navajos had taken an unloaded rifle and aimed it at a calf outside, then at a boy, then at one of the white customers inside. Another white man saw the move and drew his pistol, believing a threat existed. A Navajo seized the rifle from the one pointing it around, showing it was unloaded. The disarmed man called to Ba'álílee outside, saying, "These Americans are going to kill me." Ba'álílee strode toward the store, gun in hand. The threatened white men drew their weapons and opened fire. The Navajo who had done the pointing died instantly. Sound of gunshots brought Mitchell's son and another man from the nearby fields; upon seeing the problem, one of them fired, hitting Ba'álílee in the forehead, most likely with a ricochet, and knocking him unconscious. The Indians rushed out of the store. The whites followed, firing in all directions and hitting one man in the elbow as he jumped a fence. Caroline Mitchell assisted the two Navajo women trapped in the store to escape out a backdoor. Although they were fired upon while running, neither woman was hit. Ba'álílee revived, then escaped, as did the remaining wounded Indian, who later died.[12]

The Navajos took advantage of the incident to run off twenty-nine horses belonging to Mitchell, who saw it as an opportunity to claim the loss of fifty mounts, recruit twenty-three Colorado cowboys to stay at his establishment, and have a military force stationed there, too. A group of Utes who had pitched camp nearby also joined in, riding four miles upriver to another post to tell two hired hands that a fight had broken out. The men fled the store, providing a wonderful opportunity for the Indians to appropriate an estimated $2,400 worth of supplies.[13] Another fourteen miles upriver, Oen Edgar Noland, who had been ordered to leave, closed up the doors and windows of his post in preparation for a Ute attack.

Six days after the confrontation, Lt. J. F. Kreps arrived with a detachment; one week later Capt. Hiram Ketchum from Fort Lewis descended on Mitchell's store with one company and a month's rations, as did Capt. Allan Smith from Fort Wingate, New Mexico, with three weeks' rations. Once on the scene, all agreed that there was no need for a force of this size and that much of what happened was caused by Mitchell and greatly exaggerated. In the meantime, Kreps learned that the Indians wanted to "kill the white gentile [non-Mormon] settlers," and that the Utes desired plunder, while the Navajos wanted plunder and revenge for the previous shootings.[14] Captain Ketchum discerned the main cause of the problem when he reported "that the Mitchells have not the faculty of preserving friendly relations with the Indians; they are quick tempered, especially the sons. The question naturally arises why should they have trouble with the Navajos and no other San Juan trader, there being several on the river. These other traders have little quarrels and bickerings with the Indians but they manage to settle their affairs without spilling of blood and then sending for troops."[15] By mid-May, Sgt. Christian Soffke, a corporal, and ten privates from B Company, Twenty-second Infantry, received instructions to remain at Mitchell's, create a defensive position from which to "make a stubborn fight" if necessary, and prevent Indians from having access to his position.[16]

The stubborn fight never occurred. Mitchell continued to fuel incidents, many of which increased the profits of his store, but the spring of 1884 dampened his ardor and, by 1885, he had moved back to his ranch at Mitchell Springs, Colorado, approximately thirty-five miles away, at the head of McElmo Canyon, and three miles south of today's Cortez. During May and June of 1884, the San Juan River had washed over its banks and begun gobbling up everything in its path. The river's floodstage peaked on June 18, the torrent carrying everything before it. The water that had attracted Mitchell and other settlers from Colorado gushed over its banks and tore away farms, irrigation systems, homes, trading posts, roads, and any other element of civilization that it could reach. Homesteaders along its course became instantly destitute, with only a small handful having the energy or desire to rebuild. Most packed whatever belongings they had remaining and moved away from this unpredictable tyrant.[17] Henry Mitchell's oldest son, Porter, returned in 1885 to build a post near the first location, but this time higher on the bank, away from the floodplain.

A Different Approach: James L. Davis

In 1879, a year after Henry Mitchell established his post at Riverview, a group of settlers arrived at his doorstep. Twenty-seven men, two women, and eight children composed an advance scouting party for a large contingent of Mormons, over two hundred, who would settle along the San Juan River the following year. The scouting party was to determine the best route for this group to take as well as to locate land in the Montezuma Creek area for settlement. Among this band of travelers were Henry H. Harriman, his wife, Sarah Elizabeth Hobbs Harriman, and four children. The party stayed for a month, built a riprap dam to help Mitchell direct water out of the river and onto his crops, but never succeeded in completing the dam before it washed away—a hint of things to come. They also began building what came to be known as Fort Montezuma, a series of single-room cabins, approximately two miles above the junction of the creek and the river, while continuing to explore the area.[18] The scouting party departed in mid-August, taking a northerly route. They left Harriman and family at Montezuma Creek while sending for a second couple, James L. Davis and his wife, Mary

Elizabeth Fretwell Davis, both in their mid-to-late thirties. Because of health reasons, this family had stopped earlier with their four children at Moenkopi. Now they joined the other family and waited for the main body to arrive the next year, 1880.[19]

James Davis and wife lived a hand-to-mouth existence, but after the arrival of the main party of settlers, they opened a trading post. This operation was small in scale and short-lived, spanning the same period as Mitchell's post. Davis provides a marked contrast in relationships with American Indians to that of his neighbor; he is also representative of other small posts established around the same time. Davis's journal provides an interesting glimpse of life along the San Juan. Shortly after the scouting party left, Navajos, who were very friendly to the new families building homes at the time, warned that, because of the Ute uprising that had killed Agent Nathan C. Meeker, along with ten agency employees and eleven soldiers in Colorado, there would be angry parties of Utes traveling through the country. The Navajos offered to hide the two families, but the settlers decided to stay where they were. The women wanted to flee, the men wanted to prepare, and everyone felt that prayer and divine intervention would be the main thing that kept them alive. That night, the Utes arrived, crossing the river a mile above the newly established homesteads, then continuing on their way to Navajo Mountain, a well-known sanctuary for those in trouble. The Davis and Harriman families were safe.

Davis maintained an open-door policy with all traveling Indians. One time, even though his family was sick, he invited three men on foot to have dinner and spend the night in his home, leaving his loaded gun above the mantle where they slept. Following breakfast, as he bid them farewell, "They did not know how to thank me enough. They had hard work to keep their tears back, they hugged me up and said 'Good friend.' Friends told me I ran more risk with Indians than they would."[20] This same attitude protected Davis during the conflicts at Mitchell's, especially during the killing of the man in the trading post. Navajos came to Davis's post and told him of their intent to kill a white man in revenge for what had happened. Upon hearing this, the trader had the strong impression that what he needed to do was to go into his store and unload his rifle, which he did. Soon a group of Indians (most likely Utes) arrived, acted aggressively, and wanted to know why the store was closed. Davis's son, Ted, who did not want to open the post, argued that these visitors would steal everything; only reluctantly did he do his father's bidding. The warriors were quarrelsome, and Ted kept answering back against his father's wishes:

> One of the Indians was very mad. Ted asked him if he was sick; he thought Ted told him he would make him sick. Many of them think the Mormons talk with the Great Spirit and can make them sick. He drew his gun on Ted, but I jumped in front of him. Ted made for the needle gun but it was gone. The Indians knew I was in the employ of the government as postmaster and had to write out their passes and they were a little afraid I could give them trouble if they hurt me. But I am sure if I had not hidden the gun, Ted would have been killed. I talked to the Indian and he put up his gun, his eyes filled with tears. I told them all to come in the house and I would give them something to eat and talk with them. We parted good friends, but they killed a cowboy and a government scout shortly after.[21]

All through these turbulent years, Davis remained neutral. Soldiers operating in the area were aware of his relationship with both the Navajos and the Utes trading at his store, and so they approached him about talking to Indians on behalf of the military. He insisted that he stay out of the conflict, but assured the soldiers that if they left the Indians alone, peace would prevail. The next morning, Corporal Kelly, a somewhat conceited cavalryman riding a beautiful horse and sporting a pearl-handled pistol, visited with Davis, telling him that he was going to talk with the Indians and, if successful, would get a greatly desired promotion. Davis pointed him in the right direction, then awaited his return. At sunset, a distant figure leading a horse appeared at Davis's post. Corporal Kelly—with a yearling colt in tow, wearing old Indian clothes, and without his pearl-handled pistol—reported he had visited with the Indians. When asked if he had been trading, he retorted, "Trading be damned. They made me trade." No doubt, he received his promotion for bravery.[22]

Not all traders maintained peaceful relationships with their customers. Amasa Barton, a Mormon settler who eventually opened his own post, with dire consequences, told Davis he had noticed how Davis seemed to "make pets of the Indians . . . he just despised them. After

I have done trading with them I want them to clear out," he said. He would never let them in his home or view them on the same "level with white men." Barton eventually died from wounds sustained in a trading-post confrontation. Another store above Riverview, operated by two men named Spencer and Doolittle, also ran into conflict, when Indians raided it, took all of the goods they wanted, then burned the building. Spencer's son, who was running the store at the time, escaped out a window. None of this seemed to affect Davis. While others were moving into nearby Fort Montezuma for protection, he remained at his post. Once, nine Indians showed up at midnight, wanting to know why he was not afraid like all of the other settlers. He told them that he felt there was nothing to be afraid of, that he had treated them well and knew that they would reciprocate. He then invited them inside to get something to eat, while they shook hands and warned him to stay inside his fence where he would be safe.[23]

Another time, a group of Indians traded into the evening, and since it was cold, asked if they could sleep in one of his outbuildings. He let them, but during the night, when the door to the post blew open, the visiting women and children slept inside. The store was well stocked with crackers, cheese, silver ornaments, tobacco, and more, but in the morning, when Davis resumed business, he found that nothing was missing. Yet another time, he fixed an Indian's rifle, using parts from some of his own weapons. The three visiting Native Americans appreciated it, "one of them putting his arms around me and could not express his joy, wanting me to take a nice blanket. Brother Dunton's team got away; they spent some days hunting it, brought it to him, then went and killed a nice fat sheep, all to pay for fixing their gun. We did not charge a cent; they were always our friends after that."[24]

Unified Mormon Efforts: William Hyde and the Bluff Co-op

At the same time Davis was experiencing Navajo friendship, there were others who had similar relations, in the same general area and in stark contrast to Mitchell and Barton. Men like Henry Holyoak and William Hyde, the latter having been officially charged by the Mormon Church to "establish a trading post and depot for the purchase of wool and the sale of supplies to the Navajos. . . . [who] are extensively engaged in wool growing and have no depot in their neighborhood where they can dispose of it."[25] William's son, Ernest B. Hyde, tells of his father's work on the San Juan River in what he termed, "a life of hardship." For four years (1880–84) William maximized trade possibilities near Montezuma Creek. He built a ferry system on a cable to bring Navajos with their wool and blankets across the river to trade. At times, his visitors would leave the boat on the far side, forcing him to send his son, Ernest, to cross partway by hand on the cable, get to its middle, then drop off and swim the rest of the way to the boat. The young man loved to sing and whistle, and so received the Navajo name of "*Tł'éé'jí Hataałii*," or Night Singer. Both Ernest and his father learned to speak the Navajo language and served as interpreters for different groups of white men meeting with these people.[26]

In order to water crops along the river without getting involved in extensive, expensive, and easily destroyed irrigation systems, William built a Noria waterwheel sixteen feet in diameter, with a twelve-foot reach that lifted twenty-three thousand gallons of water an hour into a sluice that fed the ditches.[27] By 1882, there were six such waterwheels along the San Juan, all fastened to the shore, where there was sufficient rock base to provide a stable anchor. In 1884, however, the power of the river proved too great, sweeping all of them away in the flood, along with the homes and land improvements. Half of the homesteads and agricultural lands disappeared in the roiling, muddy deluge. Within a year's time, settlements along this part of the river were abandoned, with only a few people remaining at Riverview, where Porter Mitchell built a new post well above the high-water mark; Hyde established another store above Riverview at a site in Marble Canyon, where he remained for four more years.[28] Francis Hammond, a Mormon leader who lived in Bluff, said of Hyde's work following the 1884 disaster, "He lost all he had in the flood, but with indomitable pluck and energy, he and his family went to work and established a trading post at this very point. The trade consists of wool and goat skins purchased from the Navajo Indians who live just across the river and own immense herds of goats, sheep, and horses. Brother Hyde has put on a good ferry at this point and is doing quite an extensive business, and also doing much good to the Indians through his association with them. He has a good knowledge of their language and is very highly respected by them."[29]

There is no doubt that the most successful Mormon bartering venture on the northern boundary of the Navajo Reservation at this time was the Bluff Co-op, also known at various times in its history as the San Juan Co-operative Company, the San Juan Co-op, and the San Juan Mercantile, Stock Raising, and Manufacturing Company. On April 6, 1880, the main body of Mormon settlers reached Bluff and felt no desire to travel the eighteen miles upriver to Fort Montezuma. Their harrowing six-month adventure through the Hole-in-the-Rock and the canyon country of southeastern Utah had taken its toll and sapped their energies. This spot on the San Juan River was good enough. The settlers divided the land, built a fort of connected cabins, and began a series of individual and cooperative farming projects. After five years, however, it proved to be almost impossible to make a living beyond a hand-to-mouth existence.

In order to raise money to sustain themselves in the broader American economy, the townspeople organized the San Juan Co-op on April 24, 1882—a business that kept its doors open for over forty years. Influential men in the town's Mormon hierarchy composed the first board—Platte D. Lyman, president; Bishop Jens Nielson, vice president; Charles E. Walton, Kumen Jones, and Hyrum Perkins, directors, and Joseph H. Lyman, salesman.[30] Individuals bought shares in the store and then took turns freighting for it in order to pay for materials obtained from Mancos, Durango, and Alamosa, Colorado, in the summer and towns in New Mexico like Gallup and Albuquerque in the winter, since in that direction there was less snow and no mountains to cross. Besides having a larger group of participants to draw upon for operational needs as opposed to a single-family trading post, the store offered a wider variety of goods, spread its wealth in dividend payments in the town, decreased the possibility of competition between individual traders, allowed people to sell their locally manufactured products, and provided employment in the community.[31]

To trace the many fluctuations in the fortunes and misfortunes of the co-op over a lengthy period of time moves well beyond the scope of this chapter. Suffice it to say that there were struggles between individuals and factions within the town. Local and general economic trends, including depressions and recessions, fluctuations in specific markets, and issues over rangelands also affected the success of the operation. On

The San Juan Co-op at Bluff, photographed in 1914 by a member of the Byron Cummings archaeological expedition, served Utes (pictured here), Navajos, local Anglos, and visitors exploring southeastern Utah. Because of its cooperative nature and the involvement of many residents of the town, it was able, on occasion, to return a healthy dividend to its investors. (Courtesy San Juan County Historical Commission.)

the other hand, given the need for a unifying force in the community and the economic problems created by isolation, the co-op generally expanded and achieved entrepreneurial success. Following the first five months of operation, the store paid a 10 percent dividend to its shareholders; from 1887 to 1890 it paid a 40 percent dividend at the end of each of those years.[32] In 1880, the Mormon settlers had begun in Bluff with one thousand head of livestock; in 1887, the store had its own herd of thirty-two thousand cattle, eleven thousand sheep, and a capital stock of $150,000.[33] The leadership had also established strategic outlying operations to maintain control of rangelands obtained from local Utes; diversified its businesses by selling cattle, sheep, tanned hides, wool, and manufactured products to withstand fluctuations in the market; purchased livestock from bankrupt cattle companies and sheep from Navajo neighbors, whose flocks were expanding rapidly; and weathered the storms of some years when the business paid no dividend and was even in arears with the banks of Durango.[34]

Even with all of this varied activity, trade with the Navajos was one of the most important elements of the co-op's business. Shortly after its formation, the store sent wagons to freight supplies from Durango, a terminus of the Denver & Rio Grande Railroad, with the express purpose of "commanding the trade of the Indians who have large quantities of wool, sheep, and goat skins to sell."[35] Two years later, following the disastrous flood of 1884, many people moved away from Bluff, drawing out their invested capital. Those who remained had only seven hundred dollars to keep the store's doors open; by 1893, its value had risen to thirty-one thousand dollars. The reason for its success: "It is estimated that half the profits to the store accrued to the shareholders through trading with Indians."[36] In 1885, Salt Lake's *Deseret News* encouraged others to come to San Juan, where "the Indians in that region are very peaceable, and a great proportion of the trade which the co-operative store at Bluff City receives is from the Navajos."[37]

That same year, because of its success, the co-op hoped to foster related enterprises: "Here, too, is a fine opening for the establishment of a woolen factory, to work up the wool, which is the great product of the Navajo Indians, who are our neighbors just across the river. Some of them own as many as 12,000 to 15,000 head of sheep and goats. The wool can be purchased at the rate of five cents for white and three cents for black wool per pound. Here also the tanning business can be established with profit as the hides and goats-skins are plentiful and cheap, and a shrub called mountain rush, grows in abundance all over the country, which forms a strong substance, full of the tanning principle."[38] Sour dock, a large, yellow root, and an oak extract imported from the

East were added to the tanning process, and although the business never became highly successful, it provides an example of the entrepreneurial spirit of the co-op and its intention to capitalize on trading with the Navajo.

This business was not just a group of white men insensitive to Navajo culture and out to make money. The store followed the same pattern as other posts, doing what it could to foster good trade relations. Albert R. Lyman, born in Bluff in 1880 and intimately familiar with the business, described a number of its operational facets. "On the river's sandy bank, a lumber boat rocked and floated at the end of a rope tied to a sapling. In this doubtful bark, Navajos made thrilling voyages over the rolling quicksand to trade their blankets, wool, pelts, and jewelry to the San Juan Co-op. The L-shaped counter in the little store allowed them a space about eight by twelve feet, and in this narrow area they jostled each other, smoking and laughing, and giggling with the clerk in their high-keyed lingo for higher prices on their wares."[39] Martha Nez, a Navajo elder over one hundred years of age at the time she was interviewed, remembered the boat trip well, saying that she had taken it "many times." This was before 1909, when bridges were built along the Lower San Juan. "When there was a lot of water, [the boat] was the only thing used to cross. Sometimes the river would have sand waves. It was a scary experience crossing over it. The water sloshed against the boat. The water would slop over the edge of the boat. There was a man who floated [rowed] the boat. He used to live close to the boat. His name was *Hastiin Chaanii Yázhí*. Sometimes he was given five dollars for taking people's belongings to the other side."[40]

Another positive element for Navajos trading in Bluff was that there were Mormons who had served as missionaries, spoke the language, and understood the culture. A number of these men had extensive experience working with Indians and held strong friendships among them. Thales H. Haskell, Christian Lingo Christensen, and Kumen Jones were three such individuals, all of whom worked for the co-op during different periods. Kumen Jones's wife also brought good relations to the business. A newspaper of the time reported, "'Aunt Mary' is our good natured clerk in the Co-op store and Indians and whites, alike, are pleased to see her in her old accustomed place behind the counter.

The Indians would rather sell their goat skins, sheep pelts, and blankets to 'Tomskeezy' [most likely *Adzą́ą́ Tsék'izí*—Woman from a Narrow Canyon] than to any other trader on the San Juan River."[41] Lyman also gives a good description of Haskell, who served as a mediator between the Mormon settlers while trading with Navajos and Utes. "He could employ their language to better advantage than the Utes and Navajos themselves, and his superior knowledge, combined with his fearless personal bearing, made him a person of awe and majesty among them." Lyman again wrote, "In the year '89, Haskell clerked in the San Juan Co-op, in which capacity he could not only attract Indian customers, but could find ample time for the laconic declarations and impressive sermonettes he wished to deliver. He could out-Indian the red men themselves, and from his beaded moccasins to the firm lines of his fine old face, they found the tacit dignity which impelled them to concede to him the superiority they otherwise would have assumed in silence for themselves."[42]

Indeed, the preceding descriptions of this early commerce are reminders of the qualities of good traders discussed in previous chapters—speaking the language, understanding the culture, providing convenient transportation, bantering in the bullpen, respecting women traders, and never showing fear.

Violence Begets Violence: Amasa Barton

Not everyone had the skills of Haskell and Jones. In 1883, William Hyde from Montezuma Creek opened a second trading post seven miles below Bluff, with an eye to capturing the Navajo trade crossing the river at the junction of the Chinle and Comb washes. A gravel bottom ford, which in the summer might have only two or three feet of water flowing over it, was an integral part of travel over the two canyons' trails. This made an ideal spot for a store. During high water in the spring and fall, Hyde built a large, flat-bottomed boat with a shallow draft, its dimensions being thirty feet long and twelve feet wide. He attached the craft to a cable that spanned the river. This allowed "the Indians to [ride] with their loads on their ponies, sit there, fifteen to twenty of them at a time to come over."[43] For eighteen months the post and the ferry system operated at this site until the 1884 flood washed it all downstream. Shortly after the waters subsided, William's two sons, Frank and Ernest, went into business with Joseph and Amasa Barton, the latter having married Parthenia Hyde, William's daughter. The newly formed Hyde and Barton Company decided to use the simpler system of an oar-propelled skiff, half the size of the large ferry just lost. They built a new post on a high rock shelf overlooking the river and named the site Rincon. To stock the facility, supplies came in from Santa Fe during the winter months, requiring a round-trip of from six to eight weeks, and from Alamosa, Durango, or Animas, Colorado, during the summer, requiring a two-to-three-week round-trip. A waterwheel assisted their agricultural efforts; the men also owned a flock of sheep and a herd of cattle to extend their trading-post efforts.

Amasa, working the store at Rincon, did not have the temperament suitable to befriending Indian customers. Large in stature, physically powerful, and quick to anger, he was a trader destined for trouble. It came on June 9, 1887, when a Navajo named "Bad Eye" or "Old Eye" visited the post with a friend. He was well known to the Hydes, since he worked for them on Amasa's farm next to the post. That morning, the two Navajos ate breakfast with the Bartons, then went to the post for business. Bad Eye wanted to retrieve some jewelry that his wife had pawned, and offered an old pistol in exchange, asking for a reduced price. An argument ensued, Barton ordered the men out of the store, then stooped beneath the counter and stepped into the bullpen, allowing Bad Eye to cast a rope around his neck and begin choking him. A wrestling match ensued, the unnamed Indian drew a pistol and shot at the wrestling pair, hitting Bad Eye, who soon died. He next shot Barton in the head, went out to see how his friend was doing, then returned to the store and placed a second round in the trader's brain. Parthenia, her mother-in-law, and the children watched the episode unfold, as the dead Navajo was loaded into the skiff, and the assailant departed. She sent for help, but before it arrived, five other Indians had plundered the store, as the women helplessly watched. On June 16, Amasa died from his painful wounds.[44] Shortly after, a band of sixty Navajos came to Bluff, ready for a fight. Diplomacy on both sides averted further bloodshed, and the incident came to a close. The traders soon abandoned the Rincon site, although it would reopen a few years later for a short time.[45]

Mormon Trading Advantages

What can be understood from the foregoing examples of the early trading-post experience along the Lower San Juan River? There are a half-dozen points that can be drawn from what might appear at first as random incidents involving a variety of personalities. The first is to understand the importance of the landscape in determining the location of posts. Water drew traders to the banks of the Lower San Juan, its floodplain appeared to make agriculture profitable, boats made it practical when water was high, canyon systems channelized the traffic, gravel-fed fording points allowed low-water access, and both summer- and winter-accessible supply depots made feasible the restocking of goods. Another prominent point is that of relationships (*k'é*) with both Ute and Navajo customers. The Mitchell and Davis experiences—at the same time and place—underscore how both Indian groups did all they could to run off Mitchell's livestock, besiege his store, and take every opportunity to get even for the events that occurred at his post, while the same Navajos and Utes were warning Davis to remain in certain places for safety and to listen to their warnings if something bad was about to occur. This also happened to other settlers who had made friends and treated the Indians fairly. There was safety in friendship.

Parallel to these relations with the Indians was a third point—one that is found in other parts of the Southwest at the same time—the cohesive nature of Mormon traders in forming a network of support and economic stability. Just as the San Juan Co-op did not compete, but actually supported the efforts of the Hydes and other Mormons trading with the Navajos, similar arrangements are found in the Farmington/Fruitland area, the Gallup and Albuquerque region, and in settlements along the Little Colorado River, virtually any place a group of Mormons trading with American Indians was found. This is not to suggest that there was not competition between individuals, families, or groups, but only that there was more often a network of assistance that had non-Mormon traders complaining and competing.[46] This connectedness suggests a fourth point, which is that they had more investment capital and the ability to try different ventures to provide stability to the overall operation. Every trader faced the issue of obtaining products that could be sold in the larger economy and that would encourage stability in sales.

The San Juan Co-op is an excellent example of a group using its expertise to diversify its business, allowing it to not be solely dependent upon sheep, wool, and associated products. That is why the co-op maintained their own flocks and herds, started a tanning business, built boats during a short-lived gold rush, marketed dairy and agricultural products in Colorado towns, sold lumber, assisted in processing Church tithing, and generally maintained a viable economy in Bluff, one in which the townspeople not only participated but benefited as shareholders. Compare this with Mitchell's activity of encouraging conflict and then selling supplies to soldiers as his means of "diversifying."

Another point is the benefit in having people who spoke the Navajo and Ute languages, understood the culture, and appreciated their customers. The Haskells and the Joneses had the abilities and qualities to maintain positive relationships, whereas Amasa Barton paid with his life and other traders not in tune with their clientele almost did as well. A sixth, somewhat unique part of this trading experience is the role the San Juan River played. On May 17, 1884, Chester A. Arthur, through an executive order, extended the northern limit of the Navajo Reservation to the river. Well before that official act, Navajos were bringing their wares across to trading posts in sufficient amounts that every store had its own boat during the high-water seasons of the year. Literature about trading posts seldom mentions that, until bridges began to span these rivers, boats were an important part of the travel experience for Navajos in this area—the only means to get their products across the water to their point of sales. This was also true of stores in New Mexico along the San Juan River. We have seen how the river was both a blessing and a curse, drawing people in a desert environment to a constant source of water, while at another time, wiping out through a flood every vestige of man's work upon the land.

Problems with Off-Reservation Posts

The final point, and one that needs to be further discussed, is that all of these posts were off the reservation and so the government exercised little, if any, control. In the earliest years of off-reservation stores in southeastern Utah, there were few people in the area, communication was slow, agency influence minimal, and the number of Navajos with their flocks relatively small compared with future growth. As the land became settled, resources more utilized, and interaction between American Indians and settlers more intense, there was greater potential for conflict. All of the controls exercised by agents—approving goods and prices, receiving letters of reference, ensuring the trader had a ten thousand dollar bond, and keeping him under continual scrutiny—were not in effect. As Agent D. M. Riordan complained in 1883, "the Indians are persistently encouraged to leave the reservation by the small traders living around the country surrounding the reserve. These men generally treat the Indians pleasantly and the Indians listen to them. It is 'business' pure and simple with the trader."[47]

Agents did what they could to curb the desire to leave the reservation as well as to control the trade, but met without much success. The plight of Agent E. H. Plummer in 1893 provides an example, this one centering around ferries and trade. The initial spark occurred on April 5, at the Riverview post operated by brothers James F. and William W. Daugherty. The store sported a ferry that ran across the river, with a suspended cable to maintain control. Two Navajo men commandeered the boat and set off for the south shore, but William, fearing they would swamp it, called them back. They refused. He then fired two shots in front of the craft, which forced them to return. Soon the angry men reappeared with a group of thirty warriors to back up their demand for two hundred dollars in exchange for not burning the store. Since the five white men at the post were heavily outnumbered, they paid the money and sent for the agent. A few days later, one of the Navajos, encouraged by some alcohol, decided to burn the crib that supported the cable on the far bank of the river and then threatened to kill William. By the time Plummer arrived, tempers were so heated on both sides that only the suggestion of introducing cavalry calmed the Navajos. Eventually, the two guilty Indians surrendered and went to Fort Defiance to stand trial in the tribal Court of Indian Offense.[48]

The incident prompted a series of letters between Plummer and the commissioner of Indian Affairs that brings into focus the controversy surrounding trading posts on the San Juan. The agent pointed out that the ferries were used to haul wool across the river, serving as magnets to the Indian population. He recommended that ferries run by posts either be licensed or forbidden to operate, depending on the owner's reliability.

The Aneth trading post, circa 1890 here, illustrates many of the qualities associated with an off-reservation store. The business had numerous owners and a steady flow of Navajo and Ute customers. It served as an agent for change, was involved in sporadic violence, and promoted economic activity. It remains today as a convenience store and the oldest continuing business in San Juan County, Utah. (Courtesy San Juan County Historical Commission.)

Those licensed stores would carry goods sold at cost, plus transportation and clerk hire; the wool, hides, and so forth bought from Indians would be sold by the agent or clerk in charge; and the traders who carried three thousand dollars worth of goods would be bonded at ten thousand dollars and receive a salary of two thousand dollars per year. This plan, therefore, allowed substantial savings for the Indians.[49]

Acting Commissioner M. Armstrong did not like the idea. He felt that the ferries were not detrimental to peace or the Navajos' welfare, because the Indians, he argued, should have "the widest latitude in bartering and trading" and should be able to bring their produce and articles to the nearest town to sell. Plummer responded that he was not suggesting the Navajos' freedom be curtailed, but that he wanted to foster the development of "responsible, reliable, worthy traders" and avoid the "unlicensed, unlimited and unregulated' commerce that encouraged "illegal traffic, too much freedom to unauthorized roaming over the country north of the river for illegitimate purposes, ready access to gamblers who infest the north bank of the river at this season of the year, when the Indians have money from the sale of wool or other products."

Plummer then explained that he knew of Indians who left the reservation with money, pony, rifle, and goods but returned shortly after with only a G-string, having fallen into the clutches of the professional gambler. He concluded by saying:

> The theory of Indians having the widest latitude in bartering and trading is excellent or would be if all traders were honest or the Indians competent to protect themselves and understand their rights in trading. But where a trader offers a drink of intoxicating liquor for every sack of wool brought to his store or allows his ferry to be used for transporting liquor, while blankets worth from ten to forty dollars are bought by traders for from two to ten dollars; silver belts worth fifty dollars pawned for fifteen to twenty dollars are sold when opportunity offers; while the reservation is surrounded by traders and gamblers who are reaping profits of thousands of dollars annually at the expense of poor, half-starving, ignorant Indians, I must continue to believe that a somewhat more limited regulated freedom in trading facilities would be more beneficial.[50]

Thus the agent had a far different, and perhaps more realistic, perception of the problem than did the commissioner in Washington.

There were other sources of conflict. As Navajos gravitated toward the boundaries of their reservation to trade, they also brought with them large holdings of livestock—always in search of grass. While traders anxiously purchased wool and hides, those Anglos in the livestock industry viewed Indian animals as direct competitors to their own livestock. In 1878, Mitchell and other non-Mormon settlers lodged a complaint against the Navajos and their twenty thousand sheep, which during the previous ten months had ranged along the San Juan and its back country.[51] During 1881, one settler reported two Navajo herds, one of which numbered six thousand sheep, grazing far beyond the river.[52] Two years later, ranchers complained that the Navajos "crossed with their countless herds of sheep and goats, and from the San Juan to the Blue Mountains—north 40 miles—they eat every particle of vegetation . . . causing great suffering and loss among livestock belonging to the Mormons." In another two years, a similar letter, signed by twenty-three men from Bluff, requested that Navajo herds of sheep and horses be removed from the north side of the river since they were "crossing in great numbers onto our stock range and doing us great damage by way of eating up our grass and crowding our stock off of our range."[53] Similar complaints arose often throughout the remainder of the 1880s and 1890s and into the twentieth century.

Yet another source of conflict occurred over the hunting of game. Navajos, Utes, and Paiutes from southeastern Utah and southwestern Colorado began preying on the deer herds, taking an ever-increasing toll of animals.[54] The first of three annual hunts started in 1884, with an estimated three hundred Indians killing deer by the hundreds and drifting thousands of others south and east to the La Sal Mountains. According to one Anglo report, there were so many carcasses left rotting that cattle and horses would no longer range in those areas.[55] The drives of 1885 and 1886 added more fuel to the fires of resentment that continued to smolder in subsequent years. A petition signed by sixty-four men from McElmo Canyon complained that the Indians would not allow the whites to kill game, while reports claimed that more than two hundred Utes, "armed to the teeth," were hunting in the Blue and La Sal Mountains.[56] Each spring and summer saw additional groups of Indians setting out for the hunt. One party returned in July with "lots of buckskins"; another forty people set out in August with seventy-five to one hundred horses to help pack the meat and hides back home. At the same time, eighty Utes went north and killed over two hundred deer. Many of these animals were fawns whose skin sold for twenty-five cents each. Only a tenth of the meat was taken. White settlers again complained bitterly about this wanton destruction.[57]

In December 1889, the military sent 2d. Lt. George Williams to Blue Mountain to investigate. Although Williams saw no Indian hunters, he estimated that two hundred to three hundred Navajos and Utes had been hunting there but had returned to their reservations. These Indians, he reported, had "killed a good many deer as is shown by the number of hides they have sold to the trader."[58] The twelve families living in Monticello, at the base of the mountain, reported that the Utes hunted for hides and meat, the Navajos primarily for hides. The trader, Mons Peterson, felt the latter sold more green hides than the Utes because of superior horses and hunting techniques. Many of the cowmen complained that with all of the Indians chasing through the woods, the livestock had grown wild and harder to herd.

Indian accounts of the number of deer killed are sketchy, but they do exist. In the fall of 1890, Old Mexican, a Navajo man from the Montezuma Creek–Aneth area, tells of hunting with a group of relatives on Blue Mountain for thirty-three days, during which time they killed a total of seventy bucks and does. A few days after his return home, he left again with a party of three. They hunted only for skins and killed sixty-seven more animals. He personally had twenty-two hides, twelve of which he sold to a trader at fifty cents apiece. Ten years later, he could have sold two hides at the Aneth post for $7.00, but chose to sell them at Crystal, New Mexico, farther inside the reservation, for $30.75.[59] Left Handed provides another example. When he hunted with a party of eleven men over a week's time, the group killed seventy-one animals. At that point, the leader said it was time to stop because the men were getting tired. Sometime later, Left Handed and three other men hunted for nine days and killed sixteen deer. The leader of this party, when asked how long they would hunt, replied, "It all depends on how the deer will be. If we can't get anything, then we'll just turn around and come back. If we kill some, and we keep on killing some, then we'll stay until we think we can't get anymore."[60] By the early 1900s, reports of overhunting began to dwindle, as did the deer herds.

Hunting for hides-only was not an accepted practice in traditional Navajo and Ute teachings. Both cultures had spiritual laws regarding the taking of game, but they did not address the issues raised by a foreign capitalist system. The sanctions applied in a traditional setting were spiritual but not focused on herd reproduction and maintenance. Hunting solely for hides was an outgrowth of an economy that provided desirable goods in exchange for materials the market demanded. Traders accepted whatever sold and were not necessarily concerned about what took place beyond the confines of their post.

The early days of trading posts in the upper Four Corners region were part of the last days of the nineteenth-century West. Changing social and cultural patterns; the intensification of the market system; the growing dependence and desire for manufactured and processed goods; the fluctuations of an economy controlled by regional, national, and world events; the shifting boundaries of an expanding Navajo reservation accompanied by white settlement of heretofore open lands; the shenanigans of unprincipled Indians and whites alike; the lack of government control and oversight; and the fickleness of human nature all added to the unrest during the waning years of this century. In many instances, trading posts were either at the point of, or at least involved in, the resulting conflict. As a system of commerce, it was, for the most part, individualized and highly dependent upon the personality of those involved in it. Strong personalities often led to strong measures. With the twentieth century dawning over the Southwest, conflict diminished and more harmonious relations reigned. The golden age of the trading post was beginning.

CHAPTER TEN

A Different View at the Posts

Ute and Navajo Trade, 1880–1940

Often overlooked as customers in the posts of the upper Four Corners between 1880 and 1940 were the Utes and Paiutes. Before discussing the golden days of Navajo trading (1900–1940), the reader is asked to move from the Navajo experience to that of these culturally different yet important participants who frequented the posts and shared the trade with their neighbors. A quick view of Ute trading highlights a somewhat different set of expectations emanating from the bullpen. The presence of these Indians contributed significantly to the economy of the traders and added to the colorful history of this era.

Without exception, all of the posts in this region served both peoples, yet little is said about the Utes for two reasons. The first is that they never developed their herds of goats and sheep to the extent that the Navajos did, keeping their flocks relatively small. Posts buying wool from the Utes received comparatively little, while Navajo offerings were substantial. The Utes also did not weave rugs, make silver jewelry, or raise large numbers of lambs for sale. In short, they had less to offer the mainstream American economy. Tanned buckskins, woven baskets, and beadwork sold well in the tourist trade, but the volume of production was low. The second point is that the Navajo, as a people and culture, captured the imagination of the tourist industry, whereas the Utes had few advocates promoting their history or lifestyle. With extensive marketing available to the Navajos—tour guides working in a dramatic landscape, the Harvey Houses associated with the Santa Fe Railroad, and the bright, colorful products that sold themselves through fine craftsmanship and national promotion schemes—these American Indians attracted far more attention.

Historic Roots and Comparative Trade Relations

In spite of the steady interest in trading with Navajos, the Utes and Paiutes have a long history of exchanging products with their neighbors—Navajo and Anglo alike. Friendly relations after the Long Walk period grew through trade, marriage, and shared proximity. The Paiutes of Monument Valley and Navajo Mountain received horses and ceremonial services in exchange for baskets and buckskins. They viewed Navajos as people with strong supernatural healing powers and so had them perform various curing rites. Fred Yazzie remembers his father conducting ceremonies and healing the sick. "Lots of Paiutes said my father's ceremonies were real and got well from them. . . . In this way we had gotten to know them."[1] Paiutes also herded sheep, carded and spun wool, cared for Navajo gardens, and performed general chores. They traveled back and forth to Blue Mountain, although "their horses were usually skinny with sores on them."[2]

The Utes played a somewhat different role. Slim Benally remembers trading with the Utes in Bluff, Montezuma Creek, and Aneth. "They used to ride among the Navajo, bartering for sheep, corn, and other kinds of food and paying in money."[3] Ella Sakizzie, as a young girl, participated in Ute Bear Dances under the cottonwood trees at Ira Hatch's trading post in Montezuma Canyon and often saw Utes and Navajos gambling in card games. "I used to see them ride their horses carrying bundles of long sumac stems tied to their saddles behind them. I did not know what they were for back then, but now I make baskets out of them, too."[4] Centenarian Maimi Howard remembers Navajos and Utes calling each other by kinship terms: "They used to live together in the same place and they loved each other. . . . They shared their knowledge with others. They got together for the Enemy Way Ceremony and made the ceremony work easier. They were very good at it, too."[5] And trader Alan Whitmer estimated that Navajos hired by Utes may have performed as much as half of the herding of Ute livestock, especially sheep, in the later years.[6]

Like the trading-post experience of the Navajos, the Utes visited all of the trading posts in southeastern Utah and southwestern Colorado, and in some instances were the primary clientele. The proliferation of posts between 1880 and 1940 was in part due to the fact that the Utes and

Paiutes frequented these establishments, especially so in the later years, when they were able to buy more with money as well as trade goods, whereas the Navajos depended more on barter. Both clientele traded in Bluff, Montezuma Creek, Hatch, Ismay, Monticello, Blanding, Allen Canyon, Aneth, McElmo, Four Corners, Tanner Mesa, Mancos Creek, Towaoc, Cortez, Mexican Hat, Monument Valley, Oljato, Kayenta, Navajo Mountain, and elsewhere. Many of these posts were on reservation edges, where they could avoid the stricter government regulations required of those on Indian land. Each store depended on the whims of the mainstream economy and, characteristically, had a large turnover of proprietors with a convoluted history of ownership. Strategically located to capture the flow of customers traveling along trails, visiting a source of water, or grazing livestock, most posts sprang from the land to meet a need. The number of clientele they served varied—the Bluff trading post operated by Frank Hyde served 65 Utes and 950 adult Navajos, only half of whom lived within a sixty-mile radius; the Hatch trading post in Montezuma Canyon serviced 23 Navajos and 22 Ute camps because of its closer proximity to the Ute Mountain Ute Reservation; the post at Towaoc served almost entirely Ute customers.[7]

When comparing the trade experience with Utes and Paiutes to that with the Navajos, there is a mixed review, many traders having varied but definite opinions. Parley Oscar Hurst, after forty-three years of running a store in Blanding, had no doubt as to whom he trusted—and that was the Utes. "There was many a time when one came in that I had to leave him alone in the store. If it was a Navajo, I didn't dare leave. I could just say to a Ute, 'You look after it until I get back.' The Ute has a personality that is different from a Navajo. They're more jovial and can see a joke."[8] Frank Pyle, a trader with the Ute Mountain Utes, allowed those who traveled long distances by horse or wagon to sleep in the post's bullpen overnight, with much of the store's merchandise unsecured. He never lost a thing.[9] Ira Hatch agreed that the Utes were generally trustworthy, while his brother, Stewart, who worked in the Allen Canyon post, did not see much of a difference between them and the Navajos.[10]

On the other hand, Alan Whitmer felt the Utes, as a people, were more aggressive.[11] Ray Hunt also fell into this camp. He tells of moving to Bluff with his father in 1919 and having to learn "ways of buying that I was not accustomed to" because he was used to working with the Navajos." The things they bought were similar to those bought by the Navajos, but they were "loud and over-bearing at times." His father, John, "knocked one Ute down because he wanted to come in back of the counter and took him to the floor and grabbed him by the heels and dragged him out. Then people said, 'We knew very well we shouldn't have sold this store [San Juan Co-op] to you; you should not treat people like that.' My father said, 'All you have to do is give me my money back. I didn't want the damn place anyway, but as long as I own it, I am going to run it.'"[12] Perhaps the best way to summarize these varying opinions is to accept the *Cortez Sentinel*'s statement: "The Indian as a rule is as conservative a buyer as the white man and he can be depended upon to pay his bills just about as well as does his pale face brother. A great amount of credit is extended the tribes by the posts and very few accounts are lost."[13]

Some posts serving primarily Navajos used tokens to keep their clientele tied to a particular store, but those trading mostly with Utes did not generally use them. When pawning became necessary, the Utes offered some colorful items. Earle Forrest described the pawn he encountered in the backroom of the Billy Meadows post in 1902:

> Before we went to bed, the trader showed me the finest collection of beaded buckskin clothing and war bonnets I have ever seen. There were coats, vests, moccasins, and buckskin and red flannel chaps or full-length leggings, all covered with colored beads, dyed porcupine quills, and long fringe. The finest coat in the collection was decorated with scalp locks of enemies killed in battle, and the buckskin leggings with it adorned with long fringe and scalp locks, evidence that the owner had been a great warrior in his day. All this material had been pawned, and when the Indians wanted it for some dance or festive occasion, they borrowed it, just as the Navajos borrowed the pawned medicine basket from Billy Meadows.[14]

Stewart Hatch provided a second example of how pawning with the Utes worked, which also illustrated mutual respect. The Ute Baby Deer entered the Allen Canyon post and approached Stewart's brother, Joe Hatch, about releasing his pawned .22 rifle, then in hock for two or three dollars. Joe agreed and also gave Baby Deer ammunition. In three hours the hunter was back. He returned the rifle and the box of bullets with one missing, gave a choice piece of deer meat to the trader, and went home with the rest of the deboned meat wrapped in the hide.[15]

The ethnographic scene in a trading post—where two cultures met to barter—provides additional insight into the values of the participants. While some traders felt there was little variance between the Navajos and Utes during exchanges, others indicate a difference.[16] Trading for both store owner and Utes was leisurely, each customer purchasing one item at a time, then resting. Some store owners, however, found Ute trade more direct. A husband and wife would enter the post, bring their items to the counter, and work together with the trader to reach a satisfactory price. If there were no products to sell and it was necessary to pawn an item, then the couple might discuss what to do before deciding, whereas Navajo ownership was more individualized. On the other hand, an eyewitness account of Ute trading given by John Q. Cannon in 1895 makes the Ute approach very comparable to that of the Navajo:

> In the Monticello store I had an illustration of the Indian manner of trading. Their sole medium of exchange seemed to be buckskins, of which each family of purchasers had a goodly number lying in a heap at their feet or in a sack upon which they kept vigilant watch. The trading was done principally by the squaws and the white man's side of the negotiations was certainly a test of patience. The native woman would produce one skin at a time, which the storekeeper spread out upon the counter, examining it for bullet holes or knife cuts, after which—perhaps taking the additional precaution to weigh it—he would indicate by a show of fingers how much he was willing to pay. If the figure was acceptable, the squaw pushed the skin out of her way and proceeded to specify the various articles she wanted in exchange. These consisted nearly always of a small supply of tobacco, a scoopful of flour, two or three yards of bright-colored calico, ten or fifteen cents worth of sugar, etc., until the storekeeper signified her capital was exhausted; whereupon the counter would be cleared off; the purchaser placing her parcels in her pack, the merchant tossing his buckskin under the counter. Then the former would produce another buckskin and exactly the same procedure would be repeated, the buyer investing in precisely the same goods and to the

> same amount of quantity. Thus at the end of the transaction—which usually required the better part of half a day for each purchase—the storekeeper would have all her buckskins and she would have perhaps a dozen pieces of the same kind of calico, a dozen little parcels of flour and sugar and tobacco, etc., in like proportion. There was no use trying to hurry her or force upon her anything that she did not want, nor would any success have attended the effort to induce her to trade in two or more buckskins at once.[17]

While some traders spoke both Ute and Navajo, and a few traders only Ute, the Navajo language was the lingua franca when broken English would not suffice. Even in gambling or transactions solely between Navajos and Utes, the Navajo language prevailed. Alan Whitmer, who traded with both groups, estimated that 75 percent of the older Utes he knew spoke Navajo, but he did not know of many Navajos who spoke Ute.[18] Trader Ray Hunt agreed, saying that he never bothered to learn Ute because "all the old time Utes spoke Navajo."[19] There was, however, some Ute vocabulary that entered in at different times. For example, the Navajos classified money by its appearance, so that a penny was a "red," nickel a "yellow," and a dime a "blue." For the Utes, a dime was "*pavoqa-r*" (shiny), a nickel "*tupwí-ker*" (rock), a penny "*aká-tupwí-ker*" (red rock), fifty cents "*türágwako*" (at middle—i.e., half-dollar), and a dollar "*suíspanáqar*," or one shiny metal. Whenever they requested an item in English, the patron tacked on the word "mont" after it, as in "coffee–mont" and "shoes–mont." Most likely this is the Ute pronunciation of "want," as they understood what was said in English.[20]

Depending on the period of history, buckskin, beads, baskets, and later, wool and sheep hides were the primary objects of trade. As government per-capita payments from land settlements became available, cash took on a greater role as a medium of exchange. Because the Navajos did not receive individual payments, they retained much more of a barter system until they entered the wage economy, beginning in the 1940s and 1950s. As money and barter mixed, the Utes often separated the two in their transactions. They purchased food with money, but when baskets or deerhides went to the trader, their value bought clothing or other hard goods. For instance, in the Allen Canyon post, "They did not pay their [food] bill with baskets. Maybe he [Ute customer] could get a new pair of Levis or a shirt. . . . Navajos always bought Pendleton shawls, but the Utes wanted a thinner, different type, made back East. The Ute shawl was altogether different than the Navajo shawls. They were really colorful, which the Utes really liked."[21]

The women were deliberate in their purchase of cloth to make dresses. They selected four yards of soft, colorful cloth. According to Stewart Hatch, four yards was immutable. "That is exactly what it took to make a dress, two in the front and two in the back. I sold a lady four yards of cloth and in a little while she came back into the store wearing a dress she had just pinned together with safety pins. It was always four yards of cloth, which held true when we [Hatches] were in Towaoc, too."[22] Once they were ready to sew the dress, the garment came together quickly.

Ute women developed a high level of craftsmanship in beadwork. Traders evaluated their products in a systematic way, just as Navajo woven blankets were scrutinized for certain qualities. The smaller cut-glass beads had sharper angles that reflected light and could be more closely sewn together than the rounded seed beads. Purchased in large hanks by the traders, then broken into smaller amounts for sale, the beads added color to a variety of objects. Everything from cradleboards, belts, moccasins, purses, pants, shirts, and dresses to rabbit's feet acquired unique Ute artistry. If the beadwork were sewn on hand-tanned hides, as opposed to commercially tanned, the value of the object increased. The Utes used many of these articles for themselves; however, the rabbit's feet were strictly for white men who wanted good luck. The people of Allen Canyon made hundreds of these key-chain fobs, each with an individualized beaded pattern, then strung them, a dozen to a cord, to sell to the trader who, in turn, moved them to the general economy.[23]

Early Trader to the Utes: Oen Edgar Noland

Rather than sift through a myriad of names of the men and women staffing these posts, one can look at Oen Edgar Noland as an example of one of the most successful traders to the Utes as well as the Navajos. Noland's interaction with these people spanned over forty years. His activities illustrate the concern he had and the variety of ways in which he was able to serve them while maintaining positive relations. Born September 25, 1852, in Independence, Missouri, he arrived in Colorado in 1873 to work in the mining camps and as a freighter. In 1882, he took out a loan of ten thousand dollars to open a post on the San Juan River, with the understanding that he would sign over a life insurance policy of thirty-five thousand dollars as collateral. One of the lenders, Pete Schifferer, warned, "The Utes and Navvies are bad; that region is Hell's own backyard," to which Noland replied, "I'm going down there to be a trader, not a hired gun buzzard after bounty scalps."[24] Noland proudly wrote in his personal history: "Within two years I had it [the debt] all clear."[25]

He first established a post in Riverview (today's Aneth) which he allowed his father-in-law, Henry L. Mitchell, to operate. He started his own post around the same time, eighteen miles upstream and two miles below the Four Corners Monument. His store, known as either the Four Corners trading post or simply Noland's, remained open for thirty years. Soon after establishing this site, he married Caroline (Callie) Mitchell, Henry's daughter, which gave Ed his Navajo name of Bidoni (*Baadaaní*), or Son-in-Law. He had five children by her before she died in 1895. Seven years later, he married Lolla Kutch, owned a home in Mancos, hired people to alternate with him behind the counters in the Four Corners and Navajo Springs (1895) trading posts, and was considered "the best equipped of any man on the border to carry on an Indian trading post . . . [since] he has the confidence of the entire tribe [of Utes]."[26] As a trader, he provides a classic example of a man devoted to both his Ute and Navajo clientele.

Noland first built a trading post of logs roughly a mile below the Four Corners Monument in 1883, but it was swept away by the river in 1884. Next, he selected a spot a mile downstream on a raised shelf near Cowboy Wash, giving fordable access to future customers coming from every direction. He made this second post a sturdier structure of rocks quarried from the sandstone formation to the west and on the banks of the San Juan River. Today, remains of the store still stand as impressive evidence of a once-flourishing trade. For example, the length of the western wall, the stem of this L-shaped configuration, is 117 feet long, with walls 2 feet thick and 10 to 11 feet high, while the short stem is 65 feet in length. The long stem, or western end, held the trading post and storage space, while the shorter stem had living quarters. Eight large windows dot the walls, with firing ports in places where there are no

The Four Corners Trading Post, most likely photographed in the late 1890s, was a very large, prosperous facility located beside the San Juan River. O. E. Noland constructed the building from rock quarried nearby, had large corrals for livestock, planted extensive gardens and fruit trees watered by the river, and used a lengthy network of roads and trails to encourage travelers visiting from all four states. (Courtesy Utah State Historical Society.)

doors or windows to see outside. Adobe covered the interior and still remains in the three fireplaces that heated the spacious rooms where he, his wife and children, and guests stayed. Interlopers have long since removed the large cottonwood beams that held a thick layer of compacted dirt as roofing material.

Adjoining the post stands a rock building, a residence for hired help to stay in, while the remnants of a corral with a large rubble mound to the north, possibly the ruins of a former tack room and blacksmith shop, mark the outer periphery of the site. Old hole-in-the-top food cans that contained meat, vegetables, or liquids lie scattered and rusting in sand near a weathered trash pile. The trail, called the "old Mormon road to Bluff" over which these goods once traveled is vaguely etched on parts of Cowboy Wash and the hills pointing in the direction of Mancos.[27] Much of the road used to parallel the river where Noland, and those who followed him, farmed extensively and planted a large orchard of fruit trees. Trader Stewart Hatch shared his father's recollections when he visited the post while it was in operation: "My dad said it was kind of like an oasis in the desert. He said you could get grain for your horses and people camped there going different ways and that trading post had hay and colts for sale and corn and whatever they needed that way traveling by. It was a pretty nice place and then during the 1911 flood, it took his [irrigation] ditch out and all of that land. Not an apple tree left or nothing."[28]

The history of Noland's store is just as interesting as the ruins left untouched by the river. In 1884, when Henry Mitchell had a confrontation at Noland's post in Riverview, Oen felt the reverberations eighteen miles upriver. When the Riverview post was supposedly besieged and Indians robbed a smaller store in Marble Wash run by Spencer,[29] Noland was ordered by the Utes to vacate the premises. Instead, he battened down the hatches and made ready to resist an attack. The Navajos also took advantage of the opportunity and "borrowed" five horses, which Noland feared would be ridden to death or never returned. Some of the miscreants later brought back three of the animals, promised to restore the remaining two, and said that livestock belonging to Mitchell would also be turned over to Noland, who served as an intermediary between the disgruntled factions. At the same time, Noland reported that he had bought supplies pilfered by the Utes from Spencer's store. D. M. Riordan, the Navajos' agent at Fort Defiance, bemoaned the fact that the Indians dealt with men who purchased known stolen goods. He went on to say, "I do not see what can be expected from Indians who get their only moral training with such men."[30] This evaluation of Noland was too hasty and does not reflect the general tenor of his dealings with Utes and Navajos.

Other posts arose along the San Juan River. In 1885, Peter Guillet, another Missourian, operated a store owned by Noland near McElmo Creek, working for him for a year before his brother, Herman Guilett, arrived, and together they purchased the place in 1886.[31]

Life at Noland's Four Corners post was in many respects similar to that at other posts that dotted the San Juan. Fortunately, because of the prominence of this store, there is sufficient information to paint an interesting picture of what life was like in the early days. During the summer, Noland brought his family from Mancos to spend time in this isolated setting. In other seasons, he came alone to give the men he had working behind the counters a two-week break and a chance to get away. In 1892, a group of archaeologists passing through the area noted that three men, two women, and two children staffed the store. At least one of Noland's sons, Edgar, was born there, and at one point, Noland even hired a schoolteacher to provide an education for the youngsters.[32]

This post was also noted for its livestock. One day a man with a hundred horses arrived at the store and asked to sell them. Noland jumped at the opportunity and bought the herd for twelve hundred dollars, letting them graze on the wide floodplain along the river. As the animals became accustomed to their freedom, they also became increasingly difficult to round up and corral, so Noland decided that he would sell them to one of his former trading-post employees, Benjamin Alfred "Al" Wetherill, brother to John and Richard. Al and his partner thought capturing horses looked like easy money until they tried. A usual method required keeping them away from waterholes until the animals became desperate with thirst and more tractable. The technique did not work in this instance because of the accessibility of the San Juan and the unrestrained room to roam through the canyons and over the grasslands. After a week of tiring and difficult work, Wetherill and company had only four horses to show for their efforts. Noland's herd was now a wild, free-for-all pack of horses, noted for their good qualities but difficult to catch.[33]

Over twenty years after Noland left the Four Corners post in 1895, a man named Yabani, "one of the most thrifty and prosperous Navajo Indians," visited him in Mancos. The trader asked him where he had gotten such a fine team of horses, to which the Navajo openly admitted that he had stolen a beautiful stallion that had belonged to Noland's herd. The Indian confessed that, even though he was a good friend of the trader, he had decided to take the best horse and use it to sire his future herd. Noland thought the incident humorous.[34] Wetherill, a somewhat inexperienced trader at the time, recalled another incident when tending store during the owner's two-week absence. A Navajo came in and asked to see a blanket he had pawned, took it outside, and, before the trader reached the door, the Indian was riding away. A few days later, when the culprit returned, Wetherill approached him with gun in hand, yanked the blanket from beneath the saddle, and started back to the store. A group of spectators threw the trader down, hid his rifle behind a tree, and unsuccessfully tried to explain that the white man did not understand the situation. Since Wetherill's Navajo language was none too good at the time, he waited for a few days until the "thief" returned and paid the required price. When Noland came back, the Navajos told him that he had employed "one crazy fellow at the store."[35]

That same "crazy fellow" told of when he rowed a group of Navajos in a skiff across the river while it was in flood stage. After dropping his customers off, he heard them yelling that they had left their indigo dye on the store counter. Wetherill retrieved it but was tired of fighting the sand waves and current in the boat. Since the river was too wide to throw the dye across, he slipped out of his clothes, tied the package around his neck, and did the Australian crawl through the swirling brown water to deliver the goods. The Indians were impressed with the new stroke, so that every time after, when they saw Wetherill, they waved their arms wildly over their heads in imitation.[36] Another time, Ben's brother, Richard, and companions arrived at the store after a hot, tiring trip across the desert at the base of the Carrizo Mountains. When they reached Noland's, they relaxed in the cool interior of the post, drank from the bucket on the counter, then spied a large pile of watermelons in the corner. One of the men could not resist having a second and third melon, but as he continued on his way to Colorado, nature took its revenge with such viciousness the group hired a wagon for him to complete the arduous journey.[37]

Starting in 1893, severe economic troubles surfaced along the San Juan. Drought, cold spring temperatures, and early frosts ruined Navajo crops, while a national economic depression decreased opportunities to sell goods. In 1895, Agent Constant Williams reported: "The poverty of the Navajo was so great that all of the trading posts along the San Juan River were closed except for Noland's store and Noland reported that he had no trade because the Navajos had nothing to sell."[38] That same year, he sold his stock to Arthur J. Ames and Jesse V. West, but maintained ownership of the building, beginning a typical series of transfers played out here as in many other posts of the Four Corners region. Three years later, West sold his share to John Scott, who now worked with Ames. The *Montezuma Journal* recognized this new partnership by noting that they will "continue the trading business at the old stand at Four Corners and will feed the hungry, clothe the naked, and comfort the sick and blind."[39] A year later, however, Ames left the post to Scott, who in August of 1902 turned over his inventory to Robert J. Bryce, who in 1908 sold it to Joseph A. Heffernan. Although he was the current owner of a post in Aneth (previously Riverview), Heffernan purchased this second building from Noland in 1908.

During this time, a presidential executive order in 1905 made this portion of Utah land north of the San Juan River part of the reservation. Heffernan failed to file for legal title to the property, although the executive order recognized the right of previously established settlements to do so.[40] Oblivious to this legal procedure which soon became an issue, Heffernan hired Charles Fritz to act as trader at the Four Corners post, while he managed his other holding downstream. Fritz was not a newcomer to the region. As early as 1900, the *Montezuma Journal* referred to him as "an old time San Juaner whom we worked with on the San Juan way back in the '80s, trading with Navajos and old Hatch's band of Utes."[41]

For about a year everything went well, but in November, 1909 tragedy struck. A husky Navajo man named Zhonne (*Nizhóní* or Beautiful), member of the *Tó dích'íinii* (Bitter Water People) clan, visited the store. He had been travelling and was now hungry, so he decided to stop at the post to get something to eat. His statement of what follows, attested to by three white men and three Navajos, explains in detail what happened next. Fritz gave his visitor some food, then the two men brought in some kindling for the fire, and the trader set to work sharpening a saw. As Zhonne stood by the stove, he decided, for no particular reason, to kill and rob his benefactor. He went outside, made sure no one was coming, obtained his .22 caliber rifle from his horse, and shot the trader as he reentered the store with more wood. A round in the back of the head, then two more, ensured Fritz was dead. The Navajo cleaned out the trading post's cash drawer ($22.15) along with some silver buttons ($18.35) and some pawned jewelry ($12.00), all of which added up to slightly over $50, then rode to his home west of Teec Nos Pos, twenty miles away. Agent William T. Shelton, trader M. R. Butler, and Government Farmer W. O. Hodgeson met at the post the next day and sent three Navajo policemen to track down and bring in the killer. They located him herding sheep near his hogan, much of the loot buried in a nearby corral. The men also found a perfect match with the tracks of moccasins and horse hooves left at the scene of the crime. After initial denial, a detailed confession followed.[42]

Three points derived from this incident. The first underscored the vulnerability of a lone trader in an isolated post. This killing followed a standard pattern, mentioned previously, for crimes involving posts on the Navajo Reservation. Underlying the incident was not hostility toward the trader but rather the simple motivation of greed. The second point raised was what court should have jurisdiction—federal or state. Technically, the post still sat on lands excluded from reservation status because it had been built before the executive order that added lands in the Aneth area. Zhonne eventually stood trial in the U.S. district court in Salt Lake City, facing the charge of manslaughter. The court allowed this lesser plea instead of first-degree murder because "he is afflicted with an incurable tubercular infection of the throat which physicians declare will cut his life short within two years at most." He received an eight-and-a-half-year sentence in the federal prison at Fort Leavenworth, Kansas.[43]

For those hoping to see justice in full measure, disappointment lay ahead. As Marshall L. H. Smyth transferred Zhonne to Leavenworth, the prisoner showed the officer a feather "that was dear to his heart" and that he kept under his hatband. The guards at the penitentiary were not impressed, "snatching the feather from Zhonne's hat" whereupon "the Indian let out a yell that could be heard for a half a mile. At the earnest solicitation of Mr. Smyth, the men returned the feather to the Navajo, making him once more happy. Mr. Smyth says the physical condition of the Indian is pitiful and he doubts if he will live over a few months."[44] What Smyth and the guards failed to understand was the power of that feather. In traditional Navajo teachings that hearken back to the time of creation, the Warrior Twins, Monster Slayer and Born for Water, carried "life feathers" that protected them from many different types of harm.[45] Zhonne took his to prison, and three years later, sought parole, which apparently was granted. As for his sickness, there is no doubt: "His case yielded to treatment and he says he has now entirely recovered his health . . . and it is probable if the Indian is worthy, he will be given aid [to return home]."[46]

Thus is found the third point to be drawn from this incident: the Navajo version of what happened. Harvey Oliver, a Navajo elder, talked to Zhonne, whose other name was Long Slender Hair (*Tsii'agod Tsosi*), about the occurrence. He recalled, years later, that Zhonne and another man had been chasing horses all that day of the incident and had become hungry. They went to the post and encountered Fritz, whose Navajo name was "White Man's Song." According to Zhonne, Fritz had refused to feed them and would not accept credit or any type of future payment; he told the men to leave, prodded them with his rifle to get out, and otherwise threatened them until a scuffle broke out. Zhonne choked, then shot the trader, got something to eat, took what he wanted, and left. When Zhonne returned home following imprisonment, the community gave him the name of "Killed a White Man" (*Bilagáana yiyisxį*), while the store received the title of "Place Where a White Man Was Killed" (*Bilagáana sesxinídi'*).[47] Although the accounts differ, each side painting a picture most favorable to their perspective, there is no doubt that the incident had a significant impact, supplying the opening chimes of the death knell for the Four Corners trading post. Heffernan next sold his Aneth post and moved to this store, but to no avail. The Navajos avoided it because of the murder, fearing that the spirit of the deceased might be present. A massive flood in 1911 washed out the road south of the river and swept the floodplain where the traders had grown their crops. In the meantime, the establishment of a post at Teec Nos Pos and continued growth of the Aneth store drew away much of the trade.[48] By 1912, the store's doors had closed for the last time.

At this point, Noland was no longer associated with the Four Corners post. Even as the economy in 1896 was on the mend and life returning to normal, he had others taking care of the post so that he could begin an operation at Navajo Springs, the site of the new Ute Mountain Ute Agency in southwestern Colorado. This store remained open for twenty-three years (1918), until the government relocated the agency a few miles to the north at its present site of Towaoc. More abundant water, cooler temperatures, and proximity to the resources of Sleeping Ute Mountain, known to the Utes as Wee-so-gar-um (Soapweed Mountain), provided the impetus for the move. Noland loved and served the Ute people well. He and Ignacio, leader of the Ute Mountain Utes, became fast friends. Noland introduced a system by which each Indian customer had his own book. In regard to this system, he wrote, "When Ignacio came to the agency at Navajo Springs he brought five hundred dollars and gave it to me to keep for him. I entered it in his book. A row of ten ciphers—0000000000—represented $10.00. He had five squares of 100 ciphers and when he drew money, which was generally five, ten, or twenty dollars, I marked out the ciphers in his book and in mine. That way, he kept all of his accounts. (He once drew 100 dollars and bought 100 head of sheep.)"[49]

The Utes reciprocated with fairness. At one point, they owed Noland eighteen thousand dollars in charged materials. The government had failed to pay them for an entire year, but the following year, it paid them once in April and again in July. As soon as they had their money, they paid their debt.[50] Noland felt strongly that the Utes were honest people who needed to be protected against scheming white men. He was their advocate with the government, encouraging the agents to work harder on getting irrigation water for the reservation, while affirming that the Indians would be more than willing to prepare and plant the land if they had something to work with. He accompanied the Ute delegation to Washington, D.C., when deliberations to make Mesa Verde a national park were underway. At the same time, he worked to get crooked agents out of the Indian Service.[51]

As discussed previously with the traders to the Navajos, personal relations in the form of fairness, honesty, and respect were just as important to the Utes. Traders became not only a bridge to the outside world, but also representatives of that part of Anglo culture that cared. In Noland's brief life history of a little more than seven pages, he took one full page to discuss Agent Joseph O. Smith, who was in charge of the Southern Ute Agency at the turn of the century. Smith and three of his comrades wanted to skim money from the Ute payroll by keeping six thousand dollars belonging to two Indians who had died, but planned to report the money as having been paid. Noland was to keep his mouth shut. That night the trader, Ignacio, and a large group of Indians confronted the four men and demanded the money. During the ensuing argument, "one of them attempted to pull a gun but I pulled mine first." They handed the money over, two of the men leaving the area at two o'clock in the morning and never returning to the agency. Another time, the same agent, who owed Noland fifty dollars, dropped off four thousand pounds of Indian flour in payment. The trader would not accept it, and had Smith return and remove what should have been issued to his charges.[52]

Later, the Utes again proved faithful to their friend when a man spent some time stalking Noland in his store, intending to rob him. As the

Oen Edgar Noland (1852–1935) exemplifies the trader who was friend to Navajos and Utes, conversant in both languages, a profitable post owner, and a man able to span the days of rough frontier life into the twentieth-century business world. Most notable was the devotion and care he rendered to his Indian friends. (Courtesy Family Search.)

thief watched his prey, the Utes watched him, then told the trader to beware. When the adversary finally entered the post, Noland told him he had better not try anything because the Indians were ready to kill him. "He left and took a trail out of the country that was difficult and hard to travel, but kept him away from the post."[53]

Noland never tired helping his Indian friends. In 1900, he sold the Utes more flour and clothing than the government issued, while advocating that the reservation system take much better care of its charges. Newspapers reported that Noland and Joe Smith "are looked upon by them [Utes] as being their only friends," even though the reporter insisted the "Navajo Springs Utes are a better dispositioned [*sic*] people than the same number of whites would be under similar circumstances, else they would have long been on the warpath."[54] Two years later, Noland rescued eleven children on their way to the school at Fort Lewis. They had left Navajo Springs Agency crammed into a wagon with no blankets, food, or bedding for this mid-December trip, moving at a rate of twenty miles per day. After spending a frigid night around a fire in a clump of piñon trees, the children arrived in Mancos, where Noland learned of their situation, took them out to eat, and paid their train fare for the remainder of the journey.[55] And during the last illness of his friend, he again showed he cared. "Ignacio had a house about a half mile above me," the trader wrote in his journal, "and when he got sick and knew he was going to die, he came down and asked if he could put up a tarpaulin on the corral at one end of the trading post. He did this because he knew that if he died in his house, the Indians would burn everything there. He stayed at the store until he died. My sons, Frank and Edgar, built a coffin and gave him a suit of clothes. That night the Indians took his body away and buried him."[56]

A few more examples of Noland's treatment of the Indians show why they trusted and loved him. Just as he taught them how to keep their own records, he performed a similar practice at ration time, when he sold the cattle he had bought from the Indians to the agency. All the meat was cleaned, carefully divided, and distributed in fair shares. Finally, Lolla, his wife, recalled that one Christmas, as she was putting the final touches on a massive dinner for a house full of guests, Oen asked if she had enough food for eighteen Utes "dressed up in their feathers and blankets, beautiful reds and everything," with their horses tied along his fence in front of the house in Mancos. She emphatically said, "No," which set him in motion. He went to the store and prepared food baskets with bread and other assorted goods, canned meat and peaches and tomatoes, coffee, and sweet syrup. Then he set up sawhorses with planks for tables surrounded with chairs and stools in the backyard. "They had the biggest Christmas that anybody ever heard of. Everything under the sun. They were just tickled to death," right down to the last cookie.[57]

Noland's later years were bittersweet. He had become a wealthy man through his acquisition of the Bauer Mercantile, whose volume of business at the start was $60,000 a year. Seven years later, in 1909, he sold his assets, which had increased to $250,000; when added to his trading, banking interests, and other businesses, he had the financial means to live very comfortably.[58] The same year he had achieved this success, an itinerant gambler, Marion M. Baker, following a brief argument, shot the unsuspecting, unarmed Noland four times, hitting him in the chest, neck, and above the left eye, with another round grazing his right eye. He survived, but was blind for the rest of his life. The town was irate, but when the Navajos and Utes heard of what happened they put their anger into action. Lolla remembered, "They got the word at Navajo Springs, that's where our store was, and it just went through that Indian section that Bidonny had been shot. Well they came to Mancos but the man had run and hid . . . he knew they were going to mob him if they ever caught him. . . . [The townspeople found Baker and brought him to Cortez.] The Indians went to Cortez and made a raid down there on the jail but they had guards; they knew what would happen if they let him alone and wouldn't let the Indians get a hold of this Baker."[59] He eventually stood trial, received a light sentence for assault and battery, escaped from jail, so never fulfilled the remainder of his brief sentence. As for Noland, he lived the rest of his life as a respected community member, dying in 1935 at the age of eighty-eight.[60]

Later Ute Trading Posts: Mancos Creek and Allen Canyon

The story of the Mancos Creek trading post adds yet another dimension to the economic experience of the Utes. Its history starts with Frank Pyle, who first moved to Montezuma County, Colorado, to homestead. He soon took a job as a Bureau of Indian Affairs (BIA) stockman for the Ute Mountain Ute Tribe, but when drought struck the region in 1918, the government liquidated the cattle herd. Pyle bought his own livestock and leased land from the tribe for grazing. Then, in 1920, he purchased Joe Tanner's post "a dugout in the rocks" atop Tanner Mesa, where he and Jim Belmear sold goods in the winter as his herd grazed nearby.[61] To improve business, around 1923, Pyle moved his store to the place where the old road from Cortez to Shiprock crossed the Mancos River, approximately two-and-a-half miles west of where today's highway crosses the Mancos River. Here, he had stone masons (Harry Baxstrom and a Mr. Black) build a two-story trading post from locally quarried rock. In 1925, the interior of the structure burned, but Pyle used the same stone walls, replaced the roof and floor, and continued his business, "handling lots of Indian cattle." In 1928, he sold his holdings to two men, Dan Tice and Cord Bowen, who soon sold it to Sam Walker and John Claflin from Cortez.[62]

In 1932, the Great Depression forced Pyle back to the Ute Reservation to trade, but according to the government, he owed back pay for a grazing lease. Pyle insisted he had paid but that the agent had pocketed the funds. When the government denied his license, Pyle bought an off-reservation business from Lewis Ismay, where he traded until 1947. He was good friends with the Utes, spoke their language, and, on a number of occasions served as an advisor to the tribal council. He also helped to obtain funds for them by leasing lands for grazing and oil development. There is every indication that he was an upright individual, respected by those he worked with. Indeed, Frank McNitt, in his classic study, *The Indian Traders*, pays this high compliment: "When he retired from trading, Pyle continued to live at Towaoc, giving all of his active time to the interests of the tribe. Since Thomas Keams, perhaps only one other trader—Emmet Wirt—worked as hard and unselfishly for the Indians."[63]

What follows is not an attempt to besmirch Frank Pyle's reputation, but rather to illustrate the intensity of the internecine warfare waged by some traders over limited resources. As with the Navajo trade discussed previously, personality, economy, and competition contributed to the fray. The Ute Mountain Ute Reservation comprises 553,000 acres of land compared with the Navajo Reservation, which covers over 27,000 square miles. Beyond the official trading post located with U.S. government and tribal offices at Towaoc, the Mancos Creek trading post was the only other store on the reservation during the 1930s. Frank Pyle established the Ute Trading Company near the northern reservation boundary, just outside of Cortez, while there were businesses in this town that also purchased Ute products. Cattle and cash from oil royalties and land settlements and, in the 1930s, herds of sheep with their lambs and wool made business transactions with these Indians appealing and competitive. At the same time, there were a lot fewer people on the Ute Reservation, a much smaller land base to operate on, and a substantial market to contend for. Between 1932 and 1935, Samuel G. Walker of Cortez provided a litany of complaints that illustrate just how heated the competition could become.

In 1932, when Walker bought the Mancos Creek trading post on the southern end of the reservation, he attracted Ute and Navajo customers. The next year, the complaints began. According to Walker, government personnel at Towaoc, a subagency of the main headquarters of the Southern Ute Agency at Ignacio, were under the control of a clique of people who responded to the wishes of Mexicans holding influential business positions. For instance, Leo R. Chisholm, farm agent, played favorites in business decisions; Agent D. H. Wattson "is small calibered, lacks executive ability, and . . . lacks backbone and the quality to show them who is boss." But Walker saved his biggest gripe for Frank Pyle and his store. He accused Pyle of flaunting agent instructions by operating on the reservation and purchasing wool at Ute family camps; of buying three hundred Navajo ewes that were then grazing on Ute reservation land; of obtaining other livestock that were not supposed to be sold but kept for breeding purposes; of paying unfair prices; of enticing customers away from Walker, who had extended credit during the depth of the depression and now needed to be reimbursed; and of traveling to the agency on payday to secure funds individuals owed him. All Walker wanted, he moaned, was "a man capable of investigating my charges."[64]

The next year was no better. Walker accused Pyle of making false promises to encourage the Utes to bring him their wool in exchange for extensive credit, while Agent Wattson had directed that the two licensed traders on the reservation could not extend any more credit. "This act together with Pyle's propaganda just ruined us," Walker claimed. "The Utes owed us heavy accounts and knowing we could not grant them further credit, willingly fell for Pyle's talk. We offered them five cents [per pound?] for their lambs last fall on their accounts; we obtained very few. Pyle received practically all of the lambs. This spring we offered them thirty cents for their wool to clean up these accounts and we obtained 3,500 pounds, but only received nineteen cents for the wool showing a big loss."[65] Pyle was responsible for getting the remaining 20,000 pounds of wool and 1,000 to 1,500 lambs, "which worked a hardship on me [Walker] and also caused me considerable loss." A year later (1935), Walker was out of the trading business and into a grocery market in Cortez, having sold his holdings to Cole McGee and family, who operated the old store until around 1938. They then moved their business to the new Highway 666 location, abandoning the former post.[66]

Walker finally got what he asked for—"a man capable of investigating [his] charges." Belatedly, the National Committee of Indian Affairs, headquartered in New York, sent a field agent to explore how substantive Walker's claims were. In brief, the investigator exonerated Agent

Wattson and Farm Agent Chisholm of any wrongdoing, and had substantial proof that Walker had actually been buying breeding stock from the Ute herds, a practice that had officially been forbidden. He also went out to the shearing camps and took wool from the Indians without any type of control on price and quantity as part of his collection of debts. The government was supposed to have been involved in transporting the wool to the point of sale and ensuring fair prices, but as the field investigator noted, "It is the business of the trader to collect his own debts in a legal manner. There are few traders within our knowledge who have not lost considerable sums at one time in bad debts with Indians."[67] Apparently, few local people had anything good to say about Walker, while agents and locals alike accepted Frank Pyle as an even-handed businessman.[68] In fairness to Walker, he faced stiff competition and had some very real concerns. From the Walker–Pyle confrontation comes a clearer understanding of the types of issues that arose in a reservation trade environment with the Utes of southwestern Colorado.

A different example of trade with a Ute clientele at the same time in history is provided by the experience of Joe and Stewart Hatch, who, in 1931, at the request of these people, established a trading post on the boundary of Ute allotted lands in southeastern Utah. Located approximately ten miles in a straight-line distance to the west of Blanding, Allen Canyon in 1923 became the area where the government assigned White Mesa Utes to live. The people requested that Joe Hatch, who had been trading in Montezuma Creek, establish a post in order to buy their products as well as provide additional supplies that E. Z. Black, who was in charge of the subagency did not issue. The store remained open for ten years, until much of the activity in the area ceased. Built on Bureau of Land Management (BLM) land by Joseph Hatch Sr., Joseph Jr., and an Indian work crew, this post followed the same pattern as the 1926 Hatch trading post in Montezuma Canyon, which also served Utes and Navajos in that area.[69] Constructed of trimmed cedar posts, chinked with mud and sunk three feet into the ground, the store had a flat roof made of boards covered with six inches of soil. The building had two rooms—the business area and a sleeping quarters/kitchen. The bullpen boasted a fitted sandstone floor, a potbellied stove squatting in the center, and benches lining the periphery. One long wooden counter stretched most of the building's width, with shelves behind it to hold food and hardware. Located next to the road, the post became an important feature in the life of the residents of Allen Canyon between 1931 and 1941.

Joe Hatch Jr. acted as proprietor. Representing the third generation of a family of traders who had bartered on both Navajo and Ute reservations, he was well aware of what it took to keep customers happy. On the shelves sat canned goods—corned beef, Vienna sausages, peaches, pears, creamed-style corn, regular corn, and string beans. Large, one-hundred-pound sacks of sugar and flour, containers of salt pork and bacon, cases of Arbuckles' Coffee, bolts of cloth—the brighter the better—were stacked next to the cans or under the counter, with a scale at the end to weigh purchases. Each customer had his or her own account kept on a paper bag on which Joe tallied the items until he ran out of room. Very little credit needed to be extended, since his Ute customers received monthly payments from Ignacio. Joe and their agent, E. Z. Black, worked together with them to keep careful track of expenses.

Outside of the store was a place for sacking wool, which was usually purchased in the spring, as well as a shade in which to store the seven-foot-long burlap bags. Once three or four of the bags accumulated, a pickup hauled them to the Montezuma Canyon post, manned by Joe's brother, Ira. A fenced canyon provided forty acres for grazing sheep, mostly wethers, which Joe bought in the fall, at an average of thirty head per family. He developed a spring close to the store so that there was plenty of water, kept a small flock of chickens to keep the bugs down and the snakes away, built a guest hogan for travelers, made a sweat lodge for himself, and created a large flat area in front of the post for Allen Canyon residents to play games, park their wagons, and tie the horses.

People from Blanding, Ignacio, the Midwest Oil Company, and San Juan County, in general, pooled resources in 1926 to make travel easier for ever-increasing automobile and truck traffic.[70] Men from the Ute community pitched in to maintain the road system, a constant task. E. Z. recorded in his "Monthly Time Book" that he employed twenty-six men, whose work totaled 217 days of labor in March 1933, at a daily rate of two dollars a day.[71] As the road improved, a small customer base of tourists headed toward Natural Bridges National Monument, and the road was used as well by workers from the Midwest Oil Company, who were developing an oil field near the Bears Ears. Both brought business to the post. But the primary flow of traffic through the store's door was Ute and Navajo visitors.

What then passed across the counter from the bullpen to the trader? In addition to the wool and sheep already mentioned, there were products for which the White Mesa–Allen Canyon residents are still famous—baskets and beadwork. Baskets were particularly profitable. In his 1925 annual report, Agent E. E. McKean wrote, "The Indians of Ute Mountain and of the Polk and Posey Band manufacture more beadwork and baskets than any other. For these they find ready sellers and are able to provide considerable food supplies and clothing for their families."[72] E. Z. Black encouraged the industry, and the women of Allen Canyon rose to the occasion. Collecting sumac at places like Hammond Canyon, Elk Ridge, Cottonwood Wash, Montezuma Creek, San Juan River, and Comb Ridge, the weavers went to work and became some of the most successful basket makers in the Four Corners area. Just how successful, Black described in 1937, when he reported that the goal of having twenty-six women each weave twenty-five baskets in a year's time was surpassed twofold. Instead of the anticipated 650 baskets they wove 1,200. He then cited John and Tazhunie Dutchie as a "source of inspiration to all their Pah-Ute relatives and also to the white people of that territory." They were not on the annuity roll and so she made baskets and he did beadwork for their income. In addition to harvesting the sumac that often grew a long distance from Allen Canyon, there was also the peeling, splitting, curing, and dying of the materials, all of which took seven days. E. Z. estimated that if "a woman can make ten baskets in forty days, averaging $2.50 per basket, the income for forty day's hard work would be $22.50. During the past year Tazhunie has woven 109 baskets."[73]

Another popular exchange item was deerskin. Hatch believed that few other people had mastered the technique of tanning hides as well as the Utes had. Every camp in Allen Canyon had a hide-processing area. When a hunter killed a deer, he removed the meat from the bones, and piled the bones along with the antlers in one place for animals to eat. He skinned the deer completely, leaving the skin of the head and the tail attached, wrapped the meat in the hide, and brought it home. He then placed the green hide in a pit, with moistened cedar ashes on the fur side, and left it buried for a while. The tanner later removed the skin and placed the still-wet hide on a pole a foot in diameter, leaned it against a tree, and with a rock or knife scrapped the fur that now came off easily. The tanner worked the hide before putting it back in the hole and burying it again. Later, the processor removed it and rubbed it with either deer or sheep brains; then, as the final stage, he rubbed the skin with white clay to remove any smell and brighten the finished product. All of the hides sold at the trading post had the tail and face, with fur, on the hide; there could be no knife cuts, if it were to be used for Navajo ceremonials. Joe bought these skins for eight to twelve dollars and sold them for twelve to eighteen. He was always able to move his inventory quickly.[74]

Allen Canyon folks also found time for recreation. Two favorite events—horse racing and card playing—involved gambling. Racetracks, a couple hundred yards to a quarter-mile long, were located in a variety of settings, one of which was along Cottonwood Wash west of the trading post. Stella Eyetoo recalled how spectators sat on the rocks and watched two, and no more than four, riders race to a finish line at the south end of the flat. Nearby was "Under the Cottonwood Tree," where others bet on their favorite horsemen, while trying their hand at cards—usually Monte, also known as "Squaw Poker." Joe Hatch showed up to sell candy, cookies, and canned goods out of the back of his pickup.[75]

Without doubt, the biggest community event was the Bear Dance, occurring once in the spring and again in the fall after hunting season. While the ceremony and dance were performed at Towaoc, White Mesa, Montezuma Creek, and elsewhere, residents of Allen Canyon have particularly fond memories of those events held at the site one hundred yards west of the trading post. A flat, cleared area embraced by the flanks of a hill held the brush enclosure, or "Cave of Sticks." Annie Cantsee remembers Utes coming on horseback and Navajos in wagons to attend the three- or four-day festivity, with twenty-five people dancing at a time. Utes from Montezuma Creek and Towaoc, as well as a few families from Ignacio and White Rocks, also attended.[76] Stewart Hatch estimated that as many as five hundred may have participated, although this figure seems high.

The post was a major sponsor of the activity. The store donated canned goods, two or three lambs, a hundred pounds of flour, shortening, and lard for bread, as well as stocking more perishables than usual.

Joe Hatch (*second from right*) outside his "stockade style" Allen Canyon trading post that served primarily Utes from 1931 to 1941. Built mainly with native materials taken from the site and Ute labor, this building had a bullpen and counters as well as a room where the traders lived. (Courtesy Stewart Hatch.)

Cinnamon rolls were a fast snack, but particularly popular were the large bunches of bananas removed from crates and suspended on a roof beam in the post. The bananas sold at ten cents apiece; customers cut off what they wanted and paid at the counter. Perhaps this is how Joe Hatch received his Ute name of "Weece Neece," Weece being Ute for "banana," while the meaning of "neece" is unknown. To the Navajos, Joe was "*Jok Nez*," or Tall Joe. The post also became the destination for white visitors who wished to attend the Bear Dance. When CCC Company 3241, which was stationed in Blanding, held a barracks inspection and Barracks Number Six won, the government transported two truckloads of young men to the dance. "The boys who went enjoyed the ceremonies very much, something that an Easterner hears about but seldom sees." The same occurred in June 1940, when ninety CCC men in three Grazing Service trucks attended the event. For all concerned, it was a chance to make new acquaintances, while for the traders, it meant more business.[77]

Trading posts serving the Utes of the upper Four Corners provide an often ignored, but colorful page in history. Exchanging with both Navajo and Ute clientele, store owners enjoyed two different cultures and stocked a variety of products unique to each. While there were cultural differences between the two groups, they also shared many similarities—the lingua franca of Navajo, seasonal sales, pawn and credit extension, dependence on personal relationships, interest in similar store products, and a comparable environment for trade. There were also distinct differences in cultural expectations, arts and crafts, scale of sales, and lack or predominance of money. But in both instances, it was the relationships established across the counter that provided either success or failure for the traders and their customers.

CHAPTER ELEVEN

Posts as Economic Exciters

The Heyday of Navajo Trade, 1900–1935

Between 1900 and 1935, Navajo trading posts, both on and off the reservation, reached their height of activity. While the government made a conscious effort to collect and monitor data for those stores on the reservation, even their statistics are more like estimates of economic viability. There is little numerical data for the off-reservation posts at this time, and yet they, too, prospered and struggled just as their on-reservation counterparts did. A few snapshots taken at fifteen-year increments tell part of the story. In 1900, there were an estimated 401,882 sheep and goats on the Navajo Reservation; in 1915, the number jumped to 1,819,000; in 1931, with the effects of stock reduction and the Great Depression already having their impact, there were 1,370,554; four years later, the number declined to 944,910.[1]

Fluctuations in the market place caused by national events such as World War I and the Great Depression shifted demands for wool, hides, meat, and crafts, affecting what occurred at the counter. As anthropologists Garrick and Roberta Bailey noted,

> It is not surprising that when wool prices rose at the outbreak of World War I, the production of rugs declined. In 1918 the Navajos marketed only $316,643 in rugs. After the war, the price of wool fell to an average of 17.3 cents per pound, slightly more than its prewar value, while rug production increased rapidly, peaking at about $700,000 in 1920, approximately its prewar level. The market value of wool recovered somewhat by 1923 and remained relatively high through the late 1920s, but never approached wartime levels. Rug production declined

gradually during the mid- and late 1920s, and before the depression Navajos were marketing about $400,000 in rugs each year.[2]

While there can be no doubt as to the importance of these "bread-and-butter" industries for both the traders and their Navajo customers, there are yet other things to consider. The trading post in any Navajo community served as one of the central hubs around which economic activities and many aspects of local society revolved. These stores, depending on their location, resources, surrounding demographics, and community power structure, characteristically expanded opportunities for development. The heyday of this institution proved it to be an economic "exciter," fostering growth in a wide variety of ways. This chapter provides a number of examples of just how far-ranging a store's involvement could be. While not all of the activities at the posts in the upper Four Corners are presented, enough is shared to give an idea of the breadth and depth, success and failure, good and bad that occurred because of this economic institution.

Promoting Anglo Cultural Values: Case Study—The Aneth Post

The Aneth trading post provides a prime example of a store destined to foment change and to promote the desire for American goods. The *Mancos Times* in 1897, and again in 1898, reported how Buck Ames and John Scott sent word across the Navajo Reservation, and as far away as Zuni, inviting everyone to two days of festivities at the Aneth post. To attract large numbers, the traders provided 6,000 pounds of flour, 500 pounds of coffee, 500 pounds of sugar, as well as prizes ranging as high as $125 for the games—"horse races, foot races, squaw races, chicken pulls, and games of all kinds that filled up a day of strange experiences for the forty white spectators who were there." The Indians responded. Over 1,200 came, bringing "herds of ponies, cattle, and sheep and quantities of blankets."[3]

Wage Labor and Competition

Less dramatic but inexorable promotion of Anglo-American values lay in the future. In 1899, James M. Holley bought the Aneth post. Unlike many of the earlier traders, Holley took a great interest in not only developing the store as a center for the Navajo community but also in encouraging the Indians to learn new skills while helping themselves. One important contribution was his hiring of Navajos as employees. Old Mexican, a man whom Holley recognized as a hard worker and whose autobiography gives a detailed account of what transpired, shares what he observed. In 1904, the government built a road from Aneth to the Four Corners. The work required a lot of men, and so through Holley the invitation went out: "If any of you want a wagon, you have to work forty-five days, and for a shovel, one day, and an ax, one day, and a saw, one day, and a pitchfork one day, and for a scraper, five days. If you want to work with a team to earn a wagon, you have to work twenty-two days and a half."[4] Some Navajos put together their own crews and earned a wagon in seven days; others just worked for themselves. But, in either case, useful technology from the white man's world was put in their hands.

Not only did Holley provide jobs for the men improving the roads that led to his post, but he became heavily dependent upon their services as freighters. Old Mexican worked as a primary contractor to freight goods between Aneth and Cortez, Mancos, and Durango, Colorado, and Shiprock, New Mexico. For a three-day round-trip to Cortez, he received ten dollars, for a six-day round-trip to Mancos, twelve dollars. He hauled sacks of wool, blankets, and hides, and brought back two thousand pounds of flour and other supplies, including clothing and utensils for his personal use. Other Navajos complained about the freighters, saying they were making too much money and that Old Mexican, in particular, was cornering the work market. In his mind, however, that was their problem. "None of them had any stout horses. One fellow had earned a wagon by working on the road . . . but it took this fellow a long time to make a trip."[5]

Road improvement and freighting went hand-in-hand and were a huge concern to traders. Any post located in an isolated community assumed the responsibility of at least partially maintaining the section of the road system near their store. Ray Hunt gave a graphic description of what he encountered in the early days of freighting at the turn of the century. Going from Bluff to Mancos on all dirt roads was rough. The roads

. . . would get extremely rutty after a storm. If several people traveled it in wagons, they would cut deep ruts in the soft mud. Sometimes we would detour, go out around the bad spots. Sometimes you had to stay in those tracks; it was a lot easier than trying to break a fresh track. As long as the roads are dry you can go right along, but when the roads get really soaked up and wet, it's hard on your team. So sometimes you can't go as far as you're supposed to. . . . Mancos Creek would run a pretty high stream, too high to cross with a wagon and team, until you'd let it run down to about two feet deep. It would come up to the hubs on the wagon, nearly to the horses' belly."[6]

Freighting became even more complicated when a wagon could not cross a river. John Hunt and his son, Ray, had the problem of returning from Teec Nos Pos with a wagon full of goods and finding the San Juan River too high. They unloaded their wagon, disassembled it and put the box on a boat and had it rowed across. The wheels and contents followed, with the horses swimming behind the boat. It took three trips before the transfer was complete. Next, it was reassemble the wagon, reload the goods, and get underway.[7]

Years later, in 1909, help appeared in the form of steel bridges spanning the San Juan River, paid for by state and federal funds as part of road improvement. While a flood swept away a number of these bridges in 1911, they were soon replaced with more-resistant structures. The growing network of roads facilitated the introduction of the car and truck; the increased capacity of the railroad system provided more and faster transportation to distant markets; the public demand for tourism grew exponentially; and an increasing population sought improved services. While much of this story cannot be told here, the role of the trading post as a promoter of economic growth and as the identifiable hub of isolated Navajo communities cannot be dismissed. Especially during profitable times, the traders' voices played a part in obtaining graveled roads that withstood the rigors of rain, snow, and ice during some seasons and the blowing, shifting sand at other times. Since the Navajos needed a spokesperson who understood and could interface with representatives of the dominant culture to affect change, the trader became an accepted accomplice to see that it happened.

James Holley, like other traders, also coaxed the Navajos along the winding trail of economic competition for store-bought goods. Anthropologist Walter Dyk, who recorded Old Mexican's autobiography, commented on the impact his informant encountered when interacting in the dominant society:

> These trips must have played a significant role in hastening and facilitating the process of his acculturation. They brought him into frequent and direct contact with town and market, merchant and farmer, from whom he learned the white man's ways, goods, food, tools, and techniques. But the things he borrowed and accepted were highly selective. They represented superficial aspects of life and did not touch the core of his inner being. For all of his contact with white men he never learned more than a few words of English and though he welcomed more white men's clothes, he refused to the end to cut his hair, even though it were to cost him a job. These were among the symbols of his life and being.[8]

Holley also encouraged the Navajos to move into the Anglo economy by identifying for the agent in Fort Defiance, and later the superintendent in Shiprock, Navajos who would work well for them. Old Mexican and others took advantage of the opportunity, with each earning a new wagon for their efforts. Holley selected potential candidates, wrote letters of recommendation, and gave instructions about procedural matters with the government. He also rewarded good livestock care, counselled about proper marital relations, and held community meetings in his store in the winter or under the nearby cottonwood trees in the summer.[9] Like many other traders at this time, Holley also helped the government, in this case Superintendent William T. Shelton, to round up Navajo children for school at the Shiprock (Northern Navajo) Agency. One afternoon, Shelton, Holley and interpreter Robert Martin approached Old Mexican. Martin translated, "'We have been to your wives' camp. You have some good-looking children. . . . When we start school you send some of your children to school.'"[10] He and other Navajos did, taking the children in the wagons the men had earned—a fitting symbol of the ongoing acculturation process taking place.

In 1905, Holley left the trading business for employment as the government farmer stationed in Aneth, then returned as a trader to the post for a short time in 1912–13.[11] As the government farmer, he served for three years, during which he taught Old Mexican and others building skills as they constructed a government home and barns and irrigated agricultural plots. Later, he requested that Old Mexican become a policeman in the Aneth area. The Navajo would be responsible for gathering schoolchildren and helping with domestic disturbances, but the job did not appeal to Old Mexican. In his words, "I want the money all right, but the thing I don't like about being a policeman is that the Navajo are pretty hard and ornery. . . . If you don't get hard with them they will just get worse, and tell all kinds of stories on you." He refused Holley's and Shelton's offer.[12]

Following his tenure as a government farmer, Holley returned to his ranch in McElmo Canyon. The location of his stone-and-adobe house was ideally suited as a stopover for travelers moving from Utah to Colorado, and so, not surprisingly, Holley opened his door as a trader to many Anglo, Navajo, and Ute visitors. A. V. Kidder, an archaeologist investigating Anasazi ruins in 1908, described his stay at the home. The one-handed Mrs. Holley (Savilla M. Hougendoubler) was "work-worn but hospitable"; her husband was a "tall, bronzed man with a limp"; and their seven children, ranging in ages from three to thirteen, were barefoot and ragged, but "all supremely healthy."[13]

Despite her work-worn appearance, Mrs. Holley seems to have had most of the energy; she was rated by her guest as a "bang up cook" who fed them well. Holley's McElmo store was approximately halfway between Bluff and Cortez, and so was a handy stopping-off place for the stage line he operated (1909–10) that ran through the canyon. To Mrs. Holley fell the task of feeding a meal to the passengers, when she was not in the fields cutting hay, moving irrigation water, and taking care of twelve milk cows. Visitors noted that James himself seemed lackadaisical, worked very little, and provided for his family by irrigating only a few acres of alfalfa. He did, however, dig in the Anasazi ruins nearby, which netted him the nickname of "Moki Jim," although others have credited him with building a home and post in East McElmo in a rock formation that had previously housed Anasazi remains.[14] Holley continued to do some trading on the side, but he had relinquished the one site—the Aneth post—that held any real promise.

Joseph A. Heffernan bought the Aneth store in 1906 when Superintendent Shelton cautioned Holley that, as the newly hired farmer, he should not combine private enterprise with government employment. Heffernan had previously lived in southwestern Colorado and is credited with naming the Montezuma Valley, the site of his previous home.[15] The Navajos quickly accepted this new owner, who started to make improvements by excavating a well in front of the store. He hired Indian labor to start the shovel work, but once they reached an adequate depth, the crew switched to drilling, with Heffernan himself at the bottom of the hole, controlling the drill bit. Old Mexican, one of the Navajo workers, explained, "I jumped on the pump handle all day long. I got two dollars a day. I worked twelve days then quit. I was pretty tired jumping on that pole all day. We didn't get any water."[16]

Livestock Improvement and Education

During Jospeh Heffernan's first year, the government also introduced sheep-dipping vats to combat scabies and placed the vats near the Aneth post. The trader now faced a community divided over whether this medicinal process was beneficial or destructive, resulting in the death of their sheep. Those who bitterly opposed this innovation rallied around the powerful medicine man, *Ba'álílee*. A year later, the issues of sending children to school, dipping sheep, and other community concerns resulted in what is said to be the last cavalry charge in the United States against "hostile" Indians.[17] This incident is known to historians as the *Ba'álílee* Affair and to some of the participants as "The Battle of the Wounded Dog," for a canine that barked ferociously as the soldiers neared the sleeping Navajo camp and so was shot by the cavalry commander, Capt. Harry O. Williard.[18] At the base of much of this controversy lay resistance to change that opposed traditional ways.

The tip of this spear of change poised at Navajo culture was the trading post and its ally, the government. But alliances can shift, and for some time, Superintendent Shelton accused Heffernan of buying stock provided to the Navajos by the government to increase the quality of their herds. Old Mexican stood on the sidelines and watched the fray, but added his own feelings, which went far beyond livestock and into land loss, the role of education, and trade relations. Given that he was a "progressive" Navajo who accepted change and went along with the general flow of events, his remarks are revealing. After expressing Shelton's concern for the loss of breeding stock and the general practice of selling sheep and cattle to the trader, Old Mexican commented:

> We don't get the full price on anything. The store keeper is always cheating us. 'I'm worried about that,' said Shelton. 'The storekeeper is making lots of money on you and you only get half the price and the storekeeper pockets the rest.' The storekeepers are cheating us out of everything, even the springs and the rocks that are on the mountains. We have been cheated out of everything and the only way to get out of it is to put some children in school. If any of these children should be smart, when they get smart, we'll get the full price on everything we sell. . . . After your children have been through school, when they come back, then you can sell everything for regular prices. If you want to sell anything, you take this child along, who has been through school, and he can sell it for you at the regular price.[19]

Apparently the trader and agent resolved their differences, since no further correspondence discussed the issue, and two years later, Heffernan defended Shelton and his policies during a federal investigation. As for Old Mexican, he got his wish, with an increasing number of Navajo children from Aneth attending Shiprock and other schools.

During the early 1900s, interest in Anasazi ruins mushroomed, and with this came archaeologists. While John and Louisa Wetherill in Oljato, and later Kayenta, capitalized on this investigation of Anasazi material culture in their area, and trader Richard Wetherill became involved in Mesa Verde and Chaco Canyon, among other sites, there were trained archeologists who also explored McElmo and along the San Juan River. Many of them stopped at the Aneth post as a way station between Bluff and Cortez. Neil Judd visited the store in 1908 and was surprised to see a man dressed in Navajo clothes who had distinctly Negroid features. Most likely this comment refers to John Madison, "the colored man who had lived for so many years among the Navajo" and often herded for traders along the San Juan River.[20] He and his two Navajo wives were selling goat pelts, but after he left, Judd asked Heffernan about this so-called "black Mexican." The archaeologist learned that, about forty years previous, the Afro-American, who was working for soldiers passing through the country, was sold to an Indian and that by now, the black had become one of the "wealthiest Navajos thereabouts."[21]

A.V. Kidder also stopped in Aneth around the same time. He was impressed with the thick walls and sturdy beams that supported a roof, with six to eight inches of shoveled dirt on top that effectively kept out the heat of the day. Inside, and back from the door, stood the long counter that surrounded the bullpen, while in the center of the yard-wide counter was a section that could be raised for entry. Kidder summarized his impressions by saying, "During the hour or so I spent in the Aneth store, more silver dollars, I'm sure, passed one way or the other across Heffernan's broad counters than I'd seen in all my past twenty-two years."[22] Other archaeologists such as Edgar L. Hewett, Samuel J. Guernsey, and Sylvanus G. Morley followed, visiting the cool interior of the Aneth store.

In 1910, Heffernan sold the post to Charles Brown, beginning a string of owners that included Howard Antes, James Holley (for the second time), Tom Dustin, John Hunt, Robert Smith, Holly Vowell, Art Tanner, Ralph Tanner, and others who worked in Aneth then left for a "better post over the next horizon."[23] They took with them their descriptive Navajo names, like "Open Mouth," "Ugly Trader" (Holly Vowell), "Swinging Arm" (Ray Hunt), "Big Arms" (Ralph Tanner), "Bear" (Art Tanner), and "Ears" (Bob Smith), but also left behind some names of their own.[24] For instance, the Navajo, Jimmy Boatman, received his title for his long-standing service as a ferry man, hauling wool, hides, and customers across the river in a boat belonging to the Aneth post.[25] The traders, government farmer, and the Navajos sponsored his entrepreneurial efforts by sharing the cost, which ranged between a quarter and two dollars. Jimmy would start rowing on the south side of the river in this wooden boat and try to angle through the sand waves for a landing spot beneath the post. Occasionally, he missed the mark and ended downstream, much to the chagrin of the customers who had to help drag the boat to the intended landing. By mid-June, when the shearing season was over and the river flow decreased, Jimmy became unemployed, but when the waters rose, he was back in business, serving the estimated fifty to sixty families living on the far side of the river.[26]

Posts and Conflict

The Boatman family also figured prominently in a less-than-positive incident at the Aneth store. In 1916, John Hunt, known as Little Mexican (Nakai Yazzie) because of his dark hair and tanned skin and also because the Navajos said that he roamed a lot and did not stay in one place, bought the Aneth post from Tom Dustin. He got along well with his customers and many times, when he had to leave, hired a Navajo to sleep outside and watch the store in his absence.[27] Yet Hunt also had a temper and did not appreciate bullying. On August 12, 1919, the twenty-year-old son of Jimmy Boatman entered the Aneth post with an apparent chip on his shoulder. Earlier, he had boasted to the owner that he had made other traders leave and that Hunt could expect to follow suit. This time he announced that he wanted a pair of overalls and some other goods that would be paid for later. When the trader refused, the Navajo threatened to take them, came behind the counter, and swung at Hunt before going down under a well-placed punch. The storekeeper dragged him outside. The next night, the Indian died.

The Aneth community was angry, believing the trader had killed the man. Government Farmer Herbert Redshaw, serving there at the time, called the people together and all day reasoned with the crowds under the cottonwoods. For three days, the trader and his family remained on high alert, but as community members met with Redshaw, Hunt loaded his family in his car and started off to Fruitland, and eventually Shiprock. However, as they crossed McElmo Creek, water splashed onto the engine, causing it to stall. When Hunt got out to check the engine, he saw a Navajo rider approaching him with gun in each hand. John went for his pistol, but dropped it in the water. Retrieving it, he pointed it at the Indian, who stopped short, then turned away. Hunt climbed back into the car, and the family continued its journey. But John was curious; he tried shooting his pistol, and not one round fired.[28]

The government filed charges against Hunt in Shiprock. Navajo Agent Evan W. Estep (Shelton's replacement) and Dr. J. C. Braben examined the corpse in Aneth, while the trial was held in Monticello. The court summoned three interpreters—Joseph Tanner, Oswald Hunt, and Charles Ashcroft, all three traders—who accompanied the accused. Most telling was the autopsy performed by the doctor that indicated that

Jimmy Boatman's son had sustained a fractured skull when he fell off a horse two days prior to the altercation. A blood clot, which dislodged during the fight, was the actual cause of death. The court dropped the manslaughter charge and replaced it with one of assault and battery, to which Hunt pleaded guilty. Judge Oscar W. McConkie gave the defendant a maximum fine of two hundred dollars and closed the case. A few months later, in 1920, Hunt sold the Aneth post to Robert Smith and moved to Bluff, where he purchased the San Juan Co-op for six thousand dollars.[29] From a Navajo perspective, the resolution of the problem had shifted from frontier justice provided by family and community members to a court system with lawyers, a judge, an autopsy, and established fines. Traders had played a prominent role, not only because one was the defendant, but also as translators for the court, in obtaining witness statements, and when accompanying the sheriff in trips to Cortez, Aneth, Shiprock, and Fruitland.

Hunt took over the San Juan Co-op, purchasing a business that had been relatively successful during its early years. The store had always encouraged trade and promoted the local Navajo economy. For instance, in 1902 it held a fair where Navajos exhibited their rugs, jewelry, silver products, and beads. It was such a success that the Aneth post offered its own area fair, and eventually, in 1909, Superintendent Shelton sponsored and financed a Northern Agency Fair in Shiprock. By now, this activity had become a regional gathering that sported 290 exhibits, each containing from five to sixty items.[30] The Shiprock fair drew participants from as far as seventy miles away, with their products being displayed and promoted by traders from their community. All three of these fairs, and others, gave an important advertising boost to the Navajo economy, while encouraging white neighbors to view the "progress" that the Navajos were making toward acculturation.

In Bluff, the co-op occasionally hired Navajos to sort and card wool. Raw wool was not only hauled to the markets of Colorado, but was also fluffed and put in quilts or spun, dyed with roots and bark, then knitted into socks or woven into clothing. The homemade yarn and coloring never faded. Sometimes Navajo women took advantage of the situation by hiding wool under their dresses, then putting it in the bushes until it was time to return to the south side of the river. Other times,

By 1913, when this photo was taken, the Shiprock Fair had evolved into an event that brought families and entire communities together in the northern part of the Navajo Reservation. Agent William T. Shelton ensured that each group of participants had their own booth and that the prizes offered for all types of competition were valued. The traders' booths seen here were a point of pride for every individual involved in the competition. (NAU.PH. 2000.48.3, Northern Arizona University, Cline Library, Staplin Collection.)

when they ran short of wool for weaving, they just bought it back from the trader.

For roughly five years, Hunt served as the only mercantile operation in Bluff, dealing with community members as well as American Indians. For the Navajos, he provided a wooden boat to cross the river during flood time. The Utes were another story. Bluff is located near Allen Canyon, a favorite haunt for a group of Southern Utes and Paiutes, who frequented the co-op and tried Hunt's patience. There had been a long history of the townspeople losing cattle, horses, and equipment to these Indians, but peaceful coexistence remained the general policy. When the co-op passed from a collective ownership run by Kumen Jones to John Hunt on January 21, 1920, the Utes encountered someone who did not have the same temperament as its former owners. Although many of them had frequented his Aneth store, Hunt still found it necessary to establish his rules of operation in Bluff. He sent a number of them out the door by the seat of their pants because of their "loud, overbearing" and "cocky" attitudes. They soon gave up their brusque demands, the hacking on the counters with their knives, and their threats of "see you out on the range," where "accidents" happened.[31] But if trade with the Indians had its challenges, so too did dealing with Anglos. Many of them purchased items at the store on credit with a promissory note that they never redeemed. Hunt estimated his loss from these customers at two thousand dollars.[32]

It was, however, neither the Utes nor Navajos who caused the destruction of the San Juan Co-op, but rather a drifter from Texas operating under the pseudonym of Fred Star. He had wandered into town in 1922 and begun working for Hunt by managing his cattle herd. On July 19, 1925, after the store had closed for the night, Star broke in and took what he wanted. To cover his deed, he splashed kerosene or gasoline around the interior and set it ablaze. The resulting explosion blew the roof off the building and into the street, shattered all of the windows in neighboring structures, and engulfed the interior of the two-story rock store in flames. Hilda Perkins, a twelve-year-old girl at the time, explained what happened next: "We could see this man in there in back of the flames. He was standing and just screaming, 'Help me! Somebody get me out!' Rocks kept caving in. Then the flames grew so high that we could no longer see him but we could stand and hear him. Dan Perkins, who lived just across the street took a quilt and wrapped it around himself and went in to get him. . . . Fred Star was pinned by a huge rock on his leg and Dan couldn't pull him out. The quilt caught fire and so Dan had to come back out."[33] The next day, from amid the smoking rubble, townspeople retrieved Star's remains. John Hunt assessed the damage and realized that he had lost everything. That same year, his wife died from sickness, and saddened, he left the life he knew and went into mining, only to eventually return to the profession of trader in Greasewood, Bluff, and Mexican Hat. He died in October 1967.[34] While other posts sprang up in Bluff over the ensuing years, none replaced the San Juan Co-op in physical size, scope of trade, or importance to the community and its Native American customers.

The Montezuma Creek Posts

Upriver from Bluff sat the Montezuma Creek post, which by the early 1900s, had seen a succession of traders behind its counters. Ray Hunt, an active trader during this time, recalls the store's genealogy. He believed that Richard Adams initially located the post near the confluence of the San Juan River with Montezuma Creek. Around 1910, William Young ("Black Hat") assumed control and remained until 1916, changing the store from a crude shack of cedar logs to one lined with boards inside and out, with mud poured between for insulation; the building formed the familiar L-shape and was covered by a roof of heavy tarpaper, with a storage shed located to the west. The long side of the building was approximately thirty-two feet and the short stem about sixteen feet, with a fourteen-foot-square bullpen surrounded on three sides by counters. The door faced east, with windows on the north and south sides of the building. When Young left the post, he was followed in succession by Oscar Hatcher from Durango, Jesse Foutz, Chunky Tanner, Wilford Wheeler, and then Billy Meadows, after which it was vacant for a while before other traders bought it.[35]

Adams, known to the Navajos as "Batter" because he limped around with a cane shaped like a baseball bat, wanted to improve the welfare of his customers. He was a kind man who generously gave away chickens so that every Navajo camp could start its own brood. He was equally generous with goats, selling them at low prices. In the 1920s, Chunky Tanner did a similar thing, buying lambs in the spring only to sell them again in the fall in order to encourage Navajos to shop at the Montezuma Creek post. His wife sewed "squaw skirts" and blouses which Chunky peddled on horseback, trying to attract customers, but with disappointing results. Business proved to be too slow, and soon thereafter he pulled out.[36] This post at Montezuma Creek also provided a name that is now used for the entire community—Mussi (Cat). The area had first been known as Sagebrush Wash (*Díwózhii Bitó'*), but when Wilford Wheeler moved there to trade, the Navajos, who knew his mother and father, gave him the name of Son of Woman Who Looks Like a Cat (*Mósí Yázhí*—literally, Little Cat). Apparently, this woman's ears, face, and nostrils with protruding hair, reminded her customers of a cat with whiskers, and so she received the name that now denotes the town.[37]

A Navajo man named Sneak (*Biníi'ditł'oi*, or Straggle of Whiskers on His Face) provided nautical services at this post. He ran the sixteen-foot wooden boat for the store and camped on an island in the middle of the river. A large stand of cottonwood trees at his homestead provided wood, which he sold to the post for fuel.[38] Although he received the name "Sneak" because he walked around quietly and appeared when least expected, he acquired the name for yet another reason. Ray Hunt tells of a moonlit night in 1927, when he was lying in bed and heard approaching riders. He looked out the window and saw three men—Sneak and his two sons—headed toward the post. The trader sensed trouble and so slipped out of bed, stuffed two pillows under the blankets to give the appearance of a body at rest, grabbed an iron fire poker, and stepped behind a stove to watch developments. The three thieves broke into the store, Sneak posting himself by the bedroom door to see if the slumbering form in bed would awaken. Hunt, without a gun, decided just to wait out the robbery, as the men stole two hundred pounds of flour, salt, baking powder, and a few other items before departing. The next day, Hunt described to the store's owner, Oscar Hatcher, exactly what had happened and who had been involved. Hatcher talked to the Indians, saying that they had left fingerprints all over the store, and so they confessed. The trader threatened to bring them to Window Rock for discipline but gave them the opportunity of working for the cost of the goods—an option that they chose. Sneak now had another reason for his name.[39]

Around 1929, business in Montezuma Creek must have been good because Joseph Hatch Jr. established another post along the San Juan River, not far from the initial one still in operation. He received permission from an elderly Navajo known as Whitehorse, who had homesteaded in the area, named the location *Ch'ínat'a'* (meaning "Flew Back Out"), and built a two-room stockade-style structure of cottonwood logs stuck vertically in the ground. This sixteen-foot-wide by thirty-foot-long building, with its eight-foot-high ceiling, single, two-foot window, and small bullpen provided tight quarters, where Hatch purchased rugs, wool, and sheep. He one time asked Ray Hunt to mind the store while he went with some Navajo herders to Farmington to sell his flock. On the way, one of the men traded some lambs for alcohol. Angered as Joe was, he nevertheless started drinking with the herders and ended up in trouble with the law. Meanwhile, Hunt waited for the owner's return, not realizing that Hatch was in jail. Though Hatch spent eleven months in jail before being released, Hunt dutifully minded the store until its owner returned. Even so, Joe did not stay long. He abandoned the post for another one in Allen Canyon, where he served the Utes.[40]

Posts and the Anglo Economy

The active trading during the first quarter of the twentieth century had a highly beneficial effect on the general economy of the region. As early as 1896, Colorado newspapers touted the impact of the San Juan trading posts, claiming that freighting outfits "loaded out from the Bauer Store [Mancos] often $1000 worth of goods a day."[41] As thousands of pounds of wool came in to Mancos, it was either stored in large warehouses or moved to Durango, where entrepreneurs built storage facilities to keep hides and wool next to the railroad tracks. A conscious effort to woo the trade into southwestern Colorado provided hope for the continuing growth of business. For example, in 1899, the *Mancos Times* announced that "A shipment of $500 or $600 worth of general merchandise was made from Bauer's [Store] on Tuesday, destined for the San Juan River trading posts. Next spring our two mercantile companies will make effort to divert all the trade from southern Utah, northern Arizona, and northwestern New Mexico to Mancos. . . . Younger and more energetic blood will enter the competitive field, and Indians, traders, and settlers will be interviewed by 'drummers' from Mancos, who will purchase anything they may have for barter."[42] Other newspaper articles followed, announcing that the San Juan Co-op and Hyde and Barton stores had just loaded 14,500 pounds of general merchandise; that "even the Navajos have 'caught on' to the mild craze that seems to have permeated the entire blessed body that constitutes the normal institute for a demand for blankets, pottery, silversmith work"; and that "Westward for a hundred miles and more, all trade naturally gravitates in this direction and centers at this point [Mancos] and Dolores."[43]

In 1915, the *Mancos Times* received the endorsement of John Wetherill, whose post was in Kayenta, Arizona. Although he had done business in Flagstaff, Winslow, and Holbrook, Arizona, in Gallup and Farmington, New Mexico, in Bluff, Monticello, and Moab, Utah, and in Durango and Mancos, Colorado, he preferred the latter to all others. Reasonable prices, available stock, and rendered services were, according to the paper, reasons for Wetherill's satisfaction.[44] While this banter represents one town's efforts at boosterism, it also reflects the importance of the trade coming from the reservation and how, as an exciter, it was courted.

Traders, Archaeologists, and the Anasazi

Much of the discussion thus far has been about the posts along the San Juan River and dealings in Colorado. While entire books have been written about John and Louisa Wetherill's experience in Oljato and Kayenta, Harry and Mike Goulding's coming to Monument Valley in 1925, and Elizabeth Hegemann's life at Shonto, there are still some points to be made in the role they played as traders in exciting the economy in their respective areas.

John Wetherill is a particularly good example of what many traders were involved in concerning the Anasazi or Ancestral Puebloan remains scattered throughout the Four Corners area. He was instrumental in first locating, then leading expeditions into Betatakin and Keet Seel in today's Navajo National Monument, just as his brother Richard excavated heavily in Chaco Canyon and publicized his exploration of the ruins at Mesa Verde. These monumental sites boosted dramatically the tourist trade in Navajo and Ute country and provided exciting stories of "discovery." Most traders, however, were involved in the day-to-day excavation and use of these sites. There are numerous accounts indicating that both men and women operating trading posts encouraged Navajos to set aside their anxiety and traditional teachings about entering these places and guide people to the ruins and assist in the digging of artifacts, as well as attempt to locate objects on their own. Indeed, the traffic became so intense that, in the *Report of the Commissioner of Indian Affairs* in 1905, the commissioner warned the traders that these artifacts were "not private property to be disposed of at will." The report continued:

> It is well known that for some years past, Indian traders have greatly encouraged the despoliation of ruins by purchasing from the Indians the relics secured by them from the ruined villages, cliff houses,

> and cemeteries. . . . Much of the sale of such articles is made through licensed Indian traders, to whom the Indians bring their "finds." It seems necessary, therefore, to curtail such traffic upon the reservation (Navajo, Southern Ute, and Zuni) and you will please inform all the traders under your jurisdiction that thirty days after your notice to them, traffic in such articles will be considered contraband. . . . A failure to comply with these instructions will be considered sufficient grounds for revocation of license.[45]

This decree apparently had little effect on most traders, since the traffic continued unabated. A year later, the Antiquities Act, signed by President Theodore Roosevelt, again highlighted the problem, again with little impact. The legislation lacked teeth and was filled with loopholes for lawbreakers. The other problem: there were few people to enforce it.

Traders on the Navajo Reservation and surrounding areas were heavily involved in obtaining artifacts for reasons ranging from decoration in the home to sale in the public market. The tenor of these transactions varied in scope, some of the traders being less zealous than others. Elizabeth Hegemann, while working in Shonto, reported that, after extended windstorms in the spring or intense cloudbursts in the summer, Navajo herders brought into the nearby trading post pots, ladles, and bowls exposed by the storms. In exchange, the seller received five cents' worth of hard candy in a brown paper sack, the expected payment at the time. Although she did not encourage such sales, local Navajos acquired more objects to pass over the counter. One time, two Navajos took the trader to a site where they had been digging, only to find that the huge pot located at the corner of the ruin had burst into three pieces. The pressure of the sand inside had shattered the jar outward, once the surrounding dirt was dug away.[46]

Indiscriminate looting of sites not only removed valuable and, perhaps, sacred objects, many pieces were probably ruined in the excavating process. In 1906, one man took a plow and scraper and leveled a mound in order to get a few pieces of pottery to sell to the trader. He apparently destroyed much more than he saved. Commenting on the situation, archaeologist T. Mitchell Prudden recognized shifting times. "A few years ago the Indian stood in superstitious dread of these ruins and of all that they contained. . . . Now, however, all is changed. The Indian, particularly the Navajo, has learned that no harm seems to come to the

These Anasazi remains and artifacts were photographed on the shelves of a Bluff trading post in 1903. Although, by today's standards, none of this should have been disturbed, this photo depicts a lucrative trade; note the price tags, a comment on the values of this era. (Courtesy San Juan County Historical Commission.)

white man from handling these ancient bones, and carrying off the contents of the ruins and the graves. They have been employed by the whites in excavations. So at last, they too have begun to dig and devastate on their own account, destroying great amounts of valuable relics."[47]

Women were as active as men in collecting artifacts. For example, Louisa Wetherill promoted the excavation of sites, encouraging Navajos to bring in objects while guiding professional and avocational archaeologists throughout the reservation to various ruins. The danger in this activity is explained by medicine man John Holiday from Monument Valley, who tells of his grandfather, Man between the Rock (*Hastiin Tségiizh*), his wife, and other family members working for the traders. John's parents used to dig pot shards and Anasazi bones in the hills by Kayenta, then take them to the post. His mother carried around two big buckets and once they were full, she would bring them in to sell. "They did this for work and that is what killed my grandfather—the Anasazi. He went to a squaw dance one day and suddenly collapsed and died. Handling Anasazi things is dangerous and killed him. The same thing bothered my mother, who fainted quite often. I did an Evil Way ceremony on her and she got better. In fact, she lived to be 120 or so. Eventually, she just ripened then fell apart because she was too old."[48]

A Navajo guide led Hilda Faunce from her post at Covered Water to a mound peppered with shards. Seizing a piece of broken bone, Faunce unearthed a skull and some vertebrae. A Navajo woman who was watching herded her children away, fearing that a "'devil" might be present, while an old man warned Faunce to get the skull out of sight. She later found a bowl in the grave and proudly displayed it on her mantel.[49] While this was hardly in keeping with traditional Navajo values, Hilda saw nothing wrong with incorporating Anasazi materials as part of her decorating scheme. Most traders were very much aware of Navajo respect bordering on fear for the dead, yet seemed to enjoy speaking of their insensitivity to this concern. Elizabeth Hegemann tells of a trader who went to a ruin and stacked bones with a skull at the site. She writes: "Shaking his [Jot Stiles] head with a trace of a smile, he said, 'If my Navvy trade could see me now, I wouldn't have one of them left.' . . . our Navvies at that time were still very superstitious about touching the dead or having anything to do with burials, old or new."[50] One can only imagine how the Diné viewed this use of dead people's property.

Some Anasazi objects served as presents between friends. Louisa Wetherill received a finely woven basket of ancient manufacture from *Hashkéneiniihí*, a respected elder from the Monument Valley area. He had dug it up twenty-five years before, while caching some of his property, but became afraid. He recognized it was very old and so might be of interest to Louisa, who eventually donated it to the Utah State Museum. Byron Cummings, familiar with the object, felt "it was probably a mask worn as a hat by a medicine man in some religious ceremony. . . . A similar basket was found in August 1909 by Mr. [William B.] Douglass' surveying party in a cave in Sagi Canyon."[51]

Some traders dug in ruins, as Navajos watched. Franc and Arthur Newcomb owned a trading post near lands that had once been worked extensively by the Anasazi. Neighboring Navajos brought in what they found, pointed to ruins where the Newcombs could explore, and left the two to their casual excavating on Sunday afternoons. One of their faithful customers and seller-of-artifacts, Kee, brought them to a gravesite that local Navajos had known about for years. After digging four feet down, Franc and Art encountered a skeleton of what they thought was a Spaniard with copper spurs and other metal objects. But Kee was disappointed. He had hoped that, as he watched, gold and silver coins, like others had found in the area, would surface so that he could have a relative fashion silver jewelry for him. Apparently, there was no taboo associated with these goods from a grave that could not be overcome with the appropriate prayers.[52] In addition to the purchase of artifacts, traders also encouraged Navajos to enter the ruins by enlisting them to do various kinds of jobs for archaeologists. The degree of willingness varied with each individual, but many sought employment simply because of economic pressures.

Anasazi ruins and artifacts drew two different types of people into Navajo land. The first were archaeologists interested in studying these prehistoric Indians. Who could be better to take them to abandoned sites than traders or Navajos hired by traders? Harry Goulding in Monument Valley tells of some of his experiences doing this. One archaeologist from the University of Utah hired him to lead him to a little-known site. Harry knew that one called *Tsé Biyi'* fit the description of what the man was looking for; he was also aware of a pot sitting in plain view at the bottom of a deep hole in a rock cavern with a pool of water. Goulding took the archaeologist there, let him discover for himself the seemingly unobtainable relic, then watched the man shed his pack and jump into the soft sand far below. While he did not hurt himself, and the trader raised the piece of pottery unscathed out of the hole, retrieving the man presented a different problem. Goulding left the archaeologist screaming not to abandon him, went back to his post, fashioned a rope ladder, and returned "after quite a little while," to help the man to climb out of the hole.[53]

Increasing exposure of ruins by archaeologists and tourists had a growing impact on what had previously remained pristine. Goulding continued to lead professionals to the sites around Monument Valley but grew upset when they marked on the rocks as part of their site notation. The trader became angry enough at these activities that he refused to take any more groups who were likely to deface the rocks. He even went around with a piece of sandstone, scratching away any sign of their notations, trying to restore it to an "untouched" appearance. But a real disappointment came when he took a group of tourists to a favorite five-room site, still intact with the roof on and in perfect condition. He led the people to a vantage point that provided a dramatic view, telling them, "'Now look over this way.' And my God, somebody had got in there and just blowed those rooms to smithereens! Absolutely ruined! I pretty near got sick. They dynamited them! Everybody in the crowd was just sick about it. It was pretty near the nicest thing in Monument Valley."[54]

What Goulding was doing and experiencing was not limited to his world in Monument Valley. Milton Wetherill, John's nephew, also mixed trading and tour guiding. He worked at the Two Grey Hills, Oljato, and Kayenta posts, and from 1930 to 1937, he led tour groups to Betatakin and Keet Seel, just as John was doing in the Navajo Mountain and Rainbow Bridge region. The forty-mile ride from Kayenta to Betatakin was at first made in the saddle, though later, cars and busses were able to deliver tourists over a road built in 1921 from Flagstaff to Kayenta. The venture proved profitable enough for Milton to make a permanent camp at Betatakin, where he stayed all summer, taking groups through the ruins; in the winter, he worked as a trader in Kayenta. Milton also ran pack trips to Rainbow Bridge, an eight-day excursion, with horses and food provided at twenty dollars per day. This trader emphasized, however, that these were hard days on the trail for all participants. Even so, the travelers seemed to enjoy it, often giving their guide a fifty-dollar tip.[55] Everything started and ended at the door of the Kayenta trading post.

Traders and Tourism

Most traders were involved to some extent in dealing with tourists, some more than others, depending on the location of the post. But few could top the actual courting of the tourist industry done by John Wetherill. While Louisa ran the trading business with John's partner, Clyde Colville, and actively worked in preserving aspects of Navajo culture, John ran the tours and explored new areas for opportunities. Husband and wife made a winning partnership that combined elements of the "Wild West" with the gentility of eastern hospitality. Anthropologist Clyde Kluckhohn visited their home in 1925. Starting with the lawn outside the trading post—Kluckhohn saying it was the first he had seen on the Navajo Reservation—to the interior of the traders' home, visitors were awestruck. "The interior of the Wetherill home is one of the most attractive in America. The living room is cheerful and inviting, with its huge fireplace surmounted by relics of gorgeous Navajo sand paintings, its floor covered with unusual rugs, its walls hung with rare blankets and Indian handicraft of every description. But we were to have yet a greater surprise when we were told that we would be taken to a bathroom to wash; we expected the conventional desert wash basin, bucket, and soap, but here in Kayenta, Arizona, last outpost of civilization, we found a bathtub and running water!"[56] Louisa as host and John as guide impressed many other tourists in similar fashion.

As the Wetherills' fame grew, so did the flow of traffic to their door. Beside a wide assortment of generic tourists that stopped at Kayenta as they traveled through the region, there were three broad categories into which the more notable travelers can be lumped. The first included writers such as Zane Grey, poet-artists such as Everett Ruess, and wealthy Southwest aficionados like Charles Bernheimer. The second group was composed of politicians, most notably Teddy Roosevelt. Archaeologists and anthropologists such as Jesse W. Fewkes, Herbert Gregory, Byron Cummings, Earl Morris, Clyde Kluckhohn, T. Mitchell Prudden, and Alfred V. Kidder composed the third group.[57] While many of these people were interested in Louisa's understanding of the Navajos and the exploration of Anasazi ruins, Rainbow Bridge also served as a lure to an unfamiliar land. On May 30, 1910, this large rock arch became a National Monument, with John Wetherill as its first custodian.

As the Wetherills' success became increasingly well known, other traders opened their own tours, packaging them to fit in with the promotional ventures of the Santa Fe Railroad or other rail lines, the lure of Harvey House advertising, the expanding network of better roads, and the development of professional travel groups. Competition between posts to attract the burgeoning tourist industry arose, and so it was not surprising that, in 1924, the trading family of Cecil, Hubert, and S. I. Richardson explored, mapped, and built a road to within thirteen miles of Rainbow Bridge. To veteran Arizona traders, who operated posts in Blue Canyon, Cameron, Kaibeto, Shonto, Leupp, Red Lake, Inscription House, and eventually Navajo Mountain, it was only natural that they would have a growing interest in the tourist trade that had been so beneficial to John Wetherill.[58]

Hubert and S. I. received permission from the BIA and other government agencies to forge a trail into this isolated part of the reservation in order to expedite the delivery of services to Navajos in the interior. Their plan was to have tourists begin in Flagstaff, then travel to Cameron, Red Lake, and on to the western side of Navajo Mountain, where a trading post would be established. To facilitate the construction of the undeveloped part of the trail between Red Lake and Navajo Mountain, they hired John Daw, a Navajo scout for the military in earlier times. He knew well the old Ute, Paiute, and Navajo trail system in this area.[59]

At this point, according to the Richardsons, pressure began to mount for them to stop their venture. They believed that John Wetherill was using his influence with the government and the Navajos to prevent competitors from threatening his lucrative business, since he and his partner, Clyde Colville, "were failures as Indian traders."[60] Navajo workers built the road—grubbing sagebrush, dynamiting obstacles, digging out embankments, and filling in the road base—while John Daw mapped ahead.

Suddenly, the work crew disappeared, leaving Daw and the Richardsons alone to continue the task. Kayenta Navajos, in the employ of the Wetherills, had driven off the local Navajos with threats. Next followed a period of tense waiting, as the enemy stalked the camp, verbally threatened and physically attacked the small party of workers. Fistfights, rock throwing, stick bashing, and even a little dynamite-tossing resulted. Not until some of the local headmen appeared, angry that the Kayenta Navajos had moved into their territory to stop a project that they wanted completed, did the hostilities cease. The Richardsons now had a clear path to establish a trading post and guest lodge near Willow Spring on the western side of Navajo Mountain.[61]

Work continued. The Richardsons, with Navajo, Mexican, and Hopi labor, quarried local sandstone for building materials. From it, they fashioned the store, a large living room, a dining room and kitchen, and a long porch facing west. The entire structure was roofed with peeled logs and packed clay. Above the main building, they constructed guest cabins for tourists and a guide shack for the trail bosses who led trips to Rainbow Bridge. Below the post was a log barn and large corrals for the horses that they rented. And finally, there was a warehouse built from

Arbuckle Brothers' Coffee packing boxes that stored supplies brought in during October to last the trader and his wife through the long winter.[62]

The twelve-mile trail leading from Rainbow Lodge followed a relatively direct route to the bridge. At one point, the Richardsons used ten thousand dollars worth of dynamite to blast through obstacles, and they made a switchback that zigzagged down the two-thousand-foot wall of Cliff Canyon.[63] As the trail was on the west side of the mountain, much of the eastern trail, first developed by John Wetherill, fell into disuse because of this more direct route. Once the workers completed the path, the main road, which had started out from Red Lake as a one-hundred-mile trace but was eventually shortened to seventy-four miles, saw increasing automobile traffic. The last twelve miles to the bridge, however, was always by horse and mule pack train.

Over the roughly thirty-year period that Rainbow Lodge existed, it and Rainbow Bridge became a destination for approximately 8,700 tourists.[64] Touring companies were a major part of a system that moved people to this remote area for their encounter with the Wild West. Based on the rates given in a 1934 brochure, an individual could spend a fairly significant amount in a single trip to Rainbow Bridge, considering that this was during the Great Depression. Automobile transportation from Flagstaff to the lodge (332 miles round-trip) for one to four passengers cost one hundred dollars. The Fred Harvey Tours Company offered a line from the Grand Canyon, while Clarkson Tours did the same from Santa Fe, New Mexico, and Winslow, Arizona. Once at the lodge, it was two dollars a day for accommodations, three dollars a day for food, and thirty dollars for the two-day pack trip, with everything included. A five-day trip encircling Navajo Mountain cost a hundred dollars.[65]

Gradually, more and more inroads were made into the once-isolated domain of the Navajos. A trading post on the east side of the mountain soon added other amenities, as roads improved and a network of branches threaded through the piñon-and-juniper-clad mesas and hills to Navajo homes. Civilization marched boldly into the interior, bringing with it improved wells, and eventually, telephone lines, a boarding school, a clinic, and various types of commerce. Similar stories—with different characters, a slightly different setting, and their own unique posts—were being written across the landscape in the upper Four Corners. Agents of change penned the script. Some of those agents were

Navajos who had the desire to work for tools and money, to obtain more of the products that made life easier, to learn new techniques from government farmers, and to advance through education. Other agents were imposed through the white man's efforts—the control of the Shiprock Agency founded in 1903, the indoctrination of Navajo students in school, the establishment of law and order administered through a court system, the introduction of bridges and improved roads, the promotion of tourism, and the competitive market system of the national economy, as expressed through stores and sales off the reservation. Trading posts sat in the midst of this change, meeting needs and desires as expressed from both sides of the bullpen.

CHAPTER TWELVE

The End of an Era

Boom, Bust, and Livestock Reduction, 1920–1940

The golden era of trading posts in the upper Four Corners reached its height during the 1920s. With a reservation whose boundaries continued to expand (ten land additions between 1900 and 1933), with the economy and investment practices of the "Roaring Twenties," with the government infusion of assistance in the form of agents, livestock, and agricultural programs, and with a tribal council to approve business transactions, trading posts on and off the reservation mushroomed. Using Klara Kelly and Harris Francis's *Navajoland Trading Posts Encyclopedia* as the most current baseline of information concerning the location and number of Navajo posts, it can be seen that, between 1900 and 1940, there were twenty-four new stores in or near southeastern Utah and southwestern Colorado. Although there may be some discrepancies in terms of official starting dates because of the transient nature of beginning establishments, what follows paints a general outline of what was taking place. Between 1900 and 1909, four new posts started; between 1910 and 1919, five; in the 1920s, fourteen; in the 1930s, during the Depression, none; and in 1940, one.[1]

Previous chapters have shown the evolution of some of the earlier posts as they moved into fairly stable circumstances or closed, only to have another post spring up nearby. This chapter provides a brief glimpse of some of the stores that opened during the 1920s. After sharing a vignette or two about each, there follows a discussion of the impact of the Great Depression, the reasons for livestock reduction, the end of the golden days, and a redefinition of the role of trading posts. Before reaching that point, however, a quick look at five areas in southwestern Colorado and southeastern Utah during the 1920s shows how many of these "mom and pop" stores operated, and who their customers were.

The Posts of McElmo Canyon

Starting in southwestern Colorado, there were a number of posts in McElmo and East McElmo canyons belonging to James Holley, Billy Meadows, and later, Ern Hall. Today, in East McElmo, there stands a carved-rock building that overlooks a valley through which the old road from Aneth to Ute Mountain passed. This structure, built by trader Billy Meadows and his son, John, was the last of several posts that Meadows operated. He spent most of his life as a trader, starting in a stone structure he fashioned to serve as a post in St. Michaels, Arizona. Later, he built a less permanent building of wood in the Zuni Mountains and another along the San Juan River, twelve miles south of Shiprock. An account of this latter post and of Meadows's life there is found in Earle R. Forrest's *With a Camera in Old Navaholand.*[2] In 1913, he moved to McElmo Canyon, where he purchased forty acres, built a two-story stone house, farmed, and freighted for the posts at Shiprock, Bluff, and Montezuma Creek. Between1920 and 1924 he managed the store in Montezuma Creek, but desiring to have his own business and in order to be closer to home, he built the East McElmo post in 1924, where he remained for five years. An incident with a Navajo named Moppy ended his career; he endured a severe beating from which he never fully recovered. Billy went to his home in McElmo, where he remained until he died of a stroke in 1931.[3]

Given the name "Big Eyes" (*Binaatso*) by the Navajos because of his large blue eyes, Billy Meadows maintained generally friendly relationships with his customers, as did his wife, Anna Reifsnider Myers, who spoke four languages fluently, one of them being Navajo. Billy built the East McElmo post on forty acres of land, made the twenty-by-forty-foot structure from quarried stone obtained nearby, and developed a spring for water. According to his son, John, much of the trading was with Utes, who came in from Utah on their way to the Navajo Springs Agency, and later Towaoc, for their monthly rations. "They would all ride in there on ration day, which was the first of the month, and they'd mess around, play cards then go back to Utah when their money was gone." John also recalled that his father seemed to be on more friendly terms with his Navajo customers, who came to him for advice and to trade. John described the East McElmo post as a "get-by outfit"; after his father became ill and died, it was sold to Richard and Nora Wilson, as it continued to struggle.[4]

Richard passed away shortly after acquiring the post, and Nora assumed control. She became increasingly eccentric, wearing a belt with holstered pistol, which she occasionally used to shoot at passersby. She wore long-sleeved white gloves when she went to town, lived in a storage shed after the roof blew off the post, herded a large string of cats and dogs to quell her loneliness, and refused to pay taxes (which a kind neighbor did for her) because she believed she was on the Navajo Reservation. One time, Nora had a confrontation with some Indians, who lowered her into the post's well, where she remained for days before a Ute medicine man and tribal policeman, Walter Lopez, found her and pulled her out. She did not want to abandon the post, believing that her dead husband would return, and so neighbors watched each day to make sure there was smoke coming from her chimney, while Utes and Navajos sometimes brought her to town for shopping. She remained at this post until sometime in the early 1960s, when she went to live in Cortez and later in Montrose, Colorado.[5]

Farther to the west, near the Utah-Colorado state line at the junction of the McElmo and Yellow Jacket canyons, lies the Ismay Trading Post. Oral history suggests that when John Ismay built the store in 1921, it was on the foundation of an earlier post built by William Hyde in the 1800s.[6] John and his wife, Eleanor, were both descendants of trader families, Eleanor being the daughter of Joseph Heffernan and John being the son of Louis Ismay, trader to the Utes. Like other stores in the area, this husband-and-wife partnership depended on trade with Utes and Navajos traveling and camping along the canyon bottom. In 1928, a short circuit in the electrical wiring system in the attic caused a fire that, with the exception of some cash and a few articles removed ahead of the flames, destroyed most of the building, with an estimated loss of twelve thousand dollars.[7] The owners rebuilt the store, which continued to operate into the early twenty-first century.

While there is not much information about this post, historian Charles S. Peterson, when interviewing Amasa Jay Redd in 1973, learned of an incident that occurred around the same time that the store had burned. Redd and other ranchers in the Monticello area had been losing sheep to rustlers. In company with another rancher and a deputy sheriff, he started to Colorado, interviewing traders and homesteaders along the way. One night, the party camped at the Ismay store, where they questioned John Ismay about strangers driving herds of sheep through the canyons and into Colorado, but learned nothing from the friendly conversation. Further travel and visiting in the following days led back to the Ismay store and more questioning. Finally, Redd bluffed John into admitting that he had bought part of the stolen herd for half-price from a man named Fred Sharp, a known outlaw and suspected killer, who was selling the other half to a man in Dolores. The next day, the posse, with John Ismay in tow, confronted Sharp, who turned the animals over to the deputy sheriff, then left without a word. The thief was never prosecuted while John returned to his store, minus the sheep he had purchased.[8]

Hatch Trading Post

Due west of Ismay, at the intersection of Alkali Canyon and Montezuma Creek, stands the Hatch trading post. Its precursor in this location is somewhat unclear but is credited to Roy Rutherford, who built a small lumber structure with a dugout cellar for food storage to service Ute and Navajo families—about twenty-two of the former and twenty-three of the latter—living in the network of canyons and the main artery of Montezuma Canyon. Navajo community member Cyrus Begay remembers a wrangler named Jim Herrington as the first person to operate this small store, but gives no date when it started. Begay recalls that Red Mustache (*Daghaa Łichíí'*), as Herrington was called, "was a generous person, giving away sheep, goats, horses, and other valuable things to the Navajos. His store was right above the present trading post in Hatch; after him came Sam Rentz then Mister Hatch and his son."[9] In 1926, Joe Hatch Jr. purchased the land and built a stone building near the old post with the help of his father, Joseph W. Hatch Sr., a man descended from a Paiute mother (Sarah Maraboots Dyson Hatch) and Anglo father (Ira Hatch).

They also had been involved with trading, a business that Joseph Senior and his four sons continued to practice. Joe Junior's brother Ira assumed control of the post in 1929, when Joe began trading in Montezuma Creek, while Ira remained at Hatch for another thirty years. Ira earned his Navajo name, "Tall Boy" (*Ashkiísh Nééz*), as a young lad working in his father's store. The floor behind the counters was elevated three or four feet above the bullpen, and so when Ira mounted the three steps and peered down at the customers he looked very tall.[10]

Prior to assuming control of the Hatch trading post from his brother, Ira worked to earn enough money to buy the stock for the shelves. An Englishman who paid him for his labors also gave him $450 worth of tokens, or seco, that he brought to Montezuma Creek. The depression was just starting, and so the lack of money made this system of payment very appealing. Ira said, "If you done it right, you would have to be bonded before you used it. But it seemed awful well when there wasn't no money. A customer or medicine man could come to the store and get those seco dollars and carry them instead of giving them livestock. It worked good. Then they could pawn and give them that trade money. Then they would work it just like cash through one another. It worked very good." Only Bill Young in Montezuma Creek accepted this form of exchange; when he had about one hundred dollars' worth of tokens, he would go to Ira and cash them in for merchandise.[11]

The flow of patrons at this post provides a good sense of how successful business dealings were. Ira estimated he averaged a dozen customers a day, while Stewart, one of Ira's brothers, commented, "Every morning when I opened up, why I'd always think what design or what type of rug am I going to see today? And then they'd bring a rug in and you study it out. . . . You have to set a value on it and if it has no appeal, well you'll probably buy it anyway. It has to have appeal first; then you set the value on it."[12] Ira believed it was harder to trade with Anglo customers than with either the Utes or Navajos, but even then, life could be difficult. Although many of them were neighbors, "Them border [of the reservation] Navajos was pretty hard customers, hard to handle when collecting bills and staying peaceful with them. A lot of people cannot handle them. I got along well with them and had no trouble, but if you lose your temper with them, then they figure you are a little bit weak. They don't like a man who loses his temper."[13]

Mexican Hat Posts

Moving farther to the west along the San Juan River, one comes to the Mexican Hat area, named for a large, inverted sombrero-shaped rock, precariously balanced on a sandstone foundation. To the Navajos, it was known by other names, too, such as "Metal Pipe Going Across" (because of a previous culinary water system for the now-abandoned town), "Hat Rock," and "Swirling Mountain" (because of a geologic pattern of sandstone on the slope of a nearby hill).[14] The entire two-mile stretch along the river at this point was the scene of a gold-rush boomtown, starting in 1892–1893, and with continuing mining interests and oil exploration during the first quarter of the twentieth century. In the early days of the rush, Arthur H. Spencer freighted supplies to various mining camps and prospected until 1914 when he moved to the Mexican Hat area to trade with the Navajos and Utes.[15] John L. Oliver (*Tsiiyaa Nichxǫ'ii* , or Dirty or Ugly Neck) had built the Mexican Hat Rock trading post in 1911, which he hired Spencer (*Bilagáana Tsoh*, or Big Whiteman) to operate until around 1918. Those who knew Spencer referred to him as a "wandering promoter type of man" who continued his interest in mining and other business ventures. His wife, Medora, ran the post much of the time, appreciated visitors, and kept track of their five-year-old daughter, who was entirely comfortable around Indian customers but ran and hid when a white man showed up.[16] Once Spencer left, operation of the post reverted to Oliver, who managed it until 1925, when Ray Hunt leased it for a few years. By 1931, the store was abandoned and torn down.

In addition to the trading post proper, there was also a series of tents and outbuildings, which grew in number as years went by. In 1920, wealthy traveler Charles H. Bernheimer met Oliver behind the counter and described the post and his experience this way:

> The trader was Mr. J. H. Oliver, a Mormon and the first 'Wilson Democrat' I met on my travels . . . cheerful, pleasing, if filthy personality. All he had was a one-room shack built from the lumber of deserted gambling dens that at one time existed there twenty years ago during an oil boom. The chairs were boards nailed together, so was his table and bed. Many hundreds of empty tin cans lay around, and as far as the eye could reach there was neither tree nor bush to break the

Arthur H. Spencer, "Big Whiteman," displays his wares obtained from local Navajo barter at the Mexican Hat trading post. Baskets, blankets, large silver conchos, and what appears to be Anasazi pottery were for sale that day, circa 1915. (Courtesy San Juan County Historical Commission.)

> monotony of this rusty tin can trading post. . . . Supper in his shack, and I did not enjoy it . . . sand in . . . stewed prunes and bread as hard as pavonazzo marble with blue and pink mold from age . . . can you think of this man being sued for divorce and alimony by his wife? A couple of cheap Navajo horses, a dozen head of cattle, and $1,500 worth of goods in his trading store seems all the income producing values he possessed; besides he was lame. He had a fine head on his shoulders, though . . . looked like the best looking U. S. senator and almost conversed as well, only a bit more 'rough-necky,' and he could sing. And he did by moonlight after supper. . . . It would have been beautiful if it had not been so droll.[17]

John Holiday of Monument Valley provides another eyewitness account of a visit to the post in the 1920s:

> The Navajos were living around that area back then, in the red rocky hills west of Mexican Hat Rock. We used to live there, too. The people

> made an irrigation ditch all the way from the San Juan River by the Hat rock to the store so that they could have a supply of water. The trader used to buy sheep and goats from the Navajos so he kept his store well-supplied with flour, potatoes, and other groceries. I only bought striped candy canes since I was still a little boy. People bought things over the counter while the trader stood behind the counter. The store was quite large and built with wood. There was also a guest hogan for Navajo customers. The hogan was built halfway up with rocks and the rest was made with logs, bark, and sand.[18]

An amusing incident involving youngsters occurred when Ray Hunt operated the store. He had to leave the post occasionally on business, and so put his thirteen- and fourteen-year-old brothers, Emery and Jim, in charge. They decided to play a prank on Ray, and so they dug two big holes in the single-lane dirt road, laid cardboard with sand to cover the craters, rolled a tire lightly over the flimsy covering, and set up a detour sign beside it. Unsuspecting friend Dave Miller passed through with a dollar-and-a-half's worth of candy that Ray had sent down to the boys for watching the store. Ray recalled, "Down in that country, no one ever detoured for nothing. If there's a track through there, they went. Dave Miller came along in his little old Ford rattling along there, and he struck that hole and broke both springs. It almost threw him out. The kids didn't get any candy. If he could have caught them, he probably would have killed them, but they ran and hid back up in the canyon. He had to jack the car up to get it out of the hole which took him hours to do."[19]

A second store, located approximately two miles below Mexican Hat Rock at a crossing point on the San Juan River, also has a confusing early genealogy. Oral history suggests that a man named Jeff Tietjin built a small stone building near a crossing place where now a bridge stands. Soon Cord and Augusta Bowen and Dan Tyce took over the operation of the store from Tietjin. Because of pressure from his neighbor, Norman Nevills, who operated a nearby post and touring business, Tyce, who in the meantime had bought out the Bowens, sold the post to Merritt Smith, who in turn sold it to June Powell, all in a short period of time. Then, in 1938, Powell asked Ray Hunt if he would take over the operation. So Hunt with his newlywed wife, Grace, returned to the area and set up a tent to live in next to this store on the San Juan River.[20] The main attraction to this post was the bridge, described in 1928 as "a light wire suspension bridge swaying in the wind seventy-five feet over the river. Driving over it was like walking a tight-rope. At the other end the road continued along a narrow ledge actually overhanging the river and slanting dangerously downward, impassable in wet weather."[21] Located as he was on the edge of the reservation, Hunt began buying sheep that the Navajos were forced to relinquish because of the government-enforced livestock reduction. He grazed his growing flock of over a thousand animals along the banks of the river and sold them in Colorado. He also traded with Navajo customers for wool and blankets. By 1944, Ray and Grace were ready for a change and so leased the post to a man named John Johnson, who in 1947 turned it over to Jim Hunt, Ray's brother. Jim built living quarters over the trading post and added twenty-one motel units beside it for visiting tourists.

An excellent account of activities at the post during Ray Hunt's time is provided by Navajo Oshley, who worked for him. Oshley's experience gives a feeling for those difficult days when men, not machines, performed laborious tasks. It also illustrates the dependence of traders on good Navajo help, the bond of trust created between the two, the care of a trading-post flock, and the movement of animals to market. Oshley remembered, "The road to Bluff City was in poor condition in those days. I do not know how many times the trader in Mexican Hat went to Bluff to get supplies in his old vehicle, but I do know that it kept stopping on him." Ray Hunt described this same vehicle of his as a "stripped down Ford with a box on the back." Comb Ridge was so steep and difficult to traverse that he had a bicycle pump installed in the fuel system so that, as he drove, an assistant could hand-pump enough gas to the engine to propel the car up the grade. Oshley went on to describe the post's telephone service, which, by 1910, extended from Monticello through Blanding and Bluff to Mexican Hat. All calls were routed by an operator in Monticello, who, through a system of long-and-short-rings, identified which phone in the system should receive the call. The line constantly needed repair, especially the section extending to Mexican Hat. Hunt remembers going outside his post and pouring water on the ground wire to improve reception.

Oshley recalls one experience with this system:

> One evening at sunset, I had gotten the sheep in and was eating supper when the deaf white man who assisted the trader came to see me.

He told me to come in and listen, then handed me the phone. My employer was making the call from Bluff and asked me to take the sheep out and head for Bluff the next morning at dawn. He said it would take me two days to get there and he agreed that I should herd the sheep slowly and not rush them. I told him that if he wasn't joking about it, it would happen. I also told him that I had very little food left, but he said that the deaf person would prepare the camping food. I gave the telephone back and went outside to sleep.

The next morning, I took the sheep and food such as crackers, pop, and other goods, as well as my one blanket, and started to drive the sheep toward Bluff City. It was getting a little cold by this time. Across from Comb Ridge, there is a big hill [Lime Ridge], where I spent the night and kept the fire going. The following morning I herded the sheep then let them graze near Comb Ridge. By the time the sun was setting, I camped at Navajo Spring, where I spent the night with the sheep lying against the rock walls so they would not try to run off.

The next morning before dawn, I built a fire and cooked the little bit of food that I had left. I got the sheep to Bluff just as the sun came up. My employer came out, told me that my debt was paid off and then got me some food. He wrote down on a piece of paper how I was to be paid and how much I had left to pay on the price of the saddle. I was very happy to go back to Dennehotso. I arrived at the trading post just before sundown. At that point in my life I was a fast traveler. The saddle was paid off, and I had a little bit of money left over."[22]

Monument Valley and Oljato Posts

Moving south to the area of Oljato (Ool jéé'tó, or Moon Water) and Monument Valley, one encounters two posts—one at Oljato under John and Louisa Wetherill (1906–10) and one under Mike and Harry Goulding (1925 to the present)—which have had books written about them and so will not be discussed here.[23] However, there were two other posts, both in Oljato, that sprang up in the early 1920s. Joseph Heffernan, encountered previously in the discussion of Aneth and the Four Corners trading post, began a store in Oljato in 1921, which he operated until his death in 1925. His wife, Ann, stayed on for a short time thereafter with her daughter, Ana, but eventually they both moved to

McElmo to be closer to another daughter, Eleanor. Once the Heffernans departed, there followed a string of owners, including John Taylor, Jim Pierson, O. J. "Stokes" Carson, and others who kept the post operational until the 1990s.[24]

During the interim period between Joseph Heffernan's death and his wife's departure, Ann asked a visitor at the Oljato post to show her how to shoot a small automatic pistol. The man instructing her removed the clip but forgot that a round remained in the chamber. As she talked to him, saying, "And I guess this is where you pull the trigger," she shot herself in the leg. Ana, who had ridden to Kayenta miles away to get the mail, returned home to find her mother in bed, but Ann made no mention of the incident. The next day, when Ana went to make her parent's bed, she saw a bloody mess and forced the truth from her mother. Fortunately, the bullet had missed the bone. The man who had been teaching Ann how to use the pistol, encouraged her to put chewed tobacco on the wound, which must have worked, "'cause she got alright, but she finally had to tell me about it."[25]

Approximately a mile northwest and across the Oljato Wash from where the Heffernan store now stands was another post that began around the same time. The only information that exists about this store is found in the memory of Navajos who visited it at the time. The value in mentioning it here is to illustrate the ephemeral nature of so many posts that started on a shoestring, remained open for a brief period, then disappeared without much of a trace. John Holiday tells of visiting this store in 1924, when he was five years old, and meeting its owners, Rug (*Diyógí*) and Old Coyote (*Ma'ii Sání*). Rug received his name by constantly asking Navajo women if they had finished any more weaving, while Coyote used to trap animals. "When people had trouble with [coyotes], they called on him, and he would arrive with his pack mule, traps, and chains. He set up his equipment, and before too long, the coyote was sitting in the trap. He collected a lot of their skins." Holiday's father and others used to work for these two men as tour guides and assisted with their efforts to bring water from a distant spring by carving a canal in rock across the land and into a reservoir dammed with logs and a sand embankment. Old Coyote and Rug also developed an irrigated garden that grew corn, melons, squash, tomatoes, carrots, onions, turnips, and sugar beets. To process this last item, they brought in their own machinery and made syrup. These men offered produce to their neighbors, canned what they needed, and gave the Navajos access to their reservoir water. Little else is known about them and the activities at their post.[26]

The Navajo Mountain Post

Moving from the Oljato and Monument Valley area to the east side of Navajo Mountain, one finds another store, established initially as a rival of the Richardsons' Rainbow Lodge (1924) on the west side of the mountain. Ben Wetherill (One Whose Eye Fell Out—*Bináá' Haalts'id*), not surprisingly, built this second post, the Navajo Mountain Trading Post, in 1928. As both families vied for the tourist industry, with routes to Rainbow Bridge existing on both sides of the mountain, this Wetherill post also captured the trade within the Oljato–Navajo Mountain area. Ben, his wife Myrl, and two children set up a tent at Water under the Cottonwoods (*T'iisyaa Tó*), improved the spring's source, and built a two-room store. This post was one of the most isolated on the reservation, being located sixty-five miles from the post office in Tonalea, one hundred miles from Tuba City, and two hundred miles from a railroad and other amenities of civilization. It was closed during the winter months, but even in the summer there was not enough trade to support its operation, and so, in 1930, the Wetherills abandoned the finished post and an unfinished house nearby.[27]

Joe Manygoats, a resident of Navajo Mountain, gives a very personal account of his involvement with the Wetherills as they started construction on this post. Joe's candor about his situation as a twenty-five-year-old man provides an interesting perspective, not only of the development of the store but of his life and values. His mother had died recently, he was worried about the future—"I had no place to go and no one to turn to"—and he felt "shattered":

> Right about that same time, a trader from Oljato named Little Boy had moved to Navajo Mountain. He brought his food and merchandise packed on donkeys by way of the old horse trail that goes across, over and down the mesa east of Navajo Mountain. He set up and opened the first temporary tent-store across the canyon, east of

> Navajo Mountain. Later he moved closer to the mountain to build a stone house. . . .
>
> It all started one sensitive day [shortly after his mother died] when my father angrily scolded me for letting our sheep intermix with our neighbor's sheep. Our neighbors had released their group of newly-sheared sheep to rejoin the rest of their flock, when they accidently wandered into our flock. My father's painful words drove me to a deeper depression. I lost my appetite and did not care if I starved to death. The next morning I walked away from home while the sheep were still in the corral. . . .
>
> When I reached the evolving trading post, I sat on the hill overlooking the store. I observed men below, who were busy building houses. I decided to walk down to the work site to have a closer look. [He visited with a couple of men and explained his depressing state of affairs and so they helped him to get hired]. . . . I had worked for two days when my father sent a message with my brother-in-law, Mike, and my sister who were coming for me. They had brought in their sheared wool to sell. They told my boss that my father said I had run away from home and away from herding sheep and that I was to return home as soon as possible. My boss explained to them that I was working for him and that it would be impossible for me to return home, also that I was a good hard worker. They went home without me and I stayed and worked.[28]

By the spring of 1932, Raymond C. Dunn had purchased the post and moved his family to the site. Shortly after their arrival, Ray made a verbal agreement with the Richardsons that, if the Dunns stayed out of the tourist business, the Richardsons would stay out of the trading business, thus forming a cooperative bond.[29] With the exception of an eight-year interlude (1944–52), the post remained under the control of Dunn family members for almost a half century, Ray's daughter Madeline (Dunn) Cameron with her husband, Ralph, assuming the longest period (1952–79) of ownership. In 1983, Madeline sold the store to Dick Johnson, who closed it in 1993.[30] During an interview, Madeline shared her feelings about the place and people with whom she had spent so much time: "I don't particularly enjoy having a lot of people around, a lot of hustle and bustle. When I say people, I mean non-Indians. Indians don't bother me as much as white people do. . . . I don't think the trading business is any more lucrative than any other business. We have a pleasant life because of our surroundings and our association with the Navajo people, who we value very highly, but as far as making a lot of money, we do not."[31]

In summarizing these random experiences as they relate to the expansion of trading posts both on and off the reservation during the 1920s, there are five points to be made. The first is that many of these stores moved into the less-traveled, less-populated parts of Navajo land. With the establishment of communities in more centralized locations and an ever-widening network of roads, the fringe areas during this period were developing for commerce. A second point related to this is that there were fewer people in these areas, but in each case mentioned, there was at least one other post in the general vicinity that could be viewed as a competitor. The proliferation of posts improved opportunities for Navajo customers, but decreased the volume of sales in the stores, leading to the third point: many of these businesses were able to survive on their profits during good times, but those with marginal profits closed when the economy struggled, unable to weather the storm. Thus, the 1920s saw a boom, but for many, the 1930s became a bust. A fourth point is that most of the stores used as examples here were run by experienced trading families who had been in the business for at least one or two generations. The lifestyle was in the blood and that blood was passed on to the next generation. A final point is that those who succeeded had the personality and temperament for a life that others, not raised in an isolated environment, might find difficult. Those who lived on the reservation were there because they wanted to be and enjoyed their association with the Navajo people.

The Decline and Change of the Trading Post

Eventually, however, as circumstances changed—sometimes gradually, other times precipitously—the tenor of daily life shifted. In the world of traders, posts, and Navajos, the era of livestock reduction presented one of the greatest challenges. The topic is multifaceted, complex, and has been discussed extensively.[32] Here, it is approached in terms of its effect on the trading system; however, without a basic understanding of events, one cannot fully assess its impact. Briefly, the U.S. government determined, as a result of the economic and environmental disasters of the Great Depression years, that there were too many animals on the Navajo Reservation and that they had to be eliminated to save the grass, topsoil, and surrounding area from the effects of erosion and overgrazing. The Bureau of Indian Affairs in the late 1920s and early 1930s attempted to have the Navajos voluntarily reduce their herds, but when this did not happen, the Soil Conservation Service, precursor to today's Bureau of Land Management (BLM) enforced the eradication of large numbers of sheep, goats, cattle, and horses.

By the end of 1938, the mass slaughter of livestock drew to a close, with smaller numbers being removed into the 1940s. The trauma for the Navajo people created through this action was intense, compared by some to the Long Walk period of the 1860s.[33]

A few facts and figures from southeastern Utah illustrate what happened. During 1930, in the Montezuma Creek and Aneth area, 19,514 sheep and goats passed through dip vats filled with medicine to prevent scabies. The Oljato and Shonto areas produced 43,623 more animals, while some Utah Navajos' sheep undoubtedly went to vats at Kayenta, Shiprock, Dennehotso, and Teec Nos Pos. Still others probably skipped the process entirely, but if the totals from Aneth and Oljato areas are combined, at least 63,137 sheep and goats ranged over reservation lands of southeastern Utah.[34]

By 1934, the entire Northern Navajo Agency reported that government officials had killed or sold seventy thousand animals and that the Utah Navajos' herds were down to an estimated thirty-six thousand.[35] Because the nation was experiencing the depths of the Great Depression, the agent could price a sheep at only two dollars and a goat at one dollar. The annual report went on to say, "[A]n excessive number of goats and sheep were slaughtered for food. There is every reason to believe that the next dipping record will show even a greater reduction than indicated by the number sold."[36] Horses and cattle suffered a similar fate. Garrick and Roberta Bailey note in their economic history of the Navajos that "by the late 1930s, [commissioner of Indian Affairs John] Collier had been successful in implementing most of his policies. . . . Along with the inability of Navajos to secure off-reservation

These sheep drinking at Hilkitó Wash, ten miles south of Mexican Hat, illustrate the dependence on water and the lack of rich grassland that pushed the federal government to eliminate livestock on the reservation. To many Navajos it seemed unnecessary, and to all it appeared as one more heartless attempt to challenge their sovereignty—second in that regard only to the Long Walk. (Courtesy San Juan County Historical Commission.)

employment, livestock reduction had considerably mined Navajo economic self-sufficiency."[37]

What this meant in actual loss of animals, monetary sums, and sense of well-being will never be fully understood. Tribal figures indicate that dependence on agriculture and livestock had decreased to 57 percent in a little more than a decade, although this figure varied by region, by outfit, and by individual, depending on the extent of the losses.[38] In terms of slaughtering the animals, mostly round estimates exist. For an individual such as John Holiday, however, there was a clear, numbing reality. He drove 37 horses into the stock corrals and came out with only 13. Of his 600-plus sheep, he kept 354.[39] In New Mexico, one study noted that between 1930 and 1935, 61 percent of the goats—the poor Navajos' food staple—were eliminated.[40] Thus, a round estimate of 50 percent seems conservative, concerning stock loss. To maintain this number of animals grazing on reservation lands, the government, in 1936, introduced the Taylor Grazing Act to the Navajos, which divided the land into grazing sections evaluated by how well each one could support a cow, a horse, or five sheep as a unit of measure. The tribal government then allotted a family a permit to graze a certain number of animals on a specific piece of land. This limited Navajo herders to such an extent that very few remained economically self-sufficient. Men left home to earn money; women herded the sheep and goats that were left, wove rugs, and hoped their husbands would return to help keep the family intact. The end result—dependence on the wage economy and a new way of life.

What, then, was the trader's and Navajos' reaction to this sudden, dynamic shift that affected every facet of the trading business? Fundamental to the entire system of commerce was the credit extended to families dependent on a yearly cycle. By 1940, traders were offering a third less credit in pawn. Dead pawn went to pay for debts much more quickly. Family heirlooms that had previously remained on the racks of trading posts for extended periods of time were now purchased by tourists or sold to off-reservation buyers, who paid cash and made good profits by selling, in turn, to the general public. As one trader (anonymous) said, "Formerly the head of a family could pawn $250–$300 with the trader. The trader could afford to wait six months between wool clip and lamb sale. He knew exactly what economic conditions the Indians were in. . . . Now there is no economic certainty."[41] Other traders complained of what they saw. From Aneth: "40 percent of families not worth more than $30 a year credit on sheep and wool." From Shiprock: "Pawn being sold off as quick as dead." From Rock Point: "Out of 100 families last season receiving credit—only 20 will get it next season." From Toadalena: "Allowing 50 percent to 75 percent less credit now [1940]. Indians requiring 30 percent more store food now. One third of community is allowed no credit at all." To most traders, "The government never considers us on matters of policy. It's just, 'Where's the road to this place?'"[42] They felt that the government had placed too much emphasis on removing the stock without making constructive efforts to improve the herds still in operation.

Most traders sympathized with their Navajo friends, but they had to be careful, realizing that their relationship with the federal bureaucracy could be jeopardized. The first phase of reduction, up to 1934, was more voluntary, with some payment received for animals taken. But the second part of the program became ruthless, with the seizure and cold, calculating elimination of large numbers of animals with no remuneration.

Individual and group protests followed. Herbert Redshaw, the former government farmer in Aneth and friend to the Navajos, served as a county commissioner in 1938, when John Morgan, a Navajo, contacted him to organize a protest meeting in Monticello. As a concerned Navajo, Morgan wanted the power of the press to come into play against the loss of livestock by small-herd owners, who were plunging into poverty because they could not survive the percentage of loss of animals demanded by the government as well as the larger herd owners could. Redshaw willingly organized the meeting, provided a place to gather, and invited all "civic bodies of the county" to attend.[43] The commissioner, in reporting the results of the meeting of around two hundred individuals, felt that the government was using "force and coercion, something which the majority of Navajos do not want or understand." Redshaw continued, saying that he had consistently refused to "butt in" on reservation affairs, but that the Indians were being imprisoned and fined for resisting when all they wanted to do was remain self-sufficient.[44] Reduction continued.

Mildred Heflin was operating the Oljato trading post with her husband, Reuben, in 1937, when a missionary named Shine Smith arrived. He realized what was happening to the Indians' economy and wanted to help. A half-dozen Navajos were determined to travel to Washington, D.C., to present their case against continued reduction, and he offered to accompany them, since they did not speak English, had hardly been off the reservation, and had no understanding of what it would take to have any politician listen to them. The delegation pawned their jewelry for travel money, took the traders' truck to Farmington, New Mexico, where they boarded the bus to Denver, then traveled by train to Washington. Mildred recalled that as traders, "We could have gotten into very serious trouble over it, because here we were going against what the United States government was telling them to do. The Indian agent [E. R. Fryer] was quite upset, of course. Fortunately, he blamed the missionary more than he did us." Still, all the traders could do was to listen to the problems and sympathize with the Navajos. "We couldn't do any more than that, really, because we were at the mercy of the Indian agent over there in Window Rock. Any day they wanted to, they could cancel our lease out." Mildred and her husband remained in Oljato from 1937 to 1945.[45]

Ray Hunt at Mexican Hat shared similar feelings. He recalled how the Navajos "never did get it back" once reduction had run its course; how the women lulled their babies to sleep singing, "If you don't be good, John Collier will come and get you;" and how Navajo stockmen believed that Mother Nature, through drought conditions and rainy years, was really the controlling mechanism by which the herds were regulated.[46] As far as he was concerned, "I was in favor of the Indians. I hated to see them lose their stock and it left an awful hardship on some of them for a long while after that."[47] Ray found a partial solution for both himself and his customers. He bought livestock from the Navajos—to the tune of 1,100 animals—then grazed them along the San Juan River, using men like Oshley to watch the flock. He did not have a permit to range the animal over more-distant areas, but the riverbanks were free land, and so he let the animals run on the north side of the river when the reservation district supervisor for Kayenta and Oljato was in the area and on the south side when the BLM supervisor was on inspection.[48] Perhaps Mary Bailey, daughter of Jot Stiles—trader in Tuba City during this era—summarized the situation best when she said, "Well, you know there was no price of anything at that time. You know, everything was Depression. But Daddy always managed to make money with his rugs and with the trading post—it always made a profit. Like I say, he was a shrewd trader and he knew how to do it."[49]

The End of an Era

By the end of the 1930s, the old ways of trading were sliding to an end. During the last half of this decade, the government provided employment through the tribal Civilian Conservation Corps program, where young men could enlist to work on environmental improvement projects on the reservation. Harry Goulding and others helped Navajos earn money through the filmmaking industry that came to Monument Valley during the 1930s and later. The government enlisted large numbers of Navajos in World War II–related work—military and nonmilitary—that brought them into the mid-1940s. Once the depression and the war ended, Navajos sought other forms of employment with payment in wages. Traders often served as unofficial agents, providing workers not only for government programs but also for railroad construction, seasonal harvesting, mining operations, and off-reservation ranching efforts. Each form of this type of work pushed Navajo people into employment that fed into the mainstream American economy and away from the barter system of the past.

The men and women who grew up as traders were flexible enough to adapt to the shifting economic reality as they noted the changes and the passing of a former way of life. Mildred Heflin remembered, "We didn't have the same amount of sheep and wool as before. They didn't buy as much as before, until the whole economic situation changed due to the availability of outside work. . . . Before livestock reduction we were dependent primarily on the Indian economy. This is how we lived."[50] In Shonto, Elizabeth C. Hegemann shared similar notions. She eloquently opines, "My life on the reservation was coming to an end by 1939 and so were the old days of primitive atmosphere and isolation at Shonto. Perhaps we had helped in this change ourselves in the guise of progress; after 1933 it became a very definite thing and we could not have stopped it if we had wished. John and Louisa [Wetherill] still living under the spell of the old days, tried to stop it, but went down under the wave; the glamor, the charm of the untouched northwestern Navajo reservation gave way to CCC camps, truck trails, and paychecks that partially replaced the vanishing flocks of sheep and goats and general pastoral life."[51]

Many traders bemoaned the loss of what had once been; however, there were those who welcomed improvement and the change being wrought on behalf of the Navajo people. Gladwell Richardson, one such trader, summarizes succinctly, what those changes were and how they liberated the Navajo people during the second half of the twentieth century. He served in the military during World War II and came back to the Inscription House post in 1946. He was not the only person returning from this conflict, as he observed that there were six thousand young men from the reservation who were coming back with a different perspective, more interested in improving their lot in life. Already, change was evident in many facets of the store and its impact on the customers:

> The People were not forced to live in a circumscribed world peculiarly their own. Wide awake, they were ambitious and going places, acutely cognizant of changing times. Revitalized and enthused by the generation that fought the war, even the longhairs [elders] demanded

> employment. No longer were they forced to sit around their hogans hoping that a little wool woven into a blanket would buy enough coffee and flour to sustain them. Now, they not only wanted a job, but insisted on them as a right. . . . Blanket weaving became scarce, as the native craftsmen in all lines were turning to other pursuits for a livelihood.
>
> The first day I walked into Inscription House trading post after the war, the change had moved far toward what it was to become. One thing proving it most was the absence of a particular item on the shelves. Vacuum-packed coffee in all sizes of containers and assorted brands occupied space once filled with ground and whole-bean Arbuckle Brothers Ariosa coffee. The absence of the Navajo's long favorite *Hosteen Cohay* (Arbuckle Coffee) seemed to signal the end of the glamorous, even romantic period of adventurous barter-trading. This coffee had played an important role in the daily lives of the trader and Navajo alike. . . .
>
> The trading post itself had changed, also, during the war. During my absence my brother Cecil, who ran Inscription House, had put in an electric power plant. Now the post had good lights everywhere, a decided improvement over keeping sand cleaned out of the bowls and generators of gasoline lights so that they would work at least part of the time. With the juice wired into every building at the post came household appliances for better living: washing machines, refrigerators, deep-freeze boxes, soft-drink-bottle coolers, and meat saws. . . .
>
> The vastness of western Navajoland changed rapidly with new and better roads, community centers, chapter houses, and local day schools. The young people returning from the war found living standards far above those they had left.[52]

There were yet other changes, as posts over the years either morphed into today's convenience stores or closed. Some became museums of a bygone era; others, especially those in more isolated communities, maintained a flavor of yesteryear by being an important community fixture, where people shopped for a few essentials and met their neighbors for brief discussions. In *Navajo Trading, The End of an Era*, Willow Roberts Powers examines the trading business of the last quarter of the twentieth century, with its Federal Trade Commission hearings that ended the practice of pawn on the reservation, the retirement of long-standing trader families who could no longer make a living at something that had sustained previous generations, further radical changes in Navajo culture and economy, and the shifting perception of traders and trading of the past.[53] Her subtitle, *The End of an Era*, was all too true. Sometimes vilified, often romanticized, but always interesting, those bygone days are relinquished to the pages of history.

In summarizing the period from 1880 to 1940, one cannot help but admire both Navajos and traders as their lives intersected in difficult circumstances. Life in a high-country desert, with all of its extremes, was not easy for either. Yet together they made it far more bearable, with each depending on the other for the things they had to offer. The physical arrangements of the store, business demeanor, and atmosphere were tailored to the culture of the Navajos, with enough flexibility in practices to meet the Indians' needs within a yearly cycle, while allowing the traders to earn their living and meet their obligations in the economy of mainstream America. All of this revolved around relationships between storeowner and patron. While there was, at times, friction and murder, greed and graft, theft and deception—as is found among all people in most circumstances—the lingering impression is that, for traders who were fair and cared for their customers, there grew a bond of friendship and trust that extended across the counters and on both sides of the bullpen.

Epilogue
Post Trading Post

The previous chapter introduced the reader to the decline and eventual dissolution of olden-day trading posts that were based on a system of barter and steeped in Navajo cultural practices. For the past eighty years this process continued until today, when most of the posts do not exist, have become tourist attractions, or have evolved into convenience stores. Just as the old posts were an expression of a time and the cultures of those who bargained there, so, too, are the stores of today, which meet the needs of their contemporary customers. The path that led to this point was often gradual and piecemeal, but inevitable, given the events and changes in mainstream America and on the Navajo Reservation. A brief synopsis here outlines just how multifaceted this change was.

Livestock reduction opened the door, while trooping in behind it came the wage economy with the Civilian Conservation Corps, civilian and military employment during World War II, the movie industry, and contract labor. Trading posts played major roles in getting Navajo workers off the reservation to labor on railroad crews, as seasonal harvesters, with Anglo livestock, and as general itinerant employees. Those offering and those seeking jobs looked to the stores as a central meeting place for a geographically dispersed community. There, opportunities for work and workers became available and often served as the pickup and drop-off points for projects that might last for six months or longer. Ideally, when the men or the families returned, they would have money in their pockets and good reputations as employees who could be called on for future hire. For those women and family members who did not accompany their husbands or fathers, they endured an uncomfortable dependence on a wage worker who was to return and assist with needs at home. Many women still speak of the 1940s and 1950s—before educational opportunities opened new doors for them—as difficult years, when they had to wait for money to appear. They no longer had enough livestock to independently sustain themselves and were unable to earn a livelihood solely by weaving.

Uranium and coal mining, as well as gas and oil exploration, were significant industries that not only allowed Navajos to remain on the reservation, but provided sufficient money, especially when added to government assistance. They allowed people to purchase goods at the local post. By the 1950s, as extractive industries opened new doors, they also helped close the old one of barter; more and more people turned to a cash-and-carry financial practice. Individual checks arrived at the post, where the trader held them for signatures, then payment for goods obtained on credit, before releasing the remainder to the owner. Unlike the old days, where the exchange of each object was physically monitored, the use of checks, the ability to read, and higher-math calculations left some Navajo customers uncertain about the fairness of the transaction and the honesty of the trader. A growing sophistication in business created a less-personal environment and an increasing distrust.

Transportation also underwent revolutionary change. The days of horse and wagon shifted to the automobile and an ever-expanding road system that included bridges, well-maintained dirt roads, and eventually macadam highways. Industry dependent upon shipping by truck encouraged tribal, state, and federal government investment in key arteries that fed the growing wealth pouring off Navajo lands. Families adopted trucks and cars as the daily workhorse that took them with greater ease to their destination. It is not by chance that the parts of a car are named and blessed in the same way that a horse was treated in the old days, while some features, like brakes, are referred to in the same terms as corresponding elements on a wooden wagon. Navajos, always a traveling people, took full advantage of the ability to shop off-reservation. One can imagine what this did to traders extending credit, getting pressure from the government in handling checks and accounts, and competing with store prices in an Anglo business world.

The interior of the Oljato trading post blends the new and old. From the cottonwood beams and the ceiling with its hanging goods, to the bullpen, large counter tops behind which is a foot-high elevated floor space, as well as out-of-reach shelves, to the electric lights, refrigerators, and soda machines, this structure combines remnants from a romanticized era with today's reality and customer demands. (NAU.PH. 99.53.3.24, Northern Arizona University, Cline Library, United Indian Traders Assoc. Collection.)

The 1960s and 1970s were a time of social protest, with assaults on the establishment—whatever "establishment" might mean. Black, Red, and Brown Power, along with women's rights, environmental concerns, and a growing drug culture became de rigueur as government and social institutions came under attack. Trading posts, an institution of frontier economy and later viewed by some as a leech on the ever-increasingly popular Indian culture, was no exception—they, too, became targets for criticism. To some critics, the trader and his way of life was a dinosaur that needed to be confined if not destroyed. Much of this task fell to DNA (*Dinébeiina Nahiilna Be Agaditahe* Incorporated—literally, "Lawyers Moving the People's Lives"), a gratuitous Navajo legal counsel, founded in 1967. In 1972–73, the Federal Trade Commission held a series of hearings, which gave rise to increasingly restrictive regulations that governed the posts. While traders continued to operate after these hearings, the pursuing DNA fostered a climate of lawsuits and "victimization" among the Navajos. Pawn, credit, and control of checks became prime sources of contention, and few traders wished to continue complying with new government regulations. What had been an institution built on relationships had deteriorated into a source of impersonal transaction.

At the same time, expanding educational opportunities on and off the reservation challenged, as never before, Navajo language and cultural knowledge. Indeed, the dominant society's practices, in general, proved far too alluring. The tribe had its hands full in trying to accelerate reading, writing, and arithmetic skills on one hand, while, at the same time, slowing the loss of cultural identity and linguistic ability. That struggle continues. The repository for past practices and beliefs has become more and more the domain of the grandparents who had lived during the livestock economy and the medicine men familiar with traditional teachings. The trading post as an institution became even less relevant to daily life as large conglomerate markets and businesses edged onto the reservation and into the larger Navajo communities. The end of an era had arrived.

Today, trading posts still dot reservation lands and surrounding areas. In many cases, only a mound of rubble or an elder's memory can indicate where one stood during those years when this institution was in its prime and functioning between two different cultures. Some posts, such as Hubbell's, are recognized on the National Historic Register, while others are in the private hands of those who wish to maintain that air of the Old West. Still others have been gutted of their yesteryear atmosphere, and now sell only bread, cupcakes, and soda pop. Some trader families own stores, often in big cities, and carry on their forebears' activities in swank, air-conditioned, well-lit buildings sporting displays of Navajo handcrafts. Regardless of the circumstances, the trading posts of the past provide a unique heritage—one based in hard work, cultural understanding, Navajo values, and above all, relationships. Most of those who stood at the counter in those days are gone, but the memories that they left still linger on both sides of the bullpen.

Notes

Introduction

1. Frank McNitt, *The Indian Traders* (Norman: University of Oklahoma Press, 1962, 1989).

Chapter 1. Of Songs, Prayers, and Spirit: Navajo Relationships and Property Concepts

1. The reader should check the bibliography for a more complete listing of books about trading posts and traders, but some of the more important works are suggested here. For those on trading posts as an institution, see McNitt, *The Indian Traders*; Willow Roberts Powers, *Navajo Trading: The End of an Era* (Albuquerque: University of New Mexico Press, 2001); and Teresa J. Wilkins, *Patterns of Exchange: Navajo Weavers and Traders* (Norman: University of Oklahoma Press, 2008). There are many individual stories about traders and their experiences. A good place to start (given here in alphabetical order) is William Y. Adams, *Shonto: The Study of the Role of the Trader in a Modern Navaho Community*, Smithsonian Institution Bureau of American Ethnology, Bulletin 188 (Washington, D.C.: Government Printing Office, 1963); Hilda Faunce (Wetherill), *Desert Wife* (Lincoln: University of Nebraska Press, 1928, 1981); Frances Gillmor and Louisa Wetherill, *Traders to the Navajos: The Story of the Wetherills of Kayenta* (Albuquerque: University of New Mexico Press, 1934, 1979); Franc Johnson Newcomb, *Navajo Neighbors* (Norman: University of Oklahoma Press, 1966); Gladwell Richardson, *Navajo Trader* (Tucson: University of Arizona Press, 1986); Willow Roberts, *Stokes Carson: Twentieth Century Trading on the Navajo Reservation* (Albuquerque: University of New Mexico Press, 1992); Susan E. Woods and Robert S. McPherson, *Along Navajo Trails: Recollections of a Trader, 1898–1948* (Logan: Utah State University Press, 2005).

2. Joe Manygoats interview with author, December 18, 1991.

3. Nellie Grandson interview with author, December 16, 1993.

4. Sam Black interview with author, December 18, 1993.

5. Gary Witherspoon, *Language and Art in the Navajo Universe* (Ann Arbor: University of Michigan Press, 1977), 17, 47.

6. Charlotte J. Frisbie and David P. McAllester, *Navajo Blessingway Singer: The Autobiography of Frank Mitchell, 1881–1967* (Tucson: University of Arizona Press, 1978), 210.

7. Washington Matthews, *Navaho Legends* (Salt Lake City: University of Utah Press, 1897, 1994), 129.

8. George Wharton James, *Indian Blankets and Their Makers* (New York: Dover, 1914, 1974), 185.

9. Gary Witherspoon, *Navajo Kinship and Marriage* (Chicago: University of Chicago Press, 1975), 37.

10. For a lengthy discussion of *hózhǫ*, see John R. Farella, *The Main Stalk: A Synthesis of Navajo Philosophy* (Tucson: University of Arizona Press, 1984).

11. Walter Dyk, *Son of Old Man Hat* (Lincoln: University of Nebraska Press, 1938, 1967), and Walter Dyk and Ruth Dyk, *Left Handed: A Navajo Autobiography* (New York: Columbia University Press, 1980).

12. Dyk and Dyk, *Left Handed*, 139.

13. Charlotte J. Frisbie, *Navajo Medicine Bundles, or Jish: Acquisition, Transmission, and Disposition in the Past and Present* (Albuquerque: University of New Mexico Press, 1987), 100–108.

14. Robert S. McPherson and John Fahey, "Seeing Is Believing: The Odyssey of the Pectol Shields," *Utah Historical Quarterly* 76, no. 4 (Fall 2008), 374.

15. See Berard Haile, O.F.M., *Property Concepts of the Navaho Indians* (Washington, D.C.: Catholic University of America Press, 1954), 20–22.

16. Dyk and Dyk, *Left Handed*, 253.

17. Ibid., 256–57.

18. Ibid., 258.

19. Ibid., 67.

20. Gladys A. Reichard, *Social Life of the Navajo Indians with Some Attention to Minor Ceremonies* (New York: Columbia University Press, 1928), 106.

21. Gladys A. Reichard, *Navaho Religion: A Study of Symbolism* (Princeton: Princeton University Press, 1950), 271.

22. Haile, *Property Concepts*, 25–29.

23. Franciscan Fathers, *An Ethnologic Dictionary of the Navajo Language* (St. Michaels, AZ: Saint Michaels Press, 1910, 1968), 174–75.

24. Reichard, *Social Life*, 91.

25. Dyk, *Son of Old Man Hat*, 324.

26. Ibid., vii.

27. Reichard, *Social Life, 90.*

28. See Clyde Kluckhohn, *Navaho Witchcraft* (Boston: Beacon Press, 1944, 1967), for an extensive explanation about who is accused of witchcraft, different types of witchcraft, and social effects.

29. Dyk and Dyk, *Left Handed*, 16.
30. Ibid., 467, 468.
31. Ibid., 452.
32. Ibid., 455, 457.
33. John Holiday and Robert S. McPherson, *A Navajo Legacy: The Life and Teachings of John Holiday* (Norman: University of Oklahoma Press, 2005), 249.
34. Ibid.
35. Ibid., 250.
36. Dyk, *Son of Old Man Hat*, 69.
37. Rose Mitchell with Charlotte J. Frisbie, *Tall Woman: The Life Story of Rose Mitchell, A Navajo Woman, c. 1874–1977* (Albuquerque: University of New Mexico Press, 2001), 84.
38. Buck Navajo interview with author, December 16, 1991.
39. Richard Hobson, *Navaho Acquisitive Values*, Reports of the Rimrock Project Values Series No. 5, Papers of the Peabody Museum of American Archaeology and Ethnology, Harvard University, vol. 42, no. 3 (Cambridge, MA: Peabody Museum, 1954), 4.
40. Ibid.
41. Ibid., 8.
42. Ibid., 11, 15.
43. Witherspoon, *Navajo Marriage and Kinship*, 57–58.
44. Hobson, *Navaho Acquisitive Values*, 28.
45. Ibid., 29.
46. Edward T. Hall, *West of the Thirties: Discoveries among the Navajo and Hopi* (New York: Doubleday, 1994), 120.
47. Ibid., 132.
48. Broderick H. Johnson, ed., *Stories of Traditional Navajo Life and Culture by Twenty-two Navajo Men and Women* (Tsaile, AZ: Navajo Community College Press, 1977), 138.
49. Marilyn Holiday interview with author, February 14, 1992; Charlie Blueyes interview with author, June 7, 1988.

Chapter 2. Setting the Stage: Traditional Trading Practices

1. For further information concerning the Paleo and Archaic Indian experience in southeastern Utah, see Robert S. McPherson, *A History of San Juan County: In the Palm of Time* (Salt Lake City: Utah State Historical Society, 1995), 27–48.
2. An excellent overview—prehistoric and historic—of trade amongst Native Americans in the Southwest is by Richard I. Ford, "Inter-Indian Exchange in the Southwest," *Handbook of North American Indians—Southwest* 10, Alfonso Ortiz, ed. (Washington: Smithsonian Institution, 1983), 711–22.

3. Southeastern Utah archaeologist Winston Hurst conversation with author, January 8, 2015.

4. See Robert S. McPherson, *Viewing the Ancestors: Perceptions of the Anaasází, Mokwič, and Hisatsinom* (Norman: University of Oklahoma Press, 2014).

5. For a good overview of this confusing, shifting period and the resulting conflicts and slave trade, see Ned Blackhawk, *Violence over the Land: Indians and Empires in the Early American West* (Cambridge, MA: Harvard University Press, 2006); William B. Carter, *Indian Alliances and the Spanish in the Southwest, 750–1750* (Norman: University of Oklahoma Press, 2009); L. R. Bailey, *Indian Slave Trade in the Southwest* (Los Angeles: Westernlore, 1966).

6. Franciscan Fathers, *Ethnologic Dictionary*, 489–90; W. W. Hill, "Navaho Trading and Trading Ritual: A Study of Cultural Dynamics," *Southwestern Journal of Anthropology* 4 (Autumn, 1948), 374–78.

7. Ibid., 379–80.

8. Mrs. Dan Tauchin interview with J. Lee Correll, December 10, 1960, Doris Duke #659, Doris Duke Oral History Project, Special Collections, Marriott Library, University of Utah, Salt Lake City, Utah, 22 (hereafter cited as Doris Duke Oral History Project).

9. Clyde Kluckhohn, as cited in Hill, "Navaho Trading," 381.

10. Hill, "Navaho Trading," 382.

11. Ibid., 382–83.

12. Mircea Eliade, *The Sacred and the Profane: The Nature of Religion* (New York: Harcourt, Brace, and World, 1959).

13. Robert S. McPherson, Jim Dandy, Sarah E. Burak, *Navajo Tradition, Mormon Life: The Autobiography and Teachings of Jim Dandy* (Salt Lake City: University of Utah Press, 2012), 170.

14. Matthews, *Navaho Legends*, 211; Blueyes interview with author, June 7, 1988; Florence Begay interview with author, April 29, 1998; Ada Black interview with author, December 16, 1991; Fred Yazzie interview with author, November 5, 1987; Joe Manygoats interview; Editha L. Watson, talk presented March 17, 1968, Doris Duke #796, Doris Duke Oral History Project, 22.

15. Florence Begay interview, April 29, 1988.

16. Tallis Holiday interview with author, November 3, 1987; see also Blueyes interview, June 7, 1988.

17. Florence Begay interview, April 29, 1988.

18. Sally Manygoats interview with author, April 8, 1992.

19. Hill, "Navaho Trading," 386.

20. Ibid., 384.

21. Gillmor and Louisa Wetherill, *Traders to the Navajos*, 189.

22. Hill, "Navaho Trading," 386.

23. Reichard, *Navaho Religion*, 299.

24. Dyk and Dyk, *Left Handed*, 288.

25. Martha Fisher interview with David Brugge, January 5, 1961, Doris Duke #918, Doris Duke Oral History Project, 117.

26. Robert S. McPherson, *The Journey of Navajo Oshley: An Autobiography and Life History* (Logan: Utah State University Press, 2000), 74.

27. Blueyes interview with author, June 7, 1988.

28. See Sarah Hornsby and Robert S. McPherson, "'Enemies like a Road Covered with Ice': The Utah Navajos' Experience during the Long Walk Period, 1858–1868," *American Indian Culture and Research Journal* 33 no. 2 (Spring 2009), 1–22.

29. Hill, "Navaho Trading," 388.

30. Ford, "Inter-Indian Exchange," 718.

31. Hill, "Navaho Trading," 389.

32. Ford, "Inter-Indian Exchange," 720.

33. Hill, "Navaho Trading," 391.

34. Dyk and Dyk, *Left Handed*, 255.

35. Ibid., 260–61.

36. Faunce (Wetherill), *Desert Wife*, 281. Hilda Faunce was married to Ben Wetherill at the time she and her husband ran the Covered Water trading post. The marriage was dissolved, however, by the time Hilda published the account of her experiences at the post under her maiden name. In that account, she changed her then-husband's name from "Ben" to "Ken."

37. Ibid., 283.

38. Samuel Moon, *Tall Sheep: Harry Goulding, Monument Valley Trader* (Norman: University of Oklahoma Press, 1992), 44.

Chapter 3. Thinking about Architecture: Navajo Values in the Home and at the Post

1. V. B. Price, "Epilogue," in *Anasazi Architecture and American Design*, eds. Baker H. Morrow and V. B. Price (Albuquerque: University of New Mexico Press, 1997), 228.

2. Louis H. Sullivan, "The Tall Office Building Artistically Considered," *Lippincott's Magazine* (March 1896), 403–9.

3. Edward T. Hall, *The Hidden Dimension* (Garden City, NY: Doubleday, 1969), 103.

4. Aileen O'Bryan, *Navaho Indian Myths* (New York: Dover, 1993), 13.

5. Cosmos Mindeleff, "Navaho Houses," in *Seventeenth Annual Report of the Bureau of American Ethnology*, Smithsonian Institution, Part Two, 1895–96 (Washington, D.C.: Government Printing Office 1898), 488.

6. Franc Johnson Newcomb, *Navaho Folk Tales* (Albuquerque: University of New Mexico Press, 1967), 192–203.

7. Stephen C. Jett, *Navajo Architecture: Forms, History, Distributions* (Tucson: University of Arizona Press, 1981).

8. Leopold Ostermann, O.F.M., "Franciscans in the Wilds and Wastes of the Navajo Country," *St. Anthony Messenger* 12, no. 3 (August 1904), 82.

9. Peter Nabokov and Robert Easton, *Native American Architecture* (New York: Oxford University Press, 1989), 326.

10. Berard Haile, O.F.M., "Some Cultural Aspects of the Navajo Hogan," talk given at Fort Wingate, 1937, in Berard Haile Papers, Special Collections, Library of St. Leonard College, Dayton, Ohio.

11. Leland C. Wyman, *Blessingway, with Three Versions of the Myth Recorded and Translated from the Navajo by Father Berard Haile, O.F.M* (Tucson: University of Arizona Press, 1970), 15.

12. See Don Mose Jr. and Katie Smith, *The Navajo Hogan* (Blanding, UT: San Juan School District, 1996); Sam Martinez, "Hogans," in *Tsá' Ászi': A Magazine of Navajo Culture* 4, no. 3 (December 1980), 38–41; Chester D. Hubbard, *Hooghan Haz' Ą́ą́gi Bóhoo' aah* (The Learning of That Which Pertains to the Home) (Tsaile, AZ: Navajo Community College, 1977); and Berard Haile, O.F.M., "Why the Navajo Hogan?" *Primitive Man* 15, nos. 3 and 4 (July and October 1942), 39–56.

13. Hubbard, *Hooghan*, 4; Mose and Smith, *Navajo Hogan*, 3.

14. Haile, "Why the Navajo Hogan?" 41, 47.

15. Dyk, *Son of Old Man Hat*, 75.

16. Haile, "Why the Navajo Hogan?" 51.

17. Gladys A. Reichard, *Prayer: The Compulsive Word* (New York: J. J. Augustin, 1944), 27–28.

18. See William N. Fenton, *The Great Law and the Longhouse: A Political History of the Iroquois Confederacy* (Norman: University of Oklahoma Press, 1998), 135–63.

19. McPherson, Dandy, and Burak, *Navajo Tradition*, 78.

20. Jenny Francis interview with author, March 23, 1993.

21. Gilmore Graymountain interview with author, April 7, 1992; Ada Black interview with author, October 11, 1991; Mose, *Honeeshgish*, 8.

22. McPherson, Dandy, and Burak, *Navajo Tradition*, 169–70.

23. There will never be a complete listing of all the posts that served the Navajos on or near their reservation. However, one of the most complete listings to date is provided by Klara Kelly and Harris Francis at their website, "Navajoland Trading Post Encyclopedia," found at www.navajotradingposts.info (accessed June 1, 2015). Here they list 258 posts, with a disclaimer that their work at this point is ongoing and additions will follow.

24. Elizabeth Compton Hegemann, *Navaho Trading Days* (Albuquerque: University of New Mexico Press, 1963), 271.

25. Ibid., 269.

26. Leopold Ostermann, O.F.M., "Little Mission Stories from Our Own Southwest," *St. Anthony Messenger* 34, no. 12 (May 1927), 634–35.

27. Mildred Heflin interview with Dean Sundberg, June 30, 1972, O.H. 1168, Southeastern Utah Oral History Project, Utah State Historical Society

and California State University, Fullerton (hereafter cited as Southeastern Utah Oral History Project), 3, 5; Hegemann, *Navaho Trading Days*, 270.

28. Idonna Hunt Cook and John LaRay Hunt, *John Hunt Family History* (Blanding, UT: Self-published, 1993), 23.

29. Ibid., 27.

30. Faunce, *Desert Wife*, 85–97.

31. For a more complete treatment of Navajo thought concerning Ancestral Puebloans, known popularly as the Anasazi, see McPherson, *Viewing the Ancestors*.

32. Alberta Hannum, *Spin a Silver Dollar: The Story of a Desert Trading Post* (New York: Ballantine, 1944, 1972), 24–27, 44–47.

33. Roberts, *Stokes Carson*, 23–24.

34. "Navajo Trading," *Survey of Conditions of the Indians in the United States*, Hearing before the Subcommittee of Indian Affairs, U.S. Senate, August 19, 1936, 75th Congress, Part 34, 18043-44. (hereafter cited as *Survey of Conditions).*

35. Hegemann, *Navaho Trading Days*, ix.

36. Ibid., 267–68.

37. "Indian Traders," *Report of the Commissioner of Indian Affairs, 1903* (Washington, D.C.: U.S. Department of the Interior), 34; E. B. Merritt to William T. Sullivan, March 26, 1914, Record Group 75, Bureau of Indian Affairs, Western Navajo Agency Correspondence, National Archives, Washington, D.C. (hereafter cited as Western Navajo Agency Correspondence); Hegemann, *Navaho Trading Days*, 267–68.

38. "Navajo Trading," *Survey of Conditions*, 18044.

39. Newcomb, *Navajo Neighbors*, 25.

40. Hegemann, *Navaho Trading Days*, 343.

41. Richardson, *Navajo Trader*, 122.

42. Haile, "Why the Navajo Hogan?" 40.

43. The calculation of this percentage is far from scientific. I and Georgiana Simpson, who was raised in a trader family and has been in and out of Navajo trading posts all of her life, derived a list of sixty-five posts that we had visited and were familiar with. We determined the location of the door entering the bullpen and calculated percentages, finding that 55 percent of them had east-facing doors, 27 percent south-facing, 9 percent west-facing, and 9 percent north-facing doors. I then contacted Klara Kelly (see note 23 above), whose encyclopedic knowledge of posts reservation-wide no doubt differed somewhat from those I was familiar with. I did not tell her about what posts I had listed or the percentages that I obtained. Her response was that "about 55 to 60 percent" of the seventy-eight posts "all over Navajo land and all over the alphabet" had east-facing doors, confirming what I had determined.

44. Hegemann, *Navaho Trading Days*, 323.

45. Wilkins, *Patterns of Exchange*, 41.

46. Hall, *West of the Thirties*, 143.

47. Stanford L. Hassell, "Navaho Trader," unpublished manuscript, n.d., New Mexico Writers' Project, WPA #61, State Records Center and Archives, Santa Fe, 12.

48. Frank Leland Noel and Mary Elizabeth Noel, *Eighty Years in America* (Self-published, 1962), 21.

49. Arthur L. Chaffin interview with P. T. Reilly, December 24, 1966, "Trading Posts," Special Collections, Utah State Historical Society, Salt Lake City, Utah, 11–15.

50. Hegemann, *Navaho Trading Days*, 345.

51. Hall, *West of the Thirties*, 143.

52. Hall, *The Hidden Dimension*, 120.

53. Ibid., 121–23.

Chapter 4. Building Bonds, Trading Goods: The Navajo Post Experience

1. For a good overview of this period, see Gerald Thompson, *The Army and the Navajo: The Bosque Redondo Reservation Experiment, 1863–1868* (Tucson: University of Arizona Press, 1982); Clifford E. Trafzer, *The Kit Carson Campaign: The Last Great Navajo War* (Norman: University of Oklahoma Press, 1982); Lynn R. Bailey, *The Long Walk: A History of the Navajo Wars, 1848–1868* (Pasadena, CA: Westernlore, 1978); Broderick H. Johnson, ed., *Navajo Stories of the Long Walk Period* (Tsaile, AZ: Navajo Community College Press, 1973); R. C. Gordon-McCutchan, ed., *Kit Carson: Indian Fighter or Indian Killer?* (Niwot, CO: University Press of Colorado, 1996); Tom Dunlay, *Kit Carson and the Indians* (Lincoln: University of Nebraska Press, 2000). For the best collection of original contemporary documents for this period of history, see J. Lee Correll, *Through White Men's Eyes: A Contribution to Navajo History* III-VI (Window Rock, AZ: Navajo Heritage Center, 1979).

2. Gillmor and Louisa Wetherill, *Traders to the Navajos*, 72–73.

3. Dyk, *Son of Old Man Hat*, 56.

4. Mitchell with Frisbie, *Tall Woman*, 45.

5. Samuel Holiday and Robert S. McPherson, *Under the Eagle: Samuel Holiday, Navajo Code Talker* (Norman: University of Oklahoma Press, 2013), 35.

6. Moon, *Tall Sheep*, 27.

7. Paul Begay interview with Karen Underhill, February 10, 1998, NAU O.H. 75.9, United Indian Traders Association Oral History Project, Special Collections, Cline Library, Northern Arizona University, Flagstaff (hereafter cited as United Indian Traders Association Oral History Project).

8. Fred Yazzie interview with author, November 1, 1985.

9. Dyk, *Son of Old Man Hat*, 37.

10. Moon, *Tall Sheep*, 46.

11. Dyk, *Son of Old Man Hat*, 231–32.

12. Hall, *West of the Thirties*, 88, 90.

13. Louise Lamphere, *To Run after Them: Cultural and Social Bases of Cooperation in a Navajo Community* (Tucson: University of Arizona Press, 1977), xi.

14. John Ladd, *Structure of a Moral Code* (Cambridge, MA: Harvard University Press, 1957), 253–55.

15. Lamphere, *To Run after Them*, 36.

16. Hall, *West of the Thirties*, 21.

17. Hegemann, *Navaho Trading Days*, 322.

18. Yazzie interview, November 1, 1985.

19. Tom Kirk, *The Kirk Clan, Traders with the Navajo*, Brand Book no. 6, in *Peoples of the Far West* series (San Diego, CA: Corral of the Westerners, 1979), 150.

20. For an excellent study of kinship dynamics, see Mary Shepardson and Blodwen Hammond, *The Navajo Mountain Community, Social Organization and Kinship Terminology* (Los Angeles: University of California Press, 1970).

21. Deescheeny Nez Tracy, cited in *Stories of Traditional Navajo Life and Culture*, ed. Broderick Johnson, 158.

22. Hilda Wetherill, "The Trading Post: Letters from a Primitive Land," *Atlantic Monthly* 142, no. 3 (September, 1928), 289–90.

23. Lamphere, *To Run after Them*, 57.

24. Ibid., 57–62.

25. Kirk, *Kirk Clan*, 152.

26. Hilda Wetherill, "The Trading Post, Letters from a Primitive Land," *Atlantic Monthly* 142, no. 4 (October, 1928), 510.

27. Hegemann, *Navaho Trading Days*, 323.

28. Newcomb, *Navajo Neighbors*, 46.

29. Earle R. Forrest, *With a Camera in Old Navaholand* (Norman: University of Oklahoma Press, 1970), 74.

30. Faunce, *Desert Wife*, 135–36.

31. Ostermann, "Franciscans in the Wilds and Wastes," 368.

32. Walter Dyk, *A Navaho Autobiography* (New York: Viking Fund, 1947), 75.

33. Dyk and Dyk, *Left Handed*, 140.

34. Ibid., 140–43.

35. Emanuel Trockur, O.F.M., "Tangled Names," *Indian Sentinel* 24, no. 2 (February 1944), 27.

36. Berard Haile, O.F.M., as cited in *The Navajo as Seen by the Franciscans, 1898–1921: A Sourcebook*, ed. Howard M. Bahr (Lanham, MD: Scarecrow Press, 2004), 521.

37. Cook and Hunt, *John Hunt Family History*, 91; Stewart Hatch interview with author, May 7, 2010.

38. Stewart Hatch interview, May 7, 2010.

39. Cook and Hunt, *John Hunt Family History*, 28.

40. Kirk, *Kirk Clan*, 153.

41. Fern Charley interview with Dean Sundberg, July 13, 1972, O.H. 11224, Southeastern Utah Oral History Project, 13, 22.

42. Moon, *Tall Sheep*, 62.

43. Elijah Blair interview with Karen Underhill, February 9, 1998, NAU O.H. 75.11, United Indian Traders Association Oral History Project.

44. Roberts, *Stokes Carson*, 83.

45. For a more thorough understanding of these divinatory powers, see Robert S. McPherson, *Dinéjí Na'nitin, Navajo Traditional Teachings and History* (Boulder: University Press of Colorado, 2012), 13–43.

46. Newcomb, *Navajo Neighbors*, 186.

47. Ibid., 188.

Chapter 5. Standing behind the Counter: The Qualifications and Qualities of a Trader

1. "Rules and Regulations Prepared in Conformity with the Preceding Provision of Law as Contained in Section 5 of the Act of August 15, 1876," Ute Agency, Record Group 75, Regulations and Circulars on Indian Traders, Bureau of Indian Affairs, Box 11, Denver Records Center, Denver, CO, 8–9.

2. C. F. Larrabee, Acting Commissioner to Indian Agents and School Superintendents in Charge of Agencies, August 10, 1905, Ute Agency, Record Group 75, Regulations and Circulars on Indian Traders, Bureau of Indian Affairs, Box 11, Denver Records Center, Denver, CO.

3. Hegemann, *Navaho Trading Days*, 346; Noel and Noel, *Eighty Years*, 25.

4. E. B. Merritt to William T. Sullivan, March 26, 1914, Western Navajo Agency Correspondence.

5. Kelly and Francis, "Navajoland Trading Post Encyclopedia," www.navajo tradingposts.info.

6. "The Indian Trader," *Reports of the Commissioner of Indian Affairs* (Washington, D. C.: Government Printing Office, 1905), 27.

7. McNitt, *Indian Traders*.

8. "Navajo Trading," *Survey of Conditions*, 18043-44.

9. Ibid.

10. Richardson, *Navajo Trader*, 21.

11. Adams, *Shonto*, 155.

12. Vernon Jack interviews with Mark Collins, July 12 and 27, 1978, O.H. 1636, Southeastern Utah Oral History Project, 3.

13. Heflin interview, 10.

14. Ray Hunt interview with Kathy Biel, August 12, 1970, O.H. 280a, Southeastern Utah Oral History Project, 16.

15. Paul Begay interview.

16. Woods and McPherson, *Along Navajo Trails*, 45.

17. John Lorenzo Hubbell, "Fifty Years an Indian Trader," *Touring Topics* 22, no. 12 (December 1930), 28.
18. John Dick, as cited in *Stories of Traditional Navajo Life and Culture*, ed. Broderick Johnson, 188.
19. William Y. Adams, "The Image of the Trader," paper given at the Ninth Navajo Studies Conference, April 1996, Flagstaff, Arizona, in possession of author.
20. Adams, *Shonto*, 211.
21. Hubbell, "Fifty Years an Indian Trader," 28–29.
22. Richardson, *Navajo Trader*, 97–98.
23. Ibid., 76–79.
24. Hegemann, *Navaho Trading Days*, 58.
25. Elijah Blair interview.
26. Moon, *Tall Sheep*, 29.
27. Hall, *West of the Thirties*, 86–87, 146.
28. Ray Hunt interview with Kathy Biel, August 12, 1970, 4.
29. Grace Hunt interview with Marwynne Selfridge, April 15, 1987, O.H. 1910, Southeastern Utah Oral History Project, 12.
30. Cook and Hunt, *John Hunt Family History*, 53.
31. Kirk, *Kirk Clan*, 152–53.
32. Mary Bailey interview with Karen Underhill, July 13, 1999, NAU O.H. 75.41, United Indian Traders Association Oral History Project.
33. Gladys Jack interview with Mark Collins, July 25, 1978, O.H. 1637, Southeastern Utah Oral History Project, 6; Vernon Jack interview, July 12, 1978, 29.
34. Moon, *Tall Sheep*, 24.
35. Ibid., 61.
36. Hegemann, *Navaho Trading Days*, 301.
37. Adams, *Shonto*, 213.
38. Ibid.; Ray Hunt interview with Alice Maxwell, April 15, 1987, O.H. 280c, Southeastern Utah Oral History Project, 2.
39. Vernon Jack interviews, 6.
40. Gladys Yellowman interview with author, July 19, 1988.
41. Adams, *Shonto*, 213–14.
42. Emanuel Trockur, O.F.M., "What's in a Navajo Name?" *Indian Sentinel* 26, no. 5 (May 1936), 67; Emanuel Trockur, O.F.M., "Navajo Names," April 20, 1959, "Navajo Culture, Religion, Customs," box 51, fldr 3, Franciscan Fathers Collection, Special Collections, University of Arizona, Tucson.
43. Kirk, *Kirk Clan*, 152–53.
44. Carl G. Hines, "Navajo Indian Trader," manuscript #308, Glenn L. Emmons Papers, Special Collections, University of New Mexico, Albuquerque, 29.
45. Bahr, ed., *The Navajo as Seen by the Franciscans*, 68–69.

46. Hines, "Navajo Indian Trader," 30.

47. Martha Blue, *Indian Trader: The Life and Times of J. L. Hubbell* (Walnut, CA: Kiva Publishing, 2000), 112–15.

48. Forrest, *With a Camera*, 31.

49. Mrs. Roman (Dorothy) Hubbell interview with David M. Brugge, October 13–24, 1969, Frank McNitt Collection, Box 18, State Records Center, Santa Fe, NM, 57.

50. Hannum, *Spin a Silver Dollar*, 116.

51. Woods and McPherson, *Along Navajo Trails*, 45–48.

52. Cook and Hunt, *John Hunt Family History*, 100.

53. Ray Hunt interview with Alice Maxwell, April 15, 1987, 15.

54. "The Trading Posts," *Survey of Conditions*, 18042.

55. Richardson, *Navajo Trader*, 66.

56. Dyk, *Navaho Autobiography*, 65.

57. Hilda Wetherill, "Trading Post," *Atlantic Monthly* 142, no. 4 (October 1928), 519.

58. For an explanation of the Navajos' first impressions and experience with cars and planes, see Robert S. McPherson, *Navajo Land, Navajo Culture: The Utah Experience in the Twentieth Century* (Norman: University of Oklahoma Press, 2001), 84–101.

59. Vernon Jack interviews, 17.

60. Franc Johnson Newcomb, *Hosteen Klah: Navaho Medicine Man and Sand Painter* (Norman: University of Oklahoma Press, 1964), 170.

61. Hilda Wetherill, "Trading Post," *Atlantic Monthly* 142, no. 3 (September 1928), 298–99.

62. Gladys Jack interview, 26–27.

Chapter 6. Exchanging Wealth: Stock and Livestock

1. Ella Sakizzie interview with author, May 14, 1991.

2. Paul Begay interview.

3. Clyde Kluckhohn and Dorothea Leighton, *The Navaho* (Cambridge, MA: Harvard University Press, 1946, 1974), 83.

4. Richard Hobson, *Navaho Acquisitive Values*, Reports of the Rimrock Project Values, Series No. 5, Papers of the Peabody Museum of American Archaeology and Ethnology 42 (Cambridge, MA: Peabody Museum, 1954), 7.

5. For a discussion about wealth and witchcraft and other forms of antisocial behavior, see McPherson, *Dinéjí Na'nitin*, 72–99.

6. Hobson, *Navaho Acquisitive Values*, 26.

7. Census of the Navajo Reservation—1915, with letter by Peter Paquette, Film #579,683, Microfilm Division, Harold B. Lee Library, Brigham Young University, Provo, UT.

8. Robert W. Young, *The Role of the Navajo in the Southwestern Drama* (Gallup, NM: *Gallup Independent* and Robert W. Young, 1968), 66.

9. For a more complete explanation of wealth on the reservation at this time, see "Ricos and Pobres: Wealth Distribution on the Navajo Reservation in 1915," *New Mexico Historical Review* 60, no. 4 (Fall 1985), 415–34, excerpts from which are included here.

10. Blueyes interview with author, July 8, 1988.

11. Walter Runke to Commissioner of Indian Affairs, May 5, 1919, Western Navajo Agency Correspondence.

12. Stewart Hatch interview, May 7, 2010.

13. Amasa Jay Redd interview with Charles S. Peterson, July 27, 1973, CRC-C7, Charles Redd Center for Western Studies, Brigham Young University, Provo, UT, 45.

14. Kirk, *Kirk Clan*, 149.

15. Stewart Hatch interview, May 7, 2010.

16. Garrick Bailey and Roberta Bailey, *A History of the Navajos: The Reservation Years* (Santa Fe, NM: School of American Research, 1986), 115.

17. Moon, *Tall Sheep*, 70.

18. Sharp to Commissioner of Indian Affairs, January 4, 1923; Commissioner of Indian Affairs to Sharp, Feb 10, 1923; Sharp to "All Indians, Traders, and Stockmen," March 9, 1923; Sharp to Commissioner of Indian Affairs, March 9, 1923, all in Western Navajo Agency Correspondence.

19. Runke to Cato Sells, June 7, 1919, Western Navajo Agency Correspondence; F. E. Brandon, "Industrial Survey," Western Navajo Agency, October 25, 1922, Western Navajo Agency, Record Group 75, Bureau of Indian Affairs, National Archives, Washington, D.C.

20. James F. Downs, *Animal Husbandry in Navajo Culture and Society*, University of California Publications in Anthropology 1 (Los Angeles: University of California Press, 1964), 32–34.

21. Sam Bingham and Janet Bingham, *Between Sacred Mountains: Navajo Stories and Lessons from the Land* (Chinle, AZ: Rock Point Community School, 1982), 179.

22. Stewart Hatch interview, May 7, 2010.

23. McPherson, *Journey of Navajo Oshley*, 105.

24. Lamphere, *To Run after Them*, 115.

25. Roberts, *Stokes Carson*, 60–61.

26. Ibid., 61.

27. Stewart Hatch interview, May 7, 2010.

28. Faunce, *Desert Wife*, 8; Hegemann, *Navaho Trading Days*, 313.

29. Ruth Claw interview with Gary Shumway, July 11, 1968, Doris Duke #477, Doris Duke Oral History Project, 58.

30. Blue, *Indian Trader*, 49.

31. Grace Hunt interview, 14.

32. Brandon, "Industrial Survey."

33. Sharp to Commissioner of Indian Affairs, March 1, 1923 Western Navajo Agency Correspondence.

34. Bailey and Bailey, *History of the Navajos*, 149.

35. Faunce, *Desert Wife*, 278.

36. Byron A. Sharp to "Farmers, Traders, and Indians," September 30, 1922, Western Navajo Agency Correspondence.

37. Stewart Hatch interview, May 7, 2010.

38. Gladys Jack interview, 12.

39. Maria Chabot, "Some Aspects of the Navajo Problem," Report for the New Mexico Association of Indian Affairs, (Santa Fe: Museum of New Mexico, Laboratory of Anthropology, 1941), 8.

40. Moon, *Tall Sheep*, 22.

41. Dyk, *Son of Old Man Hat*, 105.

42. Hegemann, *Navaho Trading Days*, 323; John R. Winslowe, "Camps of the Nut Pickers," *True West* 17 no. 3 (January–February 1970), 67.

43. Hines, "Navajo Indian Trader," 8; Kirk, *Kirk Clan*, 149.

44. Hines, "Navajo Indian Trader," 9.

45. Winslowe, "Camps of the Nut Pickers," 37, 67.

46. Kirk, *Kirk Clan*, 149; Hegemann, *Navaho Trading Days*, 323; Richardson, *Navajo Trader*, 15–16.

47. Hassell, "Navaho Trader," 1, 13–15.

48. Blueyes interview, June 7, 1988.

49. Vernon Jack interviews, 11.

50. Mitchell with Frisbie, *Tall Woman*, 46.

51. Holiday and McPherson, *Navajo Legacy*, 41; Hegemann, *Navaho Trading Days*, 297.

52. Vernon Jack interviews, 11–12.

53. Grace Hunt interview, 17.

54. Dyk, *Son of Old Man Hat*, 73.

55. Joe Lee and Gladwell Richardson, "My Wonderful Country," *Frontier Times* 48 no. 2 (February–March 1974), 13.

56. Hegemann, *Navaho Trading Days*, 312.

57. Stewart Hatch interview, May 7, 2010; Vernon Jack interviews, 12; Ray Hunt interview with Alice Maxwell, 3; Mitchell and Frisbie, *Tall Woman*, 30; Hegemann, *Navaho Trading Days*, 271.

58. Ration, as cited in *Stories of Traditional Navajo Life and Culture*, ed. Broderick Johnson, 306.

59. Max Hanley, as cited in *Stories of Traditional Navajo Life and Culture*, ed. Broderick Johnson, 25.

60. Paul Begay interview.

61. Stewart Hatch interview, May 7, 2010; Vernon Jack interviews, 12, 31.

62. Cook and Hunt, *John Hunt Family History*, 96.

63. Ibid., 35.

64. Ration, as cited in *Stories of Traditional Navajo Life and Culture*, ed. Broderick Johnson, 304; Faunce, *Desert Wife*, 199.

65. Cook and Hunt, *John Hunt Family History*, 102.

66. Newcomb, *Navajo Neighbors*, 153–54.

67. Cook and Hunt, *John Hunt Family History*, 78.

68. Vernon Jack interviews, 18.

69. Gladys Jack interview, 27–28.

Chapter 7. Weaving a Lifestyle: Rugs and Pawn

1. For a general examination and chronology of the Navajo economy between 1868 and 1975, see Bailey and Bailey, *History of the Navajos*; for the evolution of specific trading posts and conflict emanating from them, see McNitt, *Indian Traders*. Three classics on the evolution of weaving and silversmithing are Charles Avery Amsden, *Navajo Weaving: Its Technic and its History* (Glorieta, NM: Rio Grande Press, 1934); George Wharton James, *Indian Blankets and Their Makers* (New York: Dover, 1920, 1974); and John Adair, *The Navajo and Pueblo Silversmiths* (Norman: University of Oklahoma Press, 1944, 1973). Anthropologist Gladys A. Reichard, a specialist in Navajo culture, shares her experience in living with, and learning from, a Navajo family about weaving in *Spider Woman: A Story of Navajo Weavers and Chanters* (Albuquerque: University of New Mexico Press, 1934, 1997); *Navajo Weaver and Shepherd* (Glorieta, NM: Rio Grande Press, 1984); and *Weaving a Navajo Blanket* (New York: Dover, 1936, 1974). Four books look at the role of J. L. Hubbell as a profitable trader and the issues of profiteering and honesty, while giving a general overview of trader-customer relations: Blue, *Indian Trader*; Kathy M'Closkey, *Swept under the Rug: A Hidden History of Navajo Weaving* (Albuquerque: University of New Mexico Press, 2002); Wilkins, *Patterns of Exchange*, and Powers, *Navajo Trading*.

2. Martha Nez interview with author, August 10, 1988.

3. Franciscan Fathers, *Ethnologic Dictionary*, 222.

4. Maureen Trudelle Schwarz, *Molded in the Image of Changing Woman: Navajo Views on the Human Body and Personhood* (Tucson: University of Arizona Press, 1997), 48.

5. Nez interview; Clayton Long, discussion with author, March 25, 2015.

6. Daisy Buck, conversation with author, August 18, 1989; Nakai Begay interview with Bette Benally, February 24, 1991; Rose Begay interview with Bertha Parrish, June 17, 1987.

7. Franciscan Fathers, *Ethnologic Dictionary*, 251.

8. See McPherson, *Viewing the Ancestors*.

9. Wilkins, *Patterns of Exchange*, 100–101.

10. James, *Indian Blankets*, 45.

11. Jessie E. Rogers, "Primitive Art of Navajo Women," *Home Mission Monthly* 25, no. 4 (February 1911), 88–89.

12. Hegemann, *Navaho Trading Days*, 299.

13. Mitchell with Frisbie, *Tall Woman*, 47–48.

14. Ibid., 170–71, 118.

15. Stewart Hatch interview, November 13, 2010.

16. Noel and Noel, *Eighty Years*, 21.

17. Hines, "Navajo Indian Trader," 21.

18. Kirk, *Kirk Clan*, 151–52.

19. Hassell, "Navaho Trader," 3–4.

20. Kirk, *Kirk Clan*, 149.

21. Brandon, "Industrial Survey."

22. Hegemann, *Navaho Trading Days*, 274, 317–18.

23. Stewart Hatch interview, November 13, 2010.

24. Richardson, *Navajo Trader*, 176.

25. "Navajo Blankets," Spring/Summer 1942, Sears and Roebuck Catalog, 929.

26. "Native Industries—Navajo Blankets," *Report of the Commissioner of Indian Affairs*, vol. II (Washington, D.C.: Government Printing, 1914), 36.

27. F. H. Abbott to Stephen Janus, November 10, 1909, Western Navajo Agency Correspondence.

28. "Shiprock Has First Navajo Indian Fair," *Farmington (NM) Enterprise*, October 29, 1909, 1; Dyk, *Navaho Autobiography*, 143; "Native Industries—Navajo Blankets," 36.

29. Richardson, *Navajo Trader*, 176–77; Hannum, *Spin a Silver Dollar*, 50–51; Hegemann, *Navaho Trading Days*, 362; Newcomb, *Hosteen Klah*, 114–15; Rebecca M. Valette, "Early Navajo Sandpainting Blankets: A Reassessment," *American Indian Art Magazine* 37, no. 2 (Spring 2012), 54–65.

30. Stewart Hatch interview, November 13, 2010.

31. One of the best detailed discussions about the history and evolution of basket making, with an extensive bibliography, is found in Georgiana Kennedy Simpson, *Navajo Ceremonial Baskets: Sacred Symbols, Sacred Space* (Summertown, TN: Native Voices, 2003).

32. See Harry Tschopik Jr., "Taboo as a Possible Factor Involved in the Obsolescence of Navaho Pottery and Basketry," *American Anthropologist* 40, no. 2 (April–June 1938), 257–62.

33. Simpson, *Navajo Ceremonial Baskets*, 64–65.

34. Hubbell interview, 63.

35. Cook and Hunt, *John Hunt Family History*, 103; Hegemann, *Navaho Trading Days*, 370.

36. Hines, "Navajo Indian Trader," 28.

37. Jim Dandy discussion with author, December 7, 2010.

38. Don Mose discussion with author, December 14, 2010.

39. Stewart Hatch interview, November 13, 2010.

40. See Adair, *Navajo and Pueblo Silversmiths*, for a detailed history of the development of this craft, 3–28.

41. Ration, as cited in *Stories of Traditional Navajo Life and Culture*, ed. Broderick Johnson, 329–30.

42. Bailey and Bailey, *History of the Navajos*, 152–54; E. Merritt to Walter Runke, April 4, 1919; Runke to Commissioner, March 12, 1919, Western Navajo Agency Correspondence; Hegemann, *Navaho Trading Days*, 273.

43. Hassell, "Navaho Trader," 1.

44. Ibid., 10.

45. "The Trading Posts," *Survey of Conditions*, 18042.

46. For a detailed summary of pawn and how it worked in both traditional and contemporary Navajo culture, see William S. Kiser, "Navajo Pawn: A Misunderstood Traditional Trading Practice," *American Indian Quarterly* 36 no. 2 (Spring 2012), 150–81.

47. Moon, *Tall Sheep*, 47.

48. Hilda Wetherill, "Trading Post," *Atlantic Monthly* 142, no. 4 (October 1928), 512.

49. Hall, *West of the Thirties*, 151–52.

50. Bahr, ed., *The Navajo as Seen by the Franciscans*, 541.

51. Ray Hunt interview with Kathy Biel, 10.

52. Hall, *West of the Thirties*, 152.

53. Bahr, ed., *The Navajo as Seen by the Franciscans*, 542.

54. Kirk, *Kirk Clan*, 151.

55. Stewart Hatch interview, November 13, 2010.

56. Vernon Jack interviews, 24.

57. Mildred Carson Heflin, "Indian Trading Posts," n.d., Gladwell Richardson Collection, Special Collection, Cline Library, Northern Arizona University, Flagstaff, Arizona, n.p. (hereafter cited as Richardson Collection).

58. "The Trading Posts," 18045.

59. "Statement of New Mexico Association of Indian Affairs," *Survey of Conditions*, 17829.

60. Stewart Hatch interview, November 13, 2010.

61. Adams, "Image of the Trader."

62. "Trading Regulations," Radio Broadcast from KTGM, Window Rock, AZ, April 25, 1939, Richardson Collection, box 66, fldr 100, 2.

63. Ibid., 5.

64. "The Trading Posts," *Survey of Conditions*, 18108.

65. Hall, *West of the Thirties*, 144–45.

66. "The Trading Posts," *Survey of Conditions*, 18109.

67. Paul Begay interview with Karen Underhill, February 10, 1998, NAU O.H. 75.9, United Indian Traders Association Oral History Project.

68. Hall, *West of the Thirties*, 151, 149.

Chapter 8. Social Life at the Posts: Ladies, Law, and Laughter

1. There are many books that examine the role of women in Navajo culture, but for two of the best, see Gary Witherspoon, *Navajo Kinship and Marriage* (Chicago: University of Chicago Press, 1975) and Schwartz, *Molded in the Image of Changing Woman*.

2. Hall, *West of the Thirties*, 115.

3. Faunce, *Desert Wife*, 78–79.

4. Hilda Wetherill, "Trading Post," *Atlantic Monthly* 142, no. 4 (October 1928), 510–11.

5. Gladys Jack interview, 22.

6. Heflin interview, 6.

7. Moon, *Tall Sheep*, 57–58.

8. Ibid.

9. Faunce, *Desert Wife*, 101–4.

10. Grace Hunt interview, 16.

11. Gladys Jack interview, 6–8.

12. Newcomb, *Navajo Neighbors*, 120–26.

13. Gladys Jack interview, 22; Cook and Hunt, *John Hunt Family History*, 94; Stella Tanner interview with Brad Cole, NAU O.H. 75.17, United Indian Traders Association Oral History Project; Jewel, Leona, and Lavoy McGee interview with Brad Cole, March 11, 1998, NAU O.H. 75.13, United Indian Traders Association Oral History Project.

14. Cook and Hunt, *John Hunt Family History*, 95.

15. Marilene Blair interview with Karen Underhill, February 12, 1998, NAU O.H. 75.12, United Indian Traders Association Oral History Project.

16. Gladys Jack interview, 14.

17. Two interesting accounts of her life on the reservation and work among the Navajos are found in Gillmor and Louisa Wetherill, *Traders to the Navajos*, and Louisa Wade Wetherill and Harvey Leake, *Wolfkiller: Wisdom from a Nineteenth-Century Navajo Shepherd* (Salt Lake City: Gibbs Smith, 2007).

18. Gillmor and Louisa Wetherill, *Traders to the Navajos*, 156.

19. For a more detailed explanation of the role of Navajo Mountain as a shield, see Karl W. Luckert, *Navajo Mountain and Rainbow Bridge Religion* (Flagstaff: Museum of Northern Arizona, 1977).

20. Gillmor and Louisa Wetherill, *Traders to the Navajos*, 159.

21. Genevieve Forbes Herrick, "Women in the News," *Country Gentleman* 46 (October 1939), 46.

22. Gillmor and Louisa Wetherill, *Traders to the Navajos*, 195, 199.

23. William H. Robinson, *Under Turquoise Skies* (New York: Macmillan, 1928), 515–16.

24. Gladys Jack interview, 16.

25. Ibid., 17.

26. Ray Hunt interview with Alice Maxwell, 18; Hegemann, *Navaho Trading Days*, 314; Gladys Jack interview, 16; Lee and Richardson, "My Wonderful Country," 12–13.

27. Hegemann, *Navaho Trading Days*, 315.

28. Hilda Wetherill, "Trading Post," *Atlantic Monthly* 142, no. 4 (October 1928), 516, 517.

29. Noel and Noel, *Eighty Years*, 28.

30. Vernon Jack interviews, 18.

31. Stewart Hatch interview, November 13, 2010.

32. Cecil Calvin Richardson, "Lives of the Lonely," *Arizona Highways* 24, no. 8 (August 1948), 22.

33. Hines, "Navajo Indian Trader," 26.

34. Jack Manning interview with Brad Cole, March 12, 1998, NAU O.H. 75.2, United Indian Traders Association Oral History Project.

35. Hilda Wetherill, "Trading Post," *Atlantic Monthly* 142 no. 4 (October 1928), 511–12.

36. Berard Haile, *Soul Concepts of the Navaho* (St. Michaels, AZ: Saint Michaels Press, 1943, 1975).

37. Mary Shepardson and Blodwen Hammond, *The Navajo Mountain Community* (Berkley: University of California Press, 1970), 203.

38. Hegemann, *Navaho Trading Days*, 59.

39. Woods and McPherson, *Along Navajo Trails*, 42.

40. Moon, *Tall Sheep*, 26; Richardson, *Navajo Trader*, 116.

41. Mary Jeanette Kennedy, *Tales of a Trader's Wife: Life on the Navajo Indian Reservation, 1913–1938* (Albuquerque, NM: Valiant Company, 1965), 37.

42. Bailey interview; Cook and Hunt, *John Hunt Family History*, 43; Gladys Jack interview, 21; Hilda Wetherill, "Trading Post" *Atlantic Monthly* 142, no. 3 (September 1928), 292.

43. Adams, *Shonto*, 287–88.

44. Paul Begay interview.

45. Cecil Calvin Richardson, "Navajos Are Witty People," *Arizona Highways* 27, no. 8 (August 1951), 27.

46. Moon, *Tall Sheep*, 64.

47. Cecil Calvin Richardson, "Navajos Are Witty People," 27.

48. Cook and Hunt, *John Hunt Family History*, 53; Murray Bodo, *Tales of an Endishodi: Father Berard Haile and the Navajos, 1900–1961* (Albuquerque: University of New Mexico Press, 1998), 105.

49. Powers, *Navajo Trading*, 106.

50. Gillmor and Louisa Wetherill, *Traders to the Navajos*, 184.

51. Moon, *Tall Sheep*, 63–64.

52. Philip Johnston interview with Dan Akee, Doris Duke #953, Doris Duke Oral History Project, 15–16.

53. Hall, *West of the Thirties*, 150.

54. Kirk, *Kirk Clan*, 156–57.

55. Hines, "Navajo Indian Trader," 1–2.

56. McNitt, *Indian Traders*, 322; Hegemann, *Navaho Trading Days*, 316.

57. Berard Haile, "Navajo Ethics," in *The Navajo as Seen by the Franciscans*, ed. Howard Bahr, 548, 549, 551.

58. Vernon Jack interviews, 19.

59. Woods and McPherson, *Along Navajo Trails*, 124; Vernon Jack interviews, 20; Hegemann, *Navaho Trading Days*, 314; Lee and Richardson, "My Wonderful Country," 12.

60. Philip Johnston, "Eight Stories by Philip Johnston," November 7, 1970, Doris Duke #952, Doris Duke Oral History Project, 6–8.

61. Woods and McPherson, *Along Navajo Trails*, 128.

62. Ibid., 130.

63. Ration, as cited in *Stories of Traditional Navajo Life and Culture*, ed. Broderick Johnson, 321, 322.

64. Grace Hunt interview, 23–24.

65. Hegemann, *Navaho Trading Days*, 360.

66. Bailey interview.

67. Ray Hunt interview with Alice Maxwell, 16–17.

68. Hall, *West of the Thirties*, 155–58.

Chapter 9. Beginning Relationships: Early Posts along the San Juan, 1878–1900

1. A good summary of the prehistory of these groups, as well as the introduction of the Spanish in the Southwest, is found in Carter, *Indian Alliances and the Spanish*.

2. For an encyclopedic approach to a series of complex relations during this time, see Blackhawk, *Violence over the Land*.

3. Bernard James Byrne, *A Frontier Surgeon: Life in Colorado in the Eighties* (New York: Exposition Press, 1935, 1962), 153–54.

4. Galen Eastman, "Reports of Agents in New Mexico," September 1, 1882, *Report of the Commissioner of Indian Affairs* (Washington, D.C.: Government Printing Office, 1883), 129.

5. Morris A. Shirts (descendant), correspondence with author, October 24, 1985.

6. See Robert S. McPherson, "Navajos, Mormons, and Henry L. Mitchell," *Utah Historical Quarterly*, 55, no. 1 (Winter 1987), 50–65.

7. H. L. Mitchell to Governor Thomas of Utah, December 27, 1879, Record Group 75, Letters Received by Office of Indian Affairs—Navajo Agency, New

Mexico Superintendency, 1879, National Archives, Washington, D.C. (hereafter cited as Letters Received—New Mexico).

8. David E. Miller, *Hole-in-the-Rock: An Epic in the Colonization of the Great American West* (Salt Lake City: University of Utah Press, 1975), 92–94.

9. H. L. Mitchell to Eastman, February 15, 1880, Letters Received—New Mexico.

10. Mitchell to Eastman, February 27, 1880; Eastman to Commissioner of Indian Affairs, March 8, 1880; and F. T. Bennett to Acting Assistant Adjutant General, March 22, 1880, Letters Received—New Mexico.

11. Assistant Adjutant General, District of New Mexico, to Commanding Officer, Fort Lewis, June 12, 1882, Calendar of Letters Received, Special Collections, Fort Lewis College, Durango Colorado.

12. Report of Herrero Segundo submitted to Agent D. M. Riordan, April 29, 1884, Letters Received—New Mexico.

13. Maj. R. H. Hall to Assistant Adjutant General at Fort Leavenworth, April 18, 1884, Record Group 75, Letters Received, 1881–1907, Bureau of Indian Affairs, National Archives, Washington, D.C. (hereafter cited as Letters Received–BIA).

14. 2d. Lt. J. F. Kreps to Post Adjutant at Fort Lewis, May 1, 1884, Letters Received–BIA.

15. Hiram Ketchum to Post Adjutant, Fort Lewis, May 20, 1884, Letters Received—Adjutant General's Office, 1881–1889, Microfilm #689, F-273, National Archives, Washington, D.C.

16. Lt. Theodore Mosher to Christian Soffke, May 18, 1884, Letters Received–BIA.

17. See James M. Aton and Robert S. McPherson, *River Flowing from the Sunrise: An Environmental History of the Lower San Juan* (Logan: University of Utah Press, 2000), 105–6.

18. E. Lenora Jones, ed., "Life of Parley Butt," n.d., MSS 44, box 1, fld. 21, Special Collections, Marriott Library, University of Utah, Salt Lake City, Utah, 4.

19. For a detailed rendering of these events and the personalities involved, see Ronald F. McDonald, *Fort Montezuma, 1879–1884: An Account of the First Mormon Settlers in San Juan County, Utah* (Self-published, 2015).

20. James L. Davis, "Journal of James L. Davis, San Juan Mission," MS 1640, Church Archives, Family and Church History Department, Church of Jesus Christ of Latter-day Saints, Salt Lake City, 16.

21. Ibid., 18; for a complete discussion of surrounding events and the outcome of this conflict, see Robert S. McPherson and Winston Hurst, "The Fight at Soldier Crossing, 1884: Military Considerations in Canyon Country," *Utah Historical Quarterly* 70, no. 3 (Summer 2002), 258–81.

22. Davis, "Journal," 21.

23. Ibid., 23–24.

24. Ibid., 25.

25. "Off for San Juan," June 26, 1880, *Salt Lake (City) Herald*, 5.

26. Evelyn Hyde Dunn, "William Hyde Family History, 1832–1894," in possession of family.

27. Platte D. Lyman, "Diary of Platte D. Lyman," Special Collections, Harold B. Lee Library, Brigham Young University, Provo, UT, 269, 276, 278.

28. The literature is unclear as to exactly what Hyde did after the flood. For instance, an official military mapping survey in 1886 definitely places him and one of his stores with a cable ferry system in Marble Canyon, seven miles upstream from Riverview. Local historian Albert R. Lyman in "History of San Juan County, 1879–1917," (Special Collections, Harold B. Lee Library, Brigham Young University, Provo, UT, 45) tells of Hyde moving to Peak, most likely located a little over a mile below Riverview/Aneth. Hyde also helped sponsor a post run by his sons and Amasa Barton at Rincon during the same time. This illustrates the difficulty of pinning down with surety the location of many traders in the early days. In 1888, because of poor health, Hyde sold all of his posts and moved to Mancos, Colorado, where he died in 1894.

29. "Bluff, San Juan County," January 8, 1887, *Deseret News (Salt Lake City)*, 4.

30. Kumen Jones, "Writings of Kumen Jones," Special Collections, Harold B. Lee Library, Brigham Young University, Provo, Utah, 213; P. D. Lyman, "Diary," 294.

31. David S. Carpenter, "Jens S. Nielson, Bishop of Bluff," master's thesis (2003, 2011), Department of History, Brigham Young University, Provo, UT, 86.

32. Ibid., 89, 164.

33. W. J. Forham, "San Juan County," October 12, 1887, *Deseret News (Salt Lake City)*, 3.

34. Carpenter, "Jens S. Nielson," 134–35, 196.

35. William Adams, "Bluff Report," June 26, 1882, *Deseret News (Salt Lake City)*, 3.

36. "San Juan Stake History," Church Archives, Family and Church History Department, Church of Jesus Christ of Latter-day Saints, Salt Lake City, UT, 34.

37. Francis A. Hammond, "The San Juan Country," March 12, 1885, *Deseret News (Salt Lake City)*, 3.

38. Francis A. Hammond, "Letter to the Editor," September 2, 1885, *Deseret News (Salt Lake City)*, 1.

39. Lyman, "History of San Juan," 64.

40. Nez interview.

41. "Bluff Items," October 21, 1904, *Montezuma (CO) Journal*, 2.

42. Lyman, "History of San Juan," 20, 67.

43. Frank H. Hyde, "Testimony," October 1930, 1208; Ernest B. Hyde, "Testimony," October 1930, 700–707, Colorado River Bed Case microfilm, Utah State Historical Society, Salt Lake City.

44. Francis A. Hammond to Col. P. T. Swaine, June 23, 1887, Record Group 94, Records of the War Department, Department of New Mexico, National Archives, Washington, D. C.; Lyman, "History of San Juan," 51–52.

45. Lyman, "History of San Juan," 51–52; Jones, "Writings of Kumen Jones," 206–7.

46. For a brief examination of the extent of Mormon traders in the Southwest, see Woods and McPherson, *Along Navajo Trails*, 2–10.

47. D. M. Riordan to Commissioner of Indian Affairs, December 31, 1883, Letters Received—BIA.

48. W. W. Daugherty to Lt. E. H. Plummer, April 5, 1893, Record Group 75, Bureau of Indian Affairs, Consolidated Ute Agency Records, Federal Records Center, Denver, CO (hereafter cited as Consol. Ute Agency Records); Plummer to Commissioner of Indian Affairs, May 20, 1893; Plummer to Post Adjutant, June 29, 1893, Letters Received—BIA.

49. Plummer to Commissioner of Indian Affairs, May 22, 1893, Letters Received—BIA.

50. L. M. Armstrong to Plummer, June 2, 1893; Plummer to Commissioner of Indian Affairs, June 8, 1893, Letters Received—BIA.

51. H. L. Mitchell, E. B. Mitchell, John Bruer, and C. B. Jackson, "Evaluation of Property Destroyed in Kane County, Utah," December 24, 1879, Consol. Ute Agency Records.

52. Charles S. Peterson, *Look to the Mountains* (Provo: Brigham Young University Press, 1975), 57.

53. Cass Hite to Galen Eastman, April 17, 1883; Affidavit of Twenty-three Bluff Settlers to John H. Bowman, November 2, 1885, Letters Received—BIA.

54. This is a complex topic in both an historical and a cultural sense. A fuller treatment of both aspects is given in McPherson, *Navajo Land*, 21–43.

55. Frank Silvey, "History and Settlement of Northern San Juan County," n.d., Utah State Historical Society, Salt Lake City, 33.

56. Petition to Col. P. T. Swain, December 16, 1886; Harold Carlisle to C. F. Stollsteimer, June 12, 1887, Consol. Ute Agency Records.

57. L. M. Armstrong to Stollsteimer, July 17 and August 19, 1887; F. W. Knoege(?) to Honorable Secretary Lamar, September 19, 1887, Consol. Ute Agency Records.

58. George M. Williams to Post Adjutant, December 11, 1889, Letters Received—BIA.

59. Dyk, *Navaho Autobiography*, 40, 75.

60. Dyk and Dyk, *Left Handed*, 35, 396–401.

Chapter 10. A Different View at the Posts: Ute and Navajo Trade, 1880–1940

1. Yazzie interview with author, November 1, 1985.

2. Graymountain interview.

3. Slim Benally interview with author, July 8, 1988.

4. Sakizzie interview.

5. Maimi Howard interview with author, July 19, 1988. For a list of individuals and Navajo clans in the Monument Valley area with their Paiute relations, see Holiday and McPherson, *Navajo Legacy*, 232–34.

6. Alan Whitmer interview with author, September 12, 2001.

7. E. A. Sturges to Adjutant of Black Mountain Expeditionary Forces, August 12, 1908, Record Group 98, Records of the War Department, Department of Colorado, U. S. Army Commands; Ira Hatch interview.

8. Parley Oscar Hurst interview with Sandy McFadden and Gary Shumway, July 17, 1971, O. H. 697, Southeastern Utah Oral History Project.

9. Whitmer interview.

10. Ira Hatch interview.

11. Whitmer interview.

12. Ray Hunt interview with author, January 21, 1991.

13. "Utes and Navajos Making Progress on Reservation," *Cortez (CO) Sentinel*, June 9, 1932, 1.

14. Forrest, *With a Camera*, 191.

15. Stewart Hatch interview with author, August 5, 2009.

16. For a discussion of Navajo trading, see W. W. Hill, "Navaho Trading and Trading Ritual: A Study of Cultural Dynamics," *Southwestern Journal of Anthropology* 4 (Autumn 1948), 371–96; Robert S. McPherson, "Naalyéhé bà Hooghan, 'House of Merchandise,' Navajo Trading Posts as an Institution of Cultural Change, 1900–1930," in *Navajo Land, Navajo Culture*, 65–83.

17. Gen. John Q. Cannon, "When the Utes Invaded Utah," *Improvement Era* 32 no. 1 (November 1928), 41–46.

18. Whitmer interview.

19. Ray Hunt interview with author.

20. Stewart Hatch interview, August 5, 2009.

21. Ibid.

22. Ibid.

23. Whitmer interview; Stewart Hatch interview, August 5, 2009.

24. D. B. McGue, "Ed Noland Insured His Life to Finance Indian Trading Post in Early Days," *Cortez (CO) Sentinel*, n.d., n.p.

25. "O. E. Noland (Bidonna)," a personal statement, in possession of author.

26. *Mancos (CO) Times*, May 15, 1895, 4.

27. Anthony L. Klessert, "Inventory Report—BIA," Report # BIA—NAO NTM 89-2005, August 17, 1989, Navajo Preservation Office, Window Rock, AZ.

28. Stewart Hatch interview with author, May 7, 2010.

29. This post provides another good example of the problem of pinning down with accuracy the location, ownership, and activities associated with a certain location. Spencer's store was likely located on the floodplain at the

mouth of Marble Wash, at its juncture with the San Juan River, approximately five miles above Aneth. It is in the same area as the William Hyde post found on an 1886 map previously referenced. On a 1903 map in the Wetherill–Grand Gulch archives (Edge of the Cedars Museum, Blanding, UT), the old road going from the Four Corners trading post to Aneth is shown following the river on its north side. Now Spencer's store was called Berlin; in 1907, during a small confrontation between the cavalry and the Navajos concerning a powerful medicine man known as Ba'áliee, military accounts mention this store as being run by M. [Mont] R. Butler. Agent William T. Shelton in Shiprock confirmed that, in 1910, Joe Lee was running the store and that, in 1918, he died near Red Lake during the influenza epidemic. Navajos testify that this post was in operation between 1907 and 1922, when it burned down (Klessert, "Inventory," Site SJC-446). The site is now called "Burned House" (*Kin Díílidí*) by the Navajos. Elder Mary Jay (interview with author, February 27, 1991) said, "A trader named Silver (*Béésh Łigai*) used to live there until he got mad at some people who threw him out." Florence Begay (January 30, 1991, interview with author) noted that the Utes used to trade there, too.

30. Lt. Kreps to Maj. R. H. Hall, April 21, 1884; O. E. Noland to D. M. Riordan, April 26, 1884 Herrero Segundo, Navajo Scout, April 29, 1884, Letters Received—BIA.

31. Ira S. Freeman, *A History of Montezuma County* (Boulder, CO: Johnson Publishing), 128–29.

32. Warren K. Moorehead, "In Search of a Lost Race," *Illustrated American* (July 16, 1892), 411; Edgar Noland interview with Floyd A. O'Neil and Gregory C. Thompson, September 5, 1967, Doris Duke #197, Doris Duke Oral History Project,

33. Maurine S. Fletcher, ed., *The Wetherills of the Mesa Verde: Autobiography of Benjamin Alfred Wetherill* (Lincoln: University of Nebraska Press, 1977), 80.

34. "Prosperous Navajo: An Honest Injun," *Mancos (CO) Times-Tribune*, November 9, 1917, 1; McNitt, *Indian Traders*, 309.

35. Fletcher, *Wetherills of the Mesa Verde*, 68–69.

36. Ibid.

37. Frank McNitt, *Anasazi: Richard Wetherill* (Albuquerque: University of New Mexico Press, 1957), 95–96.

38. Constant Williams to Commissioner of Indian Affairs, January 26, 1895, Letters Received—BIA.

39. "Note," June 24, 1898, *Montezuma (CO) Journal*, 1.

40. William T. Shelton to Booth, January 17, 1910, as cited in "Navajo Use and Occupation of Lands North of the San Juan River in Present-day Utah to 1935," ed. David M. Brugge, in author's possession. Brugge compiled this document from BIA materials now housed in the J. Lee Correll Collection in the Navajo Tribal Museum, Window Rock, AZ.

41. "Note," February 2, 1900, *Montezuma (CO) Journal*, 4.

42. William T. Shelton, "Statement," attached to letter to U.S. District Attorney (Salt Lake City) December 9, 1909, Letters Received—BIA.

43. "Navajo Given Light Sentence," April 21, 1911, *Grand Valley (UT) Times*, 1.

44. "Feather Gladdens the Heart of a Dying Indian," May 5, 1911, *Grand Valley (UT) Times*, 8.

45. Washington Matthews, an early ethnographer on Navajo topics, wrote in 1897: "By life-feather or breath feather (*hyiná biltsós*) is meant a feather taken from a live bird, especially one taken from a live eagle. Such feathers are supposed to preserve life and possess magic powers. They are used in all of the rites. In order to secure a supply of these feathers, the Pueblo Indians catch eaglets and rear them in captivity; but the Navajos, like the wild tribes in the north, catch full-grown eagles in traps and pluck them alive" (Matthews, *Navaho Legends*, 232 n.107).

46. "Zhonne Asks Parole," February 13, 1914, *Grand Valley (UT) Times*, 5.

47. Harvey Oliver interviews with author, March 6, 1991 and May 7, 1991; Marley Shebala, "Local Anglo Trader Killed," March 31, 2011, *Navajo Times (Window Rock, AZ)*, C-1.

48. Marsha Keele, "Trading Post in Ruins, but It Won't Be Forgotten," June 5, 1979, *Deseret News (Salt Lake City)*, B-1.

49. "O. E. Noland (Bidonna)," 3.

50. Ibid., 4.

51. *Mancos (CO) Times*, January 15, 1904, 3; Lolla Kutch Noland interview by grandchild (family member), no date, in possession of Madeline Noland McCrum and given to author.

52. "O. E. Noland (Bidonna)," 6.

53. Ibid., 7.

54. "Utes Are Buncoed," February 9, 1900, *Mancos (CO) Times*, 2.

55. "Note," December 26, 1902, *Mancos (CO) Times*, 1.

56. "O. E. Noland (Bidonna)," 3.

57. Ibid.

58. "Big Deal Closed," June 18, 1909, *Mancos (CO) Times-Tribune*, 1.

59. Lolla Kutch Noland interview by granddaughter.

60. "Mancos the Scene of a Tragedy," July 23, 1909, *Mancos (CO) Times-Tribune*, 1; Freeman, *History of Montezuma County*, 249; Fern D. Ellis, *Come Back to My Valley, Historical Remembrances of Mancos, Colorado* (Self-published, 1976), 126.

61. Warren Pyle interview with Floyd A. O'Neil and Gregory C. Thompson, September 12, 1967, Doris Duke #143, Doris Duke Oral History Project, 5–6.

62. Warren Pyle, "Statement on Trading Posts," March 20, 1991, in possession of author.

63. Ibid.; McNitt, *Indian Traders*, 311.

64. S. G. Walker to John Collier, October 30, 1933, Consol. Ute Records.

65. Samuel G. Walker to William Zimmerman Jr., August 8, 1934, Consol. Ute Records.

66. Field Representative of the National Association on Indian Affairs to John Collier, October 20, 1935, Consol. Ute Records, 33; Warren Pyle "Statement."

67. Field Representative of National Association on Indian Affairs to John Collier, October 20, 1935, Consol. Ute Records, 34.

68. Leo R. Chisholm to G. S. Courtright, December 23, 1932, Consol. Ute Records.

69. Unless otherwise noted, all information on the Hatch trading post in Allen Canyon comes from Stewart Hatch interviews with the author.

70. Joseph B. Harris to McKean, February 25, March 4, April 23 and 30, June 9, 1926, Road Construction, Consol. Ute Records.

71. E. Z. Black, "Monthly Time Book," 1933–1935, Department of the Interior, U.S. Indian Service, in possession of Ardelle Ostergaard (Family), Blanding, UT.

72. McKean, "Industries," Annual Narrative, 1925, Consol. Ute Records.

73. D. H. Wattson to A. C. Cooley, April 9, 1937, White Mesa Ute Project, American West Center, University of Utah, Salt Lake City, Utah.

74. Stewart Hatch interview, May 7, 2010.

75. Stella Eyetoo interview with author, November 16, 2005; Zelma Acton interview with Deborah Fellbaum and Shirley E. Stephenson, July 11, 1972, O.H. 1196a, Southeastern Utah Oral History Project; Stewart Hatch interview, May 7, 2010.

76. Annie Cantsee interview with author, August 4, 2009; Eyetoo interview.

77. "Blanding CCC News," June 23, 1938, and June 13, 1940, *San Juan Record (Monticello, UT)*.

Chapter 11. Posts as Economic Exciters: The Heyday of Navajo Trade, 1900–1935

1. Bailey and Bailey, *History of the Navajos*, 124–25.

2. Ibid., 300–301, 152.

3. "The Indian Festivities," September 23, 1897, *Mancos (CO) Times*, 1; "An Outing for Aborigine Cranks," September 2, 1898, *Mancos (CO) Times*, 1.

4. Dyk, *Navaho Autobiography*, 97–98.

5. Ibid., 37, 95–96.

6. Cook and Hunt, *John Hunt Family History*, 42.

7. Ibid., 21.

8. Dyk, *Navaho Autobiography*, 191.

9. Ibid., 72, 81.

10. Ibid., 100.

11. For a more complete understanding of the government farmer and his role in working with the Navajo, see McPherson, *Navajo Land, Navajo Culture*, 44–64.

12. Dyk, *Navaho Autobiography*, 121.

13. A. V. Kidder, "Reminiscences in Southwest Archaeology: I," *Kiva* 25, no. 4 (April 1960), 11–13.

14. Ibid.

15. Leslie A. White, ed., "Lewis H. Morgan's Journal of a Trip to Southwestern Colorado and New Mexico, June 21 to August 7, 1878," *American Antiquity* 8, no. 1 (July 1942), 20.

16. Dyk, *Navaho Autobiography*, 102, 105.

17. See Robert S. McPherson, "'Too Much Noise in That Bunch across the River:' Ba'álílee and the 1907 Aneth Brawl," *Utah Historical Quarterly* 77, no. 1 (Winter 2009), 26–51.

18. Anselm Weber, O.F.M., to William H. Ketcham, November 15, 1909, box 22, fldr 2, Arizona 500, Special Collections, Franciscan Library, St. Michaels, AZ.

19. Dyk, *Navaho Autobiography*, 124.

20. "Note," January 20, 1899, *Mancos (CO) Times*, 4. In 1893, a man named L. F. Hayes visited the Gus Honaker trading post on the San Juan River and stayed there for a number of days before continuing his exploration of Anasazi ruins. At that time, John Madison worked at that post. Hayes gives the following information about him. "[Madison] is kept for a translator. I learned that several Negroes started from Pueblo [Colorado] some 15 years ago and traveled down into the Ute Indian country. The Indians took a great liking to this one who was then but a small boy. Tis said one of the Negroes sold him to the Indians for 50 cents. He grew up there among the Utes and, of course, learned their language. Afterwards he went to the Navajo Indians and made his home with them and learned their language. He is now in demand as an interpreter and Mr. Honaker keeps him for that purpose." From L. F. Hayes, "Trip to Cliff Canyon," Special Collection, LDS Church History Library, Church of Jesus Christ of Latter-day Saints, Salt Lake City, UT, 58.

21. Neil Judd, *Men Met along the Trail* (Norman: University of Oklahoma Press, 1968), 26.

22. Kidder, "Reminiscences in Southwest Archaeology," 8.

23. Ray Hunt interview with author, January 21, 1991; testimony of Eleanor Ismay on May 18, 1966, in Navajo Tribe vs. State of Utah, on file at Edge of the Cedars Museum, Blanding, UT, 6–7.

24. Jane Silas interview with author, February 27, 1991.

25. According to an interview on June 11, 1958, with Old Lady Sweetwater, around 1923, "Ugly Trader" built a ferry with a cable at Aneth. One of

the anchor cables is still visible at the post, but the system did not last long and was washed down the river. Old Lady Sweetwater interview with J. Lee Correll, June 11, 1958, Doris Duke #13, Doris Duke Oral History, 5.

26. Ray Hunt interview with author, January 21, 1991; Dyk, *Navaho Autobiography*, 141.

27. Cook and Hunt, *John Hunt Family History*, 28.

28. Ibid., 36.

29. Ibid.; "Indian Killed at Aneth," August 21, 1919, *Montezuma (CO) Journal*, 2.

30. "Shiprock Has First Navajo Indian Fair," October 29, 1909, *Farmington (NM) Enterprise*, 1; Dyk, *Navaho Autobiography*, 85.

31. Jones, "Writings of Kumen Jones," 213; Ray Hunt interview with author, January 21, 1991.

32. "Man Killed, Store Wrecked in Mysterious Explosion," July 23, 1925, *Grand Valley (UT) Times*, 1; Cook and Hunt, *John Hunt Family History*, 48.

33. Hilda Perkins, "Remembrances"; Perkins interview with Janet Wilcox, June 24, 1987, San Juan County Oral History Project, San Juan County Historical Commission, Blanding, UT.

34. Cook and Hunt, *John Hunt Family History*, 86–90.

35. Ray Hunt interview with author, January 21, 1991; John Meadows interview with author, May 30, 1991.

36. Meadows interview.

37. Stewart Hatch interview with author, May 7, 2010.

38. Ibid.; Cyrus Begay interview with author, May 14, 1991; Ray Hunt interview with author, January 21, 1991.

39. Ray Hunt discussion with author, September 5, 1991.

40. Stewart Hatch interview, May 7, 2010; Cook and Hunt, *John Hunt Family History*, 68.

41. Freeman, *History of Montezuma County*, 209.

42. "Note," November 24, 1899, *Mancos (CO) Times*, 1.

43. "Note," April 24, 1903, *Mancos (CO) Times*, 1; "Note," August 28, 1903, *Mancos (CO) Times*, 4; "Trade Relations," April 25, 1913, *Mancos (CO) Times*, 7.

44. "Mancos Best Trading Point," *Mancos (CO) Times-Tribune*, July 9, 1915, 1.

45. "Traffic in Relics from Indian Ruins," *Report of the Commissioner of Indian Affairs* (Washington, D.C.: Government Printing Office, 1905), 29–30.

46. Hegemann, *Navajo Trading Days*, 366–68.

47. T. Mitchell Prudden, *On the Great American Plateau* (New York: G. P. Putnam Sons, 1906), 172–74.

48. Holiday and McPherson, *Navajo Legacy*, 236.

49. Faunce, *Desert Wife*, 238–40.

50. Hegemann, *Navajo Trading Days*, 59.

51. Byron Cummings, "The Ancient Inhabitants of the San Juan Valley," *Bulletin of the University of Utah* 3, no. 3 part 2 (November 1910), 4.

52. Newcomb, *Navajo Neighbors*, 168–71.

53. Moon, *Tall Sheep*, 220–21.

54. Ibid., 222.

55. "Conversation With: Milton Wetherill," *Western Gateways* 7, no. 3 (Summer 1967), 43–45, 62–74.

56. Clyde Kluckhohn, *To the Foot of the Rainbow* (Glorieta, NM: Rio Grande Press, 1927), 196.

57. McNitt, *Indian Traders*, 272.

58. Ibid., 274–76.

59. Richardson, *Navajo Trader*, 33, 49–52.

60. Ibid., 52.

61. Ibid., 52–57.

62. Ibid., 41–42.

63. Maurice Kildare, "Builders to the Rainbow," *Frontier Times* 40 (June–July), 51.

64. Statistical Summary of Visitations to Rainbow Bridge, in "Rainbow Bridge—Land Exchange w/Navahos; Barrier Dam," Richardson Collection.

65. "Rainbow Bridge—Rates and Other Information," Richardson Collection.

Chapter 12. The End of an Era: Boom, Bust, and Livestock Reduction, 1920–1940

1. Kelly and Francis, *Navajoland Trading Posts Encyclopedia*, at www.navajotradingposts.info, accessed November 9, 2015. Some of the posts used in this calculation sat near the state boundary of Utah and northern Arizona (Shonto, Inscription House, Red Mesa, Teec Nos Pos, Kayenta [two]) and Dennehotso, but were used in the count, since they also attracted Utah Navajos. The main point is that there was a marked proliferation of posts during the 1920s.

2. Forrest, *With a Camera*.

3. Lorraine Hunt James, *The Meadows of McElmo: A Myers and Meadows Family History* (Self-published, 1992), 29–37.

4. Meadows interview.

5. Dixie Veach discussion with author, December 9, 2012.

6. John Wesch interview with Ronald McDonald, June 15, 2015, statement provided to author.

7. "Old Trading Post Once in Utah, Now in Colorado," April 24, 1979, *Deseret News (Salt Lake City)*, 1; "Ismay Trading Post Destroyed by Fire," June 28, 1928, *Cortez (CO) Sentinel*, 1.

8. Redd interview, 10–12.

9. Cyrus Begay interview with author, May 14, 1991.

10. Ira Hatch interview with author, May 30, 1991.

11. Ibid.

12. Stewart Hatch interview, November 13, 2010.

13. Ira Hatch interview.

14. Holiday and McPherson, *Navajo Legacy*, 41.

15. Arthur H. Spencer Testimony, *United States vs. Utah* (1931) Colorado River Bed Case, Special Collections, Library, Utah State Historical Society, Salt Lake City, 181, 196.

16. Lyman P. Hunter, "San Juan Remembered," MS 374, Box 1 Book 3, Special Collections, Marriott Library, University of Utah, Salt Lake City, 35.

17. "Charles Bernheimer Field Notes—1920 Expedition," Bernheimer Collection, Library, Utah State Historical Society, Salt Lake City, 14–15.

18. John Holiday interview with author, February 24, 2001.

19. Ray Hunt and Emory Hunt interview with James D. Redd, July 13, 1971, O. H. 1088, Charles Redd Center for Western Studies, Harold B. Lee Library, Brigham Young University, Provo, UT, 17.

20. Cook and Hunt, *John Hunt Family History*, 92.

21. Charles Kelly, "Sand and Sagebrush," unpublished manuscript, Charles Kelly Papers, Special Collections, Marriott Library, University of Utah, Salt Lake City, 76.

22. McPherson, *Journey of Navajo Oshley*, 103–6.

23. Gillmor and Louisa Wetherill, *Traders to the Navajo*, and Moon, *Tall Sheep*.

24. Stokes Carson purchased the Oljato post in 1938, becoming the first in a long line of owners. Since this goes beyond 1940, these subsequent owners will not be discussed here. Those interested in the later years should read Roberts, *Stokes Carson*, 99–111.

25. Ana Heffernan interview with Margie Connolly and Fred Harden, February 11, 1994, in possession of Halene West, Cortez, CO, 9.

26. Holiday and McPherson, *Navajo Legacy*, 37.

27. James H. Knipmeyer, "The Dunn Family and Navajo Mountain Trading Post," *Utah Historical Quarterly* 68, no. 2 (Spring 2000), 127.

28. Joe Manygoats interview.

29. Knipmeyer, "Dunn Family," 127, 137.

30. Kelly and Francis, *Navajoland Trading Posts Encyclopedia*, at www.navajotradingposts.info.

31. Madeline Cameron interview with Gary Shumway, June 14, 1968, Doris Duke #422, Doris Duke Oral History Project, 10.

32. For more on Navajo livestock reduction of the late 1920s and 1930s, see Kenneth R. Philp, *John Collier's Crusade for Indian Reform, 1920–1954* (Tucson: University of Arizona Press, 1977); Richard White, *The Roots of Dependency: Subsistence, Environment, and Social Change among the Choctaw, Pawnees, and Navajo* (Lincoln: University of Nebraska Press, 1983); Ruth

Roessel and Broderick Johnson, eds., *Navajo Livestock Reduction: A National Disgrace* (Tsaile, AZ: Navajo Community College Press, 1974); Donald L. Parman, *The Navajos and the New Deal* (New Haven, CT: Yale University Press, 1976); Lawrence C. Kelly, *The Navajo Indians and Federal Indian Policy* (Tucson: University of Arizona Press, 1968); and L. Schuyler Fonaroff, "Conservation and Stock Reduction on the Navajo Tribal Range," *Geographical Review* 53, no. 2 (April 1963), 200–223.

33. To understand the cultural impact of livestock reduction from the Navajo perspective, see Robert S. McPherson, "Navajo Livestock Reduction in Southeastern Utah, 1933–1946: History Repeats Itself," *American Indian Quarterly* 22, nos. 1 and 2 (Winter/Spring, 1998), 1–18.

34. Annual Report, 1930, Bureau of Indian Affairs, Navajo Archives, Edge of the Cedars Museum, Blanding, UT, n.p. (hereafter Navajo Archives).

35. Annual Report, 1934, Navajo Archives.

36. Ibid.

37. Bailey and Bailey, *History of the Navajos*, 197.

38. Richard White, *Roots of Dependency*, 312.

39. John Holiday interview.

40. Maria Chabot, "Some Aspects of the Navajo Problem," New Mexico Association of Indian Affairs Report, 1941, in Museum of New Mexico, Laboratory of Anthropology, Santa Fe, 6.

41. Ibid., 16.

42. Ibid., 19–20.

43. "Navajo Indians Plan a Mass Protest Meeting," May 5, 1938, *San Juan Record (Monticello, UT)*, 1.

44. Herbert Redshaw to Senator William H. King, June 25, 1938, copy in possession of author.

45. Heflin interview, 17–19.

46. Ray Hunt interview with author.

47. Ray Hunt interview with Alice Maxwell, 8.

48. Cook and Hunt, *John Hunt Family History*, 76.

49. Bailey interview.

50. Heflin interview, 20.

51. Hegemann, *Navaho Trading Days*, 382–83.

52. Richardson, *Navajo Trader*, 181–83.

53. Powers, *Navajo Trading*.

Bibliography

In order to make the reader's search for sources easier, this bibliography is divided into five sections: Manuscripts, Interviews, Government Documents, Books and Articles, and Newspapers.

Manuscripts

Adams, William Y. "The Image of the Trader." Paper given at the Ninth Navajo Studies Conference, April 1996, Flagstaff, AZ, in possession of author.

Bernheimer, Charles. "Charles Bernheimer Field Notes—1920 Expedition." Bernheimer Collection, Library, Utah State Historical Society, Salt Lake City, 14–15.

Black, E. Z. "Monthly Time Book," 1933–1935. Department of the Interior, U.S. Indian Service, in possession of Ardelle Ostergaard (Family), Blanding, UT.

Brugge, David M., ed. "Navajo Use and Occupation of Lands North of the San Juan River in Present-day Utah to 1935." J. Lee Correll Collection, Navajo Tribal Museum, Window Rock, AZ.

Carpenter, David S. "Jens S. Nielson, Bishop of Bluff." Master's thesis (2003, 2011), Department of History, Brigham Young University, Provo, UT.

Chabot, Maria. "Some Aspects of the Navajo Problem." Report for the New Mexico Association of Indian Affairs. Santa Fe: Museum of New Mexico, Laboratory of Anthropology, 1941.

Davis, James L. "Journal of James L. Davis, San Juan Mission." MS 1640, Church Archives, Family and Church History Department, Church of Jesus Christ of Latter-day Saints, Salt Lake City, UT.

Dunn, Evelyn Hyde. "William Hyde Family History, 1832–1894." In possession of family.

Haile, Berard, O.F.M. Correspondence. Special Collections, Franciscan Library, St. Michaels, AZ.

———. "Some Cultural Aspects of the Navajo Hogan." Talk given at Fort Wingate, 1937. Berard Haile Papers, Special Collections, Library of St. Leonard College, Dayton, OH.

Hassell, Stanford L. "Navaho Trader." Unpublished manuscript, n.d. New Mexico Writers' Project, WPA #61, State Records Center and Archives, Santa Fe.

Hayes, L. F. "Trip to Cliff Canyon." Special Collections, LDS Church History Library, Church of Jesus Christ of Latter-day Saints, Salt Lake City, UT.

Heflin, Mildred Carson. "Indian Trading Posts." Gladwell Richardson Collection, Special Collection, Cline Library, Northern Arizona University, Flagstaff, n.d., n.p.

Hines, Carl G. "Navajo Indian Trader." Manuscript #308, Glenn L. Emmons Papers, Special Collections, University of New Mexico, Albuquerque.

Hunter, Lyman P. "San Juan Remembered." Special Collections, Marriott Library, University of Utah, Salt Lake City.

Johnston, Philip. "Eight Stories by Philip Johnston," November 8, 1970. Doris Duke #952, Doris Duke Oral History Project, Special Collections, Marriott Library, University of Utah, Salt Lake City.

———. "Tales from a Navajo Trading Post," November 7, 1970. Doris Duke #953, Doris Duke Oral History Project, Special Collections, Marriott Library, University of Utah, Salt Lake City.

Jones, E. Lenora, ed. "Life of Parley Butt." N.d., MSS 44, box 1, fld. 21, Special Collections, Marriott Library, University of Utah, Salt Lake City.

Jones, Kumen. "Writings of Kumen Jones." Special Collections, Harold B. Lee Library, Brigham Young University, Provo, UT.

Kelly, Charles. "Sand and Sagebrush." Unpublished manuscript, Charles Kelly Papers, Special Collections, Marriott Library, University of Utah, Salt Lake City.

Klessert, Anthony L. "Inventory Report—BIA." Report # BIA—NAO NTM 89-2005, August 17, 1989. Navajo Preservation Office, Window Rock, AZ.

Lyman, Albert R. "History of San Juan County, 1879–1917." Special Collections, Harold B. Lee Library, Brigham Young University, Provo, UT.

Lyman, Platte D. "Diary of Platte D. Lyman." Special Collections, Harold B. Lee Library, Brigham Young University, Provo, UT.

Noland, Oen. "O. E. Noland (Bidonna)," a Personal Statement. In possession of author.

Pyle, Warren. "Statement on Trading Posts," March 20, 1991. In possession of author.

"Rainbow Bridge—Rates and Other Information." Gladwell Richardson Collection, Special Collections, Northern Arizona University Library, Flagstaff.

San Juan Stake History. Church Archives, Family and Church History Department, Church of Jesus Christ of Latter-day Saints, Salt Lake City, UT.

Shirts, Morris A. Correspondence with author, October 24, 1985.

Silvey, Frank. "History and Settlement of Northern San Juan County." N.d., n.p. Special Collections, Library, Utah State Historical Society, Salt Lake City.

Statistical Summary of Visitations to Rainbow Bridge. "Rainbow Bridge—Land Exchange w/ Navahos; Barrier Dam." Gladwell Richardson Collection, Special Collections, Northern Arizona University Library, Flagstaff.

"Trading Regulations." Radio Broadcast from KTGM, Window Rock, AZ, April 25, 1939. Gladwell Richardson Collection, Box 66, Fldr 100, Special Collections, Cline Library, Northern Arizona University, Flagstaff.

Trockur, Emanuel, O.F.M. "Navajo Names," April 20, 1959. "Navajo Culture, Religion, Customs," Box 51, Fldr 3, Franciscan Fathers Collection, Special Collections, University of Arizona, Tucson.

Watson, Editha L. Talk presented March 17, 1968, Doris Duke #796. Doris Duke Oral History Project, Special Collections, Marriott Library, University of Utah, Salt Lake City.

Interviews

Acton, Zelma. Interview with Deborah Fellbaum and Shirley E. Stephenson, July 11, 1972. O.H. 1196a, Southeastern Utah Oral History Project, Utah State Historical Society and California State University, Fullerton.

Bailey, Mary. Interview with Karen Underhill, July 13, 1999. NAU O.H. 75.41, United Indian Traders Association Oral History Project, Special Collections, Cline Library, Northern Arizona University, Flagstaff.

Begay, Cyrus. Interview with author, May14, 1991.

Begay, Florence. Interview with author, January 30, 1991, and April 29, 1998.

Begay, Nakai. Interview with Bette Benally, February 24, 1991, used with permission.

Begay, Paul. Interview with Karen Underhill, February 10, 1998. NAU O.H. 75.9, United Indian Traders Association Oral History Project, Special Collections, Cline Library, Northern Arizona University, Flagstaff.

Begay, Rose. Interview with Bertha Parrish, June 17, 1987.

Benally, Slim. Interview with author, July 8, 1988.

Black, Ada. Interview with author, October 11 and December 16, 1991.

Black, Sam. Interview with author, December 18, 1993.

Blair, Elijah. Interview with Karen Underhill, February 9, 1998. NAU O.H. 75.11, United Indian Traders Association Oral History Project, Special Collections, Cline Library, Northern Arizona University, Flagstaff.

Blair, Marilene. Interview with Karen Underhill, February 12, 1998, NAU O.H. 75.12. United Indian Traders Association Oral History Project, Special Collections, Cline Library, Northern Arizona University, Flagstaff.

Blueyes, Charlie. Interview with author, June 7 and July 8, 1988.

Buck, Daisy. Conversation with author, August 18, 1989.

Cameron, Madeline. Interview with Gary Shumway, June 14, 1968. Doris Duke #422, Doris Duke Oral History Project, Special Collections, Marriott Library, University of Utah, Salt Lake City.

Cantsee, Annie. Interview with author, August 4, 2009.

Chaffin, Arthur L. Interview with P. T. Reilly, December 24, 1966. "Trading Posts," Special Collections, Utah State Historical Society, Salt Lake City, 11–15.

Charley, Fern. Interview with Dean Sundberg, July 13, 1972. O.H. 11224, Southeastern Utah Oral History Project, Utah State Historical Society and California State University, Fullerton.

Claw, Ruth. Interview with Gary Shumway, July 11, 1968. Doris Duke #477, Doris Duke Oral History Project, Special Collections, Marriott Library, University of Utah, Salt Lake City.

Dandy, Jim. Discussion with author, December 7, 2010.

Eyetoo, Stella. Interview with author, November 16, 2005.

Fisher, Martha. Interview with David Brugge, January 5, 1961. Doris Duke #918, Doris Duke Oral History Project, Special Collections, Marriott Library, University of Utah, Salt Lake City.

Francis, Jenny. Interview with author, March 23, 1993.

Grandson, Nellie. Interview with author, December 16, 1993.

Graymountain, Gilmore. Interview with author, April 7, 1992.

Hatch, Ira. Interview with author, May 30, 1991.

Hatch, Stewart. Interview with author, August 5, 2009; May 7 and November 13, 2010.

Heffernan, Ana. Interview with Margie Connolly and Fred Harden, February 11, 1994. In possession of Halene West, Cortez, CO.

Heflin, Mildred. Interview with Dean Sundberg, June 30, 1972. O.H. 1168, Southeastern Utah Oral History Project, Utah State Historical Society and California State University, Fullerton.

Holiday, John. Interview with author, September 9, 1991, and February 24, 2001.

Holiday, Marilyn. Interview with author, February 14, 1992.

Holiday, Tallis. Interview with author, November 3, 1987.

Howard, Maimi. Interview with author, July 19, 1988.

Hubell, Mrs. Roman (Dorothy). Interview with David M. Brugge, October 13–24, 1969. Frank McNitt Collection, Box 18, State Records Center, Santa Fe, NM.

Hunt, Grace. Interview with Marwynne Selfridge, April 15, 1987. O.H. 1910, Southeastern Utah Oral History Project, Utah State Historical Society and California State University, Fullerton.

Hunt, Ray. Discussion with author, September 9, 1991.

———. Interview with Kathy Biel, August 12, 1970. O.H. 280a, Southeastern Utah Oral History Project, Utah State Historical Society and California State University, Fullerton.

———. Interview with Alice Maxwell, April 15, 1987. O.H. 280c, Southeastern Utah Oral History Project, Utah State Historical Society and California State University, Fullerton.

———. Interview with author, January 21, 1991.

Hunt, Ray, and Emory Hunt. Interview with James D. Redd, July 13, 1971. O.H. 1088, Charles Redd Center for Western Studies, Harold B. Lee Library, Brigham Young University, Provo, UT.

Hurst, Parley Oscar. Interview with Sandy McFadden and Gary Shumway, July 17, 1971. O.H. 697, Southeastern Utah Oral History Project, Utah State Historical Society and California State University, Fullerton.

Hurst, Winston. Conversation with author, January 8, 2015.

Jack, Gladys. Interview with Mark Collins, July 25, 1978. O.H. 1637, Southeastern Utah Oral History Project, Utah State Historical Society and California State University, Fullerton.

Jack, Vernon. Interview with Mark Collins, July 12 and 27, 1978. O.H. 1636, Southeastern Utah Oral History Project, Utah State Historical Society and California State University, Fullerton.

Jay, Mary. Interview with author, February 27, 1991.

Long, Clayton. Discussion with author, March 25, 2015.

Manning, Jack. Interview with Brad Cole, March 12, 1998. NAU O.H. 75.2, United Indian Traders Association Oral History Project, Special Collections, Cline Library, Northern Arizona University, Flagstaff.

Manygoats, Joe. Interview with author, December 18, 1991.

Manygoats, Sally. Interview with author, April 8, 1992.

McGee, Jewel, Leona, and Lavoy. Interview with Brad Cole, March 11, 1998. NAU O.H. 75.13. United Indian Traders Association Oral History Project, Special Collections, Cline Library, Northern Arizona University, Flagstaff.

Meadows, John. Interview with author, May 30, 1991.

Mose, Don. Discussion with author, December 14, 2010.

Navajo, Buck. Interview with author, December 16, 1991.

Nez, Martha. Interview with author, August 10, 1988.

Noland, Edgar. Interview with Floyd A. O'Neil and Gregory C. Thompson, September 5, 1967. Doris Duke #197, Doris Duke Oral History Project, Special Collections, Marriott Library, University of Utah, Salt Lake City.

Noland, Lolla Kutch. Interview by grandchild, no date. In possession of Madeline Noland McCrum and author.

Old Lady Sweetwater. Interview with J. Lee Correll, June 11, 1958. Doris Duke #13, Doris Duke Oral History Project, Special Collections, Marriott Library, University of Utah, Salt Lake City.

Oliver, Harvey. Interview with author, March 6, 1991, and May 7, 1991.

Perkins, Hilda. Interview with Janet Wilcox, June 24, 1987. San Juan County Oral History Project, San Juan County Historical Commission, Blanding, UT.

Pyle, Warren. Interview with Floyd A. O'Neil and Gregory C. Thompson, September 12, 1967. Doris Duke #143, Doris Duke Oral History Project, Special Collections, Marriott Library, University of Utah, Salt Lake City.

Redd, Amasa Jay. Interview with Charles S. Peterson, July 27, 1973. CRC-C7, Charles Redd Center for Western Studies, Brigham Young University, Provo, UT.

Sakizzie, Ella. Interview with author, May 14, 1991.

Silas, Jane. Interview with author, February 27, 1991.

Tanner, Stella. Interview with Brad Cole. NAU O.H. 75.17. United Indian Traders Association Oral History Project, Special Collections, Cline Library, Northern Arizona University, Flagstaff.

Tauchin, Mrs. Dan. Interview with J. Lee Correll, December 10, 1960. Doris Duke #659, Doris Duke Oral History Project, Special Collections, Marriott Library, University of Utah, Salt Lake City.

Veach, Dixie. Discussion with author, December 9, 2012.

Wesch, John. Interview with Ronald McDonald, June 15, 2015. Statement provided to author.

Whitmer, Alan. Interview with author, September 12, 2001.

Yazzie, Fred. Interview with author, November 1, 1985, and November 5, 1987.

Yellowman, Gladys. Interview with author, July 19, 1988.

Government Documents

Annual Report. Bureau of Indian Affairs, 1930 and 1934. Navajo Archives, Edge of the Cedars Museum, Blanding, UT.

Census of the Navajo Reservation—1915, with letter by Peter Paquette. Film #579,683, Microfilm Division, Harold B. Lee Library, Brigham Young University, Provo, UT.

Eastman, Galen. "Reports of Agents in New Mexico." September 1, 1882, *Report of the Commissioner of Indian Affairs* (Washington, D.C.: Government Printing Office, 1883).

"The Indian Trader." *Reports of the Commissioner of Indian Affairs*. Washington, D. C.: Government Printing Office, 1905.

"Indian Traders." *Report of the Commissioner of Indian Affairs, 1903*. Washington, D.C.: U.S. Department of the Interior.

Ismay, Eleanor. Testimony, May 18, 1966, in *Navajo Tribe v. State of Utah*. Edge of the Cedars Museum, Blanding, UT.

"Native Industries—Navajo Blankets." *Report of the Commissioner of Indian Affairs*, vol. II. Washington, D.C.: Government Printing, 1914.

"Navajo Trading." *Survey of Conditions of the Indians in the United States*. Hearing before the Subcommittee of Indian Affairs, U.S. Senate, August 19, 1936, 75th Congress, Part 34. Washington, D.C.: Government Printing Office, 1936.

Post Calendar of Events. Assistant Adjutant General, District of New Mexico, to Commanding Officer, Fort Lewis, June 12, 1882, Calendar of Letters Received. Special Collections, Fort Lewis College, Durango, CO.

"Traffic in Relics from Indian Ruins." *Report of the Commissioner of Indian Affairs*. Washington, D.C.: Government Printing Office, 1905.

United States v. Utah (1931), Colorado River Bed Case. Utah State Historical Society, Salt Lake City.

U.S. Government. Letters Received—Adjutant General's Office, 1881–1889, Microfilm #689, F-273, National Archives, Washington, D.C.

U.S. Government. Record Group 75, Letters Received by Office of Indian Affairs—Navajo Agency, New Mexico Superintendency, 1879, National Archives, Washington, D.C.

U.S. Government. Record Group 75, Letters Received, 1881–1907, Bureau of Indian Affairs, National Archives, Washington, D.C.

U.S. Government. Record Group 94, Records of the War Department, Department of New Mexico, National Archives, Washington, D. C.

U. S. Government. Record Group 98, Records of the War Department, Department of Colorado, U. S. Army Commands, National Archives, Washington, D.C.

Ute Agency Records. Record Group 75, Box 11, Bureau of Indian Affairs, Federal Records Center, Denver, CO.

Western Navajo Agency. Correspondence. Record Group 75, Bureau of Indian Affairs, National Archives, Washington, D.C.

White Mesa Ute Project. American West Center, University of Utah, Salt Lake City.

Books and Articles

Adair, John. *The Navajo and Pueblo Silversmiths*. Norman: University of Oklahoma Press, 1944, 1973.

Adams, William Y. Adams. *Shonto: The Study of the Role of the Trader in a Modern Navaho Community*. Smithsonian Institution Bureau of American Ethnology, Bulletin 188. Washington, D.C.: Government Printing Office, 1963.

Amsden, Charles Avery. *Navajo Weaving: Its Technic and Its History*. Glorieta, NM: Rio Grande Press, 1934.

Aton, James M., and Robert S. McPherson. *River Flowing from the Sunrise: An Environmental History of the Lower San Juan*. Logan: University of Utah Press, 2000.

Bahr, Howard M., ed. *The Navajo as Seen by the Franciscans, 1898–1921: A Sourcebook*. Lanham, MD: Scarecrow Press, 2004.

Bailey, Garrick, and Roberta Bailey. *A History of the Navajos: The Reservation Years*. Santa Fe, NM: School of American Research Press, 1986.

Bailey, L. R. *Indian Slave Trade in the Southwest*. Los Angeles: Westernlore, 1966.

———. *The Long Walk: A History of the Navajo Wars, 1848–1868*. Pasadena, CA: Westernlore, 1978.

Bingham, Sam, and Janet Bingham. *Between Sacred Mountains: Navajo Stories and Lessons from the Land*. Chinle, AZ: Rock Point Community School, 1982.

Blackhawk, Ned. *Violence over the Land: Indians and Empires in the Early American West*. Cambridge, MA: Harvard University Press, 2006.

Blue, Martha. *Indian Trader: The Life and Times of J. L. Hubbell*. Walnut, CA: Kiva Publishing, 2000.

Bodo, Murray. *Tales of an Endishodi: Father Berard Haile and the Navajos, 1900–1961*. Albuquerque: University of New Mexico Press, 1998.

Byrne, Bernard James. *A Frontier Surgeon: Life in Colorado in the Eighties*. New York: Exposition Press, 1935, 1962.

Cannon, John Q. "When the Utes Invaded Utah." *Improvement Era* 32, no. 1 (November 1928): 41–46.

Carter, William B. *Indian Alliances and the Spanish in the Southwest, 750–1750*. Norman: University of Oklahoma Press, 2009.

Cook, Idonna Hunt, and John LaRay Hunt. *John Hunt Family History*. Blanding, UT: Self-published, 1993.

Correll, J. Lee. *Through White Men's Eyes: A Contribution to Navajo History*, vols. III–VI. Window Rock, AZ: Navajo Heritage Center, 1979.

Cottam, Erica. *Hubbell Trading Post: Trade, Tourism, and the Navajo Southwest*. Norman: University of Oklahoma Press, 2015.

Cummings, Byron. "The Ancient Inhabitants of the San Juan Valley." *Bulletin of the University of Utah* 3, no. 3, part 2 (November 1910).

Downs, James F. *Animal Husbandry in Navajo Culture and Society*. University of California Publications in Anthropology 1. Los Angeles: University of California Press, 1964.

Dunlay, Tom. *Kit Carson and the Indians*. Lincoln: University of Nebraska Press, 2000.

Dyk, Walter. *A Navaho Autobiography*. New York: Viking Fund, 1947.

———. *Son of Old Man Hat*. Lincoln: University of Nebraska Press, 1938, 1967.

Dyk, Walter, and Ruth Dyk. *Left Handed: A Navajo Autobiography*. New York: Columbia University Press, 1980.

Eliade, Mircea. *The Sacred and the Profane: The Nature of Religion*. New York: Harcourt, Brace, and World, 1959.

Ellis, Fern D. *Come Back to My Valley: Historical Remembrances of Mancos, Colorado*. Self-published, 1976.

Farella, John R. *The Main Stalk: A Synthesis of Navajo Philosophy*. Tucson: University of Arizona Press, 1984.

Faunce, Hilda (Wetherill). *Desert Wife*. Lincoln: University of Nebraska, 1928, 1981.

Fenton, William N. *The Great Law and the Longhouse: A Political History of the Iroquois Confederacy*. Norman: University of Oklahoma Press, 1998.

Fletcher, Maurine S., ed. *The Wetherills of the Mesa Verde: Autobiography of Benjamin Alfred Wetherill*. Lincoln: University of Nebraska Press, 1977.

Fonaroff, L. Schuyler. "Conservation and Stock Reduction on the Navajo Tribal Range." *Geographical Review* 53, no. 2 (April 1963), 200–223.

Ford, Richard I. "Inter-Indian Exchange in the Southwest," in *Handbook of North American Indians—Southwest* 10, ed. Alfonso Ortiz (Washington, D.C.: Smithsonian Institution, 1983): 711–22.

Forrest, Earle R. *With a Camera in Old Navaholand*. Norman: University of Oklahoma Press, 1970.

Franciscan Fathers. *An Ethnologic Dictionary of the Navajo Language*. St. Michaels, AZ: Saint Michaels Press, 1910, 1968.

Freeman, Ira S. *A History of Montezuma County*. Boulder, CO: Johnson Publishing, 1958.

Frisbie, Charlotte J. *Navajo Medicine Bundles or Jish: Acquisition, Transmission, and Disposition in the Past and Present*. Albuquerque: University of New Mexico Press, 1987.

Frisbie, Charlotte J., and David P. McAllester. *Navajo Blessingway Singer: The Autobiography of Frank Mitchell, 1881–1967*. Tucson: University of Arizona Press, 1978.

Gardner, Helen. *Art through the Ages*. New York: Harcourt, Brace and World, 1926, 1959.

Gillmor, Frances, and Louisa Wetherill. *Traders to the Navajos: The Story of the Wetherills of Kayenta*. Albuquerque: University of New Mexico Press, 1934, 1979.

Gordon-McCutchan, R. C., ed. *Kit Carson: Indian Fighter or Indian Killer?* Niwot: University Press of Colorado, 1996.

Haile, Berard, O.F.M. *Property Concepts of the Navaho Indians*. Washington, D.C.: Catholic University of America Press, 1954.

———. *Soul Concepts of the Navaho*. St. Michaels, AZ: Saint Michaels Press, 1943, 1975.

———. "Why the Navajo Hogan?" *Primitive Man* 15, nos. 3 and 4 (July and October 1942): 39–56.

Hall, Edward T. *The Hidden Dimension*. Garden City, NY: Doubleday, 1969.

———. *West of the Thirties: Discoveries among the Navajo and Hopi*. New York: Doubleday, 1994.

Hannum, Alberta. *Spin a Silver Dollar: The Story of a Desert Trading Post*. New York: Ballantine, 1944, 1972.

Hegemann, Elizabeth Compton. *Navaho Trading Days*. Albuquerque: University of New Mexico Press, 1963.

Herrick, Genevieve Forbes. "Women in the News." *Country Gentleman* 46 (October 1939): 46.

Hill, W. W. "Navaho Trading and Trading Ritual: A Study of Cultural Dynamics." *Southwestern Journal of Anthropology* 4 (Autumn, 1948): 371–96.

Hobson, Richard. *Navaho Acquisitive Values*. Reports of the Rimrock Project Values Series No. 5, Papers of the Peabody Museum of American Archaeology and Ethnology, Harvard University, vol. 42, no. 3. Cambridge, MA: Peabody Museum, 1954.

Holiday, John, and Robert S. McPherson. *A Navajo Legacy: The Life and Teachings of John Holiday*. Norman: University of Oklahoma Press, 2005.

Holiday, Samuel, and Robert S. McPherson. *Under the Eagle: Samuel Holiday, Navajo Code Talker*. Norman: University of Oklahoma Press, 2013.

Hornsby, Sarah, and Robert S. McPherson. "'Enemies like a Road Covered with Ice': The Utah Navajos' Experience during the Long Walk Period, 1858–1868." *American Indian Culture and Research Journal* 33 no. 2 (Spring 2009): 1–22.

Hubbard, Chester D. *Hooghan Haz' Ą́ągi Bóhoo' aah* (The Learning of That Which Pertains to the Home). Tsaile, AZ: Navajo Community College, 1977.

Hubbell, John Lorenzo. "Fifty Years an Indian Trader." *Touring Topics* 22, no. 12 (December 1930): 24–29, 51.

James, George Wharton. *Indian Blankets and Their Makers*. New York: Dover, 1914, 1974.

James, Lorraine Hunt. *The Meadows of McElmo: A Myers and Meadows Family History*. Self-published, 1992.

Jett, Stephen C. *Navajo Architecture: Forms, History, Distributions*. Tucson: University of Arizona Press, 1981.

Johnson, Broderick H., ed. *Navajo Stories of the Long Walk Period*. Tsaile, AZ: Navajo Community College Press, 1973.

———. *Stories of Traditional Navajo Life and Culture by Twenty-two Navajo Men and Women*. Tsaile, AZ: Navajo Community College Press, 1977.

Judd, Neil. *Men Met along the Trail*. Norman: University of Oklahoma Press, 1968.

Kelly, Klara, and Harris Francis. Website entitled "Navajoland Trading Post Encyclopedia (in progress)" found at www.navajotradingposts.info (accessed June 1, 2015).

Kelly, Lawrence C. *The Navajo Indians and Federal Indian Policy*. Tucson: University of Arizona Press, 1968.

Kennedy, Mary Jeanette. *Tales of a Trader's Wife: Life on the Navajo Indian Reservation, 1913–1938*. Albuquerque, NM: Valiant Company, 1965.

Kidder, A. V. "Reminiscences in Southwest Archaeology: I," *Kiva* 25, no. 4 (April 1960): 1–17.

Kildare, Maurice. "Builders to the Rainbow." *Frontier Times* 40 (June–July, 1966): 14–17, 48–52.

Kirk, Tom. *The Kirk Clan: Traders with the Navajo.* Brand Book no. 6, *Peoples of the Far West* series. San Diego, CA: Corral of the Westerners, 1979.

Kiser, William S. "Navajo Pawn: A Misunderstood Traditional Trading Practice." *American Indian Quarterly* 36, no. 2 (Spring 2012): 150–81.

Kluckhohn, Clyde. *Navaho Witchcraft.* Boston: Beacon Press, 1944, 1967.

———. *To the Foot of the Rainbow.* Glorieta, NM: Rio Grande Press, 1927.

Kluckhohn, Clyde, and Dorothea Leighton. *The Navaho.* Cambridge, MA: Harvard University Press, 1946, 1974.

Knipmeyer, James H. "The Dunn Family and Navajo Mountain Trading Post." *Utah Historical Quarterly* 68, no. 2 (Spring 2000): 125–38.

Ladd, John. *Structure of a Moral Code.* Cambridge, MA: Harvard University Press, 1957.

Lamphere, Louise. *To Run after Them: Cultural and Social Bases of Cooperation in a Navajo Community.* Tucson: University of Arizona Press, 1977.

Lee, Joe, and Gladwell Richardson. "My Wonderful Country." *Frontier Times* 48, no. 2 (February–March 1974): 6–15, 62–64.

Luckert, Karl W. *Navajo Mountain and Rainbow Bridge Religion.* Flagstaff: Museum of Northern Arizona, 1977.

Martinez, Sam. "Hogans." *Tsá' Ászi': A Magazine of Navajo Culture* 4, no. 3 (December, 1980): 38–41.

Matthews, Washington. *Navaho Legends.* Salt Lake City: University of Utah Press, 1897, 1994.

M'Closkey, Kathy. *Swept under the Rug: A Hidden History of Navajo Weaving.* Albuquerque: University of New Mexico Press, 2002.

McDonald, Ronald F. *Fort Montezuma, 1879–1884: An Account of the First Mormon Settlers in San Juan County, Utah.* Self-published, 2015.

McNitt, Frank. *Anasazi: Richard Wetherill.* Albuquerque: University of New Mexico Press, 1957.

———. *The Indian Traders.* Norman: University of Oklahoma Press, 1962.

McPherson, Robert S. *Dinéjí Na'nitin: Navajo Traditional Teachings and History.* Boulder: University Press of Colorado, 2012.

———. *A History of San Juan County: In the Palm of Time.* Salt Lake City: Utah State Historical Society, 1995.

———. *The Journey of Navajo Oshley: An Autobiography and Life History.* Logan: Utah State University Press, 2000.

———. *Navajo Land, Navajo Culture: The Utah Experience in the Twentieth Century.* Norman: University of Oklahoma Press, 2001.

———. "Navajo Livestock Reduction in Southeastern Utah, 1933–1946: History Repeats Itself." *American Indian Quarterly* 22, nos. 1 and 2 (Winter/Spring, 1998): 1–18.

———. "Navajos, Mormons, and Henry L. Mitchell." *Utah Historical Quarterly,* 55, no. 1 (Winter 1987): 50–65.

———. "Ricos and Pobres: Wealth Distribution on the Navajo Reservation in 1915." *New Mexico Historical Review* 60, no. 4 (Fall 1985): 415–34.

———. "'Too Much Noise in That Bunch across the River:' Ba'álílee and the 1907 Aneth Brawl." *Utah Historical Quarterly* 77, no. 1 (Winter 2009): 26–51.

———. *Viewing the Ancestors: Perceptions of the Anaasází, Mokwič, and Hisatsinom*. Norman: University of Oklahoma Press, 2014.

McPherson, Robert S., Jim Dandy, Sarah E. Burak. *Navajo Tradition, Mormon Life: The Autobiography and Teachings of Jim Dandy*. Salt Lake City: University of Utah Press, 2012.

McPherson, Robert S., and John Fahey. "Seeing Is Believing: The Odyssey of the Pectol Shields." *Utah Historical Quarterly* 76, no. 4 (Fall 2008), 357–76.

McPherson, Robert S., and Winston Hurst, "The Fight at Soldier Crossing, 1884: Military Considerations in Canyon Country." *Utah Historical Quarterly* 70, no. 3 (Summer 2002): 258–81.

Miller, David E. *Hole-in-the-Rock: An Epic in the Colonization of the Great American West*. Salt Lake City: University of Utah Press, 1975.

Mindeleff, Cosmos. "Navaho Houses." In *Seventeenth Annual Report of the Bureau of American Ethnology*, Smithsonian Institution, Part Two, 1895–1896 (Washington, D.C.: Government Printing Office, 1898): 475–517.

Mitchell, Rose, with Charlotte J. Frisbie. *Tall Woman: The Life Story of Rose Mitchell, A Navajo Woman, c. 1874–1977*. Albuquerque: University of New Mexico Press, 2001.

Moon, Samuel. *Tall Sheep: Harry Goulding, Monument Valley Trader*. Norman: University of Oklahoma Press, 1992.

Moorehead, Warren K. "In Search of a Lost Race." *The Illustrated American* (July 16, 1892): 411.

Morrow, Baker H., and V. B. Price. *Anasazi Architecture and American Design*. Albuquerque: University of New Mexico Press, 1997.

Mose, Don, Jr. *Honeeshgish: A Navajo Legend*. Blanding, UT: San Juan School District Media Center, 2006.

Mose, Don, Jr., and Katie Smith. *The Navajo Hogan*. Blanding, UT: San Juan School District, 1996.

Nabokov, Peter, and Robert Easton. *Native American Architecture*. New York: Oxford University Press, 1989.

Newcomb, Franc Johnson. *Hosteen Klah: Navaho Medicine Man and Sand Painter*. Norman: University of Oklahoma Press, 1964.

———. *Navaho Folk Tales*. Albuquerque: University of New Mexico Press, 1967.

———. *Navajo Neighbors*. Norman: University of Oklahoma Press, 1966.

Noel, Frank Leland, and Mary Elizabeth Noel. *Eighty Years in America*. Self-published, 1962.

O'Bryan, Aileen. *Navaho Indian Myths*. New York: Dover, 1993.

Ostermann, Leopold, O.F.M. "Franciscans in the Wilds and Wastes of the Navajo Country." *St. Anthony Messenger* 8, no. 11 (April 1901): 366–69.

———. "Franciscans in the Wilds and Wastes of the Navajo Country." *St. Anthony Messenger* 12, no. 3 (August 1904): 80–82.

———. "Little Mission Stories from Our Own Southwest." *St. Anthony Messenger* 34, no. 12 (May 1927): 634–35.

Parman, Donald L. T*he Navajos and the New Deal.* New Haven, CT: Yale University Press, 1976.

Peterson, Charles S. *Look to the Mountains.* Provo, UT: Brigham Young University Press, 1975.

Philp, Kenneth R. *John Collier's Crusade for Indian Reform, 1920–1954.* Tucson: University of Arizona Press, 1977.

Powers, Willow Roberts. *Navajo Trading: The End of an Era.* Albuquerque: University of New Mexico Press, 2001.

Prudden, T. Mitchell. *On the Great American Plateau.* New York: Putnam's Sons, 1906.

Reichard, Gladys A. *Navaho Religion: A Study of Symbolism.* Princeton, NJ: Princeton University Press, 1950.

———. *Navajo Weaver and Shepherd.* Glorieta, NM: Rio Grande Press, 1984.

———. *Prayer: The Compulsive Word.* New York: J. J. Augustin, 1944.

———. *Social Life of the Navajo Indians with Some Attention to Minor Ceremonies.* New York: Columbia University Press, 1928.

———. *Spider Woman: A Story of Navajo Weavers and Chanters.* Albuquerque: University of New Mexico Press, 1934, 1997.

———. *Weaving a Navajo Blanket.* New York: Dover, 1936, 1974.

Richardson, Cecil Calvin. "Lives of the Lonely." *Arizona Highways* 24, no. 8 (August 1948): 22–25.

———. "Navajos Are Witty People." *Arizona Highways* 27, no. 8 (August 1951): 26–29.

Richardson, Gladwell. *Navajo Trader.* Tucson: University of Arizona Press, 1986.

Roberts, Willow. *Stokes Carson: Twentieth-Century Trading on the Navajo Reservation.* Albuquerque: University of New Mexico Press, 1992.

Robinson, William H. *Under Turquoise Skies.* New York: Macmillan, 1928.

Roessel, Ruth, and Broderick Johnson, eds. *Navajo Livestock Reduction: A National Disgrace.* Tsaile, AZ: Navajo Community College Press, 1974.

Rogers, Jessie E. "Primitive Art of Navajo Women." *Home Mission Monthly* (Saint Michaels) 25, no. 4 (February 1911): 88–89.

Schwarz, Maureen Trudelle. *Molded in the Image of Changing Woman: Navajo Views on the Human Body and Personhood.* Tucson: University of Arizona Press, 1997.

Shepardson, Mary, and Blodwen Hammond. *The Navajo Mountain Community: Social Organization and Kinship Terminology*. Berkeley: University of California Press, 1970.

Simpson, Georgiana Kennedy. *Navajo Ceremonial Baskets: Sacred Symbols, Sacred Space*. Summertown, TN: Native Voices, 2003.

Sullivan, Louis H. "The Tall Office Building Artistically Considered." *Lippincott's Magazine* (March 1896): 403–9.

Thompson, Gerald. *The Army and the Navajo: The Bosque Redondo Reservation Experiment, 1863–1868*. Tucson: University of Arizona Press, 1982.

Trafzer, Clifford E. *The Kit Carson Campaign: The Last Great Navajo War*. Norman: University of Oklahoma Press, 1982.

Trockur, Emanuel, O.F.M. "Tangled Names." *Indian Sentinel* 24, no. 2 (February 1944): 25–27.

———. "What's in a Navajo Name?" *Indian Sentinel* 26, no. 5 (May 1936): 67–68.

Tschopik, Harry, Jr. "Taboo as a Possible Factor Involved in the Obsolescence of Navaho Pottery and Basketry." *American Anthropologist* 40, no. 2 (April–June 1938), 257–62.

Valette, Rebecca M. "Early Navajo Sandpainting Blankets: A Reassessment." *American Indian Art Magazine* 37, no. 2 (Spring 2012): 54–65.

Wetherill, Hilda. "The Trading Post: Letters from a Primitive Land." *Atlantic Monthly* 142, no. 3 (September, 1928), 289–300; no. 4 (October, 1928): 510–21.

Wetherill, Louisa Wade, and Harvey Leake. *Wolfkiller: Wisdom from a Nineteenth Century Navajo Shepherd*. Salt Lake City: Gibbs Smith, 2007.

Wetherill, Milton. "Conversation With: Milton Wetherill." W*estern Gateways* 7, no. 3 (Summer 1967): 43–45, 62–74.

White, Leslie A., ed. "Lewis H. Morgan's Journal of a Trip to Southwestern Colorado and New Mexico, June 21 to August 7, 1878." *American Antiquity* 8, no. 1 (July 1942): 1–26.

White, Richard. *The Roots of Dependency: Subsistence, Environment, and Social Change among the Choctaw, Pawnees, and Navajo*. Lincoln: University of Nebraska Press, 1983.

Wilkins, Teresa J. *Patterns of Exchange: Navajo Weavers and Traders*. Norman: University of Oklahoma Press, 2008.

Winslowe, John R. "Camps of the Nut Pickers." *True West* 17, no. 3 (January–February 1970): 34–37, 66–68.

Witherspoon, Gary. *Language and Art in the Navajo Universe*. Ann Arbor: University of Michigan Press, 1977.

———. *Navajo Kinship and Marriage*. Chicago: University of Chicago Press, 1975.

Woods, Susan E., and Robert S. McPherson. *Along Navajo Trails: Recollections of a Trader, 1898–1948*. Logan: Utah State University Press, 2005.

Wyman, Leland C. *Blessingway, with Three Versions of the Myth Recorded and Translated from the Navajo by Father Berard Haile, O.F.M.* Tucson: University of Arizona Press, 1970.

Young, Robert W. *The Role of the Navajo in the Southwestern Drama.* Gallup, NM: *Gallup Independent* and Robert W. Young, 1968.

Newspapers

Cortez (Co) Sentinel, 1928–1932.

Deseret News (Salt Lake City), 1882–1979.

Farmington (NM) Enterprise, 1909.

Grand Valley (UT) Times, 1911–1925.

Mancos (CO) Times, 1895–1904.

Mancos (CO) Times-Tribune, 1909–1917.

Montezuma (CO) Journal, 1898–1919.

Navajo Times (Window Rock, AZ), 2011.

Salt Lake (UT) Herald, 1880.

San Juan Record (Monticello, UT), 1938–1940.

Index